Home and the World

Harvard-Yenching Institute Monograph Series 82

HOME AND THE WORLD

Editing the "Glorious Ming" in Woodblock-Printed Books of the Sixteenth and Seventeenth Centuries

Yuming He

Published by the Harvard University Asia Center
Distributed by Harvard University Press
Cambridge (Massachusetts) and London 2020

Printed in the United States of America

The Harvard-Yenching Institute, founded in 1928, is an independent foundation dedicated to the advancement of higher education in the humanities and social sciences in Asia. Headquartered on the campus of Harvard University, the Institute provides fellowships for advanced research, training, and graduate studies at Harvard by competitively selected faculty and graduate students from Asia. The Institute also supports a range of academic activities at its fifty partner universities and research institutes across Asia. At Harvard, the Institute promotes East Asian studies through annual contributions to the Harvard-Yenching Library and publication of the *Harvard Journal of Asiatic Studies* and the Harvard-Yenching Institute Monograph Series.

Library of Congress Cataloging-in-Publication Data

He, Yuming.

Home and the world : editing the "Glorious Ming" in woodblock-printed books of the sixteenth and seventeenth centuries / Yuming He.

pages cm. — (Harvard-Yenching Institute monograph series ; 82)

Includes bibliographical references and index.

ISBN 978-0-674-06680-9 (hardcover : alk. paper); ISBN 978-0-674-24454-2 (paperback : alk. paper)

1. Block books, Chinese—History—16th century. 2. Block books, Chinese—History—17th century. 3. Printing—China—History—16th century. 4. Printing—China—History—17th century. 5. Publishers and publishing—China—History—16th century. 6. Publishers and publishing—China—History—17th century. 7. Book industries and trade—China—History—16th century. 8. Book industries and trade—China—History—17th century. 9. Books and reading—China—History—16th century. 10. Books and reading—China—History—17th century. I. Title.

Z240.H425 2012

092.09'031--dc23

2012031803

Index by Bruce Tindall

♾ Printed on acid-free paper

Last figure below indicates year of this printing

29 28 27 26 25 24 23 22 21 20

For Robert

Contents

Illustrations

Chapter 3

Chapter 4

Conclusion

Appendix I

Acknowledgments

The seed for this project was planted when, as a graduate student at UC Berkeley, I came across Roger Chartier's *The Order of Books* in a campus bookstore. My research and training had been primarily focused on the history of Chinese drama, but from this point I began to expand my attention to reflect on the material artifacts that provided the primary sources for my research—that is, Ming books—and to see that these possess a history of their own, a history not simply of the making and selling of books, but also a history of the use of books to shape visions of the world and of the reader's place in it. For unstinting support and mentorship during this period and since, I owe a deep debt of gratitude to my dissertation advisor, mentor, and friend Stephen West. I would also like to offer a general, but nonetheless heartfelt, thank you to all the mentors, students, colleagues, friends, and audience members over the past several years for all the questions, clarifications, suggestions, objections, corrections, and conversations that have helped shape this book. The title of this book was suggested to me by the novelist and scholar Anuradha Marwah during one of many delightful and fruitful conversations at Bellagio in August 2010. And if the themes of my book should seem far removed from those of the Tagore novel from which I've borrowed its title, perhaps I may excuse myself in part with the observation that versions of this sort of cheeky borrowing, recycling, and de- and re-contextualizing were key features of the early modern Chinese book culture examined here.

In bringing this project to completion I received generous support from the Rockefeller Foundation Bellagio Center and from the Franke Institute for the Humanities at the University of Chicago. My residency in summer 2010 at the Bellagio Center was an unforgettable experience of intensive intellectual labor, natural beauty, and lively fellowship with scholars from around the world. A grant from the Franke Institute during the 2010–11 academic year gave me a period free of teaching responsibilities during which to complete the manuscript, and the opportunity to exchange ideas with other Institute fellows helped both to sharpen my thinking on this project as well as to provide ideas and inspiration for future ones. More recently, I have received a timely grant from UC Davis to facilitate the latter stages of the book's production.

I would like to thank the following venues for their invitations to present work at various stages as this book has taken shape: the Centers for Chinese Studies at UCLA, UC Berkeley, the University of Michigan, and the Fairbank Center for Chinese Studies at Harvard University; the 2006 conference "Collecting 'China': Objects, Materiality, & Multicultural Collectors" at the University of Delaware and Winterthur Museum and Country Estate, organized by Vimalin Rujivacharakul; the 2008 workshop on "Chinese Zoomorphic Imagination" at Harvard University, organized by Eugene Wang; and the 2010 "West Coast Premodern Chinese Literature and Culture Workshop" at UC Berkeley, organized by Paula Varsano. I would also like to individually thank Richard von Glahn, Wilt Idema, Xiaofei Tian, Andrew Jones, Wen-hsin Yeh, and Christian de Pee for providing opportunities to present at their institutions.

It would have been impossible to finish this book without the generous help and advice from colleagues in various libraries and schools: Peter Zhou, Deborah Rudolph, Bruce Williams, and He Jianye at the C. V. Starr East Asian Library at UC Berkeley, Yuan Zhou and Eizaburo Okuizumi at the East Asian Collection at the University of Chicago Library, Martin Heijdra at the East Asian Library and Gest Collection at Princeton University, Guo Lixuan at the Shanghai library, and Zhou Xinhui at the Beijing Capital Library. Stephen West and Edward Shaughnessy read versions of chapter four and gave valuable suggestions for revision. A version of that chapter appeared as an article in the spring 2011 issue of *Asia Major*, and I would like to thank the three anonymous reviewers and the journal's editor, Howard Goodman, for their valuable feedback and suggestions. Yuhang Li and Bingyu Zheng provided timely help in assembling some key source materials, and Bruce Tindall prepared the index. Finally, the Harvard University Asia Center has made the publication process a true delight. The two anonymous authors of reports on the manuscript for the Center provided invaluable advice and encouragement, and caught several embarrassing errors that would no doubt have otherwise escaped my notice. William Hammell, Kristen Wanner, and Robert Graham, of the Asia Center Publications Program, have patiently and expertly guided a novice through the process of turning a manuscript into a book. Kristen Wanner's meticulous and judicious editorial presence, in particular, is in evidence on virtually every page.

Y.H.

Home and the World

Introduction

其書摭拾諸史及諸小說而成，頗多疏舛。如占城役屬於安南，乃云安南爲占城役屬，殊不足据，其他敘述亦太寥寥。

This book is composed of cobbled-together fragments of the various histories along with various collections of apocryphal tales, and is quite full of oversights and inconsistencies, as, for example, when it says that Annam is an administrative subdivision of Zhancheng, though Zhancheng is really an administrative subdivision of Annam—such a text is decidedly not to be relied on as a source of information. In other instances its relation of events is also too cursory.

General Catalog to the Complete Library of the Four Treasuries, Qing dynasty[1]

The above comment on the unreliable and bastardized nature of a book known as *Yiyu tuzhi* 異域圖志 (Illustrated record of foreign lands) is found in the *General Catalog* accompanying the massive eighteenth-century *Siku quanshu* 四庫全書 (Complete library of the four treasuries) compilation, the last and grandest of a succession of imperially sanctioned efforts to collect and account for the totality of worthwhile books in China. In the above passage, the *Siku* editor presents the rationale for concluding that the *Yiyu tuzhi* has no lasting value, and the text was accordingly excluded from the compilation. The attitude of the *Siku* editors toward the *Yiyu tuzhi* is typical of their general attitude toward a particular sort of "worthless" book that seemed to them to be closely associated with—indeed, typical of—the book culture of the preceding dynasty, the Ming (1368–1644). Again and again, Ming books and Ming editions were criticized, often in still harsher language, for sloppy editing and failure to properly cite sources, and for their crass commercial orientation. Indeed, a generally critical or dismissive attitude toward Ming books was to become rather prevalent during the Qing (1644–1911) and, to some extent, afterward. Expressions such as "when the Ming people produced a book, then that book died" (*Ming ren ke shu ze shu wang* 明人刻書則書亡), or "Ming people did not know how to produce an imprint" (*Ming ren buzhi keshu* 明人不知刻書), first uttered by Qing bibliophiles, still enjoy a vigorous afterlife as part of the stock of quasi-proverbial catchphrases shared by Chinese bibliographical scholars up to the present day.[2]

Such scorn of Ming book culture, reflected pervasively in comments by *Siku* editors, accords with a larger eighteenth-century and later critique of Ming culture as decadent and inferior in comparison with the Qing, and it reveals as much about the specifically Qing-era processes whereby these opinions were formed and articulated as it does about Ming books themselves.[3] It was through these eighteenth-century processes that Ming encyclopedic compilations, for example, came to be criticized by *Siku* scholars as "absurd," "made-up," "stealing from the ancients to benefit oneself," and as reflecting "Ming people's habitual practice to plunder and steal, to delete and exaggerate at whim."[4] In short, Ming book producers, viewed from this developing eighteenth-century perspective, were a species of cultural hooligans and bandits. In a reversal of the suppressed narrative of Ming loyalists, who saw the Manchu Qing as a regime of violent barbarians that destroyed a civilized Chinese empire, the *Siku* scholars articulated a view of book history in which the Ming itself has become a barbarian other that must be controlled and excluded to maintain the order of the world of Chinese books.

Such a tendency to deny Ming books the status of "real" books would clearly stand in the way of any attempt to gain a closer understanding of those books on their own terms, and recent developments in Ming book history have begun to redress this entrenched dismissiveness.[5] When the value judgments implicit in Qing invective against Ming books are set aside, however, these attacks themselves may provide helpful clues for an inquiry into the particular characteristics of Ming book culture. One of the most recurrent and colorful epithets used by *Siku* editors in reference to Ming texts is *baifan* 稗販, meaning roughly "hucksterish." This phrase, deployed by the *Siku* scholars with great gusto, points to two problematic dimensions of Ming textual activity. Etymologically, *bai* refers to rice-like grass that grows with and harms rice, and the traditional designation of "*bai* officials" (*bai guan* 稗官) refers to low-ranking officials tasked with collecting *xiaoshuo*, that is, "small talk" not deemed worthy of more serious consideration. In short, *bai* designates something that resembles the real thing but is not. The term thus warns of something that is, at best, light and trivial but that, if mistaken for the real thing it resembles, may prove positively harmful. The term *fan* 販, meaning "peddler" or "to peddle," more directly points to the commercial and pecuniary aspect of the Ming publications given the epithet *baifan*. Thus when the *Siku* editors denounce a text as *baifan zhi xue* 稗販之學, they are calling it "bastardized peddler-learning"—or, to return to our rough one-word equivalent, "huckster-scholarship."

These Qing scholars, editors, and bibliographers clearly used such language vituperatively. But when one's perspective and aims in tracing a history of Ming books differ significantly from those of Qing critics, might even such vituperative language suggest directions for a reappraisal of Ming books—texts, pictures, pages, and volumes—and the role they played in the reading culture of the time? The broad direction of inquiry carried out in this book suggests an answer in the affirmative. Although one need not concur with the *Siku* editors in their condemnation of Ming book culture, or their judgment that many typical Ming books were not really "proper" books at all, one can acknowledge that the Qing critics did identify some of the habitual practices of Ming book producers and recurrent characteristics of Ming books. In the following chapters I will attempt a fresh look at some of these "hucksterish" Ming productions in terms of both dimensions suggested by the term *baifan*—first, in terms of a book culture that struck those eighteenth-century scholars as shockingly lax, cavalier, unscrupulous, and heterodox; and second, in the context of the motivations and strategies of production, promotion, and consumption driven by a burgeoning and unkempt marketplace for a bewildering variety of woodblock publications. In other words, I will explore the possibilities that arise when *baifan* is treated not as a term of dismissive invective, but rather as a point of departure for examining a historical moment in Chinese book culture that is worthy of exploration and appreciation on its own terms.

During the sixteenth and seventeenth centuries, particularly what is known as the late Ming (roughly 1570s–mid-1600s), explosive population increases, rapid urbanization, expanded commercial networks, and volume of trade made the Ming a major force in the initial phase of a modern global economy. The accompanying transformations of social and economic life gave the late Ming Chinese themselves a sense of living in a special historical moment, and of sharing in a sophisticated and cosmopolitan vision of the world. In terms of the guiding position that commercial activity began to play in shaping both social structures and outlooks on the world, and of the expansion in range and volume of interaction with far-flung regions of the world, this is a period that has seemed a natural focus for exploration of the dynamics of China's early modernity.[6]

The late Ming was also the period when commercial woodblock print publications attained unprecedented diversity and popularity, and impacted Chinese cultural life in profound ways. The discussions in the following chapters often attempt to place developments in Ming printing culture in a larger historical framework, but it will become evident that the preponderance of our primary source material is centered in the late Ming period. The lives of many of the publishers, compilers, illustrators, and block carvers who were directly involved in creating and marketing the most distinctive Ming books are now datable only through the period of their surviving imprints, and the most common single period designation is that of the Wanli reign, extending from 1573 to 1620, and thus the reign period most squarely situated in what we term the "late Ming."

Qing critics were not in fact the first to compare Ming book-makers to peddlers. The Ming scholar and historian Wang Shizhen 王世貞 (1526–90) drew the analogy between the production of certain sorts of Ming book and the peddling of consumer goods through a far-flung distribution network much earlier, and in a laudatory tone. For Wang, the ability of a good encyclopedia compiler to make rare or important texts available to a broad public rivals the business acumen of a successful trader.[7] The very features that made many Ming books easy prey for critique under the standards of evidential scholarship, or for suppression by state censorship, are those that, if viewed afresh, offer insight into the texture of Ming printing culture. Where Qing scholars saw slipshod, irresponsible, or even heretical treatment of the textual legacy of the past, others might enjoy irreverent wit, exuberant imagination, clever parody, and textual hybridity. What critics condemned as crass commercialism, others might appreciate as these books' ability to vividly evoke their particular cultural moment—as exemplified by the phrases *shishang* 時尚 (the fashion of these days) or *xinxing* 新興 (newly in vogue) that so frequently adorn the often lengthy and exuberantly boastful titles of Ming publications.

Even what later came to be viewed as "hucksterish" books were in many instances quite authoritative in their own time, and they shaped the ways in which Ming Chinese viewed themselves and their world, as well as the ways in which readers in other regions of the world viewed Ming China. In fact, the difficulty of drawing clear lines of demarcation between "highbrow" authoritative books and "lowbrow" books for play or entertainment is a recurrent theme in Ming books. Like Student Zhang in the *Story of the Western Wing*, who, in one of the favorite moments of Ming theatergoers, readers, publishers, joke-tellers, and illustrators, perches astride the wall of his beloved Cui Yingying's garden, Ming books seem perpetually to have one foot in the serious world of knowledge production and timeless cultural values and the other foot in the playful and ephemeral world of the marketplace. The very qualities that make these books unreliable as sources of ostensibly timeless knowledge about Chinese tradition may provide a window for us to see how actual human beings lived with, and within, that tradition at a distinctive and transformational historical moment.

The type of cultural mastery reflected and celebrated in many Ming woodblock books is not that of the rigorous and ascetic scholar, but rather that of the urbane city dweller with his savvy command of cosmopolitan fashions and entertainments of the time. Ming books offer a sort of "pulp scholarship" that is a protean hybrid of classical texts and traditional poetry, along with more popular lore such as dramatic literature and musical performance, drinking games, and witty repartee. To express this double-sidedness in terms of a pair of literary analogues, in Ming popular imprints the world of Chen Zuiliang 陳最良, the famous pedantic tutor in the preeminent late Ming play *Peony Pavilion*, is inextricably interwoven with the world of Ximen Qing 西門慶, the infamous merchant, libertine, and local power broker in the novel *Plum in the Golden Vase*.

Siku scholarship on Ming books remains a subject of heated debate, involving revered intellectual figures and even state leaders,[8] and although modern scholars have revisited Qing assessments of Ming books, the eighteenth-century condemnation of Ming book culture has had undeniably real and lasting consequences. Several of the Ming books I have chosen for discussion in the following chapters have largely, if not completely, disappeared from the map of Chinese bibliographical tradition. This historical amnesia is partly due to the simple fact that Qing valuation of these texts has "stuck" in subsequent generations, albeit largely by default. A more fundamental factor underlying the forgetting of these books, however, is the fact that the very categories to which they belonged in the minds of Ming publishers and readers have also been lost. To these lost categories of publication, moreover, correspond not only lost niches in the Ming book market but, more basically, forgotten modes of consumption of books—that is, ways of using and interacting with books. Therefore, my basic approach will be to start from the books themselves to recapture the varieties of reader-consumer use and interaction they inspired. Each of the following chapters takes on a discrete aspect of this problem, beginning from a book or type of books and working outward to delineate the mechanisms of use and meaning-generation that correspond to each. Because these texts were so fluid, and because interpenetration among texts and categories of texts, as well as among kinds of knowledge, was so common, starting from case studies and moving outward in this way does in fact allow us to build a coherent general view of some of the distinctive ways in which books and their producers and readers interacted during the period.

The broad aim of this study, then, will be to suspend judgment about what Ming books are or ought to be, and to attend instead to the clues that these books offer about the historical contexts in which they were produced and used. In keeping with this aim, I will refrain from relying on various sorts of distinctions, such as that between poetry and musical drama or that between text and picture, that might be justified in other contexts. Many Ming book-makers themselves, including the most prominent figures such as Chen Hongshou 陳洪綬 (1598–1653) and Yu Wentai 余文台 (fl. Wanli reign), or somewhat lesser-known figures like Liu Ciquan 劉次泉 (fl. Wanli reign) and Zhu Dingchen 朱鼎臣 (fl. Wanli reign), all excelled in different areas of art and craftsmanship related to the world of books, including painting, woodblock engraving, fiction-writing, music, and theater. In reflecting on the range of readerly interactions with books, moreover, I will eschew any clear-cut distinction between literacy and illiteracy, or between reading and non-reading uses of books, in favor of a looser and broader notion of conversancy with the printed page that encompasses both high-level scholarly mastery of ancient and modern texts and various sorts of "knowing what to do with books" that might or might not include full reading mastery.

This approach also illuminates ways in which material dimensions of a book and the content of the book interact to create market appeal and cultural fashion. After all, in the Ming as in other ages, books might be objects of aspirational or prestige ownership just as easily as they could be a medium for communicating fixed written "content," and as the circulation histories of many of the books to be discussed here bear out, it is useful to think of a spectrum or field of possible or projected uses or modes of consumption for a given book (even including "abuse" or other sorts of use not anticipated by the producers), rather than to imagine each book as having a narrowly specified audience or stable and definable use value. If the possibility of virtually limitless reproduction, and the accompanying risk of books falling into the "wrong" hands, was a central feature in the historical impact of printing technology in general, then the Ming culture of woodblock printing, which was also to a high degree a culture of promiscuous reprinting, recompilation, and recycling, would be the place in Chinese book history where these tendencies were played out to the greatest degree—to the great discomfort of many guardians of cultural authority and legitimacy.[9]

Another reason for thinking in terms of "book conversancy" rather than "literacy" in a narrow sense when reflecting on Ming books is that the books themselves often invite us to interact with them in ways that go beyond straight reading of text. The interactions among text and illustrations, for example, or the preference for multi-register page layouts that bring together often widely disparate sorts of texts, along with the strong orientation toward active use rather than passive reading implicit in textual types such as riddles and drinking games with model solutions, all call for thinking in terms of multiple ways in which readers might engage with and appropriate the book, rather than simply in terms of correct or incorrect reading of textual content.

The inquiry into Ming "book conversancy" may also benefit by drawing on conceptual tools developed in recent work on the history of other print and book traditions, such as Robert Darnton's notion of the "communication circuit" or Roger Chartier's model of the "community of readers."[10] The notion of "communication circuit" aims to map out intellectual, socio-economic, and legal-political factors that impact the perpetual circuit of the making and consuming of books, involving both material and intellectual activities such as paper supply and publisher's strategies, while the idea of "community of readers" draws attention to the specific mechanisms that distinguish the various communities of readers and traditions of reading, and to the ways in which communities are shaped by shared reading experiences that transcend classifications of social status.

By emphasizing that meaning-making is a dynamic process, such conceptual tools remind us that a wide range of economic, political, and symbolic factors constantly contribute to and reshape both the form and content of the book and the interpretive community encompassing both book-makers and readers, whose ongoing and interactive process of coding and decoding gives their books meaning. Studying these processes of coding and decoding by case and in detail may, in turn, allow us to understand how a text, picture, or book functioned for a group or groups of readers within its particular historical and cultural milieu. The categories of book-users and book-makers are especially fluid and overlapping in the case of the "hucksterish" Ming books to be studied here, where reuse and reappropriation is a particularly prominent mechanism in both the production and consumption of the texts and images that make up the book.

To see how books in the "hucksterish" Ming book world defy commonplace assumptions about texts, consider the case of the *Shanhai jing* 山海經 (Classic of mountains and seas). When most people now think of the *Shanhai jing*, they are thinking of a notionally fixed and "correctly" collated text derived from a medieval recension of ancient cosmographic and religious traditions.[11] This notionally "correct" text in turn serves as a standard authority for documenting early Chinese beliefs about various exotic creatures and localities. In the Ming, however, though the *Shanhai jing* was an important and authoritative reference text, several quite distinct versions of the book circulated under a variety of headings or titles. The most widespread and influential version perhaps also qualifies as the most hucksterish: its text very frequently diverges from what is now recognized as the *Shanhai jing*, and it derived its influence and popularity not least from the fact that it was illustrated. It was also quite open and fluid, incorporating pictures and descriptions from other sources as well as providing material for a range of other titles. Thus for Ming readers, *Shanhai jing* was one designation among a protean web of pictures and descriptions of exotic lands and creatures, always subject to change in the context of use or appropriation in any given book.[12]

Moreover, it was these open and fluid clusters of texts and images, and not the notionally fixed medieval text that the title connotes for us today, that impacted how early modern Europeans understood Chinese views on the cosmos and its inhabitants. The Jesuit missionary Gabriel de Magalhães (1609–77, Chinese name An Wensi 安文思) gave the following account based on Chinese records of Xiaoren guo 小人國 (Kingdom of little people): "Siao gin que [Xiaoren guo], or the Kingdom, the Inhabitants of which are all Dwarfs, and so little, that they are constrain'd to tie themselves several in a bunch together for fear of being carry'd away by the Eagles and Kites."[13] The detail that the inhabitants of Xiaoren guo often tie themselves in a bunch for fear of being snatched up by fierce birds appears nowhere in our familiar *Shanhai jing*. If we lose sight of the influence and popularity of the Ming *Shanhai jing*, and its permeability in relation to other books, we might fault the Europeans for relying on their own fantasies in reporting Chinese views of the world, though extant Ming materials do in fact describe and envision Xiaoren guo precisely as reported by Gabriel de Magalhães (fig. IN.1).[14] The *Shanhai jing* was a key cultural reference both within and without China during the Ming, and yet at that time its status as a reference did not mean that it required a carefully collated, fixed, and autonomous text as the guarantee of its authority.

The *Qian jia shi* 千家詩 (Poems by a thousand masters) is another example of how a text we may think is quite familiar was conceived of and handled in quite alien ways by Ming readers. Whatever preconceived notions one holds of what a poetry primer is or is for, looking at the specific form in which it circulated during the Ming (fig. IN.2) forces us to reexamine what we think we know about this text. The page layout itself is an indication of a distinctive mode of interacting with the text:

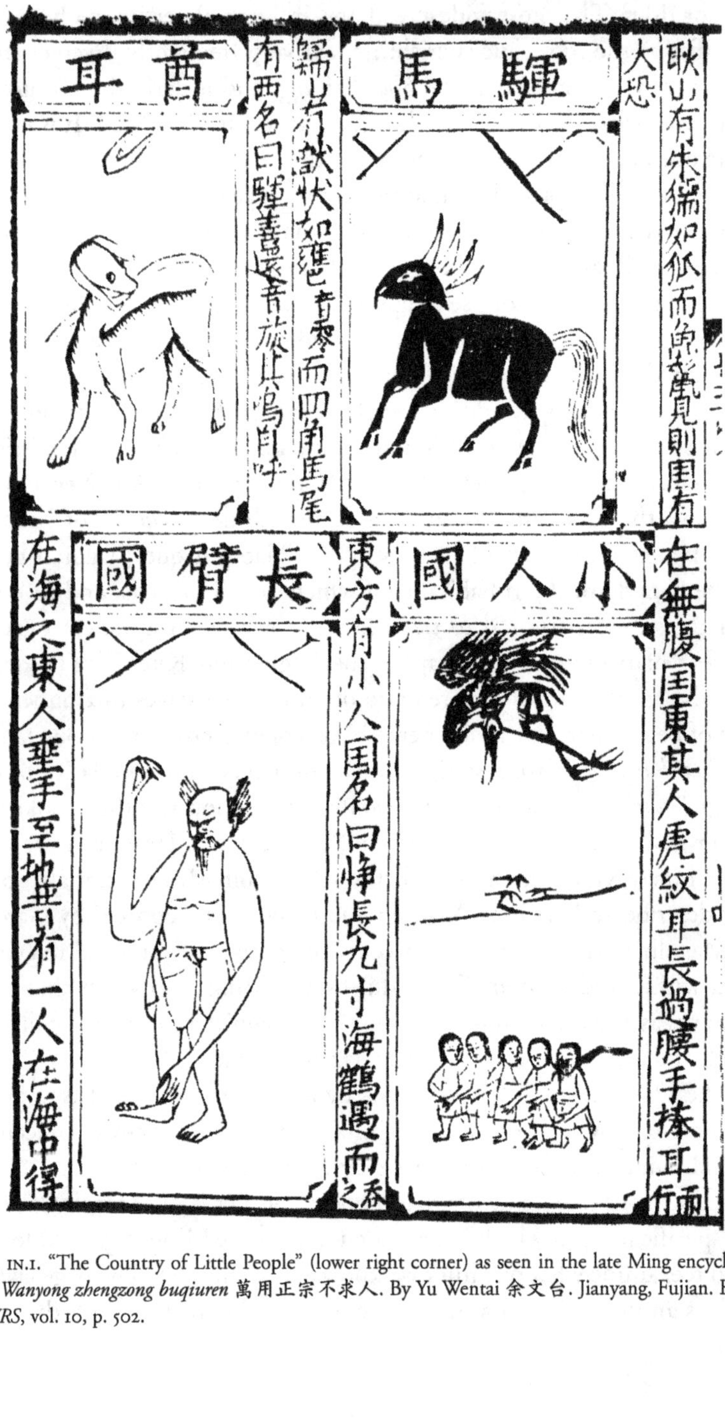

Fig. IN.1. "The Country of Little People" (lower right corner) as seen in the late Ming encyclopedia *Wanyong zhengzong buqiuren* 萬用正宗不求人. By Yu Wentai 余文台. Jianyang, Fujian. From *CNRS*, vol. 10, p. 502.

the page is divided into a lower main register, where the poems are interspersed with elucidations of each poem's meaning, and a higher register occupied by illustrations and response poems whose rhymes match those of the anthologized works. These response poems, provided as a model for the sort of imitative composition the reader should strive to produce, indicate that this Ming version of the anthology is geared much more toward particular kinds of interactive use rather than toward simple reading. It is the elucidations, however, that offer the greatest surprise to latter-day conceptions of poetry or the category of the "poetic" in the way they gloss the poems' meanings in terms of the Daoxue 道學 (Learning of the Way) discourse on self-cultivation most closely associated with the world of the eight-legged essay and the imperial examination system. Taken together, these aspects of the Ming *Qian jia shi* reflect an orientation toward guiding the reader to reproduce poems in response, as well as a set of implicit assumptions of what poetry is and what it is for that appear far removed from our own.

One way of approaching this Ming book would be to treat it as one exemplar of a notionally singular text titled "*Qian jia shi*" and to collate the instances in which its texts of the anthologized poems deviate from other sources. Such an approach would offer an intriguing look at some of the variant readings and interpretations of these poems in the Ming. But another approach would be to attempt to come to terms imaginatively with the whole of the book, with its extra registers and supplementary materials, as a way of envisioning how Ming readers used the text. What distinctive idea of "poetry" was in play for readers who were adept in the complex of reading practices (or, more generally, uses) that this book, with its unique organization and layout, reflects? This second approach, the effort to come to terms with the seemingly alien or nonsensical aspects of Ming books on their own terms, is the one I will pursue in the following chapters.

Working outward from Ming books themselves to map the webs of historical practice through which they were produced, circulated, and put to various uses is in some ways like attempting to reconstruct the rules of a complexly intertwined set of games. In this sense, the *Boxiao zhuji* 博笑珠璣 (Pearls to evoke laughter) is a logical beginning point for the studies undertaken here, since this book, with its highlighting of riddle and game texts, often raises questions less about the texts' meaning than

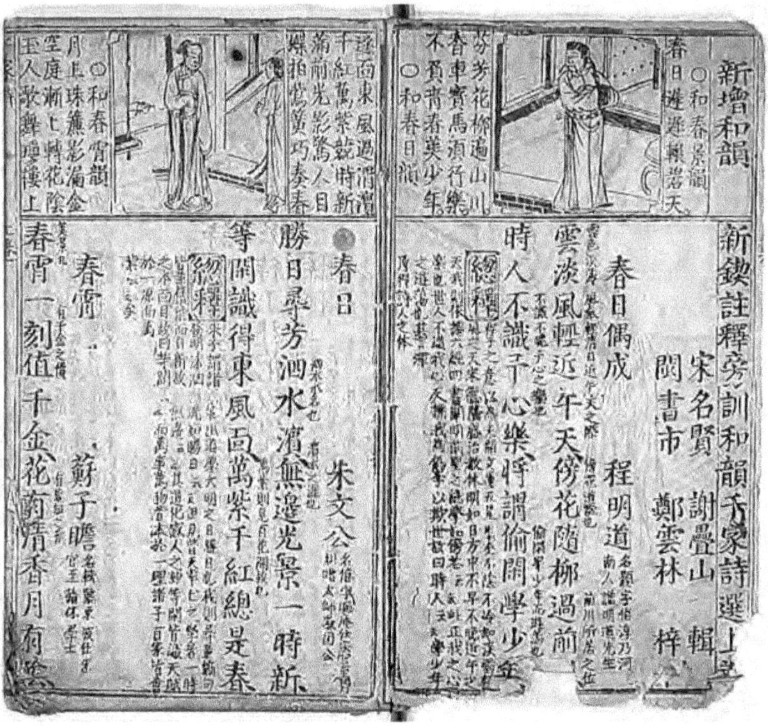

新增和韻

新鍥註釋旁訓和韻千家詩選上卷

宋名賢 謝疊山 輯

閩書市 鄭雲林 梓

春日偶成 程明道

雲淡風輕近午天 傍花隨柳過前川

時人不識予心樂 將謂偷閒學少年

春日 朱文公

勝日尋芳泗水濱 無邊光景一時新

等閒識得東風面 萬紫千紅總是春

春宵 蘇子瞻

春宵一刻值千金 花有清香月有陰

Fig. IN.2. A Ming block-printed edition of the *Qian jia shi* by Zheng Yunlin 鄭雲林 (fl. Wanli reign), Fujian. The title advertises the primer as standing in for a teacher in its attention to all aspects involved in studying a poem: annotation, elucidations relating the poems' significance in terms of orthodox scholarship, and model response poems. Photo courtesy of the Kyoto University Library.

about their range of intended use. Thus chapter 1 focuses on delineating the spaces of performance and use projected by the *Boxiao zhuji*. This line of inquiry reveals not only a constellation of canonical reference texts that is markedly different from the groupings that commanded authority in later periods, but also a brand of cultural practices that put those various sorts of canonical materials into play in displays of cultural mastery as well as in coded languages of pleasure and entertainment. The *Boxiao zhuji* contains vivid and often amusing examples of the ways in which Ming readers might have been encouraged to generate new meanings from long-established textual traditions; it also reflects some of the distinctive ways Ming readers categorized and prioritized the fields of verbal art and traditional knowledge as they conceived them.

Chapter 2 focuses on another print format in which the sorts of drinking games included in the *Boxiao zhuji* often appeared, namely, the distinctive Ming printing phenomenon now known as the "drama miscellany." The drama miscellany was printed in a unique triple-register page layout, with the top and bottom registers filled with excerpts of plays and the narrower middle register displaying a variety of amusing, bawdy, or practical texts such as drinking games, riddles, jokes, and even instructions for brothel visitors. The above combination of format and content elicits such questions as, What kind of audience did these texts anticipate or create? Why and how did these books include what they did? What made them possible and profitable?

On one hand, the page layout of the drama miscellany seems to promote desultory, segmented browsing over linear, sustained reading, and to invite readers to claim individualized experience with the book through the spontaneous choice of order and emphasis in their reading. Such segmental reading encourages a sense of ownership (as the text becomes uniquely the *reader's* text) and a taste for repeated viewing, a connoisseuristic gesture of appreciation (*wanwei* 玩味). On the other hand, the drama miscellany only became fully legible as a print genre through its complex associations with contemporary practices of private performance, encompassing both theatrical playacting and social gaming and role-play. In this sense, the triple-register format served as a textual analogue to the real linkages between fashionable modes of social behavior (modeled in its narrower middle register) and theatrical performance (represented by the dramatic excerpts in its top and bottom registers). In short, the page layout of this publication genre, both novel in its time and ephemeral within the broader trends of Chinese book history, reflects the ways in which social and theatrical performance merged in a new concept of the "performative self" whose central thrust was the ideal of being simultaneously at home and in the world. This ideal is reflected, for example, in the verbal and visual rhetoric of the drama miscellanies' title pages, which present visions of private domestic entertainments shared among a small group of intimates, while simultaneously gesturing toward the reader, inviting him to vicariously participate in that intimate circle via the medium of the book and to "make himself at home" within this vision of genteel elegance and cosmopolitan sophistication.

Chapter 3 takes up several connections that emerge from the first two chapters in a study of the patterns of circulation and (re)production of Ming woodblock printing. Building from specific cases (such as the reuse of blocks and the reenactment of the famous "Student Zhang

Jumps over the Wall" episode in the *Story of the Western Wing*), this chapter examines a "poetics of error" through which the circulation and reappropriation of common motifs and imitable and reusable material becomes not merely a matter of convenience and cost-effectiveness in the business of book production, but also a distinctive generative technique in the production of new meaning.

Texts and pictures were repeatedly recycled and re-edited, each iteration aiming to capture a sense of novelty and freshness for the reader. Each local text, then, is to be situated in relation to other texts or books in the same family, and further to other works in a universe in which a diverse range of genres and registers of text participate. In the meantime, motifs and scenes were transposed throughout a wide spectrum of materials, both textual and visual, and formed a new system of signs and symbols that gained currency in the late Ming reading world. Particularly revealing of these universalizing signs and symbols is the process by which the pictorial depiction of the screen and the hall, emblems of comfortable living and domestic respectability, is transposed to pictorial imagination of imperial court ceremonies, thus domesticating, both literally and figuratively, spaces, persons, and spectacles that were beyond the reach of commoner readers.

Chapter 4 looks at how some of the patterns of reproduction observed in chapter 3 operated to create one of the bestselling and most authoritative books about the broader global world to circulate in the Ming—the *Luochong lu* 臝蟲錄 (Record of naked creatures)—a comprehensive pictorial on foreign lands and peoples. In many ways—in its spatial layout, its subversive humor, or in the sense it conveys of a fresh glimpse into a world of knowledge that is both deeply traditional and in step with the latest fashions—the *Luochong lu* is a typical Ming book, though in the centuries since the Ming it has fallen into almost total neglect. It is this very book, in fact, that, under its alternative title *Yiyu tuzhi*, was the object of the *Siku* editors' vituperation in the epigraph with which this Introduction began. During the Ming, nonetheless, this odd text enjoyed very widespread popularity and exercised a tangible influence on both popular and elite imagination of the exotic.

From the fifteenth to the eighteenth century, the *Luochong lu* and its reprints in various types of publications were circulated widely both in China and throughout broader East Asia, extending even to global book markets. The creators of these pictorials and their critics included emperors, princes, diplomats and local bureaucrats, literati, commercial publishers, and woodblock illustrators. This chapter first traces the production and circulation routes of these pictorials and then examines the changes in patterns of reading that accompanied and sustained this phenomenon. In bringing to light the lost history of this bibliographical niche, I hope to recover a sense of its specific relevance to the cultural and social world of late Ming China, as well as observe how, in going beyond China, these texts formed part of a global system of exchange involving not only material objects, but also forms of cultural fashioning.

What emerges in this chapter is a picture of a new book culture that provided a malleable yet enduring space for filing and disseminating fantastic ethnographical, zoological, and cosmological information, especially visual representations of exotic beings. In turn, these images and their accompanying descriptions became exotic collectibles in a milieu that valued the novel, the fascinating, and the "informative"—reflecting the flux and dynamism in the cognitive models for explaining and understanding one's own place in the world via classifying and reflecting on the cultural and geographical Other. The printing history of these pictorials points to a period in which the book market valued text as a museum-like repository, creating a communication circuit in which pictures and descriptions of things beyond most readers' immediate experience were gathered and displayed for convenient viewing. For the Ming reading public, the *Luochong lu* became a cabinet of curiosities housed in a book.

The *Luochong lu* is perhaps the most vivid example of the ways in which Ming books domesticated the broader world for Ming readers, but this dynamic may be seen at work throughout the range of popular Ming woodblock texts. These books often explicitly marketed themselves as counterparts to, or substitutes for, the material objects of luxurious consumption that carried cosmopolitan prestige but were probably beyond the reach of many readers.[15] The books also persistently engaged the reader with fantasies of pleasure and cultural mastery on the grand stage of the city, whether in brothel manuals that modeled the style of the urbane and worldly wise playboy or in popular reenvisionings of grand state rituals in which foreign tribute was submitted to the emperor. Often Ming woodblock texts show the imprint of particular regional home affiliations and express mythologies of local pride within and against the frame of the broader cosmopolitan Ming imperial sphere. Popular imprints of this era afforded readers visions of feeling at home in the world, at ease or ill at ease as the case might be, by offering them the chance to create and inhabit texts, pictures, and books that reflect and give meaning to their own experience. The phrase "Glorious Ming" (*Huang Ming* 皇明) became a favorite touchstone in such visions of the Ming home-world. For Ming book-makers and users, such language could be employed with simple pride, but it was just as often tinted with a mockery or self-mockery that served less to debunk the imperial vision than to mark it as the particular possession of the ordinary book reader. For us, in turn, the term "Glorious Ming" and its like may come to stand as an emblem of the lost world of Ming reading, since Qing scholarship and politics would later erase the phrase from book titles, or simply destroy books whose titles contained such phraseology.

The mass production of woodblock texts from the sixteenth to seventeenth century drove, and was shaped by, corresponding changes in the habits and skills of readers. The books studied here, and the extended textual and visual families associated with them, are connected to one another in various ways: they appear in the same book or category of books, and they overlap with or borrow from one another, attesting to the so-called "copy and paste" compiling style that was to become a major complaint of Qing scholars. In their novelty—and, for the uninitiated reader, their opacity—these books presented to their readers a complex code of social and cultural meanings that could only be realized through a correspondingly complex constellation of interpretive skills. They stimulated new modes of readerly imagination and called forth new modes of social display and cultural dominance with their own strategies and sensitivities. By situating these books within the context of transmission and circulation in China and, next, to East Asia and beyond, this study interprets the ways in which they became culturally meaningful in a variety of period-specific contexts in the sixteenth and seventeenth centuries. By extension, it examines the rise of a particular type of book conversancy, a skill of reading and using books both as material objects and as linguistic and visual structures that enabled readers to bring grand and global visions into the ambit of their own domestic sphere.

CHAPTER ONE

The Boxiao zhuji *and the World of Late Ming Popular Texts*

My survey of the world of late Ming textual culture begins with a publication entitled *Boxiao zhuji* 博笑珠璣 (Pearls to evoke laughter, see fig. 1.1). Compiled sometime during or after the Jiajing reign (1521–66), this text subsequently went through multiple block editions,[1] including one printed by Xiong Chongyu 熊沖宇 (fl. Wanli reign) of a printshop known as the Zhongde tang 種德堂 in Jianyang, Fujian,[2] and another marked as a production of a printshop called the Wende tang 文德堂.[3] In this chapter, I will examine an exemplar of a Wende tang edition.[4] At first glimpse this text might seem an odd choice: with its mishmash of riddles, jokes, and drinking games, it seems to go out of its way to disavow any serious intent. It is also in many ways far from original, being largely composed of bits and pieces of other commercial publications thrown together haphazardly. Beyond a doubt, it epitomizes many of the characteristics of Ming woodblock texts that would give this period in book history such a bad reputation in the eyes of later scholars: low production quality, muddled pedigree, copious transcription errors, a general tone of commercial hyperbole, and insouciance about sourcing.

But it is precisely the playfulness and ephemerality of this text, and its lack of interest in preserving textual authenticity or legitimacy, that aid our efforts to recapture the whimsical, hyperbolic, and intensely commercial world of the Ming woodblock print. Its brand of humor reveals much about the late Ming world of books, because its jokes and witticisms often

新興咲談
華筵聚樂篇篇錦
博笑珠璣
博笑珠璣種種新

Fig. 1.1. Title page of the *Boxiao zhuji.* Courtesy of the Shanghai Library.

play on bodies of shared knowledge that were familiar to readers of the era but that, in many cases, have subsequently been buried in neglect. Its effectiveness often hinges on moments of irony or incongruity in which language shifts abruptly from one frame of reference to another, and in *Boxiao zhuji* this sort of moment typically involves a shift in genre or stylistic register as well. One of the most recurrent types of witty display involves the juxtaposition of citations from disparate source texts. In its focus on these moments of textual crossing, the *Boxiao zhuji* foregrounds the role of the performer—whether it be the teller of a joke, the player of a drinking game, the editor of a book, or the resourceful reader—who creates a new and playful text by finding or establishing previously unsuspected connections among far-flung sources. The variety of textual games presented in the *Boxiao zhuji* is particularly suggestive, and these games will provide the point of departure for the discussion below.

From the outset, the *Boxiao zhuji* conveys the characteristic commercial tone of Ming book culture, with its emphasis on novelty amid a marketplace of rapidly shifting fashions. Its title page (see fig. 1.1) touts the "new vogue in laughter and banter" (*xinxing xiaotan* 新興笑談) to be found within and uses a parallel couplet—echoing the couplets employed at the end of dramatic works to announce their "title" and "name" (*timu* 題目 and *zhengming* 正名)—to highlight the charm and novelty of the game texts it assembles:

華筵聚樂篇篇錦
博笑珠璣種種新

Delightful gatherings at splendid banquets: every piece is brocade;
pearls to evoke laughter: each variety is novel.

The *Boxiao zhuji* fulfills the lavish promises of its title page in four volumes.[5] These volumes include collections of drinking games, riddles, along with witty expressions called "winsome sayings of the rivers and lakes" (*jianghu qiaoyu* 江湖俏語),[6] jokes, a collection of humorous verses entitled "Selected Comical Poems" (*Xiaotan shixuan* 笑談詩選), a manual for dice games, and a poetry collection called *Huang Ming shixuan* 皇明詩選 (Anthology of poetry of the Glorious Ming). Taken together, these materials reveal a great deal about the rather quirky canon of authoritative texts that were drawn on for banquet games and repartee, as well as about the protocols governing the use and composition of texts that would have been deemed acceptable in the "current vogue" (*shishang* 時尚) of the era. For its original readers, the *Boxiao zhuji* promised to provide not only an indication of the range of textual command one needed in order to keep up with the fashion of the day, but also a demonstration of the manner in which this command was to be displayed. For later readers like us, it provides clues about the bibliographical terrain of Ming book culture and provides a valuable glimpse into the style of performance through which the mastery of books was put on display.

The full extended alternate title of the *Boxiao zhuji* appears on the book's first page:[7]

> 新刻時尚華筵趣樂談笑酒令
>
> A New Printing in the Latest Fashion, Charm and Delight for Splendid Banquets: Banter and Drinking Games

The notion of fashion invoked here is one that combines a repertoire of reference to popular literature and a fondness for lavish consumption. For Ming readers, the elusive notion of charm (*qu* 趣) featured in this full title of the *Boxiao zhuji* seems to have been associated particularly with the sort of fortuitous or even absurd combinations of vastly disparate types of language that Ming drinking games often required of their players. This art of blending required virtuosic skill as well as audacious wit, as reflected in the following example:

> 一令要二曲牌名問答，又要一比名出物押韻。
> 何人來賀壽？便是倘秀才。甚麼禮物？一錠滴滴金，一匹蘇州綾。
> 何人來賀壽？便是三學士。甚麼禮物？一對金錢花，一匹杭州紗。
> 何人來賀壽？便是雙聲子。甚麼禮物？一對撲燈鵝，一匹福州羅。
>
> [*Rule*] This drinking game requires two tune titles to form a question and answer, along with a place name and its local product to rhyme.
> [*Sample solutions*:]
>
> 1. Who has come to the birthday celebration? / It is the "Would-be Budding Talent." What gifts (has he brought)? / One Ingot of "Drip-Dripping gold,"/ One roll of Suzhou silk.
> 2. Who has come to the birthday celebration? / It is the "Three Scholars." What gifts (have they brought)? / One pair of "Gold Coin Flowers," / One roll of Hangzhou gauze.
> 3. Who has come to the birthday celebration? / It is the "Twin Kids." What gifts (have they brought)? / One pair of "Lamp-plunging Moths," / One roll of Fuzhou brocade.[8]

The model responses in this drinking game combine the resourceful recasting of phrases from current literary culture—specifically, the world of the stage—with the language of luxurious commodities. Put another way, the glitter of the words and the glitter of the goods reflect and enhance each other's charm.[9] This imagined space of cultural mastery and material consumption conveys the overall tenor of the world of Ming books, of which the various constituent texts making up the *Boxiao zhuji* are typical. The following sections examine some of these constituents in detail, to see what they reveal about the circulation of knowledge, fashions, and commodities in the late Ming.

The World of Books as Imagined in the Boxiao zhuji

In one of the drinking games presented in the *Boxiao zhuji*, the participant is to compose an impromptu poem meeting the following requirements:

> 一令要手中拿著甚麼詩書，遇見古人貫意。
>
> [Rule:] Holding a certain volume of classical literature in hand, one encounters an ancient person; the composition is to be made coherent in conception.[10]

The sample response that follows reflects some of the basic characteristics of the world of books as presented to readers of that text:

> 手中拿本李白詩，遇見古人是朱熹，說道今年科舉好，相邀同去步雲梯。
>
> Holding in hand a volume of Li Bai's verse,
> The ancient he encounters is Zhu Xi.
> Saying, "this is a good year to enter the exams,"
> They invite one another to climb the ladder to the clouds together.

Scenes in which classmates invite one another to participate in the civil service examinations abound in Chinese drama and were often played for comic effect, as in the *Jingchai ji* 荊釵記 (Tale of the thorn hairpin), where the humor derives from the student's ill-prepared state.[11] In this version, the invitation to set out for the exams is staged as a sort of wish-fulfillment fantasy. With the perfect book in hand (the poetry of Li Bai 李白 [701–62]) to signal his literary talents, the protagonist meets just the right figure of cultural authority, the patron of late imperial orthodox scholarship, Zhu Xi 朱熹 (1130–1200), and, upon exchanging familiar greetings, they venture together into the field of scholarly pursuit and worldly ambition.[12] If such fantasies often bespeak latent anxiety, moreover, this one speaks eloquently about anxiety over one's relation to the world of books, a form of unease that was naturally brought to the fore by the ascendance of printed texts in late imperial China.[13] How does one orient oneself in a proliferating sea of books? How does one create one's own texts, one's own speech, and one's own place within this new textual and cultural environment?

The game text suggests some answers to these questions. In its improbable configuration of prop (the book), characters (the protagonist and Zhu Xi), dialogue, and event (accidental meeting on the road), the game text comments on books, authority, and examination culture, while displaying a ready wit. The result is a kind of historical comedy: the quotidian act of *shuo* 說 (speaking) instead of the antiquarian sounding *yue* 曰 (saying) and the unornamented and colloquial choice of *keju hao* 科舉好 (a good year to enter the civil service examinations) convey an air of impertinent ease—armed, of course, with a good book in hand—before a powerful authority figure (Zhu Xi) who appears here to be of the same class of examinees. This historical comedy frees one from the constraints of historical time, factuality, and probability. In this way it provides the social release of laughter in the face of pent-up pressure felt by actual and would-be examination takers, and engages in a kind of self-mockery of students and their consuming absorption in that particular world of texts, knowledge, and desire. The *Boxiao zhuji* promises its readers that it can fill this need and desire to know the right books and, better yet, lets readers envision a world in which they themselves engage in elegant and witty discursive mastery of those books. And as is typical in the *Boxiao zhuji*, the vision of mastery in the world of books displayed in this game text reflects a subversive wit that delights in violating proprieties of register and genre, and makes all sorts of books and book knowledge the objects of play.

Many of the stylistic registers and textual categories that form the constellation of references in the *Boxiao zhuji* are particular to the period, and the specific late-Ming meanings of terms such as *guwen* 古文 (ancient compositions), *suyu* 俗語 (common speech), *jianghu qiaoyu* 江湖俏語 (winsome sayings of the rivers and lakes), and the like will be explored in detail later in this chapter. But given their central status in education, in the civil service examination system, and in the ideology of both popular and imperial morality, it is no surprise that the orthodox *Four Books* (*Si shu* 四書) dominate as points of reference in the *Boxiao zhuji*.[14] Consider, for example, the following drinking game, one among many of similar form:

一令要論語二句，要君子二字，下句又要頂針。
君子務本。本立而道生。
君子有三畏。畏天命。
君子有三樂。樂節禮樂。[15]

[Rule:] This game requires two lines from the *Analects*. (The starting line) must contain the phrase "A Gentleman," and the ending line must follow "thimble phrasing."[16]
[Example solutions:]
"A gentleman attends to the fundamental. The fundamental is established and the Way grows."[17]
"A gentleman has three fears. Fear the will of Heaven."[18]
"A gentleman has three delights." "Delight in the due ordering of ritual and music."[19]

The first two answers quote sentences that are consecutive in their original source. The third answer assembles two quotations from two sources: the *Analects* and the *Mencius*. This contradicts what the game rule requires, namely that the answer has to be from the *Analects*. This slippage, corrected in other publications,[20] is typical of the sloppiness of low-quality commercial books, which undoubtedly often deserved the criticism they received on this account in subsequent centuries of bibliographical history.[21] It also suggests the general looseness of the game regulations—in these games, the successful gesture is often more important than strict textual accuracy.

For all its leniency with regard to rules, however, this game demands important knowledge and skills from its players. To come up with such answers, one needs not only to memorize the canonical texts but also to be able to reorganize that memory on command to satisfy arbitrary criteria at the level of verbal form, or of secondary connotations that would be extraneous or even deviant in relation to straight readings of the canonical text in its orthodox interpretive context. Such an exercise of memory might certainly have been helpful in exam preparation, or possibly even in further inculcating the moral lessons expressed in the texts, but it is ironic that the use of quotation within this particular game transgresses precisely the behavioral code prescribed in the cited texts. A gentleman should "enjoy the due ordering of ritual and music," but playing drinking games would probably not be counted as the proper "ordering" of ritual and music. The *Analects* itself, in the continuation of one of the very passages quoted in the sample answer above, reads, "delight in unrestrained pleasures, delight in roaming excursions, and delight in banquet entertainments—these are deleterious."[22] In gaming, the orthodox risks losing its intended doctrinal force, becoming one of many texts that can be dissolved and re-assembled in the pursuit of amusement.

Another important aspect of play is its emphasis on compositional skills. This specific game requires the compositional technique of "thimble phrasing" (*dingzhen* 頂針), where the beginning of one line must echo the end of the preceding line. Essentially, playing drinking games is making text, displaying both knowledge of books and creative wit to forge new lines of verse or prose. Throughout the book, the player is asked to pick out formal resemblances in phraseology (as in directives such as "two phrases from the *Four Books*, sharing the same three final characters" 一令要四書二句, 下要三字相同)[23] or broad analogies in meaning (as in "state a common aphorism, followed by a citation from the *Four Books* to explicate its meaning" 一令上要說成語, 下要以四書解意),[24] and to follow a number of abstruse rules governing relations among pairs or chains of multiple citations (such as "coherence of basic idea" 貫意, "combined main idea" 合意, "implied relation of question and answer" 暗藏問答之意,[25] or "dissecting [i.e., explicating] the idea" 破意[26]). Added to this are requirements for rhyming and rhythm (as with rules requiring rhyme 押韻),[27] improvisation (as with rules for recitation tailored to an object or event present at the moment of performance 對景生情),[28] or rhetorical or acoustic effects (as with rules regarding "ingenious phrases" 巧語[29] or "phrases with the same sound but different meanings" 同音異義).[30]

In addition to such ultra-canonical texts as the *Four Books*, other books essential for success in the *Boxiao zhuji* games include the Ming state legal canon, the *Da Ming lü* 大明律 (Great Ming code),[31] poetic primers such as the *Qian jia shi* and the *Shen tong shi* 神童詩 (Poems of child geniuses), basic literacy primers such as the *Qian zi wen* 千字文 (Thousand character classic) or the *Bai jia xing* 百家姓 (Hundred surnames), and other educational and ethical primers such as the *Meng qiu* 蒙求 (Initial searches) and Zhu Xi's *Xiaoxue* 小學 (Elemental learning). In various ways, all these became foundational texts that shaped the textual landscape for Ming readers across a wide range of social and educational strata.[32] The use of these textual authorities in the *Boxiao zhuji*, however, persistently reflects a delight in dislocation and crossing of boundaries of genre and register:

一令要千家詩一句，下取大明律一句斷之：
春日一刻值千金，高抬時價。
夜半鐘聲到客船，越度關津。
紫薇花對紫薇郎，同姓通婚。[33]

[Rule:] This game requires one line from *The Poems by a Thousand Masters*, then a line from the *Great Ming Code* to deliver a judgment.
[Exemplary solutions:]
"A moment of springtime is worth a thousand in gold"[34]—"Price-gouging."[35]
"The sound of the Midnight bell reaches the traveler's boat"[36]—"Circumventing official checkpoints or ferry crossings."[37]
"Wisteria flower faces wisteria lad"[38]—"Marriage between bearers of the same surname."[39]

Though the *Da Ming lü* was a Ming state statute, and the editions issued by the court held ultimate authority over legal practice, its provisions permeated the realm of popular reading materials as well, where they were available for practical use in people's daily lives and in the business operations of commoners.[40] The Ming codes thus came to be more generally viewed as something desirable and prestigious to read and master (as reflected, too, in the use of references to Ming codes in detective and court stories in vernacular fiction of the period). Such legal statutes were also rendered into rhymed mnemonics (*gejue* 歌訣) in commercially produced books. To display knowledge of the *Da Ming lü* in these games could mean one had drawn on any number of reworkings of the *Da Ming lü* instead of, or in addition to, the state-issued editions.[41] In games like that cited above, moreover, command over this range of texts could provide verbal material for spoof and wordplay quite apart from legal or administrative purposes.

In the following riddle, whose answer is drawn from Zhu Xi's *Xiao xue*, a moral apothegm is skewed in a context where it no longer bears any symbolic weight but rather becomes a verbal surface that tests the respondent's memory and associative power:

小學謎
夜行以燭，無燭則止。
元宵遶街嬉，全憑燈火種；
燒盡銀燭炬，住步且回歸。

A riddle on *Elementary Learning*
[answer:] One travels at night with candle, when one lacks a candle one stops.[42]
[riddle:] On the night of the First Fifteenth festival one plays up and down the streets, all relying on the seed of lanterns and torches;
when one's silver candlestick burns out, one stops one's wandering steps and turns back.[43]

This sort of dissociation and recontextualization of quotes and tags from authoritative texts is part of the process whereby works such as the *Boxiao zhuji* exercised their appeal. The play of recombination in such games and riddles in the *Boxiao zhuji* provided a channel for readers/players to display both verbal command of the touchstone texts and the sort of witty mastery that could put those texts to use at one's whim. In addition, as this game indicates, quotidian detail, often more lively than orthodox interpretation would suggest, is a favored technique to create laughter and display wit when matched with such an orthodox text as the *Four Books*. A similar dynamic is at work in the following riddle when a line from the *Mencius* is mentioned:

孟子迷	Riddle on the *Mencius*
我視魚兒活潑鮮，	See the fishy, lively and bright—
囑婦勿把下油煎。	I tell the wife not to drop it in the oil to fry.
聽得廚中刀砧响，	When I hear the clash of knife and board in the kitchen,
情願長齋獻佛前。	I wish earnestly to take a vow of vegetarian fasting, and to offer it before the Buddha.[44]

The answer is: "If he [the superior person] sees it alive, he cannot bear to see it die; if he hears its cry, he cannot bear to eat its flesh" 見其生, 不忍見其死, 聞其聲, 不忍食其肉 from *Mencius* 1A.7. In the original conversation between Mencius and King Xuan of Qi, King Xuan's reluctance to see a terrified ox led off to be sacrificed becomes the point of entry for Mencius's argument that the King, albeit not apparently the brightest or most virtuous ruler, could develop this capacity for empathy and become a sage king. In the riddle, the lively fish, and the domestic conversation between a husband and wife, tells a comic story of the conflict between culinary desire, Buddhist fasting, and the notion of building merit through Buddhist offering. In the end, judging from the sound of knife and block from the kitchen, it seems that the fish did not escape its fate, and the final line may involve another layer of humor if the contemplated Buddhist offering is in fact the cooked and delectable fish. Suffice it to say that the riddle takes us into a markedly different world from that of the original *Mencius* conversation.

In other instances the quotidian reality against which the high-cultural references are framed is quite bleak, as in the following riddle-poem calling for an answer from the *Qian zi wen*:

長天雁獨飛，	Across the long sky a wild goose flies alone;
屋破雨澆灘。	a room in disrepair, rain drips and soaks.
節婦孀居苦，	A virtuous widow—her bereaved life is bitter;
傳揚天下知。	spread and exalted, her example is known world-wide.[45]

The required answer is the four-character phrase *gu lou gua wen* 孤陋寡聞, meaning "ignorant and ill-informed," most commonly as a formal expression of self-deprecation. Each line of the riddle-poem encodes one character from the expression: "lone," "crude" (hinted at in the poem both by the crudity of the dwelling described and by a pun on *lou* 陋 "crude" and *lou* 漏 "leaky"), "lacking" (in the poem with a play on the use of the character *gua* in the vernacular compound *guafu* 寡婦, or "widow"), and "hear/know about." The appeal of the riddle stems from the gap between the formal tone of the expression as it circulates in refined speech and the vivid picture in the poetic lines of lowly and despondent daily life. Through the act of making such a riddle, the anonymous authors of the material collected in the *Boxiao zhuji* found a channel to voice quotidian experience and perspectives.

Another prominent category of source drawn on in the *Boxiao zhuji* is dramatic literature. Within this category, the *Story of the Western Wing* is far and away the favorite reference text:

一令要千家詩一句，中間俗語一句，結尾要西廂一句相關合意。
一枝紅杏出墻來，如何不摘下，唱：粉墻兒高似青天。
一為遷客去長沙，路遠難得到，唱：見安排着車兒馬兒。
一任晚風相對愁，如何不勸他，唱：兩下裡都一樣害相思。

[Rule:]
This game requires one line from *The Poems by a Thousand Masters*, one line of common speech in the middle and one line from *The Story of the Western Wing* in the end to form a recapitulation.
[Exemplary solutions:]
1. "A branch of red apricot blossoms sticks out over the wall."[46]
   Why not pluck it?
   [SING:] "The whitewashed wall is as high as the blue sky."
2. "All because a demoted traveler goes off to Changsha."[47]
   How hard it is to get to such a far place!
   [SING:] "Now have been arranged carriages and horses."
3. "Let the evening breeze sorrow with me."[48]
   Why not urge them to get better?
   [SING:] "Because they both suffer from lovesickness."[49]

Using "common speech" (*suyu*) as a bridge, these games stitch together what, in traditional bibliographical systems, were one highly esteemed genre (poetry) with one problematic and suspect genre (drama), thereby disrupting the sense of hierarchy and articulation of register between them and suggesting the commensurability of the two within this particular space of textual play.[50] Here as more generally, the games collected in this sort of publication tend to challenge rather than reinforce established cultural habits, particularly by destabilizing hierarchies of genre and style. This particular sort of play involving connecting and mixing texts of different status seems to have been a persistent feature of the forms of textual gaming found at private gatherings. The reader/user of a model text like the *Boxiao zhuji* is assumed to be not a passive recipient but an active performer, as foregrounded by the fact that the game participant is expected to sing, rather than simply recite, the capping quote from the *Story of the Western Wing*.[51]

The textual status of the *Story of the Western Wing* underwent decisive changes in the Ming. One indication of the widespread popularity of the play in the period is the sheer number of separate Ming editions now known—well over a hundred.[52] In addition, episodes from the play enjoyed wide circulation in anthologies of dramatic excerpts, reaching Ming audiences ranging from theater and literary scholars to commoner theatergoers and becoming a shared reference text for all strata of Ming society.[53] As subsequent examples from Ming book culture will bear out, the *Story of the Western Wing* was not just an influential literary and dramatic work—it permeated vernacular speech, folk aphorisms, and the language of visual representation.

The sense of both the power and the paradox of such dramatic texts attaining canonicity is conveyed in games such as the one below, which juxtaposes orthodox texts with yet another Ming dramatic canon:

> 一令要曲一句，下要四書一句斷之合意。
> 倚定門兒眼望穿—未見其人也。
> 思量那日離故鄉—父子不相見。
> 百年夫婦今宵合—樂亦在其中矣。
>
> [Rule:]
> This game requires a line from an aria first, then a line from the *Four Books* to summarize it and match its meaning.
> [Sample solutions:]
> "Leaning against the door, my eyes are exhausted"—"I have not yet having met such a person."
> "I recall that day when I took leave of home"—"father and son do not meet."
> "Husband and wife for a hundred years meet tonight"—"There is also joy in this."[54]

Scholars of traditional China will recognize the capping quotations from the *Analects* and *Mencius*, but the source for the dramatic quotations reveals a peculiarity of the Ming dramatic canon: all the dramatic citations in this example derive from the early classic of southern drama, the *Story of the Lute* (*Pipa ji* 琵琶記).[55] Games like this one helped to perpetuate the lofty status of the *Story of the Lute*, a core cultural reference to be memorized and drawn on for display of one's mastery of current knowledge, as noted by Xu Wei 徐渭 (1521–93):

> 時有以《琵琶記》進呈者，高皇笑曰："五經，四書，布帛菽粟也，家家皆有；高明《琵琶記》，如山珍海錯，富貴家不可無。"
>
> At that time there was one who presented the *Story of the Lute*. The Eminent Emperor laughed and said, "The *Five Classics* and the *Four Books* are like cloth and grain—every family has them; Gao Ming's *Story of the Lute* is like delicacies of land and sea—families of the rich and noble cannot be without them."[56]

Though this anecdote is of dubious credibility, it is important because it conveys the cultural cachet of the *Pipa ji* through the voice of the emperor himself. To be able to recite or sing lines from the *Pipa ji* from memory was to participate in a fashion that enjoyed empire-wide currency, as interest in theater had become a marker of both cultural prestige and luxury consumption.[57]

Stylistic Registers and Compositional Techniques in the Boxiao Zhuji

The juxtaposition of such dramatic canons as *Story of the Western Wing* and *Story of the Lute* with the orthodox *Four Books* in the textual constellation of the *Boxiao zhuji* vividly conveys the widespread popularity and cultural prestige associated with these dramatic texts. The pervasive presence of dramatic texts and performance in the Ming book world will be felt throughout the following chapters. But the world of texts unfolding before us in the *Boxiao zhuji* contains still other dimensions that have been obscured by neglect in the centuries since the Ming, and in the remaining sections of this chapter I will examine some of them: first, the category of *guwen* 古文 (ancient-style writing), and then *suyu* 俗語 (common speech). A concluding section will explore the phenomenon of the popular anthology as exemplified by the *Huang Ming shixuan* incorporated into the *Boxiao zhuji*'s final *juan*.

Ancient-style Writing

Many of the specifications for various games throughout the *Boxiao zhuji* include references to the puzzling category of *guwen*:

一令要古文詩一句，又要一古人一地名。
子瞻謫南海/張翰去江東/蘇武在胸(sic)奴

[Rule:]
This game requires a poetic line of "ancient-style writing," which should also have an ancient person and a name of a place.
[Sample solutions:]
1. Zizhan is demoted to Nanhai.
2. Zhang Han goes to Jiangdong.
3. Su Wu among the Xiongnu.[58]

The lines offered as solutions for the game are in one of the common meters (pentasyllabic) of classical Chinese poetry, but otherwise there is little that at first glance appears discernibly "ancient," or even particularly poetic, about them. What, then, qualifies them as belonging to the category of "ancient-style writing" as stipulated in the game rules? The fragmentary phrases presented as *guwen* in the following drinking game solutions seem intermittently poetic enough, but again it seems hard to pin down exactly how they qualify for this label:

一令要古文四句，每句只三字，字意相串。
薄薄酒，勝茶湯。粗粗布，勝無裳。
一片石，數株松。遠又淡，近又濃。
吹龍笛，擊鼉鼓。皓齒歌，細腰舞。

[Rule:]
This game requires four lines from "ancient-style writing," each line with only three characters, and the meanings of the characters should cohere.
[Sample solutions:]
1. Thin wine is better than tea; coarse cloth is better than no clothes.
2. A slab of rock, several trunks of pine; what is at distance is vague, what is close is vivid.
3. Blow the dragon flute, beat the tortoise drum; white teeth sing, lithe waists dance.[59]

Some riddles require solutions drawn from "ancient-style writing":

古文四句
鄰舍養兒我也養，
聰明魯鈍一般同。
或作朝廷金帶客，

或作前呼後擁人。

兩家各生子，
賢愚同一初。
一爲公與相，
一爲馬前卒。

[To be answered in] four lines of "ancient writing"
[Conundrum:]
My neighbor raises a son, and I do, too;
in cleverness and stupidity, same in every regard.
One became a gold-belted guest at court;
the other, a lackey calling out ahead and crowding up behind.
[Sample solution:]
Two families each bear sons,
alike in worth or foolishness in their beginnings.
One is a duke and minister;
the other a foot-soldier before the horses.[60]

Again, what criteria qualify the quatrain given as the answer to this riddle as *guwen*? Might *guwen* in such contexts simply refer in a loose way to ancient writings, or to ancient linguistic style? If that were the case, then the players of such games could simply draw on whatever range of classical texts their reading experience happened to include. Closer examination of both the range of reference and the usage of the term *guwen* in *Boxiao zhuji* and other similar texts, however, reveals that it in fact refers to a single more or less stable source text known as the *Guwen zhenbao* 古文眞寶 (True treasures of ancient-style writing, see fig. 1.2). Comprising a first volume (*qian ji* 前集) containing verse and a second (*hou ji* 後集) containing prose, the *Guwen zhenbao* was a text of the "commentated anthology" (*pingdian xuanben* 評點選本) type, compiled in the late Southern Song (1127–1279) or early Yuan (1234–1368).[61] Although this text fell into neglect in China by the high Qing and has been largely ignored in modern China, it was exceedingly prominent in Ming China and remained so long thereafter in Korea and Japan.

The authors for the lines quoted as *guwen* in the above game texts include literary luminaries such as Huang Tingjian 黃庭堅 (1045–1105), Li Bai 李白, Su Shi 蘇軾 (1037–1101), Wu Rong 吳融 (fl. late ninth to early tenth century), Li He 李賀 (790–816), and Han Yu 韓愈 (768–824).[62] For most modern readers, however, those lines cohere very little either in their own intrinsic poetic qualities or in their perceived

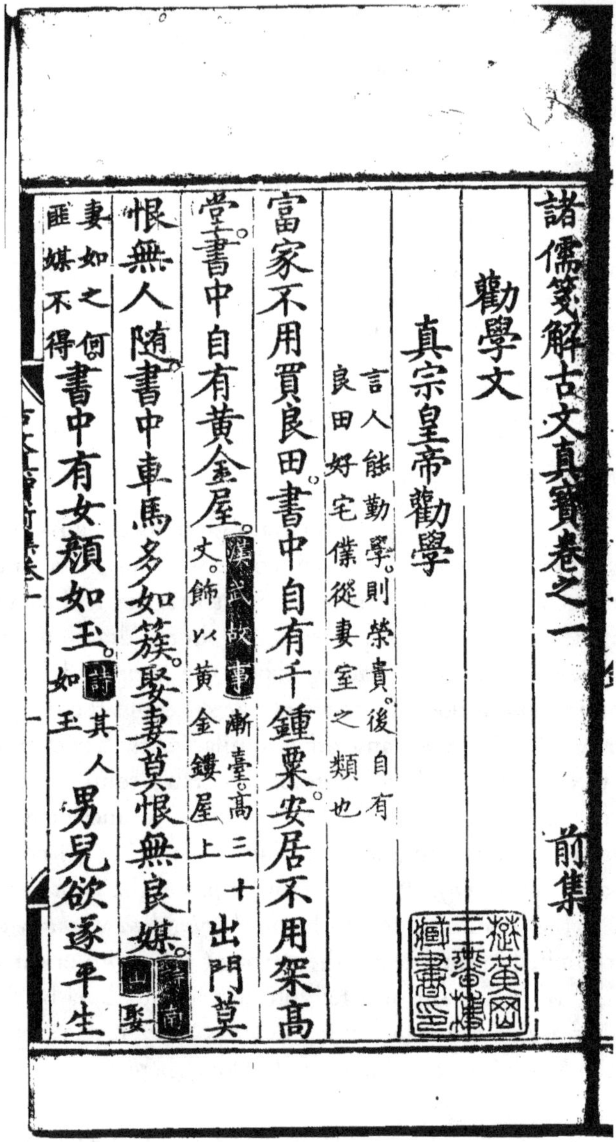
諸儒箋解古文真寶卷之一 前集

勸學文

真宗皇帝勸學

言人能勤學則榮貴後自有良田好宅僕從妻室之類也

富家不用買良田書中自有千鍾粟安居不用架高堂書中自有黃金屋漢武故事漸臺高三十丈飾以黃金鏤屋上出門莫恨無人隨書中車馬多如簇娶妻莫恨無良媒詩南山娶妻如之何匪媒不得書中有女顏如玉詩其人如玉男兒欲遂平生

Fig. 1.2. A page from an imperial edition of *Guwen zhenbao*, dated 1583. The anthology is led off by a group of *Quan xue wen* 勸學文 (Essays to exhort learning), the first of which, seen here, was attributed to the Zhenzong Emperor (968–1022) of the Song. The essay extols the practical and material benefits of learning—possession of fertile land and a good house, servants, and wife (or wives)—in addition to glory and status. This essay and the *Guwen zhenbao* itself open by borrowing the voice of an emperor (via an attribution likely to be dubious) to sanction and legitimize what might otherwise seem quite common and worldly sentiments. Photo courtesy of the Gest Collection, Princeton East Asian Library.

importance or typicality of the authors from whom they are drawn. The mere fact that literary tastes shift over time is not surprising. But beyond these shifts, the selections from ancient literature appearing in the *Guwen zhenbao* bring to light further distinctions between the elite notion of *guwen* advocated by figures such as the "Former and Latter Seven Masters" 前後七子, whose tastes and activities decisively shaped Qing and later accounts of the literary history of the Ming,[63] and the less manicured, more practical and reader-friendly notion of *guwen* reflected in the marketplace of Ming woodblock texts. And if we measure influence by the range of readership that either sort of *guwen* impacted during the Ming, it was probably this latter form that was the more influential in its own age.

Thus the *Guwen zhenbao* points to a common notion of *guwen*, one less involved in scholarly and historical debate and more geared towards the needs of average readers, as reflected by the helpful annotations and instructive commentary included along with the selections in the *Guwen zhenbao*. To conceive of this distinction as one between highbrow and lowbrow, or between standard and marginal literary tastes, however, would be not only inadequate but misleading. For the *guwen* encapsulated in the *Guwen zhenbao* was not only more wide-reaching in its impact (as seen, for example, from its infiltration of the cultures of riddling and drinking games as reflected in the *Boxiao zhuji* and other such woodblock publications), but also had its own cachet of prestige, making it eligible to serve as part of a gesture of elegance and erudition on the part of no less than the emperor himself. In the following preface to the imperial edition of the *Guwen zhenbao*, the Wanli emperor describes himself as devoting the hours of his elegant leisure to reading and annotating his own copy:

> 朕每退居清燕，游意篇章，于《古文真寶》一編，時加批閱。
>
> When We Retreat and dwell amid pure delights, disporting Our mind by roaming in *belles-lettres*, in this compilation, the *Guwen zhenbao*, We from time to time annotate and review.[64]

What a text like the *Guwen zhenbao* (or the *Boxiao zhuji*) demonstrates is that many publications from this period that by later criteria might fall outside the boundaries of serious bibliographical respectability had a breadth of impact and cultural prestige that was far more than merely marginal.

We can obtain some sense of the place of the *Guwen zhenbao* in Ming culture from a survey of its printing history. With extant editions dating back as far as the Yuan dynasty, the *Guwen zhenbao* had long captured the attention of commercial editors, publishers, esteemed court officials and scholars, and emperors in the Ming.[65] Known printings from the early Ming include one from the Jingtai period (1450–56) and another commissioned by the Hongzhi emperor (r. 1487–1505). Among the late Ming commercial developments in the printing history of the *Guwen zhenbao* are editions by three well-known publishers from Fujian province: Liu Longtian 劉龍田 (courtesy name of Liu Dayi 大易, 1560–1625), Yu Wentai of the formidable Yu publishing family, and Zheng Shirong 鄭世容 (fl. Wanli reign), whose edition was collated by the esteemed prime minister Ye Xianggao 葉向高 (1562–1627).[66] Ye was a prolific writer with a wide range of interests, one of whose defining intellectual accomplishments was his leading role in the dialogue with the Jesuit missionary Giulio Aleni (1582–1649) on Jesuit learning and Chinese beliefs, recorded in the latter's *Sanshan lunxue* 三山論學.[67] For such a prominent political figure who was pivotal in introducing and making new types of text and knowledge to have worked on the *Guwen zhenbao* gives an indication of the esteem in which that work was held in the Ming.[68]

As suggested by the above quote from the preface to its imperial edition, the *Guwen zhenbao* reached the pinnacle of its glory during the Wanli reign. The *Ming shilu* 明實錄 (Veritable record of the Ming) records that in the fourth month of Wanli year eleven (1583),

> 癸丑，大學士張四維等擬御製《古文眞寶》前序、後跋及《昭仁殿箴》、《弘德殿箴》恭進御覽。
>
> On the day *guichou* (May 22, 1583), the Grand Academician Zhang Siwei and others drafted the imperial preface and postscript for the *Guwen zhenbao*, the "Admonition for Zhaoren Palace," and "Admonition for Hongde Palace," which were humbly presented to the throne for his majesty's review.[69]

This preface and postscript graced the new imperial edition, which was printed from a set of woodblocks newly cut by the Directorate of Ceremony and entitled *Zhuru jianjie Guwen zhenbao* 諸儒箋解古文眞寶 (True treasures of ancient-style writing, commented and explicated by various scholars). Two months later, the emperor bestowed two sets of *Guwen zhenbao* on the Grand Academician Shen Shixing 申時行 (1535–1614) as a gesture of imperial favor.[70] Though the contexts are widely removed, this sort of appropriation of the *Guwen zhenbao* for the political theatrics of imperial favor is not entirely unlike the use of the same text in the riddles and game texts of the *Boxiao zhuji*: in both contexts this text serves as an emblem of cultural prestige and erudition.

A wide range of individuals and institutions took part in the production and promotion of the *Guwen zhenbao* during the Ming. The book circulated both through imperial channels, by which the court made and distributed books to its officials and libraries,[71] and in the commercial book market, as a commodity sold by bookstores and peddlers. Scholar-officials participated in the production process by working either with the imperial court (as in the case of Zhang Siwei 張四維 (1526–85)) or with commercial publishers (as in the case of Ye Xianggao). While the court ceremony of bestowing officials sets of *Guwen zhenbao* showcased the book as a text with empire-wide sanction and cachet, commercial publishing and distribution facilitated the text's wide circulation to society at large. The interdependence of imperial promotion and marketplace production was key in the making of a foundational text, with court and marketplace feeding off each other's enthusiasm for the same book.

As the publication history of the *Guwen zhenbao* suggests, conventional bibliographic distinctions of *fangke* 坊刻 (commercial imprint), *sike* 私刻 (private imprint), and *guanke* 官刻 (official imprint) may be applicable to actual printed copies, but that does not necessarily mean any given book's circulation and influence was constrained by such boundaries.[72] Rather, commercial production and circulation was but one phase of a larger field of exchange and interplay in which each edition reasserted the discursive and social significance invested in the text by various agents, institutions, and persons.[73] Throughout the history of Chinese printing, processes of canonization and popularization could work hand in hand,[74] as for example in the case of the *Song wen jian* 宋文鑑 (Mirror of Song writing), when scholars under the auspices of Emperor Xiaozong (r. 1163–89) of the Southern Song reworked a compilation that had already gained a strong reputation in the commercial marketplace, which in turn spurred another wave of commercial promotion.[75] Alternatively, as with the *Ming Code*, commercial publishers could adopt an official text for popular promotion, thereby transforming what was initially an administrative work into a touchstone reference in society at large.[76]

Several influential anthologies of "ancient-style writing" circulated during the Ming, but the *Guwen zhenbao* was often the one that a student first encountered. Ming discussions of this ubiquitous text shed light on the ways readers from various walks of life related to literary tradition and to books in general. Jiang Mian 蔣冕 (1462–1532), a high official at the court of the Zhengde emperor (1505–21), recalls in the 1520s that he first read the poem "Du Lisi zhuan" 讀李斯傳 (On reading Li Si's biography) in a commercial copy of *Guwen zhenbao*. Taking delight in the lines, he recited it often and grew very fond of it, all the while without knowing who the author of the poem was. Only when he later traveled to the capital and had access to more books did he discover that the author was Cao Ye 曹鄴 (ca. 816–ca. 875), a poet of the late Tang dynasty (618–907).[77] In this story, the *Guwen zhenbao* shaped the young man's life and relationship to books, serving as a reference point through a career of geographical and social mobility. More specifically, the *Guwen zhenbao* connected Jiang to the medieval writer Cao Ye, a connection that lasted a lifetime, as Jiang wrote, "I find it is now more than fifty years that this master's poems have not left my mind, whether asleep or awake" 蓋冕於公詩寤寐不忘者五十餘年.

In this anecdote, the *Guwen zhenbao* provides a range of texts whose prestige and popular currency are guaranteed by their inclusion in that compilation, without raising any questions, or providing any information, about the authorship and historical origins of the individual works included. Although the affinity that Jiang Mian feels for that particular poem by Cao Ye eventually leads him to seek out the author and to become a scholar of Cao Ye, the *Guwen zhenbao* initially presents that poem as part of an undifferentiated storehouse of generically "classical" writings. In this connection, the reminiscences about the *Guwen zhenbao* on the part of Sun Xu 孫緒 (*jinshi* degree 1499) are notable, since he expresses an evolving curiosity not about the authorship of an individual work first encountered in the *Guwen zhenbao*, but about the compiler of the *Guwen zhenbao* itself:

> 緒幼時先吏部口授《古文眞寶》內小詩及諸小詞，因問先公《眞寶》爲誰氏所選。先公笑曰："吾亦不知爲誰。"自是先公每詢諸執友，如東田先生，先師漳南先生，舅氏銅陵先生，皆謝不知。迨緒稍長，讀《崇古文訣》，愛其文。其編選者亦止稱曰"迂齋先生"亦不知爲誰。後爲吏部，屬匏菴吴先生寬，爲左侍郎，博學多識。暇日緒因問此二人爲誰，匏菴笑曰："《眞寶》永堅黃叔易所選，迂齋不知也。"余後閱《四明文獻錄》，見所謂迂齋嘗選《文訣》者爲樓

昉，吕東萊門人，紹熙四年陳亮榜進士，嘗論和議之非，忤姦相貶斥以終，蓋亦正人也。

When I was a child, my late father of the Ministry of Personnel gave me oral instruction on the short poems and all the lyrics from the *Guwen zhenbao*, and in that connection I asked him who had been the compiler of the *Zhenbao*. My father smiled and said, "I do not know myself who that was." From this time on, my father would often inquire of his close friends, such as Master Dongtian, my former teacher Master Zhangnan, or my maternal uncle Master Tongling, but they all confessed they did not know. As I gradually grew older I read the *Chonggu wenjue* and was particularly fond of its writings. Its compiler was also referred to simply as "Master Yuzhai," and I did not know who this was, either. Later when I served in the Ministry of Personnel it happened that the Vice Minister of the Left was Wu Kuan, known as Master Paoan, a man of wide erudition and much understanding. On a leisure day I took the opportunity of asking him who these two men were, and he smiled and said, "The *Zhenbao* was compiled by Huang Shuyi of Yongjian; as for who Yuzhai might be, I do not know." Later when reading in the *Siming wenxian lu* I saw it recorded that the man called "Yuzhai" who had compiled the *Wenjue* was Lou Fang, a disciple of Lü Donglai (i.e., Lü Zuqian 呂祖謙), who had received the *jinshi* degree in the class of year four of the Shaoxi period (1193), along with Chen Liang. He once wrote a treatise on the error of the policy of pacification with the north, and having in this way offended villainous ministers, was demoted and banished to the end of his days. One can see that this, too, was an upright man.[78]

Sun Xu's account of his personal development from a child given elementary literary instruction by his father to an established member of the political and cultural elite is shaped first around his relation to the *Guwen zhenbao*, and then to another similar compilation, the *Chonggu wenjue* 崇古文訣 (Keys to writing from exalted antiquity). From his first contact with the *Guwen zhenbao* under the tutelage of his father, the successive stages of this narrative show him gaining in both cultural expertise and social standing—as he succeeds to official service in the same ministry where his father had served before him and establishes social contacts with scholars and officials who appear at least the equals of his father's earlier circle. The oral and textual dimensions of transmission and understanding are interwoven in the account: the first instruction Sun Xu receives in the *Guwen zhenbao* is conveyed orally by his father, as is most of the ensuing inquiry about the compiler's identity. This reminds us that questions of book knowledge and questions of social circle and social prestige were intimately intertwined. The longstanding question about the compiler of the *Guwen zhenbao* is resolved quite casually as Sun Xu hobnobs with Wu Kuan 吴寬 (1435–1504),

renowned scholar, book collector, and vice-minister of one of the highest offices in the imperial bureaucracy, who had begun his career as the top-ranked scholar in the palace examination in 1472.[79] Sun Xu's eventual resolution of who compiled the *Chonggu wenjue* reads as an affirmation of his complete social and cultural autonomy, his unusual curiosity about the authorship of these touchstone anthologies having seemingly given him a sort of personal stake in his relations not only with contemporary scholarly heavyweights but with these accomplished yet seemingly little-known men of the past (i.e., the compilers) as well.

The other commentated *guwen* anthology mentioned in Sun Xu's account, the *Chonggu wenjue*, was inherited, like several such anthologies, from the Southern Song and Yuan periods, and it is in relation to these books and the conventions of textual critique they established that the *Guwen zhenbao* came to occupy its unique position. The rise of the commentated *guwen* anthology as a form in itself represented a novel intellectual current of the Southern Song. The most influential of these compilations were the *Guwen guanjian* 古文關鍵 (Pathways to ancient writing) of Lü Zuqian 吕祖謙 (1137–1181), the *Chonggu wenjue* of Lou Fang 樓昉 (1193 *jinshi*), and later the *Wenzhang guifan* 文章軌範 (Rules and models for writing) of Xie Fangde 謝枋得 (1226–89). All these compiler-commentators were established figures in their own right, and scholarly genealogy ties their compiling and commentating activities together. Lü Zuqian, as a leading scholar and a close ally of Zhu Xi, facilitated the epic meeting between Zhu Xi and Lu Jiuyuan known as the Ehu Summit (*Ehu dahui* 鵝湖大會).[80] What made Lü Zuqian distinctive among the Daoxue masters was his talent and influence in the textual refinement (*wenzhang*) of his day; along with his intellectual activities of a specifically Daoxue bent, he took on the editorship of such influential literary compilations of the time as the *Song wen jian* (see above). His *Guwen guanjian* focuses on *guwen* from the Tang and Song masters, and it served as a model for later collections. Lou Fang, a disciple of Lü Zuqian, modeled his own compilation after Lü's, expanding the scope of selection to earlier writings; Xie Fangde's compilation continued this tradition to add his own ideas and guidelines on writing, most notably the two new concepts of *fangdan wen* 放膽文 (bold writing) and *xiaoxin wen* 小心文 (careful writing). Though these three anthologies thus appeared as a linked group of model and successors, each had its own distinctive features and emphases. For example, in a gesture to link his anthology closely to the needs of examination candidates, Xie Fangde "numbered" the seven fascicles of his book with one character each from the line "王侯將相有種乎" (Are the ranks of prince, marquis, general, and minister inborn?), a classical reference that casts an aura of heroic, even naked, social and political ambition around the anthology.[81]

These commented anthologies, born of the Song *guwen* movement, were part of a general shift in the textual landscape during the Southern Song. Not only did they perpetuate the dominion of a body of model texts and writers, but they continuously aligned textual styles and models with political aspirations, imperial visions, and the tastes of the literati. The *Guwen zhenbao* was compiled at the tail end of this phenomenon, sometime during the Southern Song or Yuan.[82] In fact, the *Guwen zhenbao* is an anthology of anthologies, drawing heavily on, among other sources, the three aforementioned *guwen* anthologies.[83] Thus the *Guwen zhenbao* is a composite text, assembling commentators and models of exemplary classical style from a wide range of sources. Whereas the status of the three Southern Song anthologies mentioned above might have hinged on the prestige of their compilers, the selling point of the *Guwen zhenbao* was the more practical notion that it included everything one could possibly need to know about *guwen*.

It is perhaps for this reason that the *Guwen zhenbao* eventually superseded all other commentated *guwen* anthologies as the preferred childhood primer and reference text during the Ming. Partially based on this greater role in education, it continued to occupy an important place in the lives of the Ming general reading public. And even though it was often described as a text for beginning learners, it nonetheless enjoyed a remarkably exalted status as an emblem of the virtues of reading and classical culture more generally, as publishers of succeeding editions went out of their way to point out. Consider, for example, this encomium from the Wanli emperor's preface to the *Guwen zhenbao*:

> 朕觀前代稽古好文之主，雖雍容燕閑，不廢簡冊，非徒博覽洽聞，蓋亦定心養心之助也。
>
> We observe that all those rulers from before who were versed in antiquity and fond of cultural refinement, even in their moments of leisure and merriment, would not break off their perusal of books. This is not merely a means of gaining wide perspectives and complete information—rather, it may also be called an aid to the quieting and cultivation of the mind.[84]

The commentated *guwen* anthologies from the Song and their outgrowths in the Ming not only served as a body of model texts (*fanwen* 範文 or *wenfan* 文範) for Ming readers, but also established a basic vocabulary for critiquing and analyzing texts, a vocabulary that, in turn, extended to many other areas of literary experience. The contemporaneous development of *xiaoshuo* criticism and commentarial forms (*pingdian* 評點) is a case in point; in this later tradition, associated with late Ming figures such as Li Zhi 李贄 (1527–1602) or Jin Shengtan 金聖嘆 (1608–61), many of the technical terms, compositional rules, and even the vernacular-inflected voice of the commentators had earlier roots in the *Guwen zhenbao* and other commentated *guwen* anthologies (fig. 1.3).[85]

My purpose in emphasizing the role of these Song or Yuan commentated anthologies is not to say that Ming attitudes and insights did not contribute to the critical language and forms of the time, but rather to map these Song-Yuan commentaries onto the contemporaneous material conditions of the Ming textual world. In other words, these Song (or Yuan) commentaries were not simply chronologically earlier "sources" for Ming critical practice but rather provided significant material, in the context of the expansion of production and readership of woodblock publications during the Ming, for new uses that went beyond what their originators could have envisioned. Viewed from the experience of Ming readers, the *Guwen zhenbao* was part of their own contemporaneous world of texts and thus, in a real and material sense, a Ming book. In fact, many of its early readers knew the *Guwen zhenbao* only as a Ming book, as reflected in the *Qianqing tang shumu* 千頃堂書目 of the famous bibliophile Huang Yuji 黄虞稷 (1629–91).[86] Many of these earlier *guwen* anthologies, moreover, were updated and made more characteristically Ming by the addition of illustrations.

As a compilation of a range of earlier sources, then, the *Guwen zhenbao* was uniquely placed within this larger textual culture. In its multiple roles in Ming reading life—as a primer for children, a reader for candidates preparing examination compositions, a sourcebook for the literary inspiration of readers and writers, and, finally, as a cultural commodity embodying a prestigious brand of scholarly refinement—it molded the early reading experiences of generations of readers, shaping their tastes and reading habits.[87] This goes some way towards explaining why commentated editions, whether of *guwen*, of examination essays, of poetry, or

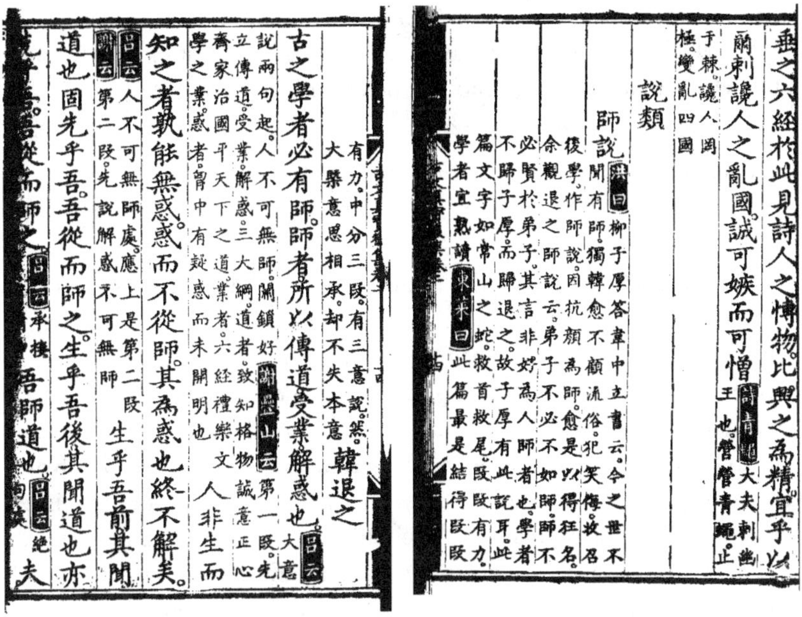

Fig. 1.3. Pages from the 1583 Sili jian edition of *Guwen zhenbao*. The pages feature Han Yu's *Shi shuo* 師說 (Discourse on teachers), upheld as a masterpiece of *guwen* style. The commentators shown here include Hong Mai 洪邁 (1123–1202), Lü Zuqian, and Xie Fangde. Technical vocabulary for elucidating expository structures, such as the "Changshan snake formation" 常山之蛇 (on the right) or the "linked chain" 關鎖 (on the left), were to become favorite terms in Ming fiction commentaries. Photo courtesy of the Gest Collection, Princeton East Asian Library.

of fiction or dramatic works, tended to enjoy a great market advantage during the Ming. The *Guwen zhenbao* in this way was emblematic of the literary culture of an age in which anthologists and commentators, as arbiters of taste and exegetes of compositional secrets, enjoyed prestige that could rival or even surpass that of the authors themselves.[88]

By the mid-Qing, the *Guwen zhenbao* had begun to fade from the Chinese reading world and bibliographical memory. Possible factors contributing to the end of its circulation in China include the rising importance of Qing anthologies such as the *Guwen guanzhi* 古文觀止 (Definitive displays of ancient-style writing) along with the generally dismissive attitude towards the book on the part of Qing bibliophiles. If we recall the sense of wonder and admiration that Sun Xu expressed as he related his search for the compiler of the *Guwen zhenbao*, we can sense the degree to which tastes and standards had shifted when we read the comments by the editors of the *Qinding Tianlu linlang shumu* 欽定天祿琳琅書目 (Imperially established catalog of the Gems of Heavenly Favor library), a catalog of Qing imperial holdings, on the work:

> 書中註釋詞意淺陋，似非名人所作。
>
> As for the annotations and exegeses in this book, both phrasing and conception are shallow and shabby, giving the impression it was not put together by anyone of much repute.[89]

The *General Catalog* to the Siku collection does not even allot the *Guwen zhenbao* an entry, and the text remained virtually unknown in China until recent years. Meanwhile, however, it has long remained an influential anthology in Korea and Japan, where modern scholars have continued to produce studies and translations of the text.[90] It was largely due to Korean scholars' studies of the various editions produced in Korea and Ming China, in conjunction with the recent burgeoning of interest among Chinese scholars in the circulation of Chinese-language texts outside China, that the text has reentered the East Asian circle of scholarly exchange to China.[91] In fact, as the evidence presented below will show, many text producers and readers in the Ming were themselves aware that the textual culture in which they participated was pan-East Asian in scope.

Let us return to the initial context in which the *Guwen zhenbao* came to our attention, namely, its prevalent use in the game texts of the *Boxiao zhuji*. Notice that all references to the *Guwen zhenbao* in those texts involve lines of poetry, and recall how the recollections concerning the *Guwen zhenbao* of both Jiang Mian and Sun Xu cited above also center on poetic selections. This reflects the prevalent way in which Ming readers seem to have used the book: as a primer of poetry in the "ancient" styles (that is, the forms without rigidly prescriptive tonal regulation) that complemented another popular poetry primer, the *Qian jia shi*, which included only "recent style" or regulated verse. Thus together these two anthologies completed the coverage of respected poetic forms for Ming readers. The dual range of the *Guwen zhenbao* as an anthology of both poetic and prose genres might have been inspired by previous anthologies with a similarly broad range of coverage, such as the *Tang wencui* 唐文粹 (Choice works of Tang literature), an influential collection of Tang dynasty writing.[92] Whatever the case, in Ming China, and elsewhere in its wider dissemination through East Asia, the *Guwen zhenbao*'s poetry and prose volumes tended to circulate separately. This is an example of how readers took the materials available and shaped and remade them to suit patterns of contemporary use.

Common Speech

Another type of verbal mastery demanded by the games collected in the *Boxiao zhuji* is *suyu* 俗語 (common speech).[93] To a certain extent, *guwen* and *suyu* represent two distinctive and complementary verbal genres within the *Boxiao zhuji*. As shown on its cover page, the *Boxiao zhuji* promises to make its embodied communicative life splendid, fresh, and charming. Accordingly, the book reveals that witty repartee demands conversancy with diverse textual canons as well as mastery of a wide range of registers and idioms, including not only the scholarly and the poetic but also the "common," "folksy," "dialect," or even "vulgar"—all qualities that, depending on context, may be included in the semantic range of the word *su* 俗. In other words, to speak artfully requires an ability to code-switch between linguistic registers with aplomb, and to speak, on a moment's notice, not only in an elegant or scholarly manner but also commonly, or even vulgarly. Just as the central skill in handling the textual canons discussed above is often a matter of nimble recontextualization and quick shifts of genre and register, the key to the successful use of *suyu* is the ability to switch between and stitch together different modes of speech and fields of knowledge quickly and cleverly. For example, the following case requires one to throw together the poetic and the common:

一令要千家詩二句拗[94]說，中間又要兩句俗語，後又要千家詩一句解合。

黄梅時節家家雨，[95]梅子黄時日日晴。[96]也不是雨，也不是晴，只是:熟梅天氣半晴陰。[97]

梅須遜雪三分白，雪卻輸梅一段香。[98]也不是遜，也不是輸，只是:梅雪爭春未肯降。[99]

子規啼徹四更時，[100]杜鵑枝上月三更。[101]也不是三更，也不是四更，只是:子規夜半猶啼血。[102]

[Rule:] This game requires two lines from the *Poems by a Thousand Masters* with contradictory points, then two lines of *suyu* in the middle, and finally, another line from the *Poems by a Thousand Masters* to resolve and bring a close.

[Sample solution 1:] In the season of the yellow plum, it rains on every household. When the plums are yellow, each day is clear. It's not rainy, and it's not clear, it's just that the weather in the plum-ripe time is half clear and half cloudy.

[Sample solution 2:] The plum petals lack three parts of snow's whiteness; the snow loses out to the plum-blossom's one whiff of fragrance. It's not lacking, and it's not losing out, it's just that plum and snow contest the spring, and neither will concede.

[Sample solution 3:] The cuckoo cries through the fourth watch of the night; the cuckoo perches on the branch, moon of the third watch. It's not the third watch, and it's not the fourth watch, it's just that the cuckoo, through the middle of the night, still cries blood.[103]

Well before the Ming, the discursive register of *suyu* had drawn its affective power from its appeal to the spoken, to common wisdom, and to the quotidian life that it so capably describes and constructs. *Boxiao zhuji*, in its frequent request for "common speech" skills, provides a window onto the scope of linguistic styling that *suyu* entails and what makes a good *suyu* utterance and a good *suyu* speaker, and suggests the kind of social energy that *suyu* embodied in the world beyond the *Boxiao zhuji*.

The range of reference of the term *suyu* in the *Boxiao zhuji* is wide: in some instances it is simply anything that is pointedly non-classical or non-literary diction or syntax, while in others it indicates the realm of folksy commonplace or moral wisdom. In many instances, phrases designated as *suyu* carry formal markers like rhyme, meter, or antithetical phrasing that help make them memorable or recognizable. Overall, *suyu* in the world of the *Boxiao zhuji* encompasses several linguistic domains. One of these includes aphorisms or dicta, the sort of expression known in Chinese as *yanyu* 諺語. The aphorisms that appear as the solutions to the following two riddles are still well known to modern Chinese speakers:

世情冷暖相交，千載不如初；萬物鮮妍開遍，一旬皆落地。
人無千年好，花無百日紅。

[Conundrum:] The coldness and warmth of the world's affairs are intermingled, but through a thousand years never as good as their beginning; the fresh lovelinesses of the myriad creatures have all flowered, and in a week all fall to the ground.

[Solution:] "Humans know no thousand-year affection; flowers have no red that lasts a hundred days."[104]

家囊消索住當街，縱有朋情不往來；十萬腰纏幽谷處，三千珠履共徘徊。
貧居鬧市無人問，富在深山有遠親。

[Conundrum:] Dwelling by the roadside with household savings in decline—even those with ties of friendship do not visit; abiding in a secluded valley with a purse holding hundreds of thousands—three thousand pairs of red slippers mill about the door.

[Solution:] "At a poor dwelling in a noisy market, none pay calls; to the rich man in a deep valley there will be distant claimers of kinship."[105]

The *suyu* maxims in the answers to the following drinking game are less familiar in modern Mandarin:

一令要一字湊成，俱要成字。用俗語二句結尾。

單同也是同，添金即是銅。除去金邊同，添重便爲鍾。俗云：現鍾不打，怎去煉銅？

單禾也是禾，添口即成和。除去禾邊口，添斗便爲科。俗云：寧添一斗，莫添一口。

單羊也是羊，添水便成洋。除去水邊羊，添易便爲湯。俗云：寧吃（開）眉湯，莫吃皺眉糧。

[Rule:] A character is to be combined from parts, with each combination forming a new character, with two lines of *suyu* to cap off.

1) *Tong* alone is *tong* (same), adding *jin* (metal) then it's *tong* (bronze); removing the *tong* by the *jin*, adding *zhong* (heavy) then makes *zhong* (bell). The saying (*suyu*) goes, "When you won't hit the ready-made bell, why go smelting bronze?"
2) *He* alone is *he* (grain), adding *kou* (mouth) then it's *he* (harmony); removing the *kou* by the *he*, adding *dou* (grain measure) then makes *ke* (rank/category). The saying goes, "Adding a measure is fine, but don't add a mouth."
3) *Yang* by itself is *yang* (goat), adding *shui* (water) then it's *yang* (ocean); removing the *yang* by the *shui*, adding *yi* (easy) on the side makes *tang* (broth/hot water). The saying goes, "Sipping broth with a carefree expression is fine, but don't eat grain with a burdened mind."[106]

These *suyu* sayings offer a selection of folksy wisdom. The point of the expression "When you won't hit the ready-made bell, why go smelting bronze?" seems to be something like "Don't reinvent the wheel"; in other words, when the necessary means for some end is already ready at hand, don't waste effort recreating it from scratch. "Adding a measure is fine, but don't add a mouth" seems to say that giving a significant amount of food is fine, but one must avoid constant "nibbling" at one's resources.[107] "Sipping broth with a carefree expression is fine, but don't eat grain with a burdened mind" is fairly transparent: it is better to accept one's lot with equanimity than to seek gain that brings worries.

The category of *suyu* also includes set or stock phrases of the sort also referred to as *shuyu* 熟語. These stock phrases do not express aphoristic wisdom but rather encapsulate a typical scene or moment:

邂逅與君會，途中勿卸鞍；東西兩手分，速出步陽關。

相逢不下馬，各自奔前程。

[Conundrum:] I encounter you by chance, on the road, let us not unsaddle; passing east and west we go our ways, quickly passing out beyond Yang Pass.
[Answer:] "On meeting we do not dismount our horses; each gallops towards his own destiny."[108]

The *suyu* given as the answer here expresses less folk wisdom than a typical moment in a stylized vision of human life, a moment of chance meeting on the road suggesting a kind of heroic abandon, or a reflection on the human condition. Other examples of stock phrases cited as *suyu* in the *Boxiao zhuji* include expressions like "Heaven and earth do not grow old" 乾坤不老, "Great shouts of 'Long live the emperor' at Mount Tai" 泰嶽山呼, and "All is peaceful and just under heaven" 太平天下.

Suyu also includes slang or vulgar expressions:

齋内書生已散歸，蕠頭燈焰自攻書。
無徒光棍。
[Conundrum:] The schools' students have scattered and gone home; by the flame of a bramble staff, he works alone at his books.
[Answer:] "A hoodlum with no resources" [lit. "bright stick, without disciples"].[109]

The answer depends on puns both on *wu tu* 無徒, which can mean either "without disciples" or "without resources," and on *guanggun* 光棍, a vernacular term for "hoodlum" or "ne'er-do-well" written with characters that allow the possibility of an overly literal rendering as "bright stick." Beyond the puns themselves, the comic effect hinges largely on the abrupt drop in register from the "poetic" image of the studious teacher working silently late into the night to the vernacular and disreputable image of the urban thug. Although the text does not quite suggest that the teacher himself is a hypocrite whose respectable image masks a sordid character, the comic effect is somewhat the same. This is a common dynamic in the jokes and riddles in the *Boxiao zhuji*, where the comic shifts involved most typically move from a high-register conundrum (*mi mian* 謎面) to a low-register solution (*mi di* 謎底) or vice versa.[110]

We may add here that the slang term *guanggun* seems to have captivated the Ming imagination and is ubiquitous in Ming lexica of slang and argot expressions, as attested by the numerous "winsome sayings" in the *Boxiao zhuji* that all hinge on this word for comic impact:

桅杆上掛紗帽－光棍老爹；
桅杆上掛擂槌－光棍打光棍；(above 2.17A)

桅桿掛燈籠－有名的光棍。(2.19B)
新插楊柳－青皮光棍。
囊無半點通宵說謊宿花街－光棍。(2.22B)

Gauze cap on a mast—hoodlum [lit. "bare stick"] old man.

Pestle hung on a mast—one hoodlum [lit. "bare stick"] beats another.

Lantern hung on a mast—a notorious [punning on *ming* 明 light/*ming* 名 "fame"] hoodlum.

Newly planted willow-shoot—skinhead hoodlum [playing on *qing* as both green and blue—as in "blue-skins," a slang term for toughs, whose exact etymology is unknown].

Without a cent in one's purse, lying one's way to a night-long stay in a brothel—hoodlum [playing on "bare stick," as well as on the notion that this would be typical hoodlum behavior].

In the Ming popular imagination, the *guanggun* became not only the object of fear and condemnation but of fantasy as well. The idea of their freedom from social constraints and their ironic manipulation of appearances and language for their own ends made them a powerfully magnetic discursive topic.

The term *suyu* also sometimes refers to characteristically colloquial syntax and grammatical patterns. For example, the following drinking game incorporates various colloquial sentence patterns for asking questions:

一令要一古人事實，中間要俗語，末要論語一句斷之合意。
顏淵陋巷簞瓢樂。俗語云：如何不憂？論語云：君子憂道不憂貧。
子路負米百里外。俗語云：何不憚勞？論語云：事父母能竭其力。
巨卿千里不失約。俗語云：怎的記得？論語云：與朋友交言而有信。

[Rule:] This drinking game requires, first, circumstances relating to an ancient person,[111] in the middle, a colloquial expression (*suyu*), and, in the end, a line from the *Analects* to pass judgment and combine the meanings.

[Answers:]

1) Yan Yuan, at the mean alley, takes delight in a single bamboo dish of rice and a single gourd dipper of drink.
   Colloquial expression: Why was he not burdened with worries?
   Analects: "The gentleman worries about the Way, and does not worry about securing food."
2) Zilu carries rice a hundred *li* away.
   Colloquial expression: Why didn't he shrink from such toil?
   Analects: "When serving father and mother, one should exhaust one's whole strength."
3) Juqing does not break the promised meeting of a thousand *li*.
   Colloquial expression: How could he remember it?
   Analects: "In dealings with friends, one should remain true to one's words."[112]

Here what qualifies the expressions in the middle positions of the answers as "*suyu*" is that they are the spoken-style (that is, non-written style or "non-classical") question expressions *ruhe* 如何 (why/how), *hebu* 何不 (why not), and *zende* 怎的 (how/why). Other examples of *suyu* structures include the "*ye bu shi . . . ye bu shi . . .*" 也不是…也不是… (neither . . . nor . . .) pattern seen in the game with opposing *Qian jia shi* citations discussed above, "*yin he*" 因何 (for what), "*ye zhi shi zhe deng*" 也只是這等 (it is just such), "*nan de*" 難得 (why is it not . . .), and "*ye shi . . . ye shi . . .*" (A is . . ., B also is . . .).

The following game provides another example of *suyu* in this sense of colloquial syntactical features:

一令要俗語一句，一字拆開合意。
堂上掛珠簾，不知是王家的朱家的。
有客到館驛，不知是官人是舍人。
半夜養孩兒，不知是子時是亥時。

[Rule:] A line of *suyu*, and an analysis of one of the characters, conforming to the sense.

[Sample solution 1:] A pearl (珠) curtain hanging in a hall: We don't know if it belongs to the Wangs (王) or the Zhus (朱).

[Sample solution 2:] A guest arrives at the posting station (館): We don't know if he's an official (官人) or a secretary (舍人).

[Sample solution 3:] Giving birth to a child (孩) in the middle of the night: We don't know if it's the *zi* (子) watch (11 pm–1 am) or the *hai* (亥) watch (9–11 pm).[113]

The main trick of the game is to separate the components of one character in the first line to be used in the make-up of the second line, and the two lines have to cohere semantically as well. The *suyu* component in each of the sample solutions offered here is the syntactical pattern for expressing alternatives "*bu zhi shi* A *shi* B" (not knowing if it is A or B).

In some instances the *suyu* reflected in *Boxiao zhuji* drinking games seem to qualify as "*su*" not only by the non-literary, non-classical, or colloquial quality of their language, but also by their connection to a world of quotidian and markedly non-elite experience:

一令上要俗語一句，下要論語一句，二要重疊結尾斷之合意。
世人貪花戀酒色—戒之戒之。
滿縣人民沾瘴氣—時哉時哉。
三歲孩兒喪爹娘—孤哉孤哉。

[Rule:] First, a line of *suyu*, and then a line from the *Analects*. The second part should be a duplicated conclusion, passing judgment and conforming to the sense.

[Sample solution 1:] People of the world crave flowers, and dote on wine and sex: "Be warned of this! Be warned of this!"[114]

[Sample solution 2:] The people of the whole county are infected with malarial vapors: "The season! The season!"[115]

[Sample solution 3:] A three-year-old child loses its Pa and Ma: "Orphan! Orphan!"[116]

While the *suyu* included in the first answer has the familiar appearance of the sort of folk maxim seen in earlier examples, the other two lines of *suyu*, although they may have had some narrative context now lost to us, seem to be ditty-like statements of decidedly ordinary and rather bleak slices of commoners' life. It appears to be some sort of quotidian typicality that qualifies them as *suyu*. Again, the author takes delight in juxtaposing such common experiences and sentiments with citations from the classics—citations that are themselves often skewed versions of their original meanings, as particularly in the third solution above, where the original text referring to *gu* 觚 (an ancient ritual vessel) is misquoted via a pun on its homophone *gu* 孤 (orphan).

As seen in several of the above examples, many of the drinking games in the *Boxiao zhuji* call for juxtaposition of *suyu* and classical citations. The *Analects* makes particularly frequent appearances in this type of context. Although the gaming use of this sort of juxtaposition often seems calculated for some sort of humorous or even irreverent effect, it is useful to bear in mind that this jumping between classical and colloquial registers characterizes not only the "recorded sayings" textual legacies of masters of Daoxue orthodoxy such as Zhu Xi, but also the more general and ongoing practice, both textual and oral, of explication of the classics (*jie jing* 解經) in the vernacular.[117] In such cases, what is typically involved is not simply stylistic juxtaposition but the translation of content that is nominally the same from one register to another. Even in patently comical instances such as the last drinking game example cited above, where the *Analects* capping quotations are deliberately and artfully distorted from their original contextual meanings, part of the rhetorical impact derives from the sense that the gaming use of the quotations is not simply inventive recontextualization but also deviant exegesis. Thus to the extent that such play carries a satirical effect, it is not narrowly directed at the canonical texts themselves but rather more broadly at the claims to monopolistic interpretive control over those texts on the part of state and educational orthodoxy.

A dramatic analogue to this sense of the vernacular as a space in which the meaning of a canonical text is at risk of ambush and cooptation is the famous schoolroom scene in the *Peony Pavilion*, where the befuddled and ineffectual Tutor Chen's stiff and pedantic interpretation of the first song in the *Shijing* 詩經 (Book of odes) is several times interrupted and subverted by the maidservant Chunxiang's free-associative and generally bawdy "exegeses" in the vernacular. The humor often hinges on comic punning misapprehensions that come about because Chunxiang hears the words naïvely—that is, outside the constraints of a written text or other interpretive authority.[118] In this sense, texts like the *Boxiao zhuji* appeal to Chunxiang rather than to Chen Zuiliang, or rather to the Chunxiang in a wide range of readers, many of whom could no doubt produce passable versions of Chen Zuiliang's language in other contexts, when the circumstances called for it. In the *Boxiao zhuji* and similar texts, the vernacular does not exist in isolation, but rather is articulated through the tension of its relation with classical and normatively bookish language.

The following riddle, drawn from another compilation whose contents overlap with the *Boxiao zhuji*, the *Zhaijin qiyin* 摘錦奇音 (Plucked brocades of wondrous tones),[119] is an extreme example of mocking and subversive explication of a classical text:

> 公媳同盆洗浴。
> 欲潔其身而亂大倫。
>
> [Riddle:] Father-in-law and daughter-in-law share the same bath.
> [Answer:] "Wishing to maintain his personal purity, he spoils the great relation."[120]

The answer is from *Analects* 18.7, where Confucius's disciple Zilu, having encountered a virtuous recluse, issues the following critique of that man's avoidance of worldly entanglements:

> 不仕無義。長幼之節，不可廢也；君臣之義，如之何其廢之。欲潔其身，而亂大倫。君子之仕也，行其義也。
>
> Not to take office is not dutiful. If the order between the old and the young cannot be set aside, how can the duty between ruler and subject be set aside? Wishing to maintain his personal purity, he spoils that great relation. A gentleman's taking office is to carry out his duty.[121]

In the riddle, the words "wishing to maintain his personal purity, he spoils the great relation" are transformed into obscenity through a literal and vernacular misreading of the line as "wishing to clean his body, he disorders proper relations (i.e., commits incest)." As both this scene and the *Peony Pavilion* schoolroom scene attest, then, sexual humor was a favorite strategy for subverting ethical pieties in a private social realm of drinking and laughter.[122] Incidentally, incest between father-in-law and daughter-in-law seems to have exerted a particular fascination in the popular imagination of scandalous and titillating sexual transgression.[123]

Many other examples show that over-literal vernacular misreading, a strategy of reducing even the most sanctified and authoritative texts to absurdity by at least the appearance of word-for-word translation, was a widespread source of humor and a vehicle for subverting educational hierarchies. In the following example, the comic misreading is explicitly presented as a teacher's attempt at exegesis:

> 宰予晝寢
>
> 昔一師喜晝睡，弟子曰：宰予晝寢之意，何解？師曰：我不講，你怎的曉得？宰者，殺也。予者，我也。晝者，晝時也。寢者，睡一覺也。合而言之，便殺我定要晝時睡一覺也。
>
> "Zai Yu slept during the day."[124]
>
> In the past there was a teacher who liked sleeping during the day. His student asked, "What is the meaning of 'Zai Yu slept during the day?'" The teacher said: "If I don't tell you, how would you know? '*zai*' means to kill. '*yu*' means I. '*zhou*' means daytime. '*qin*' means to take a nap. All these words together mean that 'even if I were going to be killed, I would still have to take a nap.'"[125]

The joke involves a comic misreading of *Analects* 5.10:

> 宰予晝寢。子曰：朽木不可雕也，糞土之牆不可杇也。於予與何誅？
>
> Zai Yu slept during the day. The master says, "Rotten wood cannot be carved; a wall of manure and earth cannot be plastered with lime. To Yu, what is the use of my denunciation?"[126]

However one interprets the satirical undercurrent of the story, the joke involves some undermining of canonical or educational orthodoxy. The most direct target of satire would seem to be the teacher, who appears not only lazy but inadequately prepared to serve as an exegete of the classics. Granting that the circumstances of the joke are rather far-fetched, though, if we choose to imagine that the teacher is aware of the creative misreading involved in his response, we might see him as adeptly parrying the student's attempt to use the accepted meaning of an *Analects* passage as implied critique of his status as teacher. To read the teacher as the winner in this imaginary exchange, however, means to invert the orthodox model of pedagogy, in which honored teachers preside over the stable translation of classical texts into vernacular explanations. In terms of the pun on *wutu guanggun* ("hoodlum without resources"/ "bright staff, without disciples") discussed above, which juxtaposes the image of the industrious schoolmaster studying late by lamplight with that of the hoodlum, to view the teacher in the above "Zai Yu slept during the day" anecdote as successfully defending his authority means to conceive of him as a schoolmaster who maintains his status by timely and audacious recourse to the linguistic resourcefulness of the hoodlum.

The games in the *Boxiao zhuji* call on knowledge of several types. The social display of this knowledge, however, is not a matter of transparent, traceless reproduction. Rather, it involves an intentional process of re-organization and play, a brand of subversive wit that challenges the orthodox impulse toward univocal interpretation by anarchically generating new meanings from classical texts. A witty speaker is not a pedant but an adroit master of both classical and vernacular language, who can switch at a moment's notice among various linguistic styles and textual genres. The array of styles designated as *suyu* bring into the game texts a set of linguistic registers and striking phraseology as well as a more loosely defined ethos of playfulness, resourcefulness, and irreverence. The game texts, then, dislodge fragments of canonical texts from their prescribed contexts of interpretation to redisplay them in a space of play that is governed by its own fashion and coded rules of speech, and possessing its own set of alternative values.

Despite the diverse types of speech it encompasses, the term *suyu* is stable in the sense that readers/players would have had a clear functional grasp of what qualified as *suyu* in any given context. Moreover, the *Boxiao zhuji* conveys an idea of *suyu* as a stylistic ideal, a mode of expression that was not only common or popular but also stylish and up-to-date. Just as *shuyu* 書語 (script speech) and *yayan* 雅言 (elegant speech) are derived and shaped by imitation of ancient classical texts, *suyu* represents not simply a lapse into ordinary speech but rather an effort of conscious styling in relation to a shared constellation of models.

The question that comes to mind, then, is whether this sense of stability was underwritten by a particular text, as seen in the relation between the category of *guwen* and the *Guwen zhenbao* discussed above. Was there a book called *Suyu* that these games quoted from? At present, it is impossible to answer definitely,[127] but it is clear that both the category of *suyu* and the widespread cultural cachet it enjoyed in the late Ming were intertwined with the larger Ming fascination with various vernacular languages, which was reflected in and shaped by the commercial book trade. In the interplay between various sorts of stylized speech and the commercial book market, novel and popular expressions became collectable and salable commodities. This period witnessed the rise to popularity of *suyu* dictionaries or reference works. Among the best known ones were *Liyan jie* 俚言解 (Explanations of folk words); *Zengding yasu jiyan* 增定雅俗稽言 (Expanded and corrected edition: a veracious account of elegant and vulgar speech); *Muqian ji* 目前集 (Before the eyes); *Changtan kaowu* 常談考誤 (Quotidian speech: examinations and corrections);[128] and an extensive *suyu* section in *Xinke Huijun yuanban zhushu zhiyin shishi tongkao* 新刻徽郡原板諸書直音世事通考 (New imprint, from the original Anhui blocks, a compilation from various books with pronunciation prompts: comprehensive examination of world affairs). Another comprehensive reference work designed for practical use was *Xinke zengjiao qieyong zhengyin xiangtan zazi daquan* 新刻增校切用正音鄉談雜字大全 (Newly cut, collated, practical, with correct pronunciations: a grand compendium of miscellaneous characters used in local conversation).[129] This vibrant bibliographical category of *suyu* reference works offers another kind of quotability, forming its own sort of canonicity that is not only invested with the authority of common wisdom and widely held views of common folk, but also represents an ideal of lively and charming speech in opposition to the pedantic and rigidly orthodox display of status or knowledge.

Interest in and awareness of distinctive kinds of diction and phraseology had been a long-standing feature of Chinese scholarly traditions,[130] but the efflorescence of this sort of title in the Ming was market-driven and reflects the distinctive social energy of the period. The specifically commercial attractiveness of *suyu*, its status as part of that up-to-date fashion trumpeted on the title pages of texts like the *Boxiao zhuji*, derived from its status as a realm of linguistic novelty among a range of verbal commodities, including "winsome sayings," jokes, market slang, and other forms of coded diction. Just as the category of "winsome sayings of the rivers and lakes" pointedly signals a sort of oppositional relation to officially sanctioned spheres of orthodox speech and knowledge, *suyu*, with its implied distinction from its counterparts such as *shuyu* (book speech) or *yayan* (elegant phrasing), has something of this oppositional appeal as well.

The ways in which *suyu* is employed in the games in the *Boxiao zhuji*, and the interpretive strategy these games foster, anticipate the type of wit and satire that is considered the signature of Li Yu's 李漁 (1610–80) narrative style. Consider one case where he (mis)represents the sage's words: in his novel *Rou putuan* 肉蒲團 (The carnal prayer mat), the narrator legitimizes the technique of "making use of lechery in putting a stop to lechery" by quoting *Mencius*.[131] The quoted conversation appears in *Mencius* 1B.5:

> 王曰："寡人有疾，寡人好色。"對曰："昔者大王好色，愛厥妃。詩云：古公亶父，來朝走馬。率西水滸，至於岐下。爰及姜女，聿來胥宇。當是時也，内無怨女，外無曠夫。王如好色，與百姓同之，於王何有？"
>
> The king said, "I have an infirmity; I am fond of sex." The reply was, "Formerly, King Tai was fond of sex, and loved his consort. It is said in the *Book of Odes*: 'Gugong Danfu, / Came in the morning, galloping his horse, / By the banks of the western waters, / As far as the foot of Qi hill, / Along with the lady of Jiang; / They came and together chose the site of settlement.' At that time, in the seclusion of the house, there were no dissatisfied women, and abroad, there were no unmarried men. If Your Majesty loves sex, let the people be able to gratify the same feeling, and what difficulty will there be in your attaining the imperial sway."[132]

The officially sanctioned *Mengzi zhushu jiejing* 孟子註疏解經 (*Mencius*: Explication of the classic, with annotations and elucidations) interprets the citation from the *Book of Odes* this way:

> 言大王亦好色，非但與姜女俱行而已，普使一國男女無有怨曠，王如則之，與百姓同欲，皆使無過時之思，則於王之政，何有不可乎？
>
> This is to say that King Tai was also fond of sex. He did not just bring the Lady of Jiang with him in his flight; he also assured that all men and women in the entire kingdom were free from resentment and dissatisfaction. If Your Majesty could model this, let the hundred surnames gratify the same desire, make sure they will not have the thought of missing their time (for marriage), then regarding your administration, what could you not achieve?[133]

In Li Yu's novel, the *Mencius* passage is presented anew in an even more markedly vernacular register:

> 想太王當走馬避難之時，尚且帶著姜女，則其生平好色，一刻離不得婦人可知。如此淫蕩之君，豈有不喪身亡國之理？他卻有個好色之法：使一國的男子，都帶著婦人避難。太王與姜女行樂之時，一國的男子婦人，也在那邊行樂。這便是陽春有腳，天地無私的王化了。誰人不感頌他？ 還敢道他的不是？
>
> Imagine that time when King Tai, although fleeing on horseback, still took his consort Jiang along with him—then the king's lifelong love of sex, so strong that he couldn't be parted from a woman even for a moment, becomes quite clear to

see. Oughtn't such a dissolute and lecherous ruler have lost both his life and his kingdom? Yet this king had a method in his love of sex: he made all the men in this country bring their women with them in their flight, and while he was making merry with his consort Jiang here, his men and women were also making merry over there. It was a case of moral influence exerted by a king who "brought springtime with him wherever he went and was unselfish in all things." Who would not be moved to praise him? Who would dare to say he was doing wrong?[134]

From the statement in the orthodox commentary to the *Mencius* that "(King Tai) assured that all men and women in the entire kingdom were free from resentment and dissatisfaction" (使一國男女無有怨曠), Li Yu gives the vernacular rendering, "(King Tai) made all the men in the country bring their women with them in their flight" (使一國的男子，都帶著婦人避難)—a detail that is nowhere found in either the *Mencius* passage or the officially sanctioned interpretations. "To let the hundred surnames gratify the same desire" (與百姓同欲) becomes "while King Tai was making merry with his consort Jiang here, his men and women were also making merry over there" (太王與姜女行樂之時, 一國的男子婦人, 也在那邊行樂). In the process of retelling the orthodox story in the vernacular, the author does more than just translate a stable "content" from one linguistic register to another. Rather, he fundamentally alters the tonality of the passage, turning the grand and weighty statement of moral principles into a carnivalesque vision of orgiastic sexual indulgence, in which the king and the lady of Jiang copulate at the same time as every other couple in the state are doing the same at some unspecified distance "over there" (*na bian* 那邊). This demonstrative "over there" clearly marks the register as vernacular and creates the effect of a panoramic view in which the reader envisions both the royal couple and the general populace disporting themselves sexually. This representative example reflects not only Li Yu's individual style but also a broader cultural dynamic in which the fascination with various forms of vernacular speech fueled a reconfiguration of the relations among high- and low-register languages and, along the way, opened spaces for the creation of alternative or subversive visions of cultural authority.

The Miniature Anthology Huang Ming shixuan

Many of the features of game texts, such as the focus on quotidian life, the subversive play with established textual or ethical orders, and the requirement to align one's responses with specific compositional techniques (e.g., quick and deft code-switching among far-flung linguistic registers) are fully on display in other sorts of texts found in the *Boxiao zhuji*. One intriguing example of such a characteristic late Ming textual form is the miniature poetry anthology, or "anthologylet." The final *juan* of the *Boxiao zhuji* includes one of these anthologies, entitled *Huang Ming shixuan* (Poetry anthology of the glorious Ming, *BXZJ* 4.6B–25B). One among many compilations circulating under similar titles, this text vividly illustrates the sorts of editorial strategies whereby new texts and new meanings were created by the recontextualization and adaptation of material in broader circulation, as well as some of the ways in which popular or casual anthologies created a reading experience distinctively different from more highbrow or elegant ones. In the discussion above I highlighted the central role of anthologies such as the *Guwen zhenbao* in the textual play of the drinking games in earlier sections of the *Boxiao zhuji*. Below I take examples from the *Huang Ming shixian* to outline some of the ways in which meanings could be shaped and generated in the compilation and layout of anthologies themselves.

To reiterate, this particular *Huang Ming shixuan* is an "anthologylet" rather than a larger, independently circulating anthology like the *Guwen zhenbao* (or, for that matter, other texts of the period sharing the title *Huang Ming shixuan* or circulating under similar titles). This sort of compressed anthology, which appeared together with a disparate group of texts in a larger compilation, appears frequently in Ming commercial imprints, where publishers crammed as much as they could onto each page and where an appearance of variety and comprehensiveness was so often a selling point. In this connection, note that the *Boxiao zhuji* uses the double-register page layout (*erjie ban* 二節版), quite common in Ming woodblock books, in which a page is divided horizontally into two running panels, each with its own sequence of texts. The *Boxiao zhuji*'s miniature anthology appears in the upper register; the lower register is devoted to a collection of jokes and banter under the heading "Banter and Laughter" (*tan xiao men* 談笑門). I will explore the dynamics of such multi-register page layouts in more detail in chapter 2. Here the discussion will focus on how the sequencing and juxtaposition of material within the *Huang Ming shixuan* creates a space of play that parodies the grandiose poetry anthology against which it defines itself.

The title *Huang Ming shixuan* signals grand ambitions: it presents a selection of poems as collectively embodying a vision of imperial splendor. A quick survey of the poems, however, reveals that this particular *Huang Ming shixuan* is not to be confused with other highly respected and serious anthologies of Ming poetry that bear the same or similar titles, of which there were many. A few examples of these works compiled by elite scholars are an independently circulating *Huang Ming shixuan* compiled by Chen Zilong 陳子龍 (1608–47), Li Wen 李雯 (1608–47),[135] and Song Zhengyu 宋徵輿 (1618–67);[136] Wang Cheng's 王偁 (1370–1415) *Huang chao shixuan* 皇朝詩選 (Anthology of poetry of this glorious dynasty); *Huang Ming Xijiang shixuan* 皇明西江詩選 (Anthology of poetry from Xijiang in the glorious Ming) compiled by Han Yong 韓雍 (1422–78), Han Yang 韓陽 (fl. early and mid-15th centuries), and Li Kui 李奎 (dates unknown); Xu Tai's 徐泰 (fl. early 16th century) *Huang Ming fengya* 皇明風雅 (Airs and Odes of the glorious Ming); Yang Shen's 楊慎 (1488–1559) *Huang Ming shichao* 皇明詩鈔 (Transcribed poems of the glorious Ming); Yu Xian's 俞憲 (1538 *jinshi*) *Sheng Ming baijia shi* 盛明百家詩 (Poems of a hundred masters of the flourishing Ming); Zhu Zhifan's 朱之蕃 (1558–1624) *Sheng Ming baijia shixuan* 盛明百家詩選 (Anthology of poems of a hundred masters of the flourishing Ming);[137] Di Sibin's 狄斯彬 (1547 *jinshi*) *Huang Ming lüshi leichao* 皇明律詩類鈔 (Categorized transcription of regulated verse from the glorious Ming); Fan Weiyi's 范惟一 (1510–84) *Mingshi zhaichao* 明詩摘鈔 (Selections of Ming poetry); and Li Tengpeng's 李騰鵬 (fl. 1573–1620) *Huang Ming shitong* 皇明詩統 (Authoritative manual for poetry of the glorious Ming).[138] These anthologies constituted a lively field in which compilers competed to present a definitive survey of the poetry of the "Glorious Ming." In their competition to be *the* anthology of the Ming poetry, they reflect visions of both poetry and society that are unapologetically elitist. At least one of these large anthologies (Han Yong's *Huang Ming Xijiang shixuan*) explicitly adopted a policy of excluding commoners' poems, with most of the rest following a similar practice even if only tacitly. It is against the background of the anthologizing practices of these more highbrow poetry collections that our *Huang Ming shixuan* articulates its own vision of the Ming, as a parody of contemporary elite anthologizing practice.

Take, as a point of comparison, the well-known large anthology sharing the title *Huang Ming shixuan*. The result of the collective effort of several elite literati over many years of preparation, this work has a heft and physical scale that seems in accord with the weightiness of its title, and the poems it includes were chosen from 453 individual authors' collections, guided by a stated principle of selection. Moreover, it is adorned with multiple prefaces using language drawn from traditional poetics to discuss poetic schools of the Ming such as the "Former and Latter Seven Masters" and to chronicle poetic forms and poets from the beginnings of Chinese poetry to the present. Our casual *Huang Ming shixuan* anthologylet, in contrast, names no editor or compiler, nor is it accompanied by prefatory materials. The selections show no pretension of contributing to poetic excellence. Rather, through its selection of a few dozen poems (58 in all) the anthologylet projects its own oppositional vision of Ming society, in which emperors are thrown together with merchants, ministers with erotic beauties, and the state valedictorian with a corpse in the river.[139] By its very choice of title, however, it establishes some sort of dialogic or satirical relation with its grander counterparts.

The small *Huang Ming shixuan*, in its single narrow register at the top of the page, unfolds from one scene to another poem by poem, with something like the visual rhythm of a painting in the traditional hand scroll format. Order and sequence are of great significance in anthologies, and this one starts with a poem from the founding Hongwu emperor, "Taizu Sets Out at Dawn" (Taizu xiaoxing 太祖曉行). This editorial decision aligns *Huang Ming shixuan*'s textual beginning with the founding of the dynasty. On the one hand, this accords with the common and long-held practice that weaves correspondence between textual order and imperial or cosmological order, a basic feature in the rhetoric of empire. On the other hand, the literary qualities of the poems included are clearly far removed from the elite taste and poetics reflected in such Ming poetry anthologies as those promoting models of the "Former and Latter Seven Masters" type.

忙着征衣快着鞭	Hurriedly donning military dress, quickly taking whip in hand;
回頭月掛柳梢邊	as I look back, I see the moon tangled in the willow's branches.
兩三點露不爲雨	Two or three drops of dew: it is not rainfall;
七八夥星尚在天	seven or eight stars: still there in the sky.
茅店雞鳴人過語	By the thatch-roofed inn the cock crows, and passers-by converse;

竹籬犬吠客驚眠 behind a bamboo fence a dog barks, startling the traveler's sleep.
等閑擁出扶桑日 Serenely emerging with its escort, the sun behind the Fusang tree:
社稷山河在眼前 the hills and streams of the nation's altars unfold before the eye.

This poem, which also appears in a Wanli-era "Emperor's Collection" (*Yu zhi wenji* 御制文集) as a work by the Hongwu emperor, adopts some of the conventional imagery of literati travel poetry, though the tone and diction are somewhat more colloquial than would be customary in ordinary literati verse of this type.[140] The lines themselves are largely a pastiche of quotation and close paraphrase from well-known poems on similar topics. Partly through the images of the final couplet and partly through the attribution to or association with the Hongwu emperor (referred to in the title by his temple name Taizu), however, it is clear that what is being described is not merely a vignette of an occasional traveler (or a group of travelers) setting out on the road at dawn, but rather an epiphanic moment wherein the sunrise that illuminates the "hills and streams" of the empire mirrors the rise of the Ming emperor taking his rightful celestial place in the firmament of a new dynasty. In this basic symbolic language, as well as in the colloquial diction, this poem is a successor to a renowned earlier poem by the founding emperor of the Song dynasty, also known by his posthumous ancestral temple name, Taizu (See Chen Yu, *Cangyi hua yu*, A.1A):

欲出未出光辣撻 About to emerge, but yet emerged, its light blazes bright;
千山萬山如火發 thousands, ten thousands, of mountains blaze like fire.
須臾走向天上來 In a short while it runs up into the sky,
逐却殘星赶却月 shooing away the remaining stars, chasing away the moon.

Regardless of whether the attributions of these two poems to the Song and Ming founders are reliable, these attributions are essential to the way the texts function, for it is precisely their colloquial tone—the very aspect in which these poems deviate from conventional notions of the "poetic," or even, in the case of the Ming Taizu poem, of originality—that marks the poems' voice as imperial: the voice may describe its own power in a poem, but it does not rely on elegant writing to do so.

Our *Huang Ming shixuan*'s opening with "Taizu Sets Out at Dawn" seems a fitting way for it to frame the poems that follow as belonging to and depicting the "Glorious Ming," even if the implicit notion of Ming identity does not conform to the standards of literary polish reflected in the grander dynastic anthologies. The parallel between the Ming and Song founding emperors on display here was part of a larger effort in the Ming to establish a lineage of legitimate rule that places the Ming as continuing the Han Chinese rule of the Song after the Mongolian Yuan dynasty. As it continues, however, our small *Huang Ming shixuan* quickly undercuts any such grand imperial vision with its second poem, entitled "Zhengde you xuanfu" 正德遊宣府 (The Zhengde emperor dallies at Xuanfu), a poem in the voice of the Zhengde emperor (r. 1505–21) who is retreating from the capital for his favorite nest—which he calls, in a jarringly common diction, simply "home" (*jiali* 家裏)[141]—in the northern frontier town of Xuanfu (modern day Xuanhua). Symbolically, he is fleeing from his role as emperor in search of a new identity and an opportunity for rebirth. Whereas in his palace in the capital, he had to fulfill his duties as an emperor and adhere to protocol, in Xuanfu he could take the role of general, a title and role he bestowed on himself and enjoyed with theatrical flair, over the objections of his court officials. More importantly, he could indulge in flirtatious and lascivious activities with women, including prostitutes. The road from the capital to Xuanfu is the path to wine and sex (*jiu se* 酒色), as the emperor confesses in the poem:

正德遊宣府	The Zhengde Emperor Dallies at Xuanfu
離了龍宮並象床，	Leaving dragon palace with its ivory couch behind,
一鞭千里馬飛霜。	a thousand *li* in a wave of my crop, my horse flies in dawn frost.
綱常高上天應天，	Norms and constants lofty and high, in layer on layered heaven;
酒色中間路更長。	yet amid drink and beauty are roads longer still.
快樂歡中圖快樂，	Within pleasure and merriment I seek pleasure and merriment more;
風光好處要風光。	where the scenes are lovely I demand more lovely scenes.
朕思浮世皆爲客，	I reflect that in this floating world all are sojourners—
何必拘拘只帝王。	why need I constrain myself to be only an emperor?

The reign of the Zhengde emperor was characterized by intrigue and scandal, largely because of his apparent restlessness in the imperial role and his desire to take on other identities. Of course, this poem was unlikely to have been composed by the Zhengde emperor himself; rather, it is a poem in the tradition of *daiyan ti* 代言體—a poem written as a dramatic monologue in the voice of another person, whether a renowned contemporary, a historical figure, or a fictionalized persona.[142] It contrasts starkly with the opening poem of the anthology: while the founding emperor rises early, rushing to put on his military travel gear so that he may gallop towards the dawning of his empire (*sheji shanhe* 社稷山河), the Zhengde emperor cannot wait to fly by night towards intoxication and debauchery, and away from the constraints of the throne and his duties as a ruler. As the Zhengde emperor reasons, why be tied down to the role of an emperor when you are just a transient visitor to a floating world?[143]

This first pair of poems gives a good indication of the tone of the collection as a whole: a normative order is established, only to be quickly undercut or ironized. The opening poem evokes the rise of the Hongwu emperor from the status of a military man enduring the hardships of campaigning to that of the dynastic founder, and then the second presents Hongwu's successor who feels constrained by his role as ruler and longs to lose himself as an anonymous pleasure-seeker. If the first poem likens the Taizu of the Ming to the Taizu of the Song, the second poem links the Zhengde emperor to Huizong (r. 1100–26) of the Song, whose infamous visits to courtesans such as Li Shishi were taken as signs and reasons for the fall of the Northern Song.[144] The vision of the "Glorious Ming" that emerges from the series of poems that follow is not without its own grandeur, but it is a vision of imperial grandeur in which mixing and permeability of roles and status categories figure prominently: the anthology includes works attributed not only to emperors but also to commoners, merchants, itinerant tutors, and Daoist immortals.

To a far greater extent than most of the independently circulating anthologies of the Ming, the small *Huang Ming shixuan* lays out for the reader the full range of other identities out there in the world that the Zhengde emperor longs to explore, including that of prostitutes. The quotidian, the lowbrow, the comical, the worldly, and the unabashedly erotic are given a vastly more prominent place than in the large anthologies. Herein lies the crucial difference between the serious, proper poetry anthologies of the Ming and our little anthologylet: while the former aim at gathering representative "good" poetry of the period, the latter is mainly interested in eye-catching scenes (defined often as humorous, scandalous, or sensational) encountered in Ming urban and court culture, with the diverse variety of voices becoming the focus of interest. It offers poems depicting fathers sending sons off to the examinations, and wives sending husbands, alongside worldly advice about avoiding litigation or about the value of a bowl of rice gruel. It expresses the pain of a daughter being sold into servitude during a bad harvest year, juxtaposed with the stark image of a corpse floating in a river. Several poems speak of the difficulties of relations between wives and concubines, or daughters and sons-in-law and their parents-in-law; and although some poems present moralizing sentiments about avoiding the perils of drink and sex, others provide frankly erotic titillation, as in a steamy series of poems on a group of paintings depicting the renowned Tang dynasty imperial consort Yang Guifei 楊貴妃: "Inscribed on the Painting 'Consort Yang Getting Up after a Night's Slumber'" 題楊妃眠起, "On a Half-body Portrait of Consort Yang" 楊妃半身圖, "On Consort Yang's Brocade Stockings" 楊妃錦襪圖, "On a Naked Portrait of Consort Yang" 楊妃赤身圖, and more.

Metrically, the poems in this *Huang Ming shixuan* are all strictly correct examples of the eight-line heptasyllabic regulated verse form. Although this form can sometimes give the effect of heightened literary tone and formality, in these poems it serves more to create a feeling of reassuring familiarity, recalling in many instances the prevalence of the heptasyllabic line in popular prosimetric storytelling or theater. As for the tonal prosody involved in the eight-line regulated form, although the technical requirements of the form are somewhat complicated, anyone who internalizes them sufficiently is able to produce verse vignettes whose metrical structure qualifies them formally as poems, even in cases where the topics and diction themselves might not seem particularly poetic. As with many of the *suyu* appearing in the model responses for the drinking games surveyed above, the verses reflect a keen interest in capturing moments from a distinctly common life, and high-register language is often contextualized in a deflating or comical way. The poem's titles or headings often clearly indicate the role and status of the supposed author, and in some cases poems of address and response form small dramatic vignettes, as in the following pair:

告丈人娶妾	Reporting to His Father-in-Law on the Intention of Taking a Concubine
愚生俯仰二儀間	My benighted existence bobs between the Two Principles;
進退於今寔兩難	yet now I face a pair of courses that both are difficult.
塵世修經三十載	In this dusty world I've studied the classics for lo these thirty years;
客窗偏向五更寒	the wayfarer's window is especially cold in the long watches of the night.
有妻娶妾皆非禮	When one has a wife, to take a concubine is indeed outside propriety,
無子傳家總是閑	yet to lack a son to carry on the family would after all be idle.
欲把瑤琴尋別調	I wish to take my jasper *qin* and seek out new tunes;
陽春一曲竟愁彈	this elegant "Warm Spring" melody in the end I feel uneasy to play.

丈人答婿	The Father-in-Law's Reply to His Son-in-Law
念汝勤勞處世間	I feel concern for your hardship in making your way in the world;
仕途勞祿立身難	on the path of service lies much toil, to establish oneself is difficult.
十年螢窗攻書苦	Bitter it is indeed to spend ten years studying by fireflies' glow;
五夜金門待詔寒	to wait in attendance in predawn dark by the Gold Horse gate is cold.
生女生男由分定	One's lot in fathering daughters or sons is all fixed by one's fate;
娶妻娶妾總皆閑	whether to take a wife or concubine is all an idle question.
善人未必終無後	If one is good, then one may in the end not die without an heir;
琴瑟調和縷縷彈	when *qin* and *se* are attuned and played with tender care.

One cannot read this exchange without mentally translating from the inflated and pompously classical-sounding circumlocutions of the two speakers into the language of the actual motives underlying their speech, motives that were in multiple senses quite "common" to contemporary readers: the son-in-law wants to take a secondary wife, and the father-in-law, anxious to protect his daughter's interests, puts his foot down. As in the case of the drinking games and riddles discussed above, the comic effect stems from this tension between conflicting registers, which causes what otherwise might appear as grand language to sound merely bombastic. Further, it is by winning this competition in poetic composition and grandiose language that the father-in-law displays his authority. To the son-in-law's clichéd complaint about the cold that a student preparing for the examinations suffers at the wayfarer's window, the father-in-law responds with an answering cliché of the cold that the court official feels while waiting for the emperor's dawn court appearance, and thereby backhandedly ridicules the son-in-law's failure to attain such glorious status. The father-in-law beats the young man at his own rhetorical game. His response poem follows the formal requirements of "harmonizing the rhyme" (*heyun* 和韻), in that it repeats the rhyming words of the original poem in the same order. But instead of harmonizing with the son-in-law's intent or aspirations (*zhi* 志) as well, as conventionally expected in this sort of poetic exchange, the father-in-law ridicules and defeats both that intent and the poem that expresses it. In this exchange, then, the father-in-law personifies the crafty play with established poetic conventions that runs throughout the collection.

Other poems depict typical scenes of daily life, often with an emphasis on its bleaker side, but the mismatch between the choice of language and the underlying situation in these poems often remains a source of humor:

小姐上太守	Young Missy's Appeal to the Governor
錢糧不納罪當誅，	For non-payment of cash and grain levies, I stand guilty of capital crime;
戰戰兢兢見大人。	full of fear and trembling, I appear before your worship.
嚴父尚書居禮部，	My strict father is a chancellor residing in the Ministry of Rites;
難兄知縣任蕪湖。	my afflicted elder brother is county magistrate at Wuhu.
當歸繡閣拈針線，	I ought to return to my ornate loft to set hand to needle and thread,
未問兒夫了稅租。	and have not inquired of husband or son about the payment of our tax.
伏望黄堂賢太守，	I humbly beseech you, worthy governor in your yellow audience hall,
放奴歸去便來輸。	release me to return home, and I will pay straightaway!

Here a "young missy" is talking her way out of trouble by appropriating the conventional self-introductory theatrical language of a daughter of a highly respectable family: her father a chancellor in the Ministry, her brother a respectable official, and herself a proper wife. In a way she resembles the beauty Luo Fu in the medieval *yuefu* poem "Moshang sang" 陌上桑, whose physical presence and verbal ingenuity captivate both her would-be seducer and her audience. The "young missy" of the poem above, however, with her fearful trembling and her awkward poetic performance, seems to fall short of Luo Fu's standard of mastery, so that the audience is moved more to sympathy than to awe.

Another poem presents a speech of encouragement and remonstrance from a wife to her husband:

妻送夫試　A Wife Sends Her Husband off to the Examinations

自古男兒志四方	From ancient times, men have set their minds on making their way in the world;
出門何必淚汪汪	why must you, on leaving home, shed streaming tears?
滿朝朱紫文章貴	Among a court full of splendidly robed ministers it is writing that holds esteem;
結髮夫妻歲月長	betrothed from youth, our time as husband and wife is long.
衾暖豈如桃浪暖	How could the quilt's warmth compare to the warmth of peach-blossom waves?
粉香寧似桂花香	How does the fragrance of face powder compare to the fragrance of cassia flowers?[145]
鰲頭尚有青錢選	And on the head of the stone-tortoise is the "green coin" selection;[146]
早遣音書返故鄉	don't delay sending news of it back to your hometown!

With a hint of comic role-reversal, the wife faces the situation bravely and exhorts her husband by appealing to what would conventionally be thought of as masculine values, and the poem presents a rather charming, if idealized, glimpse of conjugal domesticity.

Other scenes of everyday life appearing in the *Huang Ming shixuan* employ a broader comic touch, as in the following poem entitled "A Chaste Widow Fires Her Son's Tutor" 節婦辭先生:

妾本人間女丈夫	I have ever been a woman stalwart in this human world,
平生作事不模糊	and throughout my life my ways have been forthright and clear.
一身貞節天知我	As for my personal chaste and constant ways, heaven knows me;
眾口咸聲汝染吾	yet the many mouths all claim you have tainted me.
色即是空空即色	"Appearance is empty and emptiness is appearance":

無中説有有中無	amid nothing they say there is something, in something there is nothing.
春山處處堪啼鳥	Throughout the spring hills are nooks fit for chirping birds;
請抱琴書過別圖	pray take up your zither and books, and make plans elsewhere.

The widow's nimble use of poetic images charged with erotic connotation makes her a match and a mirror image of the tutor, for whom mastery over poetic language and emotional impulse is supposed to be a central professional qualification. The phraseology of the opening line is striking, as the widow uses the conventional feminine self-deprecatory term of self-reference *qie* 妾, but then immediately goes on to claim status as a *zhangfu* 丈夫, which here must be translated gender-neutrally as "stalwart," but which generally refers to a man of heroic integrity. This poem, in which a potentially vulnerable and passive woman takes poetic and social initiative in banishing the tutor from her household, is yet another example of the fascination with role-play and role-reversals—particularly those that challenge conventional hierarchies—that permeates this collection.

Regional Identity and the Tailoring of an Anthology

Along with its selection and sequential ordering of poems that create a polyphony of social and aesthetic registers, another noteworthy feature of our small *Huang Ming shixuan* is its strong regional orientation, specifically its focus on events, people, and places connected with the Jiangxi area. One figure whose profile in the *Huang Ming shixuan* is richly suggestive of the polyvalent relations between high and low and between cosmopolitan imperial space and the local space of Jiangxi is the disgraced Ming Prince of Ning (Zhu Chenhao 朱宸濠, *d. 1521)*, who before his fall from grace resided in Jiangxi. According to the historical record, he attempted to usurp the throne during the Zhengde reign, only to be suppressed in 1519 by imperial forces under the command of Wang Shouren 王守仁 (1472–1529), the same figure, better known as Wang Yangming 王陽明, who was to become one of the most influential Neo-Confucian thinkers in Ming intellectual history.[147] The following poem purports to present the rebel prince's thoughts after his capture by imperial forces, as he was awaiting execution:

寧王自嘆 Prince Ning Sighs over His Fate

懶與乾坤擔此憂， Uninterested in bearing these cares along with the world,
摳衣徐步上瀛洲。 with loosened gown and slow steps, I rise to Mt. Ying.
清風明月人三友， The pure breezes and bright moon with me form a fellowship of three,
荒草斜陽土一坵。 amid wild grass in declining light, one mound of dirt.
夢去夢來皆是夢， Dreams come, dreams go—but all is dream,
愁多愁少總成愁。 sorrows large and sorrows small—all end in sorrow.
從今別卻江西去， From this day on I depart and leave Jiangxi behind,
不管人間春復秋。 no longer concerned with the springs and autumns of the mortal world.

These closing lines depict Prince Ning's fall from grace as the opening of a path to immortality, and Jiangxi, by implication, as a place of transcendence rather than of disgrace.[148]

Jiangxi serves as a key regional point of reference throughout the *Huang Ming shixuan*, with other prominent figures from or connected with Jiangxi making frequent appearances—Jiangxi natives such as the scholar-official Xie Jin 解縉 (1369–1415) who led the compilation of the famous encyclopedic project *Yongle dadian* 永樂大典, the general Mao Bowen 毛伯温 (1482–1545) who led the military campaigns against Annam/Vietnam, and the "Valedictorian Shu" 舒狀元 of the Zhengde reign, Shu Feng 舒芬 (1487–1531), an icon of Jiangxi regional pride who is the focal point of the anthologylet's sole illustration (fig. 1.4). Since the founding Hongwu emperor's decisive battle in his rise to rulership was won in Jiangxi, at Poyang Lake, moreover,[149] there is also an implicit but crucial connection between the anthology's first poem and the Jiangxi region. Other Jiangxi references include the line "The old man turns his head to gaze out from west of the Yangzi" 老夫翹首西江望, from a poem called "A Father Sends Off His Son to the Examinations" 父送子試, and a poem entitled "The Nine Counties of Ji'an" 吉安九縣 (Ji'an was a prefecture in Jiangxi). This last poem is especially indicative of the activities of Jiangxi commoner poets, as this type of composition brings to mind the story of a blind itinerant Jiangxi poet, Liu Chonghua 劉充化, who composed similar poems on local names and legends.[150] Jiangxi editors were quite savvy in creating novel anthologies or anthologylets of playful poems, songs, and plays, and the *Huang Ming shixuan* is a particularly revealing example of this proclivity.[151]

A poem entitled Han Du's Poem on the Oriole ("Han Du ti ying" 韓都題鶯) is particularly revealing of this strong regional perspective and frame of reference. It allows us to reflect not only on the anthology's Jiangxi regional affiliation, but also on its relation to the broader world of anthology-making in its era:

韓都題鶯 自喻 Han Du's Poem on the Oriole (An Allegory for Himself)

萬里扶搖到廣西，	Riding the ten-thousand *li* whirlwind, all the way to Guangxi,
一雙玉爪不沾泥。	a pair of jade claws that are not stained by mud.
威聲唬破群鴉膽，	Its awe-inspiring cry terrifies the flock of crows;
展翅驚翻萬馬蹄。	when it spreads its wings it startles and topples the hooves of ten thousand steeds.
身在江西嫌地窄，	Confined in Jiangxi, it feels the space narrow;
氣沖斗北恨天低。	its power thrusting up beyond the Dipper, it regrets the lowness of heaven.
平生豪氣三千丈，	Its heroic air, throughout its life, three thousand fathoms' scope,
不與凡雞一處棲。	unwilling to perch together with the common fowl.

The term "Han Du" will likely strike modern readers as obscure, but to readers of the *Huang Ming shixuan*, it would have been a familiar reference to a renowned figure in local and imperial politics: contemporary usage reveals that "Han Du" is an abbreviation for the title Han Dutang "Censor-in-Chief Han," and this title belongs to Han Yong 韓雍 (1422–78).[152] As the title of the poem announces, the poem is Han Yong's own allegorical self-description, capturing the moment when he arrives at Guangxi after leaving his tenure as Censor-in-Chief of Jiangxi, where he had first become a nationally known figure. It was in Guangxi, however, when he led the Ming troops in a crackdown against rebels of the local ethnic group, the Yao, that his reputation soared, as suggested, albeit sardonically, in lines from the poem such as *fuyao* 扶搖 (whirlwind), *zhan chi* 展翅 (to spread wings), *qi chong Dou bei* 氣沖斗北 (his power thrusting up beyond the Dipper), and *san qian zhang* 三千丈 (three thousand fathoms). These military triumphs in Guangxi sealed his place in history and legend in late imperial China. This poem, appearing in *Huang Ming shixuan* decades after his death, is part of the continuous re-inscription of the iconic figure of Han Yong in readers' memory on both general and regional levels. The idiomatic reference

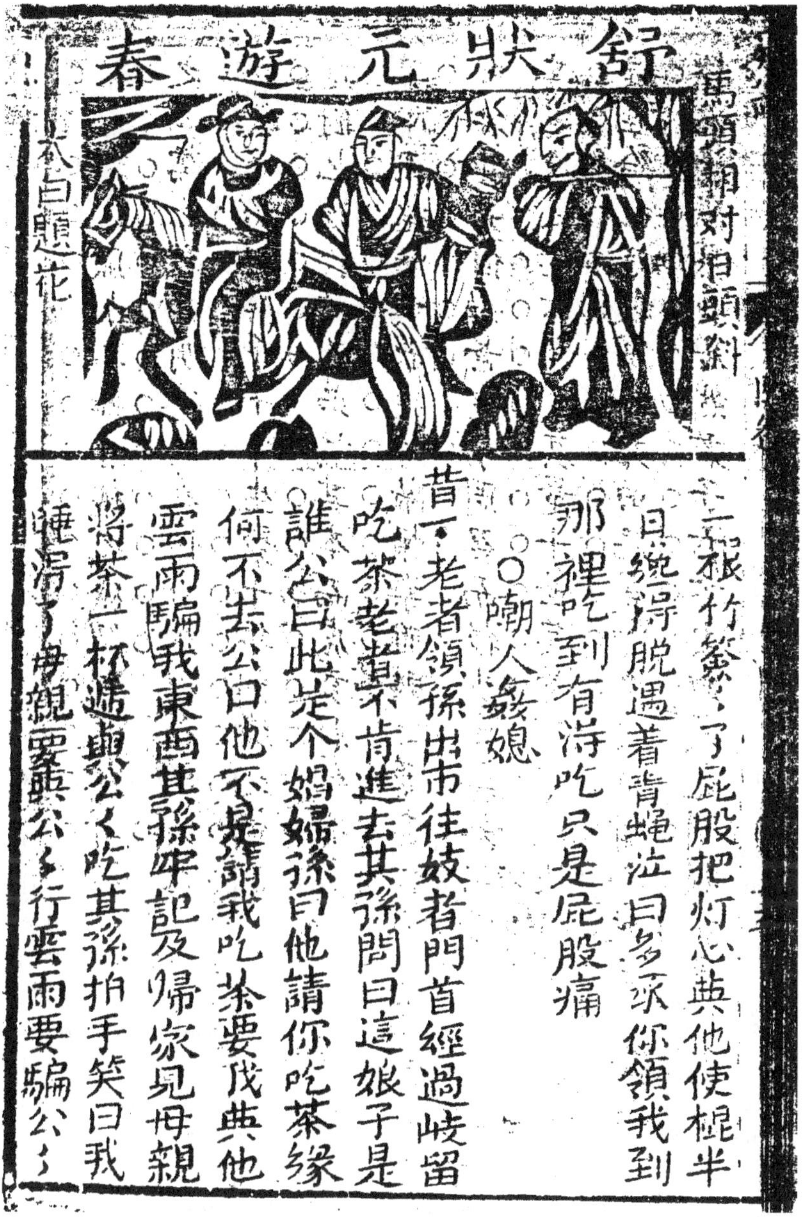
舒狀元遊春

馬頭相对柏頭斜

太白題花

一根竹篙了屁股把灯心與他使棍半
日纔得脫遇着青蠅泣曰多承你領我到
那裡吃到有滸吃只是屁股痛
○嘲人爺媳
昔一老者領孫出市往妓者門首經過岐留
吃茶老者不肯進去其孫問曰這娘子是
誰公曰此是个娼婦孫曰他請你吃茶緣
何不去公曰他不是請我吃茶要戊與他
雲雨騙我東西其孫牢記及歸家見母親
將茶一杯遞與公公吃其孫拍手笑曰我
娘涓了母親要與公公行雲雨要騙公公了

Fig. 1.4 The sole illustration in *Huang Ming shixuan*, bearing the caption "Valedictorian Shu Dallies in the Spring" in the top register. In the lower register is printed a joke ridiculing incest between father-in-law and daughter-in-law.

to Han Yong as "Han Du" signals that he is already well known to the intended community of readers and, given the Jiangxi-based perspective of the poem, reminds us that he enjoyed lasting political celebrity in that region. This is attested by a saying attributed to "people of the time" (*shiren* 時人) concerning two Jiangxi Grand Coordinators who were renowned as fierce prosecutors: "First there was Han Yong, then there was Chen Xuan."[153]

In fact, as noted above, Han Yong himself had been an active promoter of Jiangxi learning and culture during his term there, orchestrating the collection of over 1,200 poems under the title *Anthology of Poetry from Xijiang in the Glorious Ming*, the "Xijiang" of the title being an alternate designation of Jiangxi. This compilation promotes a close connection between literary and political status, reflected in the fact that the number of poems included for each author is in proportion to the author's official rank.[154] Han Yong's anthology excluded the work of commoners (called "gentlemen of the hills and forests clad in leather and plain cloth" 山林韋布之士), according to one preface to the anthology.[155] Within this context, the above *Huang Ming shixuan* poem in Han Yong's voice, likely itself the work of a commoner poet from Jiangxi who both by social status and by regional affiliation would have been one of those "common fowl" alluded to in the poem's final line, seems to be poking fun at Censor-in-Chief Han's inflated sense of self.

This is suggested most unmistakably by the disparity between the poem's bombastic language and the ostensible topic of the poem, the delicate oriole. The oriole's primary literary associations are with lovely springtime scenery and tuneful warbling, and its most common metaphorical application was to female singers, or the female voice generally—after all, the household name of the female lead in the *Story of the Western Wing* is "Oriole" (Yingying). To say that this poem on the oriole was composed by Han Yong as a metaphorical self-portrait is thus to present Han Yong as having a grossly mistaken sense of proportion or appropriateness; it suggests furthermore that Han Yong has an equally mistaken sense of his own worth and nature. This poem that purports to represent Han Yong's grand ascent to bigger and better things in his glorious career thus turns out to be a vehicle whereby those "common fowl" take rhetorical revenge for his disdain.[156]

Here and elsewhere in the small *Huang Ming shixuan*, regional and class pride and identity are inserted within the broader context of the "Glorious Ming."[157] The particular regional identity of Jiangxi, we should note, had historically fraught relations with the broader Ming order.[158] For one thing, Jiangxi had been the stronghold of Chen Youliang 陳友諒 (1320–63), a rival general and would-be dynastic founder to the Ming founder Zhu Yuanzhang during the period leading up to the latter's consolidation of power, and the people of the region had suffered reprisals in the aftermath of Chen's defeat and the Ming founding. Some Jiangxi natives at court also fought against certain state policies that did not favor the region, especially those that had made Jiangxi one of the more heavily taxed regions during the Ming.[159]

In the preceding example, the title, which also serves as an attribution of putative authorship, plays an essential role in indicating to the reader how to construe the poem's voice. The compilers of the *Huang Ming shixuan* in many cases created new meanings for material in wider circulation by the contexts they provided it. We glimpse this process at work in a poem that appears in the *Huang Ming shixuan* attributed to a Daoist immortal known as Xu Zhenjun 許眞君, who was particularly important in Jiangxi religious traditions:[160]

許眞君詩	A Poem by Xu Zhenjun
渺渺茫茫水接天	Vague and distant, water joins sky;
霏霏拂拂雨如煙	in drizzly dimness, rain like mist.
蒼蒼翠翠山堆石	Pale greys and bright greens—hills piled with stone;
白白紅紅花滿川	mingled whites and pinks—flowers fill the river.
兩兩三三沙上雁	In twos and threes—geese on the sand;
來來往往水中船	coming and going—boats in the water.
精精巧巧丹青手	Fine and skillful—painters' hands;
世世生生作話傳	generation after generation, will pass this story on.

The poem invites the reader to appreciate how an ephemeral moment achieves immortality through successive acts of depiction and commemoration, whether in painting or in narrative, both *hua* (畫/話). With the attribution to Xu Zhenjun, along with its link to a proud claim of aesthetic immortality in a Jiangxi regional context, the poem encourages its readers to reflect on the associations between the immortality of the aesthetic experience and its representations and the immortality of Xu himself. Just as in the case of the poems in the voices of Ming emperors or of Han Yong, however, these meanings arise as much from the attribution and framing given to the text within the *Huang Ming shixuan* as from the poem itself. Compare, for example, the following anecdote appearing in a Wanli-era scholar's notebook:

> 嘉靖間，倭子從終興雨中往曹娥江，賦詩曰：渺渺茫茫浪潑天，霏霏拂拂雨和煙。蒼蒼翠翠山遮寺，白白紅紅花滿川。整整齊齊沙上雁，來來往往渡頭船。行行坐坐看無盡，世世生生作話傳。"
>
> In the Jiajing reign, a Japanese who was going to the Cao'e river in the rain from Zhongxing composed a poem, which went . . . [what follows is a slightly different version of the Xu Zhenjun poem].[161]

"Isn't it remarkable that a foreigner should have composed such a poem?"—one can almost hear the compiler remark.[162] The poem suddenly acquires an altogether different significance. It is hard to pin down whether the editors of such texts were purposefully playing with attributions, or whether editors of texts like the *Boxiao zhuji* were simply adapting texts already in circulation to suit their own purposes, but it is clear that in such kaleidoscopic variation of both text and context we see the stamp of a distinctive culture of books and cultural display. Many of the poems in the small *Huang Ming shixuan* also appear in other sources, such as scholars' notebooks. Authorial attributions were not always the result of scholarly inquiry into texts' legitimate sources, but they served just as often as an effective tool for editors and publishers to create new meanings from material that happened to be ready to hand.

Conclusion

The world of text as reflected in the *Boxiao zhuji* is one with multiple types of canons and linguistic registers. Its novelty (*xin* 新) and charm (*qu* 趣) are realized by a playful recombinative energy linked to urban space and values as well as to a commercial impulse that shaped not only the production and circulation of texts but also their internal structure and composition. Along with dealing lightheartedly with various established canons (e.g., the *Four Books*), books such as the *Boxiao zhuji* reflected, and helped perpetuate, a distinctive grouping of canonical texts particular to the Ming book world, including administrative texts such as the *Da Ming lü*, anthologies like the *Qian jia shi,* dramatic texts like the *Story of the Western Wing*, and a range of other texts that have subsequently fallen into neglect, including the *Guwen zhenbao*. The *Boxiao zhuji* markets to its readers a fantasy that they can know all these texts discursively, and display their mastery of them, without really reading them. Such gesture and display became key to a theatricality of cultural fashion in which parodic mimicry of authoritative genres and discursive forms created new spaces for meaning and identity—both a larger Ming identity as well as a range of particular regional and social identities, as seen, for example, in the *Huang Ming shixuan*. In this process, the *Boxiao zhuji* reflects an intense interest in linguistic novelty, in exuberant rhetorical effects, especially parody (and even self-parody), and in the deconstruction and reappropriation of canonical texts and their prescribed system of value and social respectability. Core to this theatricality is the reading self, nimble and skilled at linking private laughter with a vision of the world at large.

CHAPTER TWO

Page and Stage: Drama Miscellanies and Their Milieu

若要認眞，
必然著假。
One who believes in the genuine
will surely be duped by the fake.
—*Brothel Instructions*, Ming dynasty

Many texts included in the *Boxiao zhuji* also appear in a variety of other Ming woodblock books.[1] In this chapter I expand the focus of discussion from the single book *Boxiao zhuji* to the broader space of publication genres within which these materials typically circulated. One of the most distinctive such genres of late Ming commercial publications is the one modern scholars refer to as the "drama miscellany" (*xiqu zashu* 戲曲雜書), which enjoyed wide popularity from the Wanli reign to the early Qing.[2]

As was the case with the *Huang Ming shixuan*, the editors of Ming commercial publications played an essential role in shaping the meanings both of individual texts and of groupings of texts, not in the mode of classicist collators striving to produce the most authentic version of a canonical text, but rather as curators, or even stage managers, in reworking, organizing, and maximizing the audience appeal of a fluid repertoire of textual and visual resources. Working with a pool of materials that was largely shared, editors of different book projects competed to produce novel and distinctive versions of widely popular textual genres. In this process they not only created their own individual books but also generated new kinds of books, rendering traditional bibliographical taxonomies insufficient to capture the vitality of their forms. To an even greater extent than with more familiar genres of texts, understanding these books must therefore mean resituating them within the complex of market dynamics and reader expectations that shaped them.

As an examination of the drama miscellany and related texts from this period will show, late Ming popular imprints reflect a relentless desire to keep up to date with current fashions—as suggested, for example, by the ubiquity in Ming book titles of terms such as *shixing* 時興 or *shishang* 時尚, both meaning "in the current fashion." To be up to date often meant to be conversant with various brands of specialized insider knowledge, and Ming publications could appeal to readers either by flatteringly treating them as initiates, or by promising to fill any potentially embarrassing lacunae in their range of expertise. Both readers and book producers were anxious to avoid being seen as a "three-pawed cat"—the Ming slang term for a person with a range of knowledge or cultural skill that lagged behind the latest standards of proficiency and style.[3]

One example of the importance of knowing the taxonomy of publishing genres is the designation *kui di qu* 簣底去, which means "going to the bottom of the basket" and which was used to refer to erotica. As Tang Laihe 湯來賀 (1607–88) recalls, these books were hidden at the bottom of the book-peddler's baskets;[4] anyone wishing to purchase such a book would have to know how to ask for it. Such publishing genres shaped and mobilized the corresponding processes of interpretation within which these books made the most sense to readers (and money for producers). The aim of this chapter's focus on the drama miscellany is to understand what aspects of the book market in this period made this particular genre possible and effective, and what sorts of know-how it would solicit from its consumers.

Figure 2.1 shows two pages from a drama miscellany entitled *Yuefu yushu ying* 樂府玉樹英 (Blossoms from jade trees of the Music Bureau), with a preface dated to 1599.

Part of the table of contents of *Yuefu yushu ying*, these pages reflect the typical triple-register page format of this print genre. In the main text, the top and bottom registers are devoted to the actual dramatic excerpts from plays that give the "drama miscellany" its name. In the *Yuefu yushu ying*, the dramas excerpted include the *Herong ji* 和戎記 (Tale of making peace with the barbarian), *Sijie ji* 四節記 (Tale of the four seasons), and

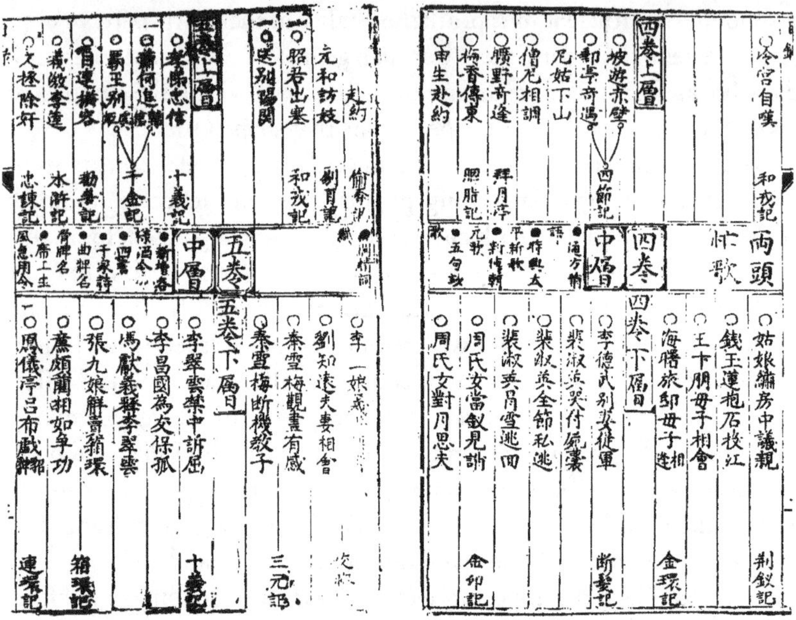

Fig. 2.1. Two pages from *Yuefu yushu ying*. 1599. Printed by Yu Shaoya 余紹崖, Jianyang, Fujian. From *HWSN*, pp. 6–7.

Baiyue ting 拜月亭 (Tale of the moonlight pavilion) in the top register, along with the *Jingchai ji* 荆釵記 (Tale of the thorn hairpin), *Jinhuan ji* 金環記 (Tale of the gold bracelet), and *Duanfa ji* 斷髮記 (Tale of severing hair) in the bottom register.

The narrow middle register, in this drama miscellany as in other exemplars of the genre, features a very wide range of text types, including popular songs, jokes and drinking games, glossaries of dialect and argot expressions, and other curiosities. Specific texts appearing in the middle register of the *Yuefu yushu ying* include "Liang tou mang ge" 兩頭忙歌 ("Busy at both ends" songs),[5] "Tong fang qiao yu" 通方俏語 (Pan-regional winsome sayings), "Shixing taiping xinge" 時興太平新歌 (New songs of great peace, in the current style), "Xin chuan chao yuan ge" 新傳朝元歌 (Newly circulated songs on a "Palace Audience at New Year's"), "Wu ju miao ge" 五句妙歌 (Marvelous songs in five lines), "Gui qing ci fu" 閨情詞賦 (Lyrics of the women's quarters),[6] "Xin zeng geyang jiuling" 新增各様酒令 (Newly added, various forms of drinking games), "Si shu" 四書 ([Drinking games on] *The Four Books*), "Qian jia shi" 千家詩 ([Drinking games on] *Poems by a Thousand Masters*), "Qupai ming gupai ming" 曲牌名骨牌名 ([Drinking games on] tune names and names of gambling tiles), and "Xishang sheng feng jiyong ling" 席上生風急用令 (Style for the banquet: drinking games for immediate use).[7] Many of the titles, and even more of the textual genres, included here overlap with those seen in the *Boxiao zhuji*.

The *Yuefu yushu ying* exemplifies how the drama miscellany typically organized and presented its material. These publications generally employ a triple-register page layout (*sanjie ban* 三節版) in which the upper and lower registers are devoted to the actual dramatic excerpts, though double-register layouts (*erjie ban* 二節版) also appear in some books.[8] What differentiates this publishing genre from the forms of drama anthology established in earlier periods (such as the *Fengyue jinnang* 風月錦囊 [Brocade bag of breezes and moonlight])[9] is the inclusion of the relatively small middle register (or, in the case of the double-register format, a small upper register) where sundry "novelty" genres (e.g., popular songs, drinking games, riddles, jokes, and other forms of incidental text) are squeezed in as a way of grabbing readers' attention.

The distinctive pages of the drama miscellanies, divided into different registers each filled with different contents, provide an alternative to the linear flow of text in the usual undivided page format. This layout creates the visual impression of a lively simultaneity of happenings within a single space, a unique textual geography where readers are prompted to take an active role in shaping a combination of reading (*du* 讀)—understanding what a single text says—along with viewing (*guan* 觀 or *lan* 覽)—taking in an overall visual arrangement of multiple texts and textual genres. The technique of dividing the page among multiple registers reshapes the experience of reading into one of visual pleasure and novelty.

The late Ming reading experience is enriched by many new and renewed types of visual materials, and the triple-register page appeals to readers' visual appetite by turning texts into components of the visual field of the page.[10] Although the divided page format had a long history that provides partial parallels to this sort of multilayered reading practice, particularly with page formats presenting a main text along with one or more layers of commentary, the late Ming popularity of the dramatic miscellany created a uniquely rich and complicated textual geography, turning the page into a field of negotiation among practices relating to print, visual images, and various types of both theatrical and social performance.

The following list encompasses the known texts of drama miscellanies. Their abbreviated titles are given first, followed by full titles:[11]

1. *Yuefu yushu ying* 樂府玉樹英
   Xinqie jingxuan gujin yuefu gundiao xinci yushu ying
   新鍥精選古今樂府滾調新詞玉樹英

   (From newly carved blocks—a meticulous selection from the ancient and modern bureaux of music, new lyrics in rapid recitative: blossoms from jade trees)[12]

2. *Hui Chi yadiao* 徽池雅調
   Xinqin tianxia shishang nanbei Hui Chi yadiao
   新鋟天下時尚南北徽池雅調

   (From newly carved blocks—the style of this age in the subcelestial realm, from north to south: elegant melodies of Huizhou and Chizhou)

3. *Yao tian yue* 堯天樂
   Xinqin tianxia shishang nanbei xindiao Yao tian yue
   新鋟天下時尚南北新調堯天樂

   (From newly carved blocks—the style of this age in the subcelestial realm, new melodies from north and south: music from the world of the sage king Yao)

4. *Cilin yizhi* 詞林一枝
   Xinke Jingban Qingyang shidiao cilin yizhi
   新刻京板青陽時調詞林一枝

   (From newly carved blocks—the capital edition of modern Qingyang melodies: a branch from the forest of lyrics)

5. *Baneng zoujin* 八能奏錦
   Dingdiao Kun Chi xindiao yuefu baneng zoujin
   鼎雕崑池新調樂府八能奏錦

   (From newly carved blocks—Music Bureau songs with new melodies from Kunshan and Chizhou: brocade performed by eight music masters)

6. *Yugu xinhuang* 玉谷新簧
   Dingke shixin gundiao geling yugu xinhuang
   鼎刻時興滾調歌令玉谷新簧

   (From newly carved blocks—in the current style of rapid recitative, arias and songs: a new reed from the jade valley)

7. *Zhaijin qiyin* 摘錦奇音
   Xinkan Huiban hexiang gundiao yuefu guanqiang zhaijin qiyin
   新刊徽板合像滾調樂府官腔摘錦奇音

(New imprint—the Anhui edition, with illustrations, in rapid recitative, the official accent of the Music Bureau: plucked brocades of wondrous tones)

8. *Yuefu wanxiang xin* 樂府萬象新
   Liyuan huixuan gujin chuanqi gundiao xinci yuefu wanxiang xin
   梨園會選古今傳奇滾調新詞樂府萬象新

   (A combined selection from the Pear Garden, *chuanqi*-drama new and old, new lyrics in rapid recitative: from the Music Bureau, a renewal of the ten thousand phenomena)

9. *Da Ming tianxia chun* 大明天下春
   Jingke huibian xinsheng yaza yuefu da Ming tianxia chun
   精刻彙編新聲雅雜樂府大明天下春

   (Finely carved—a comprehensive selection of new sounds, Music Bureau works in elegant and sundry modes: sub-celestial spring of the grand Ming)

10. *Da Ming chun* 大明春
    Dingqie Hui Chi yadiao nanbei guanqiang yuefu dianban quxiang da Ming chun
    鼎鍥徽池雅調南北官腔樂府點板曲響大明春

    (From newly carved blocks—elegant melodies of Huizhou and Chizhou, official accents of both north and south, Music Bureau works with beats marked: songs to echo the spring of the grand Ming)

11. *Shidiao Qing Kun* 時調青崑
    Xinxuan nanbei yuefu shidiao Qing Kun
    新選南北樂府時調青崑

    (New selection—Music Bureau songs from both north and south: popular tunes of Qingyang and Kunshan)[13]

Titling is a key technique for the successful production and marketing of books, and the titles of these drama miscellanies tell a great deal about the commercial publishing market of the period. Their full titles are composed both to captivate the reader's imagination and to excite the buyer's acquisitive impulse. The first part typically makes a claim of novelty, that the book in question is a new edition or new selection, drawn from newly cut blocks (*xinke* 新刻, *dingdiao* 鼎雕, *xinqie* 新鍥, *xinxuan* 新選, etc.) and current or novel melodies and lyrics (*shidiao* 時調, *xindiao* 新調, *xinci* 新詞, *xinsheng* 新聲, etc.). The second part describes the kinds of music and songs in the book (e.g., elegant melodies of Huizhou and Chizhou). The titles of these books in particular advertise that the dominant genre they include is musical drama, focusing on the popular tunes and singing styles (e.g., Qingyang and

Kunshan styles) of the day and highlighting what is called the *gundiao* 滾調—arias with insertions of rhythmic verses that are performed in rapid recitation. This was a technique much loved by contemporary audiences for its apparent spontaneity and for the space it offered to the virtuosic incorporation of familiar texts and sayings.[14]

With all their variety, these titles reflect a broadly similar syntactical structure in which a series of appealing descriptive phrases are capped at the end with an iconic or metaphorical phrase, striking in both image and sound: blossoms from jade trees (*yushu ying* 玉樹英); music from the world of the sage king Yao (*Yao tian yue* 堯天樂); subcelestial spring of the grand Ming (*da Ming tianxia chun* 大明天下春); a renewal of the ten thousand phenomena (*wanxiang xin* 萬象新), and so on. By incorporating such grand and suggestive phrases, book-makers evoked a sublime realm of imperial and cosmic grandeur for their books, while their frequent references to classical and latter-day musical lore also asserts their specialized authority and insider status in the world of music and theater. Thus, for example, *baneng* 八能 (eight abilities) is a rather archaic expression referring to eight skills such as adjusting the *yin* and *yang* energies and the five musical pitches, and the title *Yao tian yue* (music from the world of the sage king Yao) derives from a phrase for sagely rule common in imperial hymns and the like. While *wan xiang xin* 萬象新 (a renewal of the ten thousand phenomena) and *da Ming chun* 大明春 (spring of the grand Ming) sound auspicious and grandiose, phrases such as *yushu ying* 玉樹英 (blossoms from jade trees) and *yugu xinhuang* 玉谷新簧 (new reed from the jade valley) evoke images of secret rendezvous and thinly veiled erotic enticements, along with intimations of a plane of spiritual transcendence.[15]

By means of such phraseology in the titles, the producers of these books not only associated their texts with such fundamental concepts as universe (*tian* 天) and empire (*da Ming* 大明), but also plainly with desire (*yu* 玉/jade is a homonym of *yu* 慾/desire) and pleasure. Consequently, these texts map desire, fulfillable in music and play, within a sphere of values that are imperial or even cosmic in scope, and present the pleasures of dramatic performance as an alternative counterpart to the pursuit of status and prestige through orthodox learning. According to the visions presented by these book producers, drama and song were central not only to the cultural fashioning of the day but also to the manifestation of the empire's prosperity and heavenly blessings. The craft of book titling is part of the art of advertisement in the marketplace, and requires the same kind of verbal resourcefulness as the allusive play and eye-catching hyperbole displayed on store signs in Ming cities.[16]

These books' commercial success is largely due to how they textualized popular and provocative forms of entertainment that were all the rage at the time, as was also claimed by the *Boxiao zhuji*. One does see in these books ample evidence of what would become the standard litany of complaints against Ming commercial imprints: they were often produced in a rush, and missing characters, mis-transcriptions, and mis-titlings abound. The texts collected in one miscellany often overlap with those in others—in at least one case a print shop issued a "new" edition simply by making superficial changes and adding a new title to an old set of woodblocks, but on several pages neglected even to update the older title.[17] The quality is uneven, confirming the reputation for shoddy production standards in imprints from Jianyang, where most of these books were printed.[18] Characters are often crowded together, giving a general impression of a jumble aimed simply at fitting large amounts of text into a limited space, and tables of contents often do not perfectly match their accompanying texts. Scribal and printing errors are numerous, and variant forms of Chinese characters (*yiti zi* 異體字 or *suti zi* 俗體字) and phonological prompts (*baizi* 白字) can be found throughout.

To judge such features strictly as evidence of poor production quality, however, is to risk applying values that the drama miscellanies' own producers and readers never shared. Careful management of a book's "xylographic dignity" and collation of graphic forms were not priorities for this type of publication.[19] These texts did not operate within the world of classical erudition or archaist learning, but rather, as their titles tirelessly remind us, in the realm of "current fashion," and aimed to be read for pleasure and for the purpose of keeping up with the latest textual and musical trends. These texts' frequent and casual recourse to phonological prompts, for example, alludes to a world where the promise of the book was to enable oral reperformance, and where sound mattered more than orthography. Speed, affordability, and pleasure took precedence over the curation of rigorously correct text. The makers of these books therefore inserted illustrations to enhance the visual pleasure of reading and included jokes (including off-color and scatological jokes) and games, along with a rich literature of popular songs on the lives, and often in the voices, of courtesans and prostitutes. To read these books is to enter a realm where sensual pleasure reigns supreme, where the pursuit of good living—filled with drinking games, courtesans and actors, songs and plays, bodies and sounds, chatting, joking, and irreverent displays of wit and verbal invention—is the highest goal.

Filled with ephemera, these books would themselves prove ephemeral. With changes in stage fashions, anthologies of the popular singing styles of the late Ming gradually lost their appeal, and since they had never been held in particular esteem by elite bibliophiles, they fell into historical oblivion. Some of these books were taken to foreign lands, where they were stored in libraries as curious artifacts of another culture. They were not rediscovered until twentieth-century scholars, mainly scholars of drama, sought them out in the Naikaku Bunko in Tokyo, the Kongelige Bibliotek in Copenhagen, and the Österreichische Nationalbibliothek in Vienna.[20]

Many studies have been done on various aspects of these books, with a majority focused on the documentary value of the texts they include, particularly for the history of drama.[21] Here I will consider the books themselves as artifacts of a cultural moment, a site where texts responded to and helped to shape the social and cultural world around them. Centered on an examination of textual and visual field of the triple-register page layout, the core question that this chapter investigates is: how were these books coded and decoded by the late Ming communities of interpretation that were involved in their production and circulation?[22] The roles of book producers and readers were particularly interwoven in this period, as bookmaking often meant finding a novel angle for reconfiguring material the producer had read elsewhere, while the texts produced were often of a sort that solicited readers to take full ownership of the book by adapting it to their own individual needs and desires.

The Art and Business of Book-Making

The initial compilation of a book is the beginning of the process of circulation through which the book exercises its impact and realizes its cultural possibilities. How did these books come to be? Who made them? What made them possible and profitable? Why and how did they come to include the particular mix of materials that they did? What kinds of reading did they anticipate or create? I will begin answering these questions by looking at the production end of the process, to situate these books vis-à-vis the broader printing scene of the day. Looking at where, when, and by whom they were published reveals certain patterns of production that shed light on the formation of the genre. This information, summarized in Table 2.1, shows that most of the texts were printed by Jianyang commercial printers during the second half of the Wanli reign, and that the compilers were themselves often Jiangxi natives.

The neighboring provinces of Jiangxi and Fujian shared a long history of circulation of human talent.[23] The collaborative relationship between Jiangxi compilers and Jianyang publishers is telling in regard to their respective specialties in the book trade. While many Ming and Qing readers complained loudly about the poor quality of Jianyang imprints, what provoked this elite critique was Jianyang's notable commercial success in producing works of popular literature. In the broader world of Ming reading, the Jianyang imprint was a brand with widespread appeal. Chapter 1 touched on the impressive work of Jiangxi editors in making new types of anthologies. In the case of drama miscellanies, the prestige of the Jiangxi producers was further attributable to their perceived insider access to and knowledge of a regional musical tradition that lay at the foundation of both popular theater and songs of the Ming: the early southern drama, called *Yongjia zaju* 永嘉雜劇 (Yongjia variety play), took root in Jiangxi during the Southern Song and became the foundation for later development in southern theater.[24] In drama miscellanies in particular, the featured stage vogue was the Yiyang 弋陽 singing style, named for its place of origin in Jiangxi, along with its Anhui variant, the Qingyang 青陽 style. Thus attribution to a Jiangxi compiler would be a potent market-positioning strategy, suggesting to prospective buyers the authenticity and authority of the dramatic judgments underlying the selection. Jiangxi had, moreover, already established a tradition of anthologizing drama texts, marked by the printing of the *Fengyue jinnang* during the Jiajing reign, further enhancing the authority of Jiangxi editors as curators of dramatic books. Indeed, the marking of printshops and editors' native places in these publications was less a tribute to clan lineage than a publicity tool—some of these books were simply designated as made by *shulin* 書林 (forest of books), a phrase referring generally to the world of commercially produced books

Table 2.1. Publication Information on Drama Miscellanies*

Book title	Date of publication	Compiler(s) and native place	Publisher or publishing house	Place of publication
Yao tian yue	On or after 1598	Yin Qisheng 殷啓聖, Raoan 饒安, Jiangxi	Xiong Renhuan 熊稔寰	Jianyang, Fujian
Yuefu yushu ying	1599 (the 27th year of the Wanli reign)	Huang Wenhua, Jiangxi	Yu Shaoya 余紹崖	Jianyang, Fujian
Cilin yizhi	1606–7	Huang Wenhua 黄文華, Xi Xiufu 郗綉甫, Jiangxi	Ye Zhiyuan 葉志元	Jianyang, Fujian
Baneng zoujin	1607–8	Huang Wenhua, Jiangxi	Cai Zhenghe 蔡正河, Airi tang 愛日堂	Jianyang, Fujian
Hui Chi yadiao	Wanli reign	Xiong Renhuan 熊稔寰, Jianyang, Fujian	Yanshi ju zhuren 燕石居主人	Tanshui 潭水, Fujian
Yuefu wanxiang xin	Wanli reign	Ruan Xiangyu 阮祥宇, Ancheng 安成, Jiangxi	Liu Lingfu 劉齡甫	*shulin* 書林
Da Ming tianxia chun	Wanli reign	Jiangxi	Unknown	Unknown
Yugu xinhuang	1610 (the 38th year of the Wanli reign)	Jing jushi 景居士/Ba jing 八景, Jizhou 吉州, Jiangxi	Liu Ciquan 劉次泉/Tingli 廷禮	*shulin* 書林
Da Ming chun	Wanli reign	Cheng Wanli 程萬里, Zhu Dingchen 朱鼎臣	Jin Kui 金魁/Gongtang 拱唐	Jianyang, Fujian
Zhaijin qiyin	1611 (the 39th year of the Wanli reign)	Xi Zhengwo 龔正我, Huishe 徽歙, Zhang Dexiang 張德卿, Jutan 莒潭 (vols. 5 and 6 only)	Zhang Sanhuai 張三懷, Dunmu tang 敦睦堂	*shulin* 書林
Shi diao Qing Kun	Late Ming–early Qing	Huang Ruqing 黄儒卿, "Jianghu" 江湖 (rivers and lakes)	Sizhi guan 四知館	*shulin* 書林

*No publishing dates appear in *Yao tian yue*, *Cilin yizhi*, or *Baneng zoujin*. Here I follow the datings proposed by Guo Yingde and Wang Lijuan, "*Cilin yizhi, Baneng zoujin* bianzuan niandai kao."

often associated with Jianyang printshops.[25] This lack of specificity has caused difficulties for modern scholars in their attempts to pinpoint the actual places of publication of such books, but to Ming book-makers and buyers alike, *shulin* served as a good enough "place" to locate books. It seems that out of the specific places where books were printed (Jianyang, Anhui, Nanjing, just to name a few printing centers of the day) emerged a space of book trade and circulation driven by various printing centers, each possessing its own market niche and buyer appeal.[26]

As the above table of extant drama miscellanies shows, Huang Wenhua 黄文華 (fl. late sixteenth to early seventeenth centuries), who was evidently an established compiler of drama miscellanies, compiled three of the known publications of this type, *Yuefu yushu ying* (1599), *Cilin yizhi* (1606–7), and *Baneng zoujin* (1607–8), each in collaboration with a different printshop. Xiong Renhuan 熊稔寰 (fl. 1573–1620) is listed as the compiler of *Hui Chi yadiao*, and also as the printer of *Yao tian yue*, suggesting that the responsibilities of printer and compiler might overlap to some degree.[27] Some of these book-makers were in very high demand, enjoying the status of publishing celebrities. Liu Ciquan 劉次泉 (ca. 1590–ca. 1644), for example, the publisher of *Yugu xinhuang*, was better known as a renowned woodblock engraver and illustrator who had a close business relationship with the famed printing house Shijian tang 師儉堂,[28] and who counted among his accomplishments the carving of the blocks for the *Tang shi huapu* 唐詩畫譜 (Pictorial album to accompany Tang poems). Printed by the bibliophile and publisher Huang Fengchi 黄鳳池 (fl. early sixteenth century), the *Tang shi huapu* is a selection of Tang poems calligraphed, illustrated, and engraved by some of the best-known scholars, artists, and craftsmen of the day; it later became influential in the history of Japanese painting.[29] Yu Shaoya 余紹崖 (fl. late sixteenth to early seventeenth centuries) was a member of the Yu family of Jianyang, who ran a publishing business traceable back to the Song dynasty and had become the premier publisher of Jianyang.[30] As for woodblock engravers of these books, two names were inscribed in the *Cilin yizhi*: Chen Tengyun 陳騰雲 (fl. Wanli era) and (Chen) Pinzhou 聘洲 (ca. 1565–ca. 1625). Several other works of Chen Pinzhou have survived and are highly acclaimed by historians of woodblock illustrations. Like Liu Ciquan, Chen Pinzhou worked with Shijian tang. Such intertwining of the activities of known book producers suggests a dense network of printing houses with a specialized talent pool in constant migration from employer to employer in the region during this period.

Looking at other works credited to printshops such as Sizhi guan 四知館, or to named producers such as Yu Shaoya, Liu Ciquan, Chen Pinzhou, and Zhu Dingchen 朱鼎臣 (fl. Wanli era),[31] we can gain some sense of the cultural milieu in which the book-makers lived and worked. For example, Huancui tang 環翠堂, where Chen Pinzhou worked, won a reputation for finely produced and lavishly illustrated block-printed texts such as *Renjing yangqiu* 人鏡陽秋 (A mirror for humanity: lessons of history) and *Zuoyin xiansheng jingding jiejing yipu* 坐隱先生精訂捷徑奕譜 (Diagrams of shortcuts to success in *wei qi* [or *go*] playing success: carefully reviewed and approved by "Master Seated Reclusion").[32] Still more significant, "Master Seated Reclusion" himself, the Huancui tang owner Wang Tingne 汪廷訥 (also spelled Tingna, ca. 1569–after 1609) was an important member of the elite theater circle of the day, whose friends and associates included major figures in dramatic and cultural life such as Tu Long 屠隆 (1543–1605), Tang Xianzu 湯顯祖 (1550–1616), and Li Zhi 李贄 (1527–1602).

Chen Pinzhou's involvement in both Huancui tang productions and the *Cilin yizhi* attests to the sharing of production talent between what have been conventionally considered "high-end" and "low-end" publishing markets. Such overlap further suggests that the expertise involved in the crafting of the book as a material object was as important as its textual content in determining its status as a prestige item of consumption. While these book-makers were apparently involved in a broad range of publication genres and niches, some also seem to have pursued specialized interests: Sizhi guan was interested in medical treatises and military texts, and Chen Pinzhou seems to have specialized in theatrical works. Liu Ciquan cut woodblocks for popular reading materials such as plays and religious texts; his collaboration with the celebrated commercial publisher Yu Wentai (also known as Yu Xiangdou 余象斗) on Yu's own novel, the *Wuxian lingguan dadi Huaguang tianwang zhuan* 五顯靈官大帝華光天王傳 (Hagiography of the Heavenly King Huaguang, the great emperor of the five manifestations), is a clear indication of his respected status among the best commercial book-makers of the day.[33] Liu Ciquan seems to have been a particularly itinerant figure, moving from place to place as each new project demanded: he also worked as the illustration cutter for a *Sanguo zhi zhuan* 三國志傳 (Tales from the *Record of the Three Kingdoms*) compiled by Zhu Dingchen.[34] Zhu Dingchen, as noted in the above table, was also the compiler of the *Da Ming chun*. It appears that an active network of book producers moved about freely and formed ad hoc project-based teams, and an element of canny marketing opportunism was involved in the production of drama miscellanies as well.

Colloquialisms, Argot, and the Appeal of an Urban "Counterculture"

The commercially opportunistic impulse underlying the formation of these drama miscellanies is best seen in their signature innovation, the narrow middle register, and its conspicuous juxtaposition with the dramatic excerpts themselves. As mentioned above, these narrow registers draw from a pool of miscellaneous genres including popular songs, drinking games, riddles, jokes, "local expressions" used in market and pleasure quarters, "winsome sayings," brothel treatises, and geographical lists, including lists of local place names, local officials and offices, and local products. These types of texts, many of which were also present in the *Boxiao zhuji*, project the world of theater (as embodied in the drama excerpts of the top and bottom registers) into a larger world of cultural performance: musical (e.g., songs), verbal (e.g., drinking games), and social (e.g., interaction with courtesans), all wrapped in an aura of the alternative, the desirable, and the corporeal.[35] A prominent feature of many of these texts is the foregrounding of alternative nonstandard modes of speech associated with an urban milieu of alluringly dubious respectability.

One common subject matter heading in these texts is *fangyu* 方語 (local expressions), which is an abbreviation for *fangqing miyu* 方情密語 (cryptic phrases for local sentiments), also commonly referred to as *jianghu fangyu* 江湖方語 (local phrases of the rivers and lakes).[36] These categories refer to various types of argot, jargon used in marketplaces and brothels rarely represented in the official speech of early Mandarin.[37] As seen in late Ming fictional works such as *The Plum in the Golden Vase*, coded diction was frequently used in private gatherings with courtesans and singsong girls, not just because it formed a shield that kept outsiders at bay, but also because it was an esteemed mode of insider display within that social realm. Below are examples of *fangyu* as they appeared in drama miscellanies: [38]

琴家: 稱下處主人家	*Qinjia* refers to the host of one's accommodations.
墩臺: 乃其歇處	*Duntai* is one's place of temporary lodging.
犢孫: 乃做吏者	*Dusun* are government staff.
平天孫: 乃官員也	*Pingtiansun* are officials.
姑兒子: 亦官宦也	*Guerzi* are officials and affluent families.
立地子: 乃門子也	*Lidizi* are yamen-runners.

Such *fangyu* catalogs of alternative appellations for groups in power evoke the world of the *jianghu* 江湖 (rivers and lakes), a term referring to a hidden social order existing beyond and in opposition to the structure of the state, and provide lexical building blocks to articulate a distinctive perspective on social reality. Though much of the insider knowledge behind the semantics of these phrases is lost, it is hard to miss a pervasive tendency toward mockery and ridicule, especially directed at deflating the presumption of establishment elites: both phrases for officials end with the character *sun* 孫 (grandson), and *gu erzi* 姑兒子, the term glossed as officials and affluent families, is suspiciously homophonic to *gui erzi* 龜兒子 (son of a tortoise), a familiar invective term for "bastard." Such terms are thus reminiscent of the ubiquitous tendency in cursing speech to attack the target's parentage or generational rank. More generally, fascination with the world of "rivers and lakes" as a parallel universe to the state and its administrative structure is a strong drive in many of the books considered here. The following drinking game shows that *jianghu* and *langmiao* (corridors and temples, or halls of the empire, referring to the imperial buildings and offices) are two worlds in which one can exercise the right to choose one's own aspirations:

一令要江湖廊廟四字，暗藏問答之意，成詩一首。
幾年歸志樂江湖，問是何人蠡大夫。別卻廊廟懷重寶，乘舟過此號陶朱。
江湖廊廟志何如？聽說文公蓋世無。會做秀才含抱負，致令千載仰嘉謨。
樂意江湖更有誰？煙波釣叟最爲奇。忘情鷗鳥相遊戲，廊廟功勳徂不爲。

This game requires the use of the four characters *jiang hu* and *lang miao*, with an implied relation of question and answer, to form a complete poem.
[Sample answers]

A. Through many years wishing to retire, delighting in rivers and lakes; you ask what man was this?—it was the grandee Fan Li.
Leaving behind halls of empire, cherishing the greatest treasure,
he went off in a boat and passed by here, and his sobriquet is Master Tao Zhu.

B. "Rivers and lakes" and halls of empire—how do these aspirations compare? I hear there was never in the world one like Duke Wen.
A bona fide "blossoming talent" full of ideals,
so that to this day we admire his fine strategies.

C. Delighting in rivers and lakes, who else was there? The old fisherman amid mist and waves was the most wonderful.
He left human sentiments behind, and gulls flew playfully about him, as for merits of the halls of empire he left these and no longer pursued them.[39]

The category of *qiaoyu* 俏語 (winsome sayings), which partly resembles and is sometimes conflated with *fangyu*, is another verbal form reflecting an irreverent attitude expressed through colloquial styles of speech in these middle register texts.[40] Also referred to as *tongfang qiaoyu* 通方俏語 (pan-regional winsome sayings), *jianghu qiaoyu* 江湖俏語 (winsome sayings of the rivers and lakes), or *dujiao hu qiaohua* 獨腳虎俏話 (winsome sayings of a single-footed tiger), *qiaoyu* are a form of witty language game known in modern Chinese as *xiehouyu* 歇後語 (phrases omitting the end), in which a riddle is substituted for a phrase that answers the riddle, usually involving a further level of punning or wordplay. For example:

落花紅滿地—多謝.

Red of fallen flowers covers the ground—Many thanks/Many have withered.[41]

In employing this "winsome saying" in conversation, one would say "red of fallen flowers covers the ground" instead of "many thanks"—the pun in this case deriving from the fact that *xie* may mean either "to wither away" or "to thank." This language game is often grouped in popular publications with ordinary riddles and regional argot. The common thread among these categories is that to learn and use such expressions makes the reader an insider to a popular coded form of expression that could be mystifying to the uninitiated. Below are more examples of "winsome sayings" appearing in drama miscellanies:

子弟吃磨刀水—有些秀氣。
順風使帆進北京—都是南風。
銅錢孔裡打鞦韆—小人。
麥蒿吹火—小氣。
荷包裡鬼叫—是個腰精。
下雨出日頭—假情。
桅杆上掛燈籠—有名光棍。
張生跳粉墻—偷花賊。

A good-for-nothing eats knife-sharpening water—somewhat elegant (punning on *xiuqi* as "rustiness"/"elegance").
A following wind blows the sail to go to Beijing [the northern capital]—exclusively homosexual (punning on *nanfeng* as "south wind"/"male homosexuality").
Swinging in the hole of the bronze coin—a petty man (playing on literal "small person" and figurative "petty person").
Using a wheat-stalk to blow the fire—stingy (punning on *xiaoqi* as "small breath"/"stingy").
A ghost screams in an embroidered wallet—Must be a demonic sprite (punning on *yaojing* as "demonic sprite"/"waist sprite").
The sun comes out while raining—fake passion (punning on *qing* as "clear weather"/"passion").
Hanging a lantern on top of a mast—a well-known hoodlum (punning on *youming guanggun* as "light-bearing bright stick"/"renowned hoodlum").
Student Zhang jumps over the whitewashed wall—flower thief (playing on the alternate sense of the phrase to designate an illicit lover).[42]

Qiaoyu were such a staple of a variety of Ming books, not limited to drama miscellanies, that they often appear in quite elaborate taxonomic divisions. There was not just *changza qiaoyu* 常雜俏語 (common and miscellaneous winsome sayings) but also the more specific categories—not only *ma ren qiaoyu* 罵人俏語 (winsome sayings for cursing), but more refined categories for cursing specific groups, including *ma changji qiaoyu* 罵娼妓俏語 (winsome sayings cursing prostitutes), *ma guanggun qiaoyu* 罵光棍俏語 (winsome sayings cursing hoodlums), *ma xiaoren qiaoyu* 罵小人俏語 (winsome sayings cursing petty people), *ma xiaosi qiaoyu* 罵小伺俏語 (winsome sayings cursing catamites), and *ma shuohuang qiaoyu* 罵說謊俏語 (winsome sayings cursing liars).[43] *Ma*, cursing or ridiculing, is the key function of these winsome sayings, providing both an outlet for social indignation as well as a way to articulate and manage the *shiqing* 世情 (common sentiments of the world) that were also a key social aspect of Ming dynasty fiction.

The categories alone give a good indication of some of the favored objects of attention in the popular urban space of these middle-register texts: the *zidi* 子弟, a type of urban good-for-nothing who also seems to exert a potent charm (we might think of them as the Ming flancur); male homoerotic behavior and fashion; hoodlums (*guanggun* 光棍), who formed a marginal yet volatile group; and the pitfalls of "fake passion" that confuses anyone who seeks something or someone genuine. Among these contemporary figures is also the omnipresent character from the literature of the stage, Student Zhang, more often than not envisioned just at the moment when he jumps over a whitewashed wall in pursuit of a tryst.

Indeed, any lingering doubts as to the peculiar Ming taste for this exciting and morally ambiguous urban world would be dispersed by consideration of the Ming genre of the brothel treatise. The brothel treatise is entitled, in the particularly eye-catching way we often see in these commercial imprints of fashionable texts, "Fengyue jiguan qinglou jufu" 風月機關青樓罝罘 (Traps of breeze and moonlight, nets of the green lofts") in *Yuefu yushu ying,* and "Jiezhu piaojia fengyue jiguan" 解註嫖家風月機關 ("Traps of breeze and moonlight, set for brothel frequenters—with commentaries and annotations") in *Yuefu wanxiang xin*. This treatise discusses the proper ways to interact with courtesans and prostitutes.[44] It opens as follows:

男女雖異，愛慾則同。男貪女美，女慕男賢。
鴇子創家威逼佳人生巧計，撅丁愛鈔勢摧女子弄奸心。
且如尋常識見，皆由繩準之中。設若奇巧機關，更出筌綈之外。
若不運籌，定遭設網。
調情須在未合之先，允物不待已索之後。
初耽花柳，最要老成。久歷風塵，豈宜熟念。
若要認眞，定然著假。
對新妓勿談舊妓之非，則新妓生疑；調蒼姬勿憐雛姬之小，而蒼姬失意。
痛酒勿飲，寡醋休嘗。
寧使我支他，莫教他閃我。
初厚決非本心，久濃方爲實意。
欲買其心，先投所好。

Although men and women differ, in passion and desire they are the same.
Men crave feminine beauty; women admire manly worth.
As the madam builds her business:
by imposing force she compels the beauty to hatch clever plots;
The pimp loves cash:
his influence eggs on women to dally in villainy.
When everything goes according to common understanding, then affairs will proceed along the standard line; but if there are crafty ruses, then things pass beyond the grasp of ordinary conceptions.
Thus if you do not lay wily plans, you will fall into the net.
Flirting must come before mating; gifts should be granted before they are asked for.
When beginning to indulge in "flowers and willows," it is important to appear seasoned and experienced; after long indulgence in the winds and dust, one must not seem to have thought of everything.
One who believes in the genuine will surely be duped by the fake.

Don't discuss a former prostitute's bad points with a new one, lest the new one be suspicious; don't show sympathy for a young chick of a prostitute when with an older one, lest the older be disappointed.

Don't drink if there's too much wine, don't taste if there's only a little vinegar.[45]

Better that I abandon her than that she dump me.

Deep passion in the beginning is never genuine; it is true only when it thickens with age.

To buy her heart, one must first find what she likes.[46]

Each of these whimsical aphorisms of the brothel veteran's worldly wisdom takes the form of paired antithetical clauses, and each is accompanied, in a mock-serious mimicry of the manner of the canonical Confucian classics, by extensive commentary. For example, the following exegetical comments follow the statement that "Flirting must come before mating; gifts should be granted before they are asked for":

> 風月之中，以情爲先；軍武之內，以操爲最。情未調而求合，譬之三軍未曾操練馴熟而臨大敵，其敗必矣。嫖之允物，如魚之設餌，不得餌則他往。妓之索物，不得物則他求。後總與之，亦何益焉？
>
> In matters of "breeze and moonlight," passion is the primary thing; in matters of military forces, training is the ultimate. To pursue union before stirring up feelings is the same as confronting a strong enemy without first training one's three armies to the point of thorough proficiency: defeat is a foregone conclusion. A gift to a courtesan is like bait for a fish, who on finding none will go elsewhere. As for a courtesan's asking for a gift, when she is not able to secure one she will look for one elsewhere. What will be the use of a gift thereafter?[47]

Similar to the "local expressions" and "winsome sayings," the lexicon of the brothel treatise is also meant to create a realm that is linguistically outside of official speech and enclosed within a private world of desire (*siqing* 私情/secret passion or *miyi* 密意/clandestine intent), addressing the reader as an intimate companion and as a social insider by the use of terms such as *tiaoqing* 調情 (flirt), *zhuojia* 著假 (being duped by the fake), *zhi* 支 (abandon), and *shan* 閃 (dump), examples of the popular urban slang that also circulated in popular songs. The lexicon and rhetoric with which the emotional and monetary game in the brothel is played are distinctive in that they belong to an alternative world centered on desire, but the text-commentary format, the antithetical phrasing, and the floridly didactic tone of the commentary echo features familiar from canonical texts, making the brothel treatise simultaneously a whimsical wish-fulfillment fantasy and a parody of established modes of scholarly textual transmission and exegesis. Indeed, a further indication of the way in which such texts create a parodic mirror image of the world of orthodox scholarship on the classics is the fact that these commentated brothel treatises, a favored rubric of commercial printing in the late Ming, were often simply referred to as "Piao jing" 嫖經 (The Classic of whoring).[48]

The idea of the alternative spaces that such commercial imprints offered for the enjoyment of their readers is often directly expressed in geographic terms, as, for example, on the first page of *Shi diao Qing Kun* (fig. 2.2), on which various elements of place and space conjure an intriguing maze of connections and mutual shaping.

On this page, several appellations of the general notion of the world are used: *nanbei* 南北 (south and north) indicates the geographical comprehensiveness of the book's musical selections, whereas *liang jing shisan sheng* 兩京十三省 (the two capitals and thirteen provinces) invokes the spatial framework of the entire Ming realm in terms of the administrative structure of the state. Reference to the *tuchan* 土產 (local products) of each region, however, immediately orients our sense of this framework more toward mercantile activity, luxury commodities, and visions of a life of material comfort and luxury than toward interests and activities of the state. The term Qing-Kun 青崑 (Qingyang and Kunshan) of the book's title itself echoes this connection between "local product" and worldly usefulness, in that these two regional singing styles were at the forefront of stage fashions of the time. "Dallying by the Lake" and "Farewell at the Distant Pavilion" take readers to two iconic sites, Hangzhou's West Lake and the distant pavilion, with their conventionally associated human activities, excursions and farewell banquets, and with their corresponding emotional tonalities of joy and sadness.

Along with this network of commonly understood regions, territorial structures, local products of both material and cultural varieties, and iconic sites and scenes, the text presents geographical markers that hint at its origins: the compiler, Huang Ruqing, is provided with the toponymic epithet *jianghu* 江湖 meaning "of the rivers and lakes," and the printing house, Sizhi guan, is noted as situated in "the forest of books." Out of the spatial organization of the page (the triple-register page format, the title column, the publishing credits, the choice of dramatic scenes on the top and bottom and a song in the middle) and such recurrent play on multiple layers of topographical reference emerges the sense of an alternative geography unfolding before the reader's eyes. As one title of

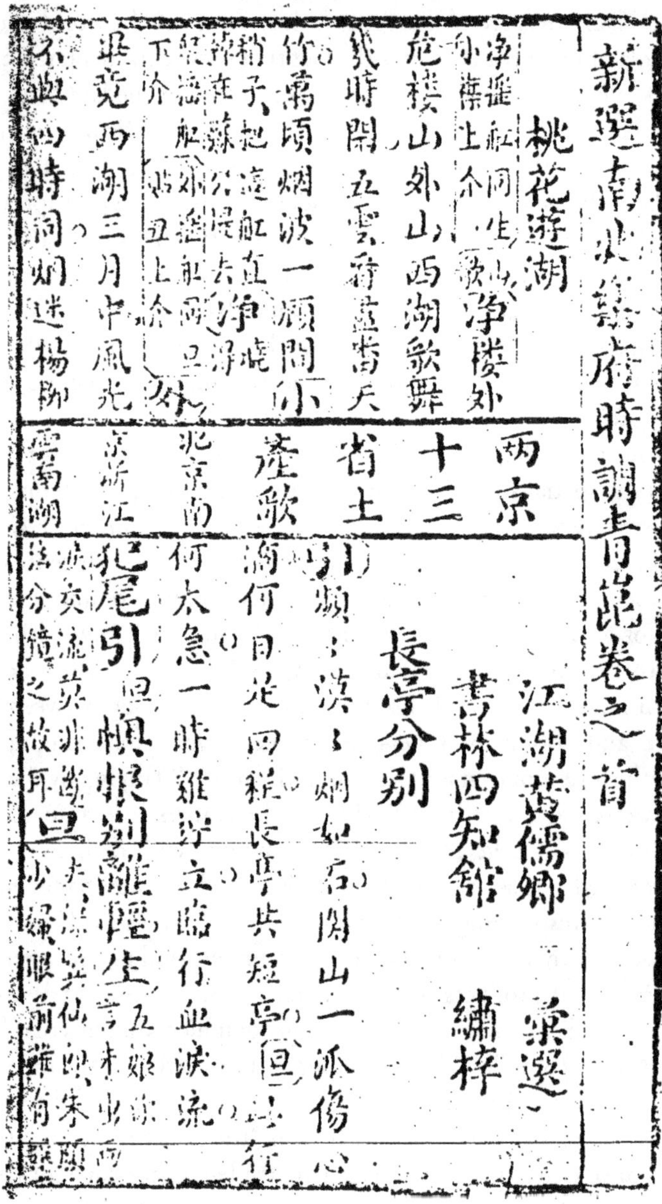
新選南北樂府時調青崑卷之首

江湖黃儒卿 彙選

書林四知館 繡梓

桃花遊湖

長亭分別

兩京 十三 省土 產歌

Fig. 2.2. The first page from *Shidiao Qing Kun*. The dramatic scene in the top register is "Taohua youhu" 桃花遊湖 (Dallying in the lake amid peach blossoms), from *Story of the Peach Blossoms*, composed by Jin Huaiyu 金懷玉 of the Ming; the scene in the bottom, "Changting fenbie" 長亭分別 (Farewell in the distant pavilion), is from one of Ming readers' favorite plays, the *Pipa ji*. From *SBXQCK*, vol. 9, p. 11.

drama miscellanies promises, this is indeed *wanxiang xin* (ten thousand phenomena made fresh).

The Daily-Use Encyclopedia

The drama miscellany's middle register is a space of fun, humor, irreverence, and oddly skewed or inverted echoes of orthodox texts and ideology. The source materials on which the drama miscellanies drew for their middle registers often reappear in another dominant publication type of this era—the daily-use encyclopedia, or, in the language of Ming people, the "wanbao quanshu" 萬寶全書 (complete book of myriad treasures),[49] a designation derived from a common title for this sort of book. In fact this connection reflects not only a shared group of source texts, but also an overlap between the groups of book-makers involved in the two publication genres. Zhu Dingchen, one of the compilers for the drama miscellany *Da Ming chun*, for example, also worked with the Xiong family printshops in Jianyang to edit several daily-use encyclopedias, including the *Xinke Yejia xincai wanbao quanshu* 新刻鄴架新裁萬寶全書 (From newly carved blocks: complete book of myriad treasures newly culled from the shelves of the Marquis of Ye)[50] (preface 1614), *Bolan qunshu* 博覽群書 (Wide-ranging survey of the crowd of books) (Wanli reign), and *Longtou yilan xuehai buqiuren* 龍頭一覽學海不求人 (One vista from the dragon's head: in the ocean of learning, seek no further)[51] (date unknown).[52]

Encyclopedias (*lei shu* 類書) had a long publishing history by the late Ming, encompassing a wide range of subtypes.[53] The daily-use encyclopedias of the late Ming represent a new incarnation of an encyclopedia type with a pronounced orientation toward practical knowledge that can be traced back to early exemplars such as the *Shilin guangji* 事林廣記 (Wide-ranging record of the forest of affairs), compiled during the Southern Song and reprinted frequently thereafter. These texts are organized by thematic divisions, starting from "Heavenly Patterns" and continuing with "Geography," "Time and Seasons," "Human Affairs," and further categories covering a wide range of topics and textual genres, ranging from astronomy to history, legal knowledge to dream interpretation, poetry anthologies to contract forms and letter templates, and so on. Its promise was to aid readers in understanding and acting independently in all aspects of everyday life.[54]

Though comparable in basic orientation to these earlier exemplars, the late Ming daily-use encyclopedias, published mainly by Fujian commercial printers, in many respects appear drastically different from earlier compilations such as the *Shilin guangji*. The new encyclopedias restructured the traditional divisions, updated the texts included, devoted a significant portion of the text to illustrations, and achieved, during their time, an unparalleled degree of popularity.[55] A short sampling of the titles of these daily-use encyclopedias may provide some indications as to their target audiences and the sorts of benefits they promised to the reader:[56]

> *Xinqie tianxia beilan wenlin leiji wanshu cuibao*, 1596. *(Wanshu cuibao for short)*
> 新鍥天下備覽文林類記萬書萃寶
>
> (From newly carved blocks—comprehensive world survey, a categorized record of the forest of literature: Splendid treasures from the myriad books)
>
> *Xinqie quanbu tianxia simin liyong bianguan wuche bajin*, 1597 *(Wuche bajin for short)*
> 新鍥全補天下四民利用便觀五車拔錦
>
> (From newly carved blocks, fully supplemented—a handy survey for advantageous employment by the four classes of the subcelestial realm: plucked brocade from the five carriages of books)[57]
>
> *Xinke tianxia quanshu bolan buqiuren*, 1598
> 新刻天下全書博覽不求人
>
> (From newly carved blocks—a broad survey of all books of the subcelestial realm: seek no further)
>
> *Xinke tianxia simin bianlan Santai wanyong zhengzong*, 1599 *(Santai wanyong zhengzong for short)*
> 新刻天下四民便覽三台萬用正宗
>
> (From newly carved blocks—a convenient survey for all four classes of the subcelestial realm: the Santai studio's authentic standard for myriad uses)
>
> *Xinqie Yantai jiaozheng tianxia tongxing wenlin jubao wanjuan xingluo*, 1600
> 新鍥燕臺校正天下通行文林聚寶萬卷星羅
>
> (From newly carved blocks, collated and corrected by Master Yantai—recognized throughout the subcelestial realm, a compendium of treasures from the forest of letters: starry array of a myriad volumes)
>
> *Xinkan hanyuan guangji buding simin jieyong xuehai qunyu*, 1607
> 新刊翰苑廣記補訂四民捷用學海群玉
>
> (From newly carved blocks—supplemented and corrected, a wide-ranging record of the garden of authors, for expeditious use by the four classes: hoarded jade from the ocean of learning)

Xinke quanbu shimin beilan bianyong wenlin huijin wanshu yuanhai, 1610 *(Wanshu yuanhai for short)*
新刻全補士民備覽便用文林彙錦萬書淵海

(From newly carved blocks, fully supplemented—a comprehensive survey for ready use by gentry and commoners, amassed brocades from the forest of letters: a fathomless ocean of myriad books)

Ke xinban zengbu tianxia bianyong wenlin miaojin wanbao quanshu, 1612 *(Miaojin wanbao quanbian for short)*
刻新板增補天下便用文林妙錦萬寶全書

(Reedition from newly carved blocks, expanded and supplemented—for ready use throughout the subcelestial realm, wondrous brocades from the forest of letters: complete book of myriad treasures)

Xinke Ai xiansheng Tianlu ge huibian caijing bianlan wanbao quanshu, Wanli reign
新刻艾先生天祿閣彙編採精便覽萬寶全書

(From newly carved blocks—a comprehensive compilation by Master Ai of the Tianlu studio, selecting the best for ready reference: complete book of myriad treasures)

Xinke Meigong Chen xiansheng bianzuan zhushu beicai wanjuan souqi quanshu, 1628 *(Wanjuan souqi for short)*
新刻眉公陳先生編纂諸書備採萬卷搜奇全書

(From newly carved blocks—compiled by master Chen Meigong,[58] drawing on the full range of books: complete book of assembled wonders from myriad volumes)

Among these daily-use encyclopedias, the earliest to have been discovered is the 1596 *Wanshu cuibao*, the only known copies of which are incomplete. An intact exemplar of the 1597 *Wuche bajin*, however, does exist. Better known to modern scholars is the 1599 *Santai wanyong zhengzong* 三台萬用正宗 (Santai Studio's authentic standard for myriad uses) compiled by the renowned publisher Yu Wentai. Jianyang is far and away the predominant place of publication for these books, and this publication trend seems to have taken off in the 1590s, closely coinciding with the period when drama miscellanies took hold.

These late Ming encyclopedias attest to a new book market where the rise of groups of commoner readers—merchants, craftsmen, village teachers, women, and others with less-than-perfect education but disposable income—created fresh opportunities for publishing. Indeed, one of the more striking aspects of the titles of these late Ming encyclopedias is the way they persistently go out of their way to make clear, with phrases such as *shimin* 士民 (gentry and commoners) and *simin* 四民 ("all four classes," i.e., scholar-officials, peasants, craftsmen, and merchants), that they are intended and suited for use not only by a (notionally) highly educated official class, but by a broader reading public made up of an inclusive swath of disparate social strata.[59] The practical goal of these books, as their titles declare, is to provide information for the myriad issues of everyday life so that one need not beg for help from others—as highlighted by the alternate designation of this print genre as a whole, *buqiuren* 不求人, or "seek no further." The implication of this commercial selling point is that these print productions promise their buyers a degree of social and cultural autonomy that they would have lacked when the knowledge they make available was accessible only to a select few. At the same time, these works reflect a pervasive fascination with collecting the most marvelous and bizarre texts and "facts," the impulse referred to in Chinese by the phrase *sou qi* 搜奇 (seeking out the marvelous). Their emergence in the book market first marked, then shaped and created, a new social space where the everyday was redefined along with its own knowledge system.[60]

An episode from the opening chapters of the *Xingshi yinyuan zhuan* 醒世姻緣傳 (Foredestined marriage bond to awaken the world), a seventeenth-century novel of uncertain authorship, is richly suggestive about the complex topography of the late Ming world of books, and about how books could generate social and psychological meanings far beyond their mere textual content.[61] The novel recounts the fate of Chao Yuan 晁源, a dissolute young playboy whose formal education does not extend much beyond basic literacy primers like the *Qian zi wen* 千字文 (Thousand-character essay). He owes his wealth and status to his father's position as a local magistrate, a position that was itself acquired not through scholarly attainment and success in the civil service examinations but rather through the *suigong* system, a mode of advancement generally viewed as readily open to those with social connections or money.

Early in the novel, the excesses of Chao Yuan's lavish and sensually indulgent mode of life have left him desperately ill and lying insensate in bed. A Doctor Yang who comes to attend to him requests a book to use to prop up the patient's wrist as he takes the pulses, and a maidservant offers up the first book that comes to hand beside Chao Yuan's pillow—an erotic picture album entitled *Chunxiao mixi tu* 春宵秘戲圖 (Pictures of secret play on spring nights). Objecting that the pages of this volume are too coarse and stiff, the doctor suggests a soft-covered book, suggesting a copy of a *Jin shen* 縉紳—a genre of social register, published as a "who's who" by and for gentry—as an option. The maid searches again by Chao Yuan's bedside and comes up instead with the *Ruyi jun zhuan* 如意君傳 (Story of the lord of perfect satisfaction), a historical fantasy about the sexual and political exploits of the seventh-century Empress Wu Zetian, and a classic of Ming erotica.[62] During a subsequent visit from Doctor Yang, when Chao Yuan is more lucid, he quickly snatches the *Ruyi jun zhuan* from the maid's hand when she produces it for the doctor, telling her to go to the eastern wing of the house to fetch a book, from which she returns bearing a daily-use encyclopedia entitled *Wan shi buqiuren* 萬事不求人 (Seek no further for a myriad of affairs). Having taken Chao Yuan's pulses using this new prop, Doctor Yang pronounces the patient "sixty to seventy per cent cured," and predicts that full recovery will soon follow.[63]

The multilayered ironies and in-jokes relating to books in this episode resist definitive decoding. Clearly the erotic pictorial and novel that lie close at hand by Chao Yuan's bedside offer a glimpse of what books are truly nearest and dearest to him, as well as giving some indication of the causes and nature of his illness. As for the doctor, his seeming incomprehension of the significance of these books other than as material objects opens the possibility of reading him as a rube or naïf, but also serves as a reminder of the real physical qualities and characteristics that differentiate one type of book from another and suit each to its proper use. The stiff material of the pictorial, coarse to the touch, is what one would expect from a book designed to withstand repeated handling and page-flipping, while the smoothness and suppleness reflective of luxury-grade paper and bindings might very well be expected qualities in a vanity publication such as the gentry social register.

Doctor Yang's mistaken supposition about the sort of text likely to be lying about in Chao Yuan's household brings to relief the range of choices available to a young well-to-do reader of the time. He assumes that Chao Yuan, as a member of a gentry family, would keep a finely produced social register, a textual reinforcement of gentry identity and prestige and a symbol of his public persona, in his home. But the texts Doctor Yang finds reveal that Chao's real identity and social status are more problematic and protean than Yang supposes. Chao Yuan is naturally ashamed to have his bedroom cache of "basket-bottom" volumes exposed, but the book he directs the maid to fetch from the eastern library as a more respectable substitute is not a social register, much less a text of orthodox scholarship, but rather precisely the sort of book that promises its readers the means to successfully manage their affairs regardless of their scholarly attainments or social class: the daily-use encyclopedia.

However one reads the ambiguities appearing in these passages, the protagonist Chao Yuan is presented in the *Xingshi yinyuan zhuan* as a basically negative figure, whose lack of moral integrity and failure to embody the virtues of the class whose status he usurps have a disruptive and destructive impact on his social world. In popular publications of the late Ming, however, the worldly sensualist who masters the verbal and behavioral vocabularies of a range of social types, and displays a subversive and satirical attitude toward social convention, often appears as a model for emulation. A primary virtue of the daily-use encyclopedias for Chao Yuan and others lies in the way they assemble new categories and styles of knowledge and imagination, and orient their readers in this new system of learning. Alongside the traditional practical categories such as guides to drafting letters or legal documents, using an abacus, categories of food and drink, or commonplace facts relating to history or religious traditions, the Ming daily-use encyclopedia foregrounds categories of knowledge or skill relating to humor and play.

New divisions appearing alongside the traditional encyclopedic categories in the late Ming daily-use encyclopedias include drinking games and riddles (*youshang* 侑觴, *jiuling* 酒令, or *miling* 謎令), jokes (*xiaoxue* 笑謔, *tanxiao* 談笑, *xiaotan* 笑談, or *xiaohua* 笑話), and brothel treatises (*fengyue* 風月 or *shanglü* 商旅).[64] The general trend of these new categories openly defies the value reflected (and stated outright) in many earlier encyclopedic works that pleasure-seeking is a menace to one's physical and spiritual well-being. For example, *Jujia biyong shilei quanji* 居家必用事類全集 (The complete collection of matters necessary for household use) quotes from *Sanyuan canzan yanshou zhi shu* 三元參贊延壽之書 (Book for extending lifespan through mutual interaction of the three principles), a Yuan-dynasty treatise on the cultivation of longevity:[65]

談笑

書云：談笑以惜精氣爲本。多笑，則腎轉腰痛○多笑則神傷；神傷則悒悒不樂，恍惚不寧○多笑則臟傷；臟傷則臍腹痛，久爲氣損○行語令人失氣；語多須住乃語。

Joking and Bantering

In books we find the following: Joking must be based on (the principle of) cherishing one's essence and vital energy. Too much laughing makes one's kidneys twist and turn and one's waist hurt. ◦ Too much laughing harms one's spirit. If one's spirit is harmed then one is depressed, unhappy, absent-minded, and fidgety. ◦ Too much laughing harms one's organs. If one's organs are harmed then one's stomach is in pain. If this continues for a long time, one's vital energy will be damaged. ◦ Babbling on makes one lose vital energy; when one speaks too much one should pause before speaking again.[66]

In the same volume, the *Complete Collection of Matters Necessary for Household Use* criticizes behavior such as ridiculing (*chaoqiao* 嘲誚) and mocking (*jixue* 稽謔).[67] These attitudes are markedly relaxed, to say the least, in the late Ming daily-use encyclopedia, where adroitness in joking and play become essential to the self-fashioning of a new urbane and trendy persona, and these categories of demimonde behavior now enjoy respectability. Knowing how to banter playfully saves one from being perceived as a dull and boring Chen Zuiliang, a pedant lacking the ability to respond with charm or wit when the conversation demands it.

These newly highlighted categories in the late Ming daily-use encyclopedias were precisely the sorts of materials that were packed into the middle registers of drama miscellanies. Figure 2.3 demonstrates how the middle-register "novelty" genres in the drama miscellanies find close parallels in the division headings of the late Ming daily-use encyclopedias: local names (*liangjing gesheng* 兩京各省) and local products (*huliang tuchan* 户糧土產) in the Geography division; drinking games (*shixing jiuling* 新興酒令) in the "Aid to Drinking" division; riddles (*qiqiao dengmi* 奇巧燈謎) in the "Gaming and Fun" division; brothel treatises

Fig. 2.3. (overleaf) The table of contents of *Santai wanyong zhengzong*. The sundry forms of literature in the middle registers of drama miscellanies can be seen here in divisions of *Diyu men* 地輿門 (Geography), *Youshang men* 侑觴門 (Aid to drinking), *Boxi men* 博戲門 (Gaming and fun), *Shanglü men* 商旅門 (Merchant and travel), and *Xiaoxue men* 笑謔門 (Laughing and mocking). Following the table of contents is a likeness of the publisher Yu Wentai, surrounded by things that signal cultural and domestic living sophistication: a paneled screen, a stove, incense burning, book pages, young maids, and plum trees. From *CNRS*, vol. 3, pp. 6–13.

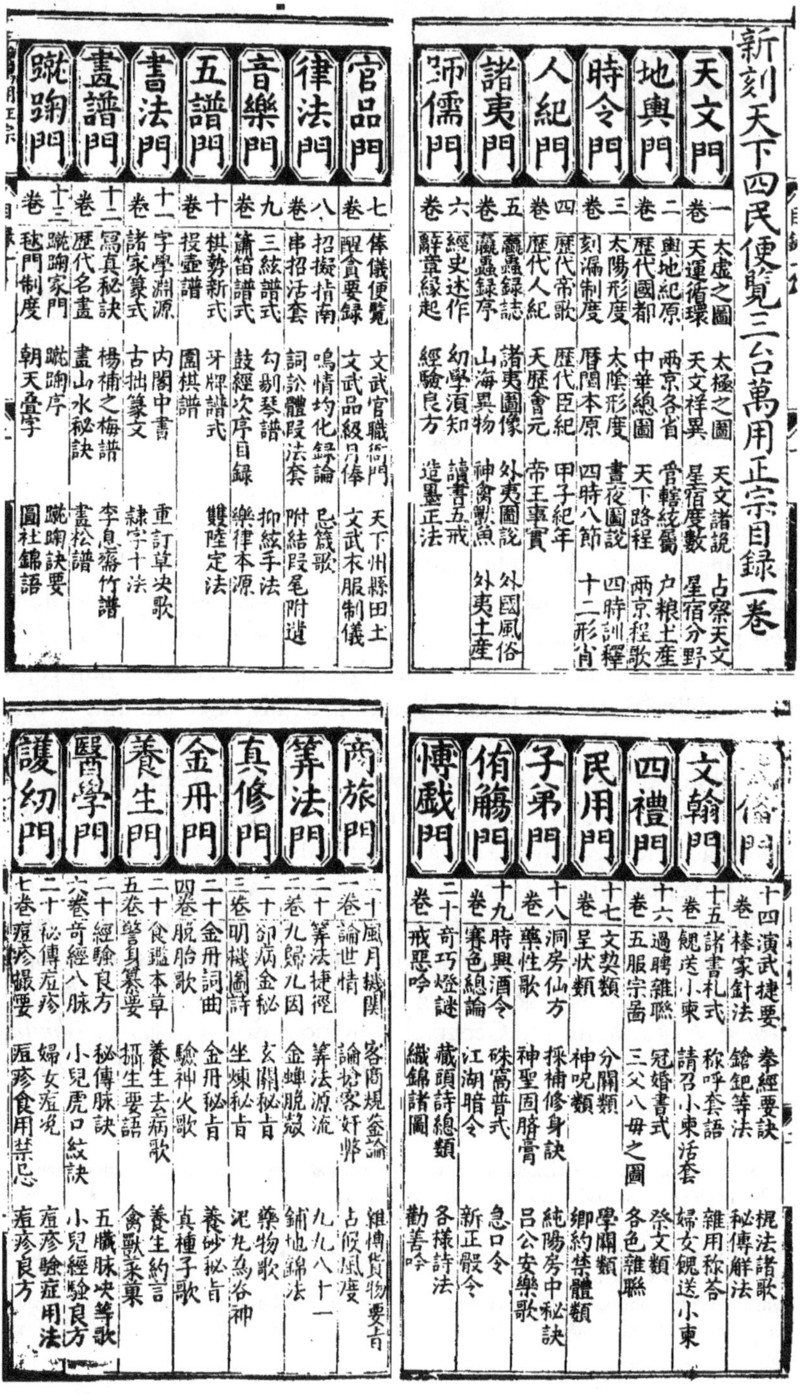
新刻天下四民便覽三台萬用正宗目錄一卷

天文門 卷一 太虛之圖 太極之圖 天文諸說 占察天文 天運循環 天文祥異 星宿度數 星宿分野
地輿門 卷二 輿地紀原 兩京各省 骨轄統屬 户粮土產 歷代國都 中華總圖 天下路程 兩京程歌
時令門 卷三 太陽形度 太陰形度 晝夜圖說 四時訓釋 刻漏制度 曆閏本原 四時八節 十二形肖
人紀門 卷四 歷代帝歌 歷代臣紀 甲子紀年 歷代人紀 天歷會元 帝王事實
諸夷門 卷五 贏蟲錄誌 諸夷圖像 外夷圖說 外國風俗 贏蟲錄序 山海異物 神禽獸魚 外夷土產
師儒門 卷六 經史述作 幼學須知 讀書五戒 辭章緣起 經驗良方 造墨正法
官品門 卷七 俸儀便覽 文武官職衙門 天下州縣田土 醒貪要錄 文武品級月俸 文武衣服制儀
律法門 卷八 招擬指南 鳴情均化錄論 忌箴歌 串招活套 詞訟體段法套 附結段尾附遺
音樂門 卷九 三絃譜式 勾剔琴譜 抑絃手法 簫笛譜式 鼓經次序目錄 樂律本源
五譜門 卷十 棋勢新式 牙牌譜式 雙陸定法 投壺譜 圍棋譜
書法門 卷十一 字學淵源 內閣中書 重訂草訣歌 諸家篆式 古拙篆文 隸字十法
畫譜門 卷十二 寫真秘訣 楊補之梅譜 李息齋竹譜 歷代名畫 畫山水秘訣 畫松譜
蹴踘門 卷十三 蹴踘家門 蹴踘序 蹴踘訣要 毬門制度 朝天疊字 圓社錦語
武備門 卷十四 演武捷要 拳經要訣 棍法諸歌 棒家針法 鎗鈀等法 秘傳解法
文翰門 卷十五 諸書札式 稱呼套語 雜用稱荅 餽送小柬 請召小柬活套 婦女餽送小柬
四禮門 卷十六 過聘雜聯 冠婚書式 祭文類 五服宗圖 三父八母之圖 各色雜聯
民用門 卷十七 文契類 分關類 學館類 呈狀類 神呪類 鄉約禁體類
子弟門 卷十八 洞房仙方 採補修身訣 純陽房中秘訣 藥性歌 神聖固臍膏 呂公安樂歌
侑觴門 卷十九 時興酒令 硃窩嘗式 急口令 賽色總論 江湖暗令 新正骰令
博戲門 卷二十 奇巧燈謎 藏頭詩總類 各樣詩法 戒惡吟 織錦詩圖 勸善吟
商旅門 卷二十一 風月機関 客商規鑑論 雜傳貨物要言 論世情 論物客奸弊 占候風度
筭法門 卷二十二 筭法捷徑 筭法源流 九九八十一 九歸九因 金蟬脫殼 鋪地錦法
真修門 卷二十三 卻病金秘 玄關秘旨 藥物歌 明機圖詩 坐煉秘旨 泥丸為谷神
金丹門 卷二十四 金丹詞曲 金丹秘旨 養砂秘旨 脫胎歌 驗神火歌 真種子歌
養生門 卷二十五 食鑑本草 養生去病歌 養生約言 警身纂要 攝生要語 禽獸桼菓
醫學門 卷二十六 經驗良方 秘傳脉訣 五臟脉決等歌 奇經八脉 小兒虎口紋訣 小兒經驗良方
護幼門 卷二十七 秘傳痘疹 婦女痘疹 痘疹驗症用法 痘疹攝要 痘疹食用禁忌 痘疹良方

胎產門
二十八卷 姙娠脉訣 產後良方 種子奇方 夫婦雲雨忌日 不育女專生男 十月懷胎形局

星命門
二十九卷 合婚要旨 六十甲子 五星指南提要 論生肖皇帝詩 起八字法 陰陽生旺之圖

相法門
三十卷 麻衣摘要 人面部相 相法秘旨 眉目部相 男女痣訣 耳鼻部相

卜筮門
三十一卷 斷易秘旨 陰陽宅賦 求卦祝文 秘傳神機 擲錢訣法 十六字例

數課門
三十三卷 五行訣課 論錢斷法 冲天數 淳風六壬課 諸葛馬前課

夢珍門
三十三卷 周公夢書 鎮日夢符 夢珍故事 厭禳符書 禳夢符呪 逐時雜斷法

營宅門
三十四卷 營造宅經 相宅吉凶 魯班經論 撥抄吉凶時 定盤詩訣 上梁致語

地理門
三十五卷 龍穴砂式 穴法論 登山[illegible]賦 水五星吉凶論 遊山倒杖經 龍穴砂水形圖

剋擇門
三十六卷 剋擇便覽 水行局例 事急不暇擇法 十二時吉凶斷 六十花甲吉凶例 二十八宿吉凶詩

牧養門
三十七卷 秘傳牛經 相良馬論 秘傳安驥集 養羊養猪法 治馬三十六證歌 牛病三十二證歌

農桑門
三十八卷 農桑便覽 付耕犁篇 農事源流 付耙勞篇 蠶繅提要 種植類

僧道門
三十九卷 釋祖源流 道派源流 禪苑清規 僧道榜文 弔慰疏狀 雜用書文

玄教門
四十卷 靈寶玄文 遊仙夢法 神仙秘旨機要 神仙戲術

法病門
四十一卷 書符秘旨 雷霆占病 淳風百怪書法 十二占病 籌病生死 籌病諸怪符法

閑中記
四十二卷 名公格言 勸世文 混沌總論 嘆世報應分明 樵談總叙 酒色財氣

笑謔門
四十三卷 嘲人笑話 戒酒文 綺席清談 方情密語 獨脚虎笑話 罵人笑話

右書目畧舉其大綱各門事類甚多目録難以備載

蓬左文庫に同一本あり
昭和三十年秋十月 調查
仁井田

(*fengyue jiguan* 風月機關) in the "Merchant and Travel" division; jokes, "local expressions" and "winsome sayings" (called here *dujiaohu xiaohua* 獨脚虎笑話) in the "Laughing and Mocking" division.[68]

These encyclopedias and drama miscellanies show considerable overlap both in the publishers involved and in their source material. Both were the products of the market conditions that determined what was deemed possible and profitable, specifically, a drive to redefine earthly life and imagine how readers ought to inhabit their personal and domestic spheres. The success of the printing genre of the daily-use encyclopedia lent legitimacy to a new body of texts as part of the vital knowledge of the day. Drama miscellanies, in collecting samplings of such texts in their middle registers, took a market share of this trend, and registered the late Ming living experience in its most personal and private moments.

By reorganizing the world of print, the drama miscellany caught on to the interest in remapping everyday knowledge and re-creating quotidian life that characterized late Ming cosmopolitan culture on many levels. The drama miscellany, along with the daily-use encyclopedia, evoked a vision of domestic living in a radically un-institutionalized and private language, outside public institutions and official structures. As signaled by the self-portrait of the renowned publisher Yu Wentai (bottom left corner of fig. 2.3), the dawning of a prosperous day takes place as he surveys the pages of a book, surrounded by emblems of domestic comfort and luxury.

Textual Circulation: The Case of Geographical Knowledge

Just as the drama miscellany and the daily-use encyclopedia overlapped in the textual sources they drew upon, both of these print genres overlapped with still other genres at different levels of literary, scholarly, or administrative textual hierarchies. In each instance of circulation, the circulated text becomes, in a real sense, a different work, with each specific printed environment (e.g., physical appearance and page layout of the text) and each specific community of readers contributing to the full social meaning of the text. One prominent feature of late Ming culture was the enormous expansion in the array of printed texts in circulation. From the classics and the orthodox canon, to the popular, the oral, the performative, the heterogeneous, the nonsensical, and the forbidden, etc., the proliferation of printing allowed for the creation of a textual storehouse from which readers and editors alike could draw at will. The process was, in many ways, a textual free-for-all, in which text as a form of raw material circulated within and among different publishing genres, only gaining its symbolic and material specificity in the process of being set on a block, printed, and bound into volumes and cases. One kind of text that frequently appeared in drama miscellanies, the catalog of place names, serves as a useful case study for examining the sources available to compilers as well as for observing how different social meanings could be set in motion when the same text was reproduced in different publication formats.

Drama miscellanies present fascinating elements related to geography, as reflected, for example, in figure 2.2. Here I will focus on one specific sort of geographical text: the seemingly matter-of-fact list of names of localities. This list is entitled variously in drama miscellanies as:

> *Huizuan Jing sheng fu zhou xian ming kaoshi*
> 彙纂京省府州縣名攷實 (in *Yuefu wanxiang xin*)
>
> (Compiled from various sources—verified record of the names of the counties, districts, and prefectures of the capitals and the provinces)
>
> *Xin zuan liang Jing ge sheng fu zhou xian ming*
> 新纂兩京各省府州縣名 (in *Da Ming tianxia chun*)
>
> (Newly compiled—the names of the counties, districts, and prefectures of the two capitals and each province)
>
> *Da Ming yitong heshu liang jing shisan sheng suoxia*
> 大明一統合屬兩京十三省所轄 (in *Zhaijin qiyin*)
>
> (Areas under the control of the two capitals and the thirteen provinces that comprise the unified grand Ming)

This list, almost identical in each compilation,[69] starts with the names of the two capitals (the southern capital, Nanjing, and the northern capital, Beijing) and thirteen provinces, and then follows with a summary of the total numbers of prefectures, districts, and counties throughout the empire, followed by each individual capital or province with the names of prefectures, districts, and counties under its administration (fig. 2.4). In conception, then, this is a comprehensive list of the names of all the localities in the Ming empire.[70] In addition to advertising their lists as newly made and solidly reliable, as indicated by the phrase "kaoshi" 攷實 (verified for factuality), compilers indicated that they gathered their lists from various sources (*huizuan* 匯纂), signaling a large pool of source material.

Fig. 2.4. Two pages from *Zhaijin qiyin*. The bottom register is an episode from Wang Jide's play *Nanhou ji* 男后記 entitled "Gu sao sijiu jiaqi" 姑嫂私就佳期 (Tryst between the [King's] younger sister and her [male] sister-in-law); the top register is the beginning of a list of geographical names under the subtitle "Da Ming yitong heshu" 大明一統合屬 (Combined constituents of the grand unified Ming). From *SBXQCK*, vol. 3, pp. 189, 192.

One of the available sources or contexts is the second division of the daily-use encyclopedia—Geography (called *diyu* 地輿, *diji* 地紀, or *dili* 地理). This division normally starts with "Dynastic Capitals through History" 歷代國都 and "History of Geographical Nomenclature" 輿地紀原. Next, a map of the empire is displayed, followed by the main body in this category: typically the top register consists of "Routes of the Two Capitals and Thirteen Provinces" 兩京十三省路程, and the bottom details "What Is under Administrative Control" 管轄統屬 for each locale in the empire (fig. 2.5), including information such as numbers and names of municipalities, the officers in charge, the kind and amount of local tribute, local products, and so on.

The lists of local names in drama miscellanies could have been derived from this division in the encyclopedias, but probably not as easily as from

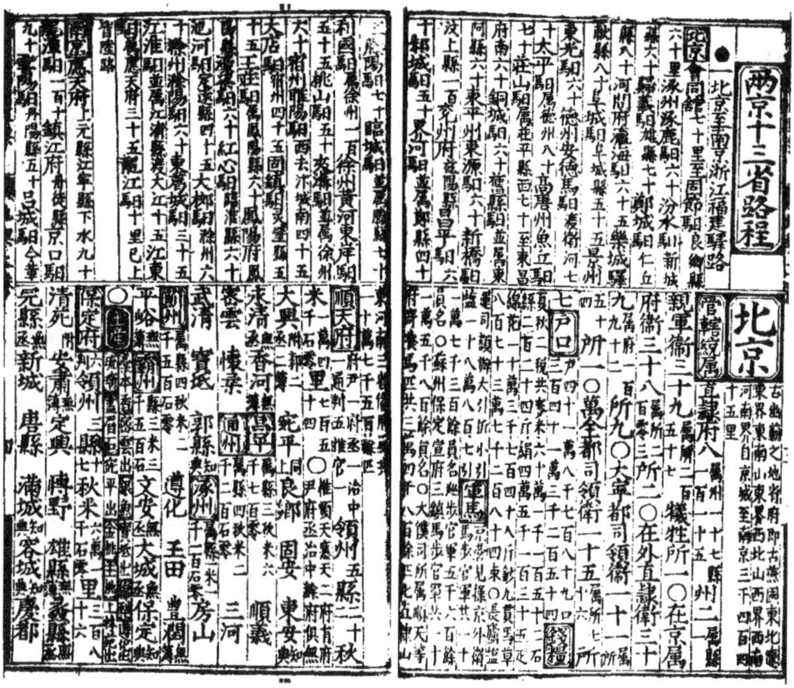

Fig. 2.5. Two pages from the *Diyu men* 地輿門 (Geography division) in *Santai wanyong zhengzong*. The bottom register incorporates the names of the capitals, and provinces and their prefectures, districts, and counties. Information such as administrative offices, populations, and the kinds and amounts of local tributes, military forces, and local products is also provided for each locale. From *CNRS*, vol. 3, pp. 52–53.

other kinds of texts that contained the information in briefer form, such as route books (*tuji* 圖記 or *tujing* 圖經), merchant manuals (*shangshu* 商書), character books (*zazi shu* 雜字書), and imperial court documents such as *Da Ming yitong zhi* 大明一統志 (The gazetteer of the unified imperium of the grand Ming). Each of these types of books shaped and captured a specific process of meaning-making for a given text.

Route books and merchant manuals became popular in the latter half of the sixteenth century. A route book, as Timothy Brook has described the form, was "a traveler's handbook of water and land routes," whose purpose was to "describe routes in terms of the places they traverse—such as towns, villages, and fords—and to give the distances between these places."[71] Often, route books became a significant part of merchant manuals, which placed the former alongside other mercantile-related texts on how to conduct business and how to survive in a competitive economy. An early mention of route books in Ming sources appears in a statement Wang Zhideng 王穉登 (1535–1612) made in 1567, "As I did not know about the routes and distances for traveling south, I went to a bookseller's and bought a *tujing*, which I packed in my trunk."[72] An early example of a Ming route book is the 1570 *Yitong lucheng tuji* 一統路程圖記 (Illustrated route book of the unified empire),[73] while a representative example of the merchant manual is the *Shi shang lei yao* 士商類要 (Essentials for gentry and merchants), dated to 1626. To obtain a better idea of the kinds of information contained in these route books and merchant manuals, consider the following excerpt from the Table of Contents of the Wanli-era *Xinke jingben hua yi fengwu shangcheng yilan* 新刻京本華夷風物商程一覽 (Newly carved capital edition: Chinese and non-Chinese products of local flavor—merchant routes at a glance; "*Shangcheng yilan*" for short) (fig. 2.6).[74] Its lower register describes over 100 travel routes, while its upper register contains the following:

> 兩京十三省府州縣名及土產；四夷土產；附各省王府及祿米俱備；天下吏員月支俸米；文官服色；武官服色；文官月俸；歷代國都；歷代歌；大明清海甸；南京城門歌；北京城門歌
>
> Names of the Counties, Districts, Prefectures, and Their Local Products of the Two Capitals and the Thirteen Provinces; Local Products of the Four Foreign Lands; Supplemented with a Complete Account of the Princely Houses of Each Province and Their Emoluments; Salary and Emoluments for Officials in the Empire; Prescribed Colors for Civil Officials' Regalia; Prescribed Colors for Military Officials' Regalia; Monthly Stipends for Civil Officials; Dynastic Capitals through History; Song on the Dynasties throughout History; The Great Ming Purifies Its Ocean Shores; Song on the Nanjing City Gates; Song on the Beijing City Gates[75]

The first entry in the upper register closely resembles what is found in the drama miscellanies.

The importance placed on knowing natural and cultural geography is underscored by the fact that it features prominently in a character book entitled *Zazi yuangui* 雜字元龜, whose full title is *Xinqie aotou beiyong zazi yuangui* 新鍥鰲頭備用雜字元龜 (From newly carved blocks—for the reference of valedictorians: compendium of characters of various types, fig. 2.7).[76] Character books (*zazi shu* 雜字書) were popular primers that combined literacy education with practical knowledge. Their contents were constantly updated to reflect the most current quotid-

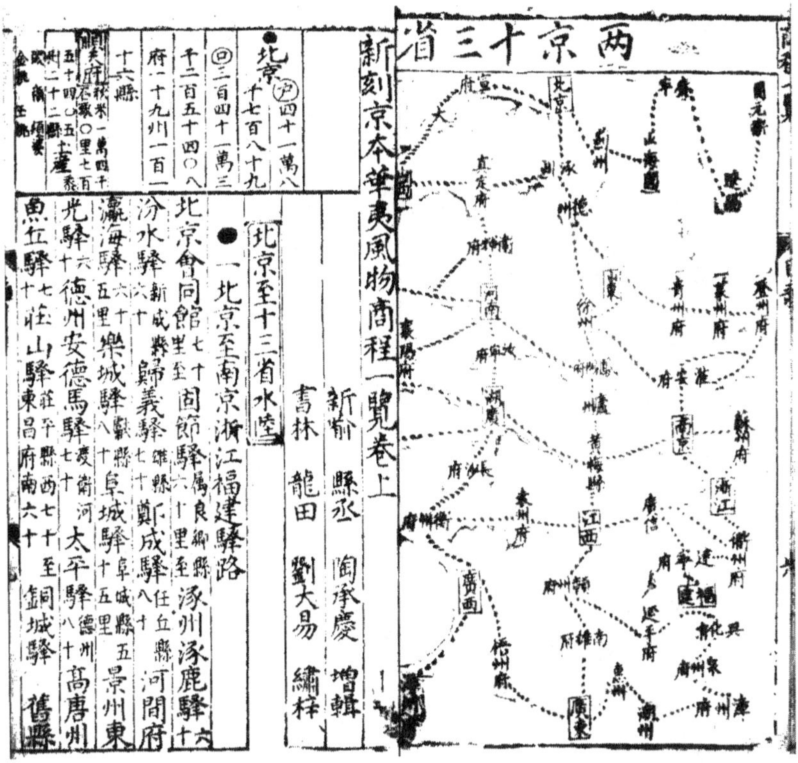

Fig. 2.6. Pages from *Shangcheng yilan*. The bottom register incorporates transportation routes, while the upper register, under the subtitle of "Liang Jing shisan sheng fu zhou xian ming ji tuchan" 兩京十三省府州縣名及土產 (Names of the counties, districts, prefectures, and their local products of the two capitals and the thirteen provinces), incorporates names of locales, their populations, and the kinds and amounts of local tributes and local products, etc. From Brook, *Geographical Sources of Ming-Qing History*, p. 9, with the permission of the author.

ian knowledge, and they likely circulated primarily among non-elite social strata.[77] The *Zazi yuangui*, dated to 1594, is laid out in double-register format, and it comprises a lexicon of individual characters and compounds that are grouped into different divisions. The lower register contains the main content, consisting of 9,000 characters or so in twenty divisions such as "Drink and Food," "Grains," "Fabrics," "Colors," and so on. The much smaller upper register consists of characters or compounds grouped under divisions such as "Heavenly Patterns," "Geography," "Human Affairs," "Auspicious Days for Traveling," and "Auspicious Days for Making Clothes." The categorization in both

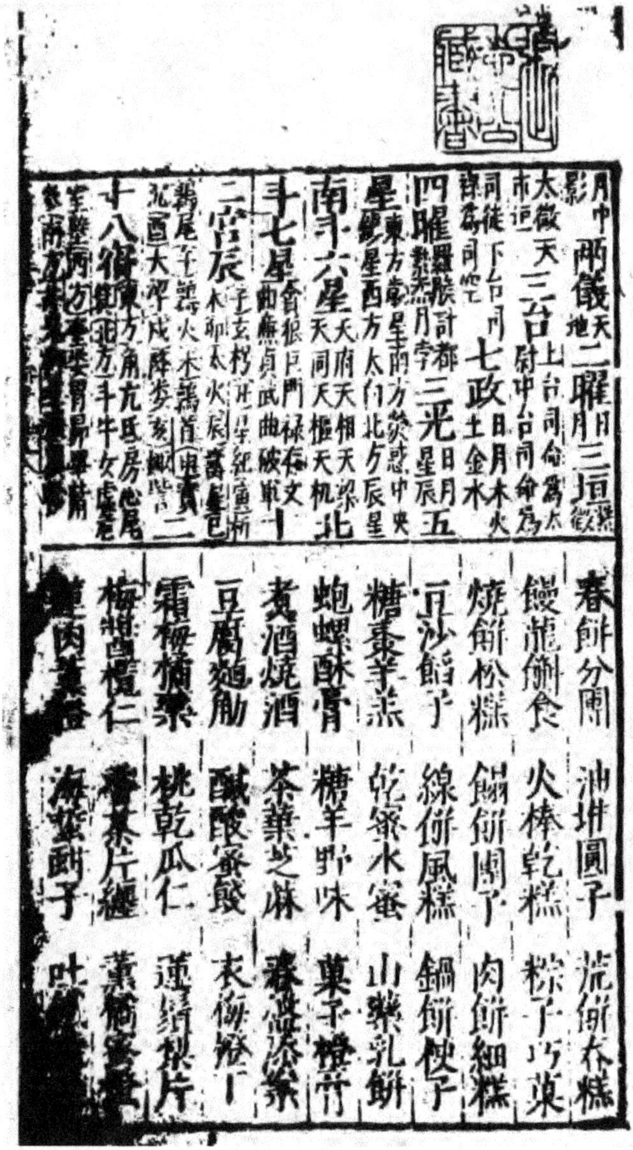

Fig. 2.7. A page from *Zazi yuangui* 雜字元龜. The upper register on this page incorporates compounds and phrases, supplemented by commentaries, in the division of "Tianwen" 天文 (Heavenly patterns). This *Zazi yuangui* is an incomplete copy, and the page shown here is the first page in the remaining body of text. The seal at the top of the page reads "Zhang Zhigong cangshu" 張志公藏書 (Personal library of Zhang Zhigong). From Lai Xinxia and Gao Weiguo, *Za zi*, p. 1.

registers mirrors that of the daily-use encyclopedia. However, instead of sentences and paragraphs, character books focus on the words and phrases of everyday life.

In the *Zazi yuangui*, under the division of "Geography," one of the texts is a list of localities entitled "Municipalities of the Two Capitals and the Thirteen Provinces" 兩京十三省郡邑. The appeal of such lists of geographical localities apparently extended beyond the fully literate reading public to reach the audience of semi-literate readers or people just learning to read who would have relied on a character book of this type. Semi-literate readers formed a significant proportion of book consumers during the Ming due to the incorporation of pictures and texts with rich mnemonic prompts in new types of literature printed and disseminated at the time. One might thus speculate that the list's multi-functionality and broad appeal contributed to its inclusion in the drama miscellany. At the same time, it is hard to determine with certainty from which publishing genre (e.g., encyclopedias, route books, merchant manuals, or character books) the drama miscellanies derived their geographical lists. In fact, such muddled origins are often the rule in the world of Ming block-printed texts, where sources were often anonymous and diffused through a space of circulation and recycling.[78]

The texts discussed above are all popular publications, which reveal only a portion of the social meaning invested in such geographical lists. The field of circulation for names of localities was certainly much wider, and was shaped decisively by a category of books called *zhishu* 制書 (imperial ordinances), specifically the *Da Ming yitong zhi* 大明一統志 (Gazetteer of the unified imperium of the grand Ming) and the *Da Ming huidian* 大明會典 (Collected statutes of the grand Ming). Both were imperial documents compiled under the direct command of the Ming emperors in the fourteenth and fifteenth centuries, undergoing revisions whenever deemed necessary at the hands of later emperors and their officials. The *Da Ming yitong zhi* was a state survey of Ming geography, incorporating geographical history, population, products, and so on for each capital and province and the places under their administrative control. Though the Hongwu emperor ordered its compilation in 1371, there is no evidence that his wishes were carried out. Later, the Yongle emperor (r. 1402–24) issued a similar order, but the book was again never finalized. The project was finally accomplished in the Tianshun reign (1457–64) of Emperor Yingzong in the year 1461. Yingzong wrote the preface and conferred the name *Da Ming yitong zhi* on the text.[79] The *Da Ming huidian* is also the product of a collective and continuous effort of Ming emperors and officials over an extended period. It was first compiled and published in the Hongzhi reign (1488–1506), with several subsequent revisions and republications. This is reflected in its Wanli edition, which retained three prefaces, dated to 1502, 1509, and 1587. Its fifteenth and sixteenth chapters, under the subheading "Districts and Counties," survey the geography of the empire.

In both these imperial documents, geographical texts, as direct textual representations of the empire's territorial and administrative structure, function as a vital tool for imperial ideology: their unitary organization and comprehensive scope convey a message of imperial unity (*yitong* 一統 or *tongyi* 統一). The more factual such catalogs appear, the more ideologically effective they are. To achieve this goal, reading and mastering knowledge (*zhishi* 知識) in these books is channeled toward internalizing and eternalizing the glory of the empire and the memory of its emperors:

> 朕於萬幾之暇，試覽閱之，則海宇之廣，古今之跡，了然盡在胸中矣。既藏之秘府，復命工鋟梓以傳。嗚呼！是書之傳也，不獨使我子孫世世相承者知祖宗開創之功，廣大如是，思所以保守之惟謹。而凡天下之士，亦因得以考求古今故實，增其聞見，廣其知識，有所感發興起，出爲世用，以輔成雍熙泰和之治，相與維持我國家一統之盛於無窮，雖與天地同其久長可也。於是乎序。
>
> In Our leisure from the myriad affairs, We once took occasion to survey and read it—and the breadth of oceans and skies, and traces of human affairs from ancient to modern, all were vividly comprehended in Our mind. Having stored it in the imperial library, We further ordered workers to make woodblock imprints in order to disseminate it. Ah! The transmission of this book is not only to make it possible for our sons and grandsons, who shall succeed to rule in coming generations, to understand that the achievement of their ancestors in establishing this realm is as grand and great as this, and to be keenly aware of how to protect this enterprise, but also to have all scholar-officials in the sub-celestial realm use it to examine and verify factual precedents from past to present, to expand upon what they themselves encounter, to enlarge their own knowledge, to be moved to rise forth and be employed in the world, to bolster a peaceful and harmonious polity, and together to maintain the prosperity of our unified realm without end, even as long as heaven and earth. And thereupon was composed this preface.[80]

This imperial preface for *Da Ming yitong zhi* lays out a set of prescriptions for the texts's proper use: upon reading the document, the princely reader will understand the greatness of his ancestors' achievement in creating such a vast realm, spurring on his aspiration to protect its unity; scholar-officials will broaden their knowledge and, consequently, be motivated to assist in the administration and protection of the permanent prosperity of a unified empire. The emperor himself embodies the figure of the exemplary reader, one who can transport what is on the page to the mind's eye—the territory and history of the empire—through a combination of both reading (*yue* 閱) the discourse and information in the book and viewing (*lan* 覽), taking in the overall layout through a roving survey of the page. While reading anchors one to a specific place (both in the book and in terms of the locality) and a local moment of understanding, viewing projects this place and moment onto the expansion of the totality of both the document and the empire.

Motivated by this rationale, both central and local governments celebrated and promoted this document. In the year 1467 a copy of *Da Ming yitong zhi* was given to a court official, Ke Qian 柯潛 (1423–73), as a reward for services rendered.[81] Meanwhile, Li Dongyang 李東陽 (1447–1516), the minister and leading scholar and poet of the day, recorded the following essay question given in the civil examination for Shuntian prefecture:

> 在我太祖高皇帝時，則有大誥三編。太祖文皇帝時，則有爲善陰騭，孝順事實，性理大全書。宣宗章皇帝時，則有五倫書。英宗睿皇帝時，則有大明一統志。及我皇上嗣位以來，則有續資治通鑒綱目。或躬御翰墨，次第成編；或分官纂修，手賜裁定。顧其首簡，必親製序文，或繼志補作，以著述作大意。天下臣民，家傳人誦，佩服而體行者，蓋已久矣。王言之博大，篇帙之浩瀚，固不可以一二指，亦不可以頃刻陳也。請問：諸書述作之大意何居？見諸序文者何說？仰窺伏讀之餘，有得於心而愿體諸身者何事？夫不知其意而徒習其辭者，雖多無益；不體諸身而徒得其意者，雖精亦且無用。皆非所望於諸士子者。盍敬陳之。
>
> At the time of our Emperor Taizu [i.e., the Hongwu emperor, r. 1368–99], there were three *Great Admonitions*. At the time of Emperor Taizong [i.e., the Yongle emperor, r. 1403–25],[82] there were the *Blessings of Good Deeds Done in Secret*, the *Testimonies to Filiality and Obedience*, and the *Great Compendium on Nature and Principle*. At the time of the Emperor Xuanzong [i.e., the Xuande emperor, r. 1426–36], there was the *Book on the Five Relationships*. At the time of the Emperor Yingzong [i.e., the Tianshun emperor, r. 1457–64], there was the *Gazetteer of the Unified Imperium of the Grand Ming*. At the time when our current emperor [i.e., the Chenghua emperor, r. 1465–88] succeeded to the throne, there was the *Outline of the Comprehensive Mirror as an Aid to Ruling, Continued*. Some emperors personally wielded brush and ink to gradually finalize the compilation; some emperors divided the work of compilation among different officials and then

determined its final form themselves. When we attend to the opening pages we find that these emperors composed prefaces by their own persons, or continued previous sovereigns' intentions in supplementing such prefaces, so as to render a faithful account of each work's guiding purpose.[83] Among officials and the people in the world, every family transmits them and everyone recites them, respects them and embodies them—it has been so for a long time now. The breadth of kingly words and the ampleness of pages cannot be explained through a single enumeration, nor can they be laid out in a short period of time. Allow me to ask, then: Where does the grand import of the making of these books reside? What accounts do you observe appearing in the prefaces? After reading the works thoroughly, what are the matters that you have understood in your heart and desire to embody in your actions? Now, simply to recite the words without knowing their significance will amount to nothing, no matter how much you do it. Simply to understand its significance without embodying it, even if you have an excellent comprehension, is still useless. This is not what is desired from you students. Why not, then, reverently lay out your views on these matters?[84]

This examination question first lists the weightiest publications produced by a succession of Ming emperors, starting from the founding emperor's *Great Admonitions*, to the sequel to Zhu Xi's *Outline of the Comprehensive Mirror as an Aid to Ruling* that had been compiled on imperial command by Shang Lu 商輅 (1414–86), under the then-reigning Chenghua emperor. This list focuses the reader's attention on a particular tier of books, the *zhishu* (books by/of imperial ordinance), whose production and circulation had taken place through the direct agency of the imperial court, and which thus occupied a unique place in the Ming reading world. It also reminds the reader of the role of the emperors as model book-makers and readers, as they participated in various aspects of the reading and making of these books.[85]

The importance of knowing the *Da Ming yitong zhi* could not be emphasized more than it is here by its appearance as one of the reference texts for civil service examination candidates—texts that earned this status because they were each in their own way held, in the language of orthodoxy and imperial power that Li Dongyang speaks here, to be reflections of Ming emperors' sagely engagement and concern with the world. The central issue in this essay question is the understanding that reading is based on a prior state of mind and that there is a certain reading response expected from those who aspire in turn to positions of authority and power. The question alludes directly to the imperial prefaces and reinforces the reading reactions modeled in those texts. In answering this question, students are expected to have memorized the imperial prefaces and to be ready to elucidate the tenets they express, and further to reflect on the degree to which those tenets are incorporated in their own personalities and impulses. The examinations are the preeminent institution for molding and enforcing the proper dissemination of textual understanding, whose final stage involves full embodiment of that understanding in the very identities of the candidates, as explicitly signaled by the recurrent phrase *ti zhu shen* 體諸身 (embody it in oneself).

The effort to produce and authenticate geographical knowledge is no less manifested in the *Da Ming huidian*. Its 1502 preface emphasizes that proper documentation, including that of geographical knowledge, is essential to achieving order and prosperity:

> 我聖祖神宗，百有餘年之典制，斟酌古今，足法萬世者，會粹無遺矣。特命工鋟梓，以頒示中外，俾自是而世守之，不遷於異説，不急於近利，由朝廷以及天下，諸凡舉措，無巨細精粗，咸當乎理而得其宜。積之既深，持之既久，則我國家博厚高明之業，雍熙泰和之治，可以並唐虞，軼三代，而垂之無窮，必將有賴於是焉。遂書以為序。
>
> Of the documents and institutions of more than a hundred years of our sagely ancestors and saintly founders, those which thoroughly examine the past and present and are sufficient to be used as a model by ten thousand generations, are comprehensively assembled in this compilation. Thus, We ordered workers to make woodblock imprints in order to issue and disseminate them both within and outside the central government in order for generations to guard it, so that they will not be moved by heterodoxies, nor rush toward short-sighted benefits; so that every act and step, big or small, of the court and the world will suit reason and attain what is proper. When this is carried out deeply and continued perpetually, then the profound and enlightened enterprise of our state and its peaceful and prosperous governance can rival that of the sage kings of Tang and Yu, exceed the three dynasties, and continue forever. In all this they will rely on this document. Thereupon We wrote this as preface.[86]

Here the emperor emphasizes that the print dissemination of these proper and comprehensive imperial documents is necessary to fend off hearsay and shortsighted opportunism and, thereby, to safeguard and guarantee the prosperity of the empire. The "Districts and Counties" section of the *Da Ming huidian* is devoted to a catalog of place names in Ming administrative geography (see Fig. 2.8), and this would have been one likely source from which compilers of late Ming popular imprints could have drawn in producing their own similar catalogs.

The endeavor of the central government to produce and promote an authoritative document on the geography of the empire had far-reaching impact, and local gazetteers were but one part of this publishing boom.

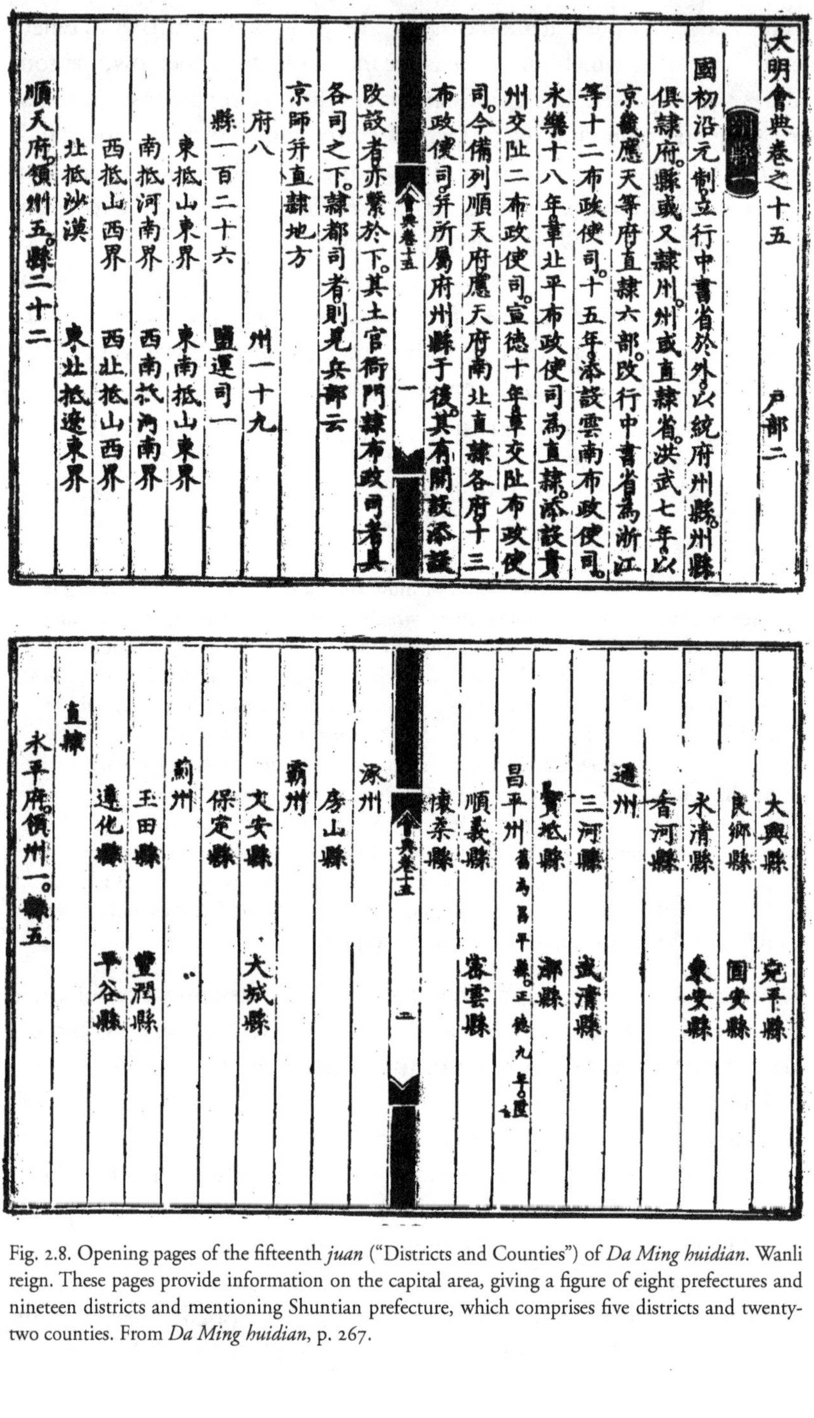

大明會典卷之十五　戶部二

州縣一

國初沿元制。立行中書省於外。以統府州縣。州縣俱隸府。縣或又隸州。州或直隸省。洪武七年。以京畿應天等府直隸六部。改行中書省為浙江等十二布政使司。十五年。添設雲南布政使司。永樂十八年。革北平布政使司為直隸。添設貴州交阯二布政使司。宣德十年。革交阯布政使司。今備列順天府應天府南北直隸各府十三布政使司并所屬府州縣于後。其有開設添設改設者。亦繫於下。其土官衙門隸布政司者。具各司之下。隸都司者。則見兵部云

會典卷十五　一

京師并直隸地方

府八　州一十九

縣一百二十六　鹽運司一

東抵山東界　東南抵山東界

南抵河南界　西南抵河南界

西抵山西界　西北抵山西界

北抵沙漠　東北抵遼東界

順天府。領州五。縣二十二

大興縣　宛平縣

良鄉縣　固安縣

永清縣　東安縣

香河縣

通州

三河縣　武清縣

寶坻縣　漷縣

昌平州 舊為昌平縣。正德九年。陞

順義縣　密雲縣

懷柔縣

會典卷十五　二

涿州

房山縣

霸州

文安縣　大城縣

保定縣

薊州

玉田縣　豐潤縣

遵化縣　平谷縣

直隸

永平府。領州一。縣五

Fig. 2.8. Opening pages of the fifteenth *juan* ("Districts and Counties") of *Da Ming huidian*. Wanli reign. These pages provide information on the capital area, giving a figure of eight prefectures and nineteen districts and mentioning Shuntian prefecture, which comprises five districts and twenty-two counties. From *Da Ming huidian*, p. 267.

Here is the court official Shao Bao 邵寶 (1460–1527) expressing his joy at having the court present him with a set of *Da Ming huidian*:

賜大明會典	On Being Bestowed a Copy of the *Da Ming huidian*
緗函新捧出天衢	*Xiang*-silk cases newly clasped, I emerge from the heavenly lanes;
十載文光照石渠	ten years' brilliant culture blazing from the Shiqu archive.
唐作一經徒託語	That Yao made a classic is mere hearsay;
周遺六典始成書	only when the Zhou left its Six Norms did they take form as books.
聖神功化三才裡	The sage's divine power transforms heaven, earth, and man;
今昔經綸萬卷餘	encompassing and ordering past and present, over a myriad scrolls.
遐想先皇初詔日	I imagine that long-ago day of our Ancestor Emperor's command:
洞觀千古欲何如	his gaze penetrating all ages—what more is there to say?[87]

Whoever did not have the good fortune to be granted a set of these volumes by the emperor, however, could easily purchase one in the marketplace.[88] Efforts by both central and local governments to promulgate authentic textual expressions of imperial vision provided both motivation and source material for popular publications in the late Ming.

However, as such geographical knowledge circulated from official documents into popular publications, the rationales underlying both compilation and reading underwent subtle transformations. If the above 1502 preface to the *Da Ming huidian* had already sounded the alarm against heresy, the Wanli preface (1587) to the same document observed a worrisome practice of unorthodox dissemination and employment of text and knowledge:

> 逮我世宗皇帝入承天序，時歷四紀，而因革損益，代有異同，乃復下詔重修……載在祕府，未及頒行。蓋至於今，又三十八年矣。歲歷綿遠，條例益繁。好事者喜紛更，建議者昧體要。甚則弄智舞文，奇請他比。自明習者，莫知所從。小吏淺聞，何有究宣。朕甚閔焉……乃命儒臣，重加修輯。芟繁正訛，益以見行事例而折衷之……

> By the time that our Emperor Shizong [i.e., the Jiajing emperor] entered to carry on the heavenly order, forty-eight years had already passed. And, because each generation had different things they changed or kept, or which were done away with or augmented, he issued an edict to recompile this text . . . It has now been

> thirty-eight years that this compilation has been stored in the imperial library, no occasion having been found for printing and disseminating it. With the passage of the years, rules and regulations have become ever more complex. Busybodies delight in making frequent alterations, and those fond of making proposals are blind to guiding fundamentals. Still worse are those who simply put on displays of cleverness or ingenious textual manipulations, invoking strange authorities and drawing far-fetched analogies. From legal experts on down, none knows what standard to follow—as for those minor clerks with limited knowledge, how could they possibly give a thorough or clear accounting? We feel the greatest concern over this! [. . .] thereupon We commanded our scholar-ministers to amend and collate it again, deleting redundancies and correcting falsehoods, and supplementing the standards and precedents as applied today, to allow for balanced judgment . . .[89]

This passage reveals that official documents could be and were (mis) used to forge and corrupt texts. The disparaging term *nongzhi* (displays of cleverness) criticizes those who abuse their knowledge and wisdom, while the equally disparaging term *wuwen* (textual manipulations, lit. "make one's texts dance") points to the means by which knowledge is abused: by falsely creating captivating documents that only appear to be true. To rectify this textual corruption, which appears as a problem of administrative corruption and a sign of moral decay (as indicated by the phrase *mei tiyao* 昧體要, blindness to the guiding fundamentals), the preface presents a dire picture of the reasons why an authoritative updating and re-authentication were necessary.

This preface offers a useful perspective on the pitfalls of official documents entering the supply stream of texts appropriated by popular publications such as encyclopedias, route books and merchant manuals, character books, and so on, making it clear how all such recirculation might be viewed as unauthorized and even unwanted offspring of official geographical publications. As a matter of fact, the imperial preface above unwittingly points out the close link between popular literature such as *xiaoshuo* and the abuse of official documents, as both were seen as typical handiwork of that type of personality labeled as a *haoshi zhe* 好事者 (busybody) whose signature mental energy is an excessive curiosity.[90] On the other hand, the inclusion of geographical knowledge in late Ming popular works attests to a real demand for geographical texts, and this demand was in part driven and legitimized by the prestige and popularity of imperial-sanctioned dissemination of such works.

From the imperial geographical documents to popular books, these publications were tailored to various readership groups, from royal house members, officials, and examinees, to commoners (encyclopedias), merchants or gentry-merchants (route books and merchant manuals), and finally to the semi-literate group who were the target audience of character books. These different reading publics, who represented different social spheres, invested divergent cultural meanings into the same geographical information. For example, in his postface to his *Yitong lucheng tuji*, Huang Bian 黄汴 (fl. mid-sixteenth century) states, "Should the gentry obtain this book, it will help them carry out the emperor's sagely commands. If merchants obtain it, it will inform them about the characteristics and problems of local areas."[91] While the first sentence reinforces the reading response subscribed to by the imperial ideology, the second identifies a separate mercantile readership with its own practical concerns unrelated to the grand projects of the empire.

The actual practical value of such texts, however, may not have been as clear-cut as the picture Huang Bian presents. Martin Heijdra, evaluating these sources in terms of their actual connection with Ming transport and economic activity, acutely points out that "one cannot see this genre [i.e., route books and merchant manuals] as having totally and only mercantile origins; nor was much of its information up-to-date, practical, or very important," and goes on to observe that "yet again another source, which on first sight promised us some direct access to the pre-modern Chinese economy, reveals itself to be a disappointment, full of cut-and-paste stereotypes."[92] In short, Heijdra , though his perspective is quite different from theirs, points out in these geographical texts many of the same general aspects of Ming book-making that had maddened Qing bibliographers and editors: material in various books often overlaps (*cuo jian* 錯見) and seems to reflect indiscriminate borrowing.

To fully understand this pattern of circulation one must consider how these books functioned not only as sources of practical information, but more generally as a form of commodity and material possession, in their own time. The proliferating book trade reshaped the social expectation of what people of various classes should read and possess, and geographical texts were one among a range of such new textual genres that became a mark of their owners' qualifications as cosmopolitan, worldly, and up-to-date. The world—whether conceived of as *tianxia* 天下 (the subcelestial realm), as *nanbei* 南北 (from north to south), or as *hainei* 海内 (all within the seas)—was not only a fixed space to be articulated by geography but a productive space that stimulated the printing of multiple varieties of texts that late Ming readers felt compelled to read and own. In this process, the reinvention of textual meanings and the proliferation of variant versions by means of print went hand in hand in the changing cultural landscape of the late Ming.

Revisiting the drama miscellanies' incorporation of catalogs of localities into their middle registers from this broader perspective, we can see these texts not as discrete informational sources but rather as a dimension of the varied ways in which these books unfolded spatial and geographical vistas before their readers' eyes. Similarly to figure 2.2, the page in figure 2.9 shows a number of spatial and topographical markers by which book producers situated their readers in relation to both the geography of the empire and to alternative spaces of culture and imagination.

This book bears numerous indicators of the geographical origins of its constituent elements. It is a "capital block-edition" (*jingban* 京板), connoting the literal "imprimatur" of the most central and cosmopolitan site of cultural and intellectual authority. The geographical marker Qingyang 青陽 links the dramatic selections themselves to one of the leading regional singing styles of the day. The toponym Gulin 古臨 (the traditional designation for Linchuan 臨川) capping the names of the compilers suggests their insider status as natives of Jiangxi, a key region in the history of the most popular operatic traditions of the day, and announces that they are also fellow townsmen of the master playwright Tang Xianzu. Gathered in the middle register are songs from Chu 楚, a region known for its long-standing status as the heartland of oppositional or alternative cultural traditions, whether it be the banished poet-minister Qu Yuan's 屈原 (trad. mid-fourth–early third c. BCE) laments or the tragic general Xiang Yu's 項羽 (232–202 BCE) hometown tunes, marking a historical legacy combining lyricism and political resistance. Finally, appearing as the coordinator and stage manager of these diverse elements is Ye Zhiyuan, the producer of this book, whose place of origin is given as "Min Jian shu lin" 閩建書林, the "forest of books" in Jianyang, Fujian, the well-known center of commercial printing. The print industry in the late Ming both reflected and contributed to the production and desire for geographical knowledge. By incorporating the names of localities, the drama miscellanies substantiate their claim

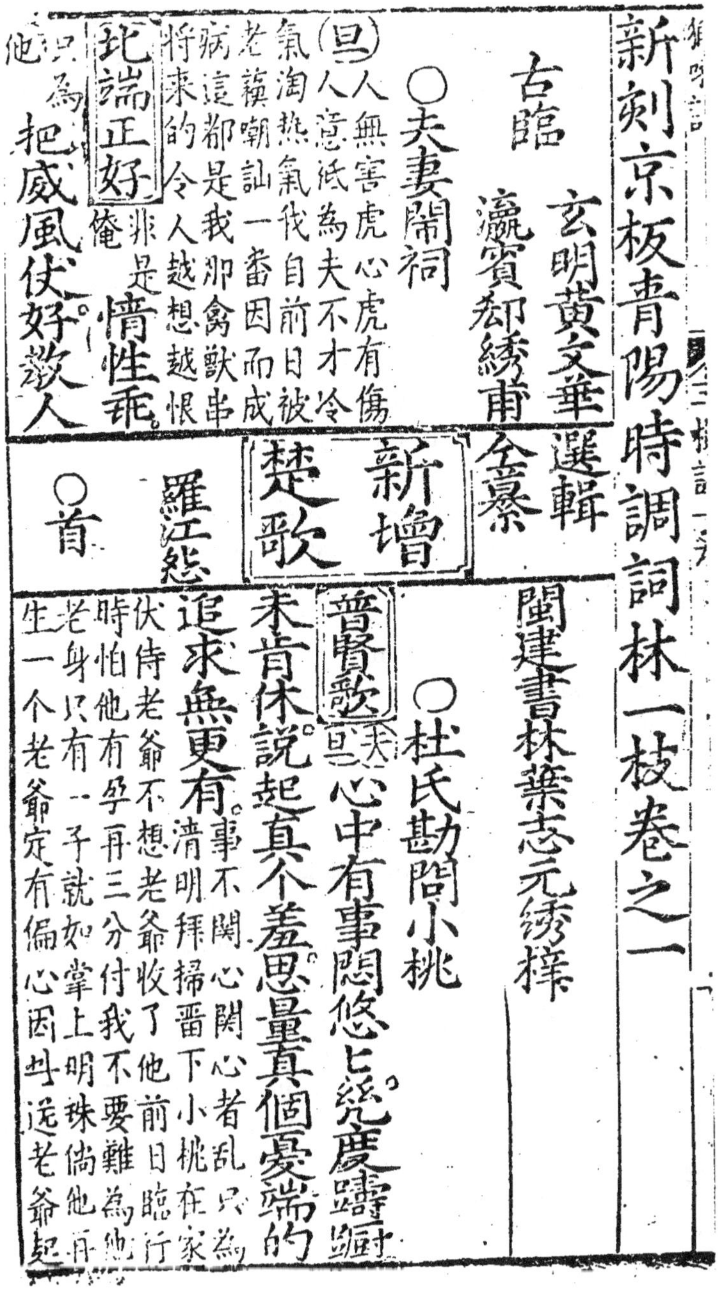

Fig. 2.9. Opening page from the drama miscellany *Cilin yizhi*. From *SBXQCK*, vol. 4, p. 8.

to be what the world now desires by articulating a geographical space that makes sense and appeals to its audience. The drama miscellanies frame their readers' experience within the cosmological and imperial space of *tianxia*, and at the same time also orient their readers in relation to various spaces of local commodities, local knowledge, and local culture.

Private Theater: The Coding of Cover-Page Designs

As Roger Chartier put it, "(T)he book always aims at installing an order, whether it is the order in which it is deciphered, the order in which it is to be understood, or the order intended by the authority who commanded or permitted the work."[93] With their openness to the broad operations of printing trends and modes of textual circulation, drama miscellanies prompt the questions Is there any underlying affinity that holds their collage of texts and pictures together as a whole? and In what order should they be read, and according to what template? At issue here is the dialectic relation between an order of a book (however inculcated, and however rigid or malleable it may be) and the openness of interpretation. The *Huang Ming shixuan*, discussed in chapter 1, provides one window into how the order of text was both evoked and ironized in the technical process of editing and anthologizing. In the case of the drama miscellanies, although at first glance they seem hardly concerned with any "order," their producers in their own ways developed a vision about the world that their texts and books allude to.

One of the ways they expressed this vision was through inviting cover-page designs. The late Ming has been acclaimed as the golden age of woodblock illustrations, and the design of frontispiece illustrations (both cover-page illustrations for separate volumes and chapter-head illustrations for subdivisions of a volume) became a particularly favored venue for commercial book-makers to create an arresting first impression on potential buyers and readers. They experimented with various design possibilities, particularly those involving the correlation between the verbal and the pictorial. In coding the range of social uses of their texts, makers of drama miscellanies used cover-page illustrations to great effect. In fact, in a departure from traditional attitudes, they generally favored the visual impact of cover-page illustrations over the prestige of written prefaces: to them, it would seem, a picture was indeed worth a thousand words.[94] Five such cover page illustrations for drama miscellanies survive, from the *Yugu xinhuang*, *Cilin yizhi*, *Baneng zoujin*, *Da Ming chun*, and *Shidiao Qing Kun*. The *Yugu xinhuang* cover page illustration is in several ways distinctive, and will be discussed in more detail in the next chapter. The other illustrations provide a good indication of their broadly shared visual rhetoric.

On the cover page of the *Cilin yizhi* (fig. 2.10) the book title itself is slightly rephrased as "Ke Cilin di yizhi" (Engraved: the first branch in the forest of lyrics), highlighting the book as the first to include the latest tunes. A short note to readers by the publisher Ye Zhiyuan substantiates this claim:[95]

> 千家摘錦，坊刻頗多。選者俱用古套，悉未見其妙耳。予特去故增新，得京傳時興新曲數折，載于篇首，知音律者幸鑒之。
>
> Bookshop imprints of the "The Tapestry of a Thousand Kinds" anthology have by now become rather numerous.[96] The anthologists all use the ancient suites, but none has produced anything really wonderful. I have made a point to omit the old and add the new, and have obtained several suites of new tunes, currently circulating in the capital with great popularity, to include at the beginning of this book. I hope that connoisseurs of music will be so kind as to render judgment about this.

These claims present the reader with the opportunity to be among the first to enjoy a newly updated sampling of popular dramatic music—following the implications of the title, a "first branch" of the flowering of a musical springtime. This idea is taken up by the cover page illustration, which depicts a group of three gentlemen and two boy servants on an outing beneath a tree. One of the men is waving to someone out of the frame of the picture, reminding us that this intimate circle is situated within the larger world and inviting anyone who notices the man waving to join them.

This double reference to the vastnesses of the outer world and to a possible intimate connection with like-minded onlookers shares an affinity with the choice of the phrase *hainei* 海內 in the anthology's extended title, rather than other designations of the world seen in other similar titles, such as *nanbei* 南北 or *tianxia* 天下. For the phrase "within the oceans" resonates with the beloved lines of the Tang poet Wang Bo 王勃 (650–76) about "someone who knows you" (*zhiji* 知己): "When within the oceans there is someone who knows you, then the ends of the earth are like one's neighborhood" (海內存知己，天涯若比鄰). In this light,

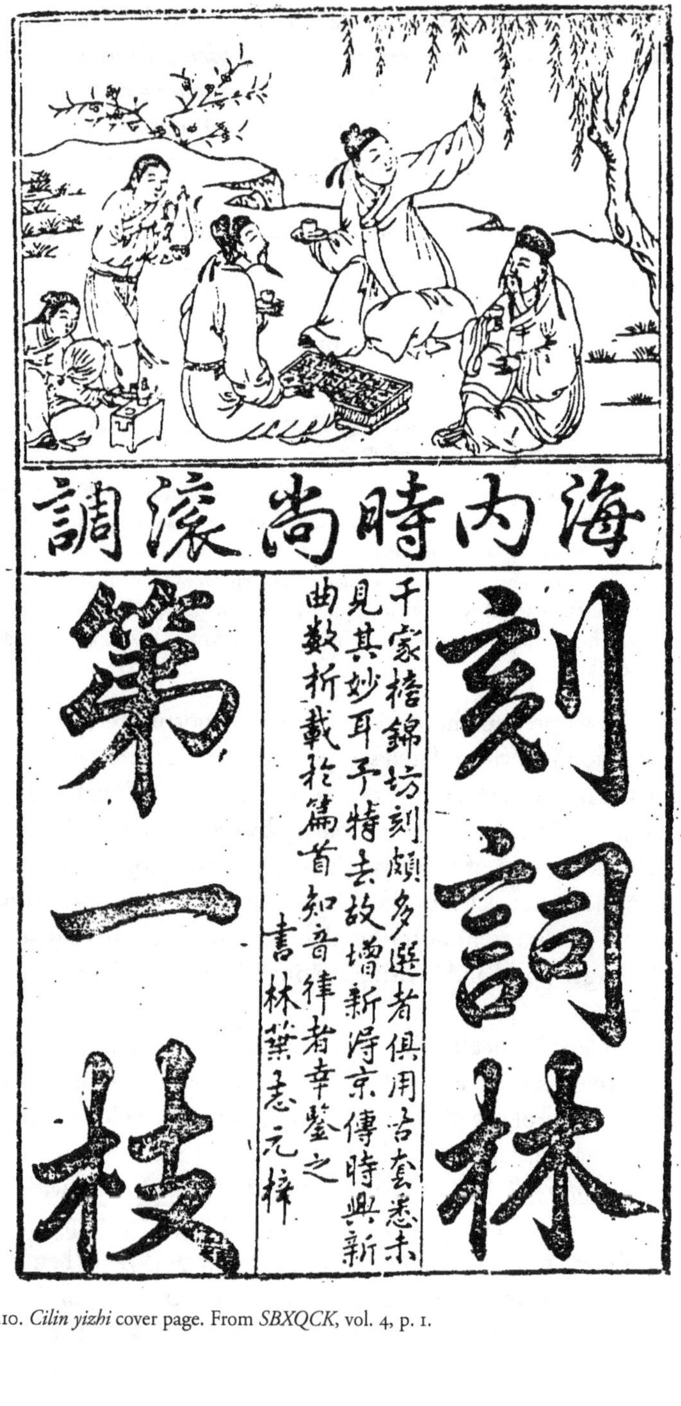

Fig. 2.10. *Cilin yizhi* cover page. From *SBXQCK*, vol. 4, p. 1.

the phrase *hainei* works in tandem with the waving hand in the illustration: we may respond to this picture as simply a picture of an outing, but if we see the waving hand as gesturing to us, then it invites us into a shared world of intimacy and pleasure. The men are seated around a portable picnic box, while the boy servants serve wine warmed by means of a portable stove (*tilu* 提爐). As it happens, both the picnic box and the portable warmer are accessories of elite leisure that became objects of connoiseuristic appreciation during the Ming (fig. 2.11).[97]

Portable things (the picnic box, the stove, the wine service) and movable bodies are here arranged to illustrate a model of floating and transportable pleasure and comfort in the earthly world, shared with kindred spirits to the accompaniment, and through the medium, of music. For this anthology and this cover page, music is important in

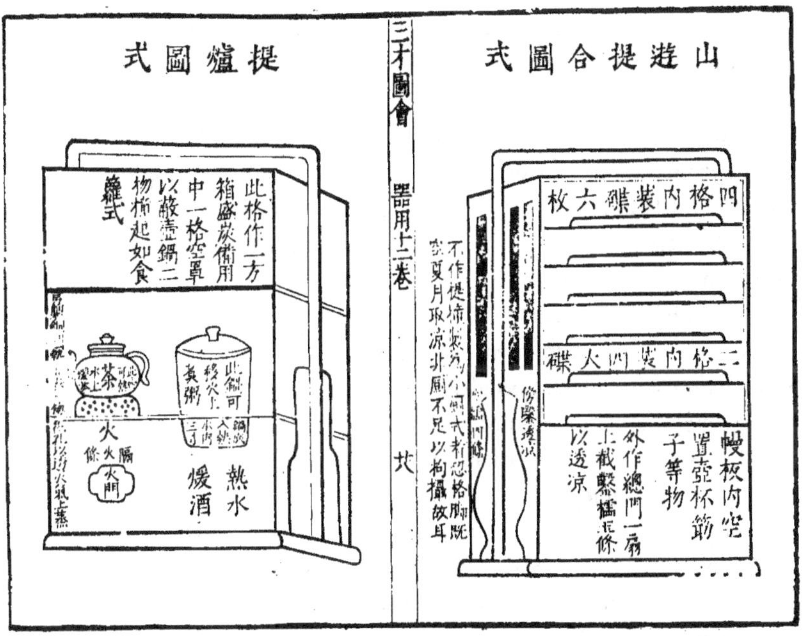

Fig. 2.11. Two portable "things" used in outings are illustrated in the late Ming encyclopedia *Sancai tuhui* 三才圖會 (Pictorial compendium of the three realms) (ca. 1609). On the right is the *shanyou tihe tushi* 山遊提合圖式 (illustrated diagram of a portable picnic-box for outings in the hills), and on the left is the *tilu tushi* 提爐圖式 (illustrated diagram of a portable stove). The same illustrations appear in Gao Lian's 高濂 *Yashang zhai zunsheng bajian* 雅尚齋尊生八牋 (Eight treatises on nurturing life of the Studio of Cultural Pursuits) and Tu Long's 屠隆 *Youju yabian* 游具雅編 (An elegant compilation of outing implements), printed in the late Ming. From *XXSKQS*, vol. 1234, p. 463.

its own right as a subject of elite connoisseurship, and just as much as a privileged metaphor for the tacit understanding that binds social intimates together—both these dimensions being embodied in the reference to "connoisseurs of music" at the end of Ye Zhiyuan's publication note on the same page. For in "connoisseurs of music" (*zhi yin lü zhe* 知音律者) we hear the phrase "knower of the tone" (*zhi yin* 知音), effectively synonymous with the "someone who knows you" (*zhi ji* 知己) of Wang Bo's poem. Thus for prospective readers of this drama miscellany, the cover page conveys a transportable and emulable scene of the latest fashion in music, living, and fellowship, the waving hand serving as an invitation to join in the fun.

Next, on the cover page of *Baneng zoujin* (fig. 2.12), two men are being entertained by eight female performers, miming the title of the book, *Brocade Performed by Eight Music Masters*. The man on the left appears to be a servant holding a fan for his master. The picture is, in effect, a visual rendering, almost a rebus, of the anthology's title, with the phrase "baneng" 八能 (eight skills) being "translated" as eight female entertainers. This visual realization—via the verbal surface of the phrase rather than through its scholarly associations with ancient and highly orthodox musical traditions—is yet another typical example of the sort of witty and subversive vernacular play with classicist tradition in these books. In addition to the female entertainers, what makes this scene lavish—the quality suggested by the term *jin* 錦 (brocade) in the title—are the folding screen creating enclosure and thus an air of intimacy, along with the table laden with plates, bowls, chopsticks, food, and wine. Here again, along with the disposition of human figures mapping social relations, we see the significant deployment of luxurious and elegant objects to create an overall spectacle of enviable style and savoir-vivre.

The next example, the cover page of *Da Ming chun* (fig. 2.13), captures the moment when a performing troupe has assembled to entertain a private party of three officials. Standing at the center of the picture, the latter are all wearing their official gowns showing the *buzi* 補子—the embroidered patches whose patterns mark the wearer's official rank—on the front. The two females and the crouching male appear to be members of a performing troupe. The booklet in the latter's hand may be read as a list of plays (*xidan* 戲單) from which the audience can select what they want to view.[98] The couplet flanking the illustration comments on the occasion:

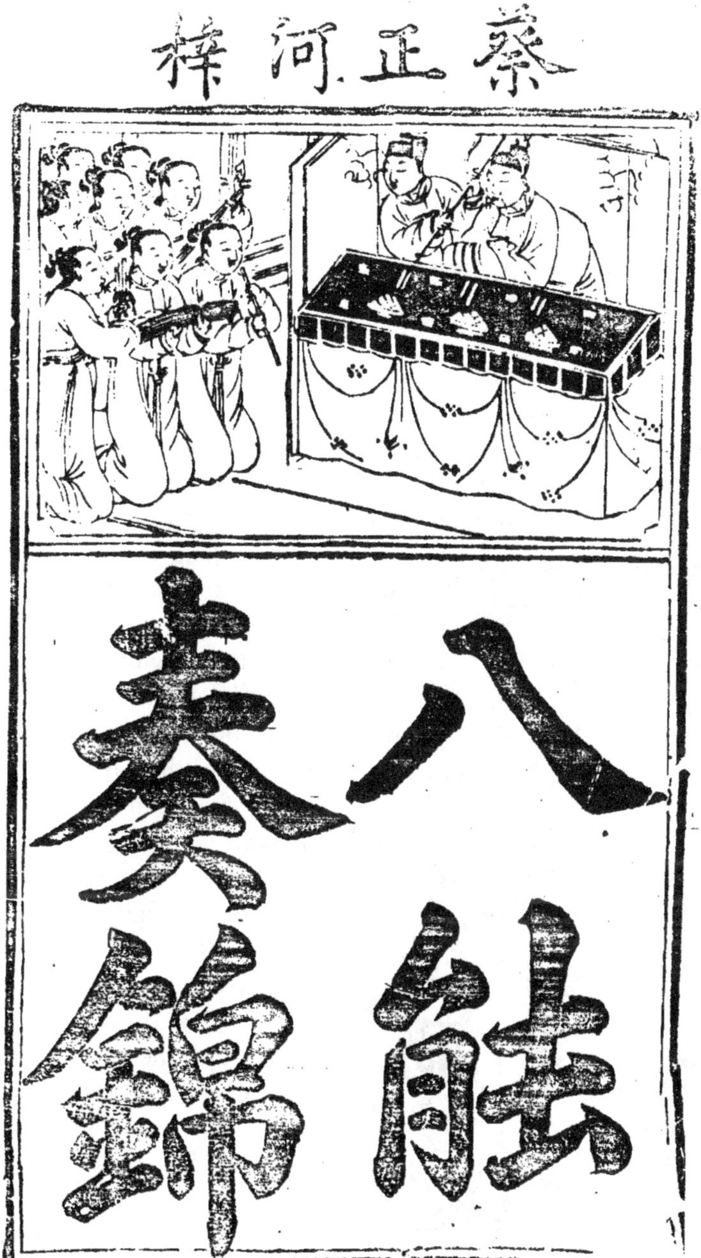

Fig. 2.12. Cover page illustration of *Baneng zoujin*. From *SBXQCK*, vol. 5, p. 1.

洒落千般調
清新萬曲音

Vigorous and bold—thousand-fold varieties of tune;
pure and fresh—tones of a myriad songs.

The officials are obviously not conducting government business, but rather enjoying a leisure moment amid their official duties. Two bow in greeting to one another, and the distracted demeanor of the third, who seems to be gazing off into an indeterminate distance, conveys the spirit of idleness and absorption in some momentary flight of fancy—an essential ingredient in the ideal of elegant leisure. The details on the clothing and the backs of the chairs as well as the dense and kinetic composition of the image suggest the sumptuousness of the setting—echoing the rephrasing of the book title appearing in oversize print in the lower half of the page: "Eternal Spring of Ten Thousand Songs to New Melodies." The dense flower patterns on the edge of the page frame the whole scene as belonging to such an eternal spring, and the effect of sumptuousness is enhanced by the overall density of inked-in space in the image, while still, like the preceding illustrations, employing the method of *yangke* 陽刻 (black figure on white ground). This visual density is also attributable to the attention given not only to the figures but to the screen behind them—an object within the scene that serves as a visual backdrop both for the figures and the viewer and that, in the material culture of the period, carried its own connotations of luxurious domesticity and leisure (fig. 2.14).

Fig. 2.13. Cover page illustration of *Da Ming chun*. From Wang Gulu, *Mingdai Huidiao xiqu sanchu jiyi*, unpaginated.

Next is the cover page of the *Shidiao Qing Kun* (fig. 2.15), in which four men are sitting at a

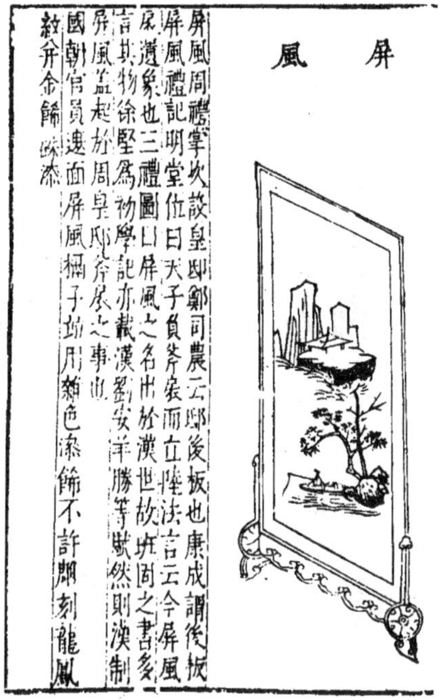

Fig. 2.14. Visual coding of the good life as represented by the screen (*pingfeng* 屏風). Illustrations of "things" and their socio-cultural history helped to code them as markers of elegant living in cover-page designs such as that of *Da Ming chun*. From *Sancai tuhui*, in *XXSKQS*, vol. 1234, p. 459.

feast. One servant boy is waiting on them, wine carafe in hand, while another male servant peeks at the banqueters from behind the screen. This figure behind the screen adds a narrative touch to the moment, as happens so often, for example, in the novel *The Plum in the Golden Vase*, where male servants are sent between Ximen Qing and his associates, wives, or singsong girls, interrupting his merry-making at some picturesque juncture. There are five female entertainers in this scene: the two on the right and the two on the left are playing musical instruments to accompany the one in the center, who dances on a patterned carpet, called *qushu* 氍毹 in Chinese and so commonly used to demarcate a space of performance that it became an alternate designation for the stage or the larger world of theater. Again, a folding screen serves not only to frame the performance as unfolding within an enclosed space for an intimate circle, but also to frame the whole scene, as perceived by the viewer of the illustration, within a specific cultural atmosphere.

The figuration on the screen shows a spread of water with rocks and islets under a serene moon and floating clouds (in Chinese, *shui* 水, *yue* 月, *yun* 雲, *shi* 石)—classic components in Chinese paintings depicting nighttime landscapes—that serve as setting and foil to the wine, food, and mortal pleasure of the banqueters' brotherhood. If the *Cilin yizhi* cover page, with its all-male group of companions, evoked ideals of universal understanding, here the presence of female entertainers encircling the male banqueters highlights their gender, evoking the sense of

Fig. 2.15. *Shidiao Qing Kun* cover page. From *SBXQCK*, vol. 9, p. 1.

a band of brothers and bringing the scene even closer to the world of Ximen Qing in *The Plum in the Golden Vase*, whose social life takes shape around the founding of his fraternity of ten.[99]

Further, the collectivity created by the scene is extended to all readers—as the caption states, it is to be "heard and enjoyed by all" (*gong tingshang* 共聽賞). The illustration's rounded framing evokes the rounded "moon-gates" of elite interior architecture, further emphasizing the luxurious domesticity of the scene and enhancing the viewer's sense of being, like the servant peeping from behind the screen, a voyeuristic witness. At the same time, the interwoven associations with the moon and with mirrors make the scene transportable between memory, imagination, and imitation. The floral ornamentation on the four corners completes this multiple framing as a vision of "lovely flowers and full moon" (*hua hao yue yuan* 花好月圓) or "flowers in the mirror, moon in the water" (*jinghua shuiyue* 鏡花水月)—bywords for the serendipitous, yet fleeting, pleasures that make life worth living.

While portraying different moments and aspects of performance, these illustrations allude to a shared vision of performance understood in its spatial dimension. The space for musical and dramatic appreciation being depicted is not a public venue such as the commercial theater (*goulan* 勾欄) or the communal and often rural festive celebrations (*she* 社). Rather, it is of an indoor, private, and personal nature: with the hall as the typical setting and the screen as the typical interior decoration, these depictions give at least as much emphasis to the social intimacy shared by the audience as to the spectacle that audience gathers to enjoy.[100] A further intimacy between audience and female performers is alluded to in *Baneng zoujin* (fig. 2.12) by the rather uncomfortable-looking poses of the figures: the female performers are stretching their heads towards their audience, while the upper bodies of the males are leaning towards the performers as if there is a magnetic attraction between them.

The Space of Private Performance

The drama miscellanies' front page illustrations exhibit a range of the material and architectural markers of the space of private theater, such as screen, hall, balustrade, or the *qushu* mat on which a dancer performs. Space is marked and shaped, still more importantly, by human activities: by how bodies are placed, words are exchanged, and delight is taken in music. This is a space in which one comes in contact with the good things in life, as imagined by the makers and readers of these books. Banqueting is as central an activity as actual musical performance in this private theater: wine, food, and conversation promote intimacy and socialization among participants. The illustrations capture moments of social interaction among an intimate group of peers, interactions for which musical performance provides both a motive and a sustaining atmosphere, piquing desire for more. These cover page illustrations provide visual clues to the excitement that permeates the space of private theater, a space that includes not only dramatic performance but also diverse kinds of social performances (e.g., drinking games, gossip, riddles, and so on). Again, it is just these disparate layers of performance whose intermingling is given its textual representation in the distinctive page layout of the drama miscellany.

Private theater was a sensation of the age, practiced and emulated across a wide swath of Ming society. The following comment by He Liangjun 何良俊 (1506–73) on his contemporary Lin Xiaoquan 林小泉 (ca. 1472–1541) gives a small indication of how the fashion for theater became integral to the kind of social performance by which the theater aficionado became an elegant personality:

> 小泉有大才，敏於剖決。公餘多暇日。好客。喜燕樂。每日有戲子一班。在門上伺候呈應。雖無客亦然。
>
> Xiaoquan had great natural talents and keenly discerning judgement. On his many days of leisure from his official duties, he loved having guests and delighted in banquet entertainment. A troupe of drama performers was on call at his gate every day, waiting for his summons. It was thus even when he had no guests.[101]

This account of how Lin Xiaoquan transformed his official residence into a private stage can serve as an explanatory note for the cover page illustrations of both *Baneng zoujin* and *Da Ming chun*, which depict officials indulging in musical performances whenever they get respite from their official duties.

To indulge one's taste for private theater was to fashion a style of living in which musical performance reshaped the daily experience of life in all of its sociality and domestic functionality. This activity created an organizing impulse for social interactions with a close circle of friends. As the above passage shows, the dramatic performances themselves are simply the crowning delight of the primarily social occasions of banqueting, referred to as *yanhui* 讌會 (banquet gathering) or *yanyue* 燕樂 (banquet gathering with music).[102] The typical site for the performance gathering is usually the main hall (*ting* 廳 or *tang* 堂) of a private dwelling. The enclosed domestic space within which the occasion unfolds fosters a social milieu with its own norms of behavior and modes of expression, offering an alluring alternative vocabulary of self-fashioning. The frequently invoked opposition between the official and off-duty personae of its elite aficionados is suggestive in this regard. In this space it was not just the singers and actors but the audiences as well who participated in a private theater of leisurely elegance. While the performance of songs and arias was ostensibly the central activity, this space was also filled with wine, food, and performers—members of family troupes, singsong girls, courtesans, etc.—and it provided a site in which uncensored linguistic and social acts could be yoked together in the form of jokes, games, and gossip.

This space was, moreover, essentially amorphous, and could take form in or among different social strata and manifest itself in various combinations: a drama performance could last several days or could be as short as a few arias; different games could be played simultaneously or could be interspersed with performance. Popular songs were sung, jokes exchanged, riddles posed and resolved. On such occasions courtesans and female entertainers held the keys to pleasure through their performance, as music and singing brought their sexuality and desirability to the fore. The sponsorship of such performances could be lavish or meager, and the venue consequently changed. Elite households sponsored extravagant private performances or raised their own family troupes just as traveling merchants cobbled together a few strings of cash to hire a singer to perform at a local inn. In the late Ming, private theater had become a quintessential marker of lavish style and sophistication for the cultured and well-to-do and, as such, was also an object of emulative desire for a far broader audience.[103]

Viewed in relation to this cultural fashion, the rhetoric of the drama miscellanies' cover-page illustrations becomes fully legible: each in its own way offers readers an opportunity to affirm a shared taste for this activity, or simply to participate vicariously by possessing and reading the book itself. To read a text is to place it within recalled space, and such space itself is a product of real-time social actions that enact textual knowledge. The social energies that flow between the text and its realization cue readers to consider text as a gateway to human activities, thus freeing it from one dominant traditional mode of interpretation: the discursive, biographical, and ethical. The cover-page design helped to transport readers into that imagination, that magic moment of *yue/le* (music/pleasure, both written with the single graph 樂).

This distinctive late Ming fascination with private theatrical spectacles that could become, in turn, the object of emulative desire for a far wider public is vividly conveyed in the short essays of reminiscence composed after the Ming's fall by Zhang Dai 張岱 (1597–1679). One telling example is Zhang's essay in the *Tao'an mengyi* 陶庵夢憶 (Dream recollections of the Master of Tao'an) on Bao Hansuo 包涵所 (*jinshi* 1586), a former intimate of Zhang's grandfather, who had spent the years of his retirement in Hangzhou in lavish and elegant fashion:[104]

> 西湖之船有樓，實包副使涵所創爲之。大小三號：頭號置歌筵，儲歌童；次載書畫；再次儲美人。涵老聲伎非侍妾比，仿石季倫、宋子京家法，都令見客。常靚妝走馬，婆娑勃窣，穿柳過之，以爲笑樂。明檻綺疏，曼謳其下，擫籥彈箏，聲如鶯試。客至則歌童演劇，隊舞鼓吹，無不絕倫。乘興一出，住必浹旬，觀者相逐，問其所止。

> The boats on West Lake with multistoreyed decks were in fact an innovation of Vice Commissioner Bao Hansuo. They come in three sizes: the large ones, for conveying waterborne musical banquets and troupes of child singers; the next size down, for bearing books and paintings; and the smallest, for carrying beautiful women. The family performers of the venerable Mr. Han were not to be classed with maids or concubines: following the household regulations of Shi Jilun and Song Zijing, he let them all interact with his guests.[105] Often they would go wandering on horseback in their most gorgeous attire, elegantly swaying and rustling, weaving through willows to pay calls, all for a merry lark. Beneath bright balustrades and filigree windows, they would intone languorous melodies; or, to the rhythm of pipes and strummed zithers, their voices would warble like young orioles. When guests arrived at Bao's household, then singing children would perform, with group dances and drum and fife bands—and all were beyond compare. Even when they went out on the spur of the moment, they were sure to tarry a week or longer. Onlookers followed them in a stream, inquiring where they would stop next.[106]

Bao Hansuo is presented as a trend-setting innovator in a specialized technology of pleasure-seeking. The differentiation in the designs of the various sorts of pleasure craft (which Zhang implies has impacted the local culture of pleasure outings down to the time of the essay's writing) is eminently practical in the sense that each type of vessel is tailored to a particular function. These functions themselves, however, are eminently impractical, in that they are oriented toward no end other than pleasure-seeking. By design or otherwise, however, they do have the effect of turning Bao's private pleasure seeking into a public spectacle.

This theme of portability, by which Bao Hansuo is enabled to enjoy private pleasures even while moving freely about in a public space, is continued throughout the essay. In the passages following the portion quoted above, Zhang describes still other innovations that Bao Hansuo applied to garden spaces to make them more amenable to dance performances, and in a concluding remark Zhang draws a contrastive analogy to the story of Emperor Wu (r. 141–87 BCE) of the Western Han dynasty (206 BCE–9 CE), who as a young boy was said to have exclaimed of a female cousin he was fond of that if he could have her as a wife he would "store her in a golden chamber." Bao Hansuo and his peers of that age, Zhang Dai reasons, because of their elegant freedom from an overly rigid division between private pleasures and public spectacle, had been able to keep West Lake itself in a golden chamber, increasing the scope of their private enjoyment by making their domestic sphere portable, and by making the boundaries between the private and the public permeable.

The underlying thematic variations on these questions of portability and private entertainment offer a perspective for understanding the point of the narration about Bao's private theater troupe; whereas others might indeed treat their domestic performers as equivalent to maids or concubines who should be confined to the inner quarters of the household, Bao Hansuo's performers circulate fluidly, enhancing their master's delight by enticing a broader circle of onlookers to participate in it vicariously. For less affluent late Ming men who lacked the resources to remodel their residences or custom-build excursion yachts, the markers of the space of private performance could be as simple as a single red carpet placed in the spot where the performer acted and sung. And within this context the drama miscellanies provided handy access to this world, as the books extended the invitation to readers to "listen and appreciate together" (*gong ting shang*).

If Zhang Dai's recollections are a reconstruction of the cultural magic of the late Ming viewed in a nostalgic retrospective, the late Ming writer whose vision of the links between private theater and the good life is most reminiscent of our drama miscellanies is certainly Wang Jide 王驥德 (1542?–1623), the premier critic of dramatic literature and performance of his age. In his classic drama treatise entitled *Qulü* 曲律 (Regulations for *qu*), much of which is taken up with sometimes forbiddingly technical concerns of dramatic and musical craft, he finds a moment to be playful:

論曲亨屯第四十

迂愚叟之志牡丹也，有“榮辱”籍焉；夫曲曷嘗不籍所遇以爲幸與不幸哉，遇則亨而不遇則屯也。戲次其事，各得四十則，附志于後，以當好事者一噱。

曲之亨

華堂，青樓，名園，水亭，雪閣，畫舫，花下，柳邊，佳風日，清宵，皎月，嬌喉，佳拍，美人歌，孌童唱，名優，姣旦，伶人解文義，艷衣裝，名士集，座有麗人，佳公子，知音客，鑒賞家，詩人賦贈篇，座客能走筆度新聲，閨人繡幕中聽，玉卮，美釀，佳茗，好香，明燭，珠箔障，繡履點拍，倚簫，合笙，主婦不惜纏頭，廝仆勤給事，精刻本，新翻艷詞出。

曲之屯

賽社，醵錢，酬願，和爭，公府會，家宴，酒樓，村落，炎日，淒風，苦雨，老丑伶人，弋陽調，窮行頭，演惡劇，唱猥詞，沙喉，訛字，錯拍，刪落，鬧鑼鼓，傖父與席，下妓侑尊，新篘酒敗喉，惡客闖座，客至犬嚎，酗酒人罵座，席上行酒政，將軍作調笑人，三腳貓人妄譏彈，村人喝彩，鄰家哭聲，僧道觀場，村婦列座，小兒啼，場下人廝打，主人惜燭，家僮告酒竭，田父、舟人作勞，沿街覓錢。

On *Qu*'s Being Blessed or Cursed, Chapter 40[107]

The record on the peony by the "Foolish and Pedantic Old Man" lists the circumstances of honor and shame on which the peony relies.[108] How could we suppose that *qu* as well do not rely on the circumstances they meet with to determine their good or bad fortune? On encountering the right circumstances, *qu* are blessed, while when not encountering those circumstances, they are cursed. Playfully I have listed the varieties in which such things occur, with 40 items on each side, and note them below to give the curious a chance to laugh a little.

On *Qu*'s Being Blessed

Splendid halls, green bowers [a term occasionally used as a euphemism for a brothel], famous gardens, waterside kiosks, snow-bound pavilions, painted boats, among the flowers, beside the willows, days of nice breezes, clear nights, bright moons, delicate throats, skilled beats, beauties intoning, catamites singing, famous performers, beautiful female leads, performers who actually understand the text, gorgeous clothes, celebrated and lettered men gathering together, beauties at the feast mat, handsome young men, guests who are connoisseurs of music, good critics, poets who compose commemorative verses, guests who can rapidly compose lyrics to new tunes, beauties listening behind embroidered curtains, jade winecups, good brew, fine tea, nice incense, bright candles, beaded curtains, embroidered slippers tapping out the beat, attuning *xiao*-flutes, harmonizing *sheng*-pipes, hostesses generous at giving performers a bonus, servants diligent at serving, refined woodblock texts, fresh versions of sultry songs.

On Qu's Being Cursed

Village grain altar celebrations, performances put on by pooling cash together, paying back a vow to a god, appeasing a dispute, official banquets, house banquets, wine lofts, rustic villages, burning sun, chilly wind, bitter rain, an ugly old performer, *Yiyang* music, tattered costumes, performing awful plays, singing bawdy lyrics, hoarse throats, mispronounced words, missed beats, dropped lines, loud gongs and drums, a vulgar man at table, low prostitutes helping with wine, newly filtered wine that hurts the throat, bad-mannered guests dashing in after it's started, dogs barking when guests arrive, drunk men cursing at their seats, playing drinking games, the judge of the drinking game playing the buffoon, a three-pawed cat [i.e., a know-it-all without real understanding] giving pointless critiques, a coarse man cheering, the sound of crying in a neighboring house, Buddhists or Daoists watching the play, village women at the table, children crying, attendees getting into fights, a host stingy with his candles, a servant boy reporting a shortage of wine, farmers or boatmen laboring away, beggars along the street.[109]

Wang's list of the "blessings" that operatic music can encounter, described in terms of the social and material conditions accompanying its performance, complements and illuminates our survey of frontispiece illustrations from Ming drama miscellanies—indeed, Wang Jide's phrases could be directly borrowed to serve as captions for those illustrations. For example, one could match the *Cilin yizhi* cover page with phrases such as "beside the willows," "a day of clear breezes," "a gathering of celebrated and lettered man," "guests who are connoisseurs of music," and "good brew"; and one could match *Shidiao Qing Kun* with "splendid hall," "among the flowers," "bright moon," "delicate throat," "skilled beat," "beauty singing," "beautiful female lead," "good brew," and "servants diligent at serving." Wang Jide's playful account of the blessings of operatic music also projects by implication a particular vision of a blessed life. Just as the blessings of music, for Wang, exclude any practical motives such as a "village grain altar celebration," "paying back a vow to a god," "appeasing a dispute," or conducting an "official banquet," the blessings of musical performance, or of the elegant life that shapes itself around such performances, are found in moments of pure pleasure of sound and beauty, and in camaraderie with a community of listeners with the discernment to appreciate them.

Conclusion

The meaning of a text is intricately tied to its materiality. Drama miscellanies form a genre of printed text that is inseparable from the print culture and popular urban culture of the late Ming, and contemporary texts play an active role in their formation and perception. As Roger Chartier has demonstrated, form plays a crucial part in the production of meaning.[110] Both in their cover page illustrations and in their multi-register page layout, drama miscellanies intermingle dramatic and musical performance with the equally complex social performances of communities of spectators and readers hoping to display their insider status in a community of connoisseurs of pleasure-seeking. Thus, in these books, textual meaning is intimately tied to performance and desire.

This chapter has shown that the space of splendor, pleasure, worldly sophistication, and subversive wit that unfolds before the reader of the drama miscellany often takes on the characteristics of an alternative empire, where private pleasure-seeking expands to fill an entire world. The *Yugu xinhuang*, instead of duplicating the simple list of administrative seats and regions, provides a group of songs extolling the tricks and characteristics of male and female prostitutes of different localities.[111] The *Da Ming tianxia chun* expands this list to include profiles of girls and lads from more localities.[112] Taken together, this song repertoire maps out a geography of sex and desire in the Ming empire, albeit in a mocking fashion. The song titles are as follows:

> Linqing sisters 臨清姐兒, Yangzhou sisters 揚州姐兒, Yizhen sisters 儀眞姐兒, Suzhou sisters 蘇州姐兒, Tianjin sisters 天津姐兒, Xiaoshan sisters 蕭山姐兒, Qiantang sisters 錢塘姐兒, Lanxi sisters 蘭溪姐兒, Hangzhou sisters 杭州姐兒, Xiangyang sisters 襄陽姐兒, Fancheng sisters 樊城姐兒, Jingzhou sisters 荆州姐兒, Bianliang sisters 汴梁姐兒, Yunnan sisters 雲南姐兒, Jiujiang sisters 九江姐兒, Guangdong sisters 廣東姐兒, Shunchang sisters 順昌姐兒, Jingzhou sisters 荆州姐兒, Xiangjiang daughters 湘江女兒, Suzhou daughters 蘇州女兒, Zhenjiang daughters 鎮江女兒, Yangzhou daughters 揚州女兒, Linqing daughters 臨清女兒, Hangzhou daughters 杭州女兒, Jiujiang daughters 九江女兒, Jianchang daughters 建昌女兒, Jinhua daughters 金華女兒, Tongcheng fellows

> 桐城小夥, Tongling fellows 銅陵小夥, Poyang fellows 鄱陽小夥, Huizhou fellows 徽州小夥, Macheng fellows 麻城小夥, Jingshan fellows 京山小夥, Shashi fellows 沙市小夥, Tuanfeng fellows 團風小夥, Qizhou fellows 蘄州小夥, Zhangzhou fellows 漳州小夥, Shangqing fellows 上清小夥, Shulin fellows 書林小夥, Tancheng fellows 潭城小夥.

As the catalog of administrative geography is skewed into a catalog of local characteristics of male and female prostitutes, geography itself is redefined as a landscape of carnal pleasure in private performance. The stable and encompassing spatial order of the empire is dissolved in this subterranean remapping. We note as well that amid this catalog of place names appears the place "shulin," or "forest of books"—likely as a designation of Jianyang, but earning its distinctive allure from the book trade itself.

The issue of form and the material aspect of printed text is also one of visuality. The matter of late Ming visuality is shaped by an impressive volume of pictorial matter in print.[113] The form of the printed page itself, meanwhile, was also part of the visual culture of the day. In the triple-register page format, a sense of "other" space is inserted into the conventional linear textual flow. This visual arrangement replaces sequential reading with segmental reading, and replaces the dominance of time on the page with the logic of space. In engaging with texts, drama miscellanies coded a way of reading that turns the page into a site where ideas and practices associated with printing, text, and theater interplay. If technique intimately registers historical experience, drama miscellanies reshaped the spaces of reading in the late Ming by the visual technique of their page format and cover page design. In this way, these books of the theater created a new theater of reading.

CHAPTER THREE

The Poetics of Error: Repetition and Novelty in the Age of Woodblock (Re)production

This book opened with an example of how the editors of the eighteenth-century *Siku quanshu* project used the term *baifan*, which I rendered as "hucksterish," to point to a complex of traits in Ming book culture that they found repugnant. For them, the term signaled irresponsible transfer and transmission of text, particularly sloppiness with regard to verifying the most authentic version of an original book (*ben shu* 本書) for reference in study, citation, or in producing new editions. The seeming willingness of Ming editors to use whichever version of a book lay most readily to hand, and the hodge-podge fashion in which they cobbled heterogeneous sorts of texts together, provoked a litany of invective from Qing scholars, whose impatience and indignation with Ming editors and Ming books in general finds expression in comments that "the source is not cited" (*buzhu chuchu* 不注出處), that a given work or section was "patched together" (*pincou* 拼凑) or "ripped apart" (*gelie* 割裂), that an editor engaged in "hawking old texts (as though new)" (*baifan jiu wen* 稗販舊文), that the "old edition was not preserved" (*jiu ben bu cun* 舊本不存), or that "references were imprecise" (*zheng shi bu xiang* 征事不詳), "the original text was not cited" (*bu ju ben shu* 不舉本書), or references "had not been traced to their origins" (*bu de shi shi* 不得事始). The Qing scholars were also fond of pointing out cases of "errors and mistranscriptions" (*cuo e* 錯訛), of "unclear documentation" (*buming gen ju* 不明根據), of "tissues of plagiarism" (*piao chuo* 剽輟), or of "credulously repeated hearsay" (*er shi* 耳食). All of these complaints point to a tangle of textual interbreeding and random borrowing that frustrate, or even make a mockery of, any scholarly effort to trace textual origins and adjudicate authenticity.

Such invective points to something distinctive about Ming book culture, at least in comparison with the scholarly and bibliographical norms of the eighteenth century and later eras. Rather than acceding to the accompanying negative value judgment implied by the tone of such language, however, I will attempt instead to ask how and why such books, with such seemingly major flaws, nonetheless held value for Ming readers. What sort of value might this have been?

It can be said of many Ming books not only that they exhibit variation, but that variation is itself the dimension in which they create their own distinctiveness and appeal.[1] When viewed in their own terms, the variation these books exhibit is not a debility arising from an overly lax attitude toward textual authority. Rather, in them one sees textual authority "coming into play" rather than merely being reproduced. In a wide range of genres and contexts, variation becomes a generative and often quite self-conscious mechanism for making something new, and the lines between corruption and creation, and between citation and parody, are often deliberately blurred.

The aspects of Ming book culture most reviled by Qing editors tend to be those that frustrate or render moot the scholarly impulse to uncover a clear line of transmission of original or authentic texts. Rather than follow those bibliographers in their preoccupation with reconstructing textual stemmata, I will here employ a notion of textual "families": groupings of texts, pictures, and books that enter into relation with one another through an intertwined process of mutual borrowing and creative derivation that does not allow us to point to any particular version as more definitive or authentic than others. The phrase *zhanzhuan baifan* 輾轉稗販 (meaning something like "back-and-forth hawking and re-hawking of the same wares" or "iterative hucksterism"), which appears as a particularly impatient and dismissive comment by a *Siku* editor describing a Ming book, in fact reveals something significant about the actual practice of many Ming editors and booksellers. Although it leaves very little ground for the scholarly retracing of legitimate textual authority, this mechanism is far from incapable of producing meaning, novelty, and excitement, as the following discussion of Ming textual families will attempt to show.

To put this in the language of Wang Jide, the Ming drama critic cited in relation to private theatrical performances in chapter 2, a fruitful dialectical relationship exists between old and new language that goes into what he calls the "ripeness of opportunity" when a given piece of verbal material is "played" for telling effect: "My words are actually new, but when people hear them, they perceive them as if they were old—this is to say that the moment of opportunity is ripe" (我本新語，而使人聞之，若是舊句，言機熟也).[2] To Wang Jide, this "ripe moment of opportunity" is the essential factor in creating new phrases so intrinsically rooted in established convention that they immediately take on an air of familiarity for the audience. In this formula of novelty, the key is to transpose perceptions built up from old material to a new composition so that the new appears familiar. This effect of familiarity, to Wang Jide, is the most exquisite achievement in dramatic writing. To apply Wang Jide's concept of the "ripe moment of opportunity" to our study of late Ming woodblock reproduction will mean to examine these works in terms of their networks of interreferentiality, built out of a common store of texts, pictures, and books across a range of types, genres, and registers, and to attempt to appreciate how each strives to capture its own ripe moment of opportunity in the complex of crossings and echoes shaped by those networks.

Of particular interest in our exploration of the dynamics of variation, or "iterative hucksterism," in Ming book culture are the complex relations between texts and illustrations. This has long been a focal topic in the study of what has been dubbed the golden age of Chinese woodblock prints. The perspective of this chapter will be to view texts and visual images as parallel and often overlapping systems that display many of the same dynamics of variation.[3] The issue of whether and how text and picture interrelate as separate representational media becomes less important than how texts and pictures work together to create something new: a new kind of chapter, a new kind of book, and eventually a new vernacular language. I thus begin my discussion of several textual "families" in the Ming book world by considering the flux and variation surrounding the frontispiece illustrations appearing in woodblock texts.

New Reeds from the Valley of Jade: *Recycling and Self-Reference in Woodblock Prints*

The process of producing illustrated woodblock texts involved a multitude of special roles including, to name a few, authors, artists, copyists, engravers, editors, publishers, illustrators, printers, binders, and sellers.

While one can often see texts and pictures being copied, modified, and recycled from one edition to another, another significant and in a sense more fundamental sort of re-use is going on behind the scenes as well: the re-use of old blocks. Dates assigned by bibliographers to woodblock books usually, as one might expect, refer to the time when the blocks were carved, and not necessarily to the time when the actual sheets were printed and bound. The simplest sort of later reuse of a set of blocks, by merely drawing new imprints from the same blocks, may generate any number of imprints after the original production date that are often indistinguishable from earlier printings. But many reprint editions reflect market forces that tended to encourage publishers to give at least token attention in such editions to the reading public's desire for all things novel and up-to-date.[4] Even where the efforts to update such editions were minimal and cosmetic, paying close attention to them can be a useful way of observing the dynamics of the fashions and tastes that shaped the Ming book world. Here I will examine the processes of reworking and adaptation reflected in the case of the drama miscellany entitled *Yugu xinhuang*.

Let us first look at the cover page illustration (fig. 3.1).[5] It portrays a man and a woman (who, by the visual conventions of this type of illustration, would probably be read as a courtesan) playing musical instruments together. Both bodies and instruments are intertwined: the man enfolds the woman in his arms and body, and the string instrument, a *pipa*, is held by the man's left hand and the woman's right hand, while the flute is held by the woman's left hand and the man's right hand. The intertwined bodies and instruments display an erotic intimacy in which the audience is invited to share voyeuristically.

As is common in cover page designs, the book title is not rendered verbatim as it appears at the beginning of the book's main text but is reworded as *Yugu tiaohuang* 玉谷調簧 (Tuning the reed in the jade valley). The point seems to be that the cover page as a whole is to effectively frame the book, or shed new light on the book, but not simply to repeat what one can readily see in it. Further, the word change from the title in the opening chapter *xin* (new) to *tiao* on the cover page also serves to highlight the central act of the picture: plucking, playing, manipulating, or teasing—all possible meanings of the action verb *tiao*.

Framing is key to the function of cover page illustrations, and serves as a key motif within this picture as well. The outer frame is the balustrade (*goulan* 勾欄) that comes at an angle right behind the Taihu rock in

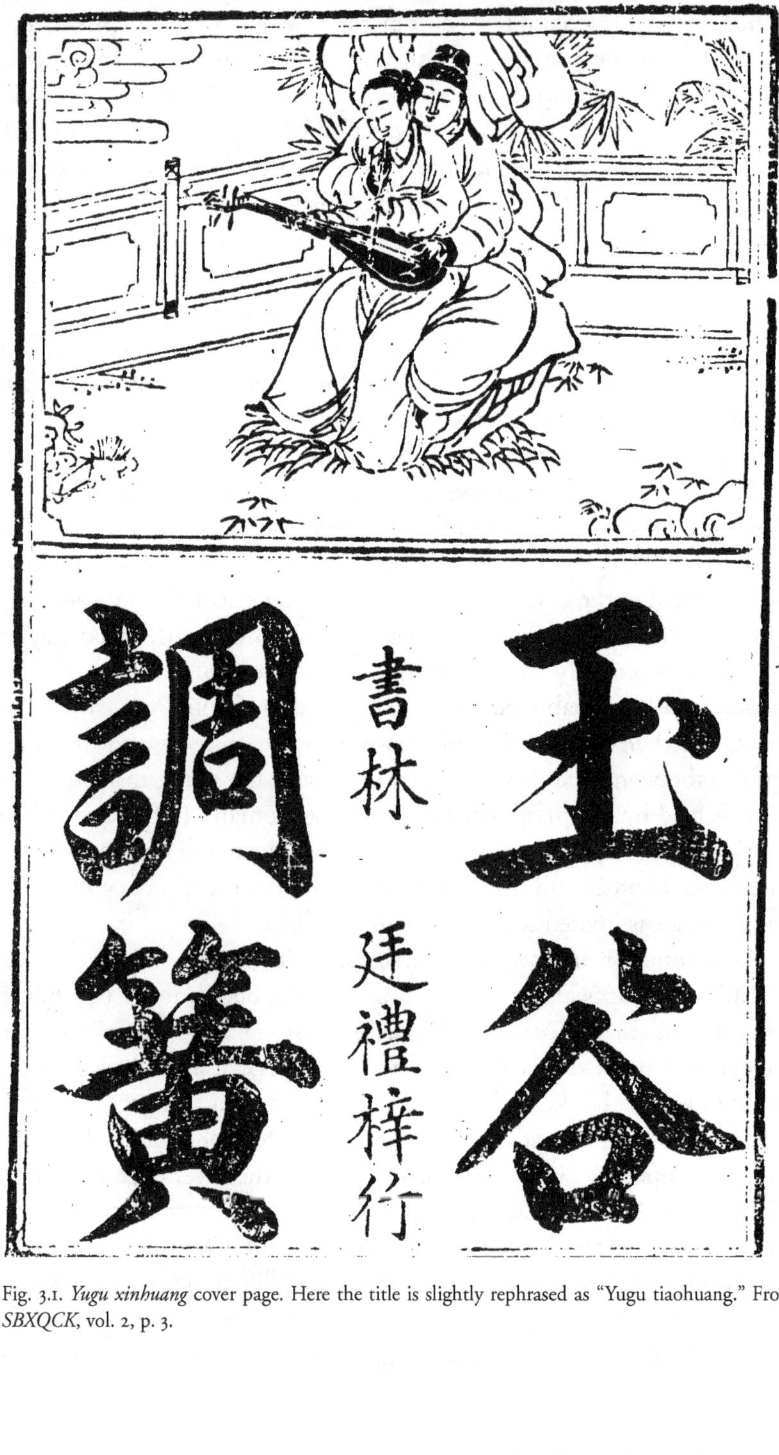

Fig. 3.1. *Yugu xinhuang* cover page. Here the title is slightly rephrased as "Yugu tiaohuang." From *SBXQCK*, vol. 2, p. 3.

the center, evoking the multiple referents of the word *goulan*, both as an aesthetic site and as an alternative designation for a theater or a brothel. The moving clouds in the upper-left corner evoke the expression *yunyu* 雲雨 (clouds and rain), a familiar euphemism for love-making. Moving from the angle of the balustrade forward to the front of the picture, the tree behind the Taihu rock, the rock itself, the male body, the female body, then the musical instruments—all these layers of things and bodies form a depth that creates an effect of *you* 幽 (quiet seclusion) and wraps the central act of playing instruments in layers of erotic insinuation.

A couple seated near or on a Taihu rock is an established commonplace in pictorial renderings of romance and sex (fig. 3.2), but in the

Fig. 3.2. Sex and books, and the Taihu rock seen in a late Ming erotic picture collected by R. H. van Gulik. From *Erotic Colour Prints of the Ming Period*, vol. 2, p. 235.

Yugu xinhuang cover illustration the crossed arms and an involved set of visual puns, instead of the outright stripping and sex on display in erotic albums, lend the motif fresh novelty and interest. These puns draw on the lexicon of sex, most obviously through the bawdy metaphors *chuixiao* 吹簫 (flute-blowing, i.e., fellatio) and *boxian* 撥弦 (strumming, i.e., manipulating the labia of the vagina). Corresponding to these puns, the stringed instrument, normally held in an upright position, now is laid horizontally, a visual reference to the phrase *heng chen* 橫陳 (horizontally arrayed), which since medieval times had been a conventional phrase to describe the woman's body in lovemaking. The flute, as a sign for *nahua* 那話 (that thing) in the language of vernacular fiction, is rightfully in its upright position in correlation with the recumbent string instrument. The illustration is thus an ingenious visual reprise of the ever-familiar traditional definition by homonym equating music (*yue* 樂) and delight (*le* 樂),[6] but emphasizing the distinctly sexual overtones of both. Overall, the design evokes the realm of *se* 色, which could refer (as in Buddhist contexts) to the bewildering realm of phenomenal appearance in general, but tended in more specific contexts to connote erotically charged appearance and sexual desire. On one hand, this vision of *se* replicates a rising urban culture in the late Ming that was fascinated with musical performance and the world of the demimonde; on the other hand, as a cover-page illustration, it also situates the book itself, an anthology of arias, songs, and drinking games, as part of this world of *se*.

At the same time, the excessiveness (*yin* 淫) and cleverness (*qiao* 巧) in the choreography of sex and musical, instrumental, and bodily intimacy in the image, with all the thinly disguised bawdy puns, challenges the reader's capacity to read these images in terms of desire or intimacy and seems to point the way beyond, into a comic mode, suggesting that the idea of "teasing" in the word *tiao* of the cover illustration's version of the title might include not just erotic titillation but also mockery. Such a possibility is immediately highlighted on the first page of the book (fig. 3.3), where, placed right in the middle is a group of satirical songs entitled "In the Latest Fashion: 'Kid-Teasing' Songs in Mockery of Prostitutes of Various Places" 時興各處譏妓耍孩兒歌. A sense of irony is further reinforced by the book title itself, *Yugu xin/tiao huang*, where *yu* 玉 (jade) is an established pun for *yu* 慾 (desire). The expression *yugu* 慾谷 (ravine of desire), or its alternate form *yuhe* 慾壑, appeared frequently in maxims

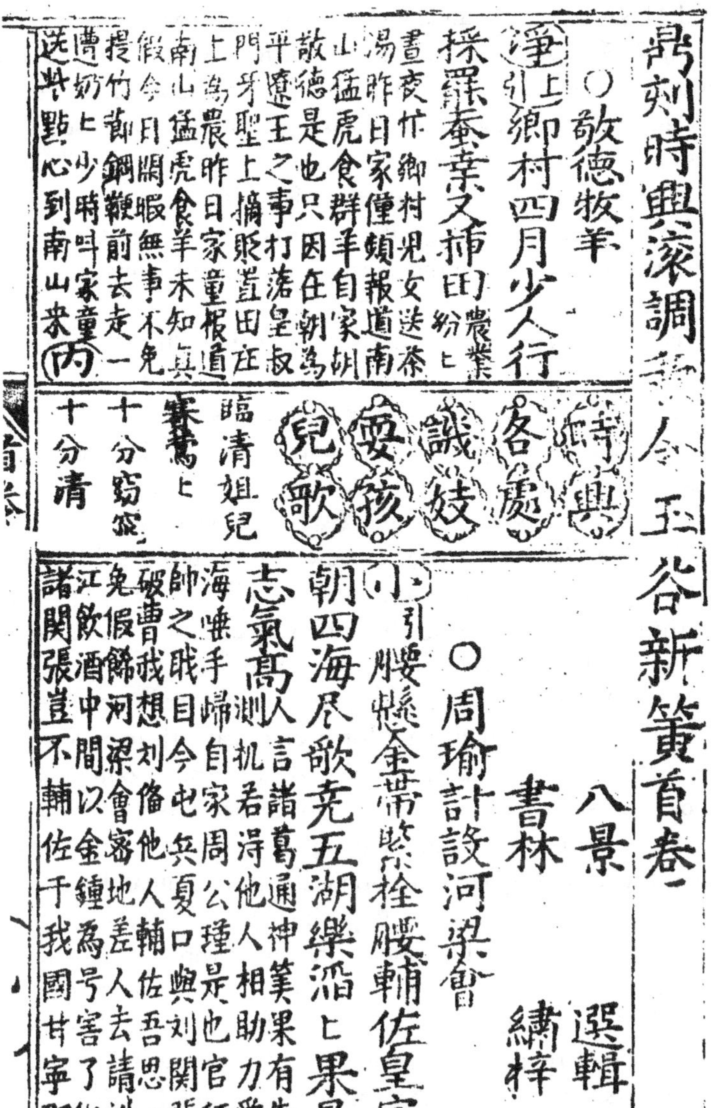

Fig. 3.3. A group of "kid-teasing" songs seen on the opening page of the first volume of *Yugu xinhuang*. From *SBXQCK*, vol. 2, p. 11.

about the insatiability of human desire—a ravine proverbially hard to fill (*nan tian* 難填) that threatened catastrophe to those who strayed into it, as *The Plum in the Golden Vase* and other erotica elaborately and graphically related for late Ming readers. Thus both with its frontispiece image and its title, the *Yugu tiaohuang* cover page suggests both a "straight" reading (*zheng du* 正讀) in terms of music-making as a site of alluring sensuality and pleasure, along with a "reversed" reading (*fan du* 反讀) as an ironic commentary on the illusory nature of the seductive world of *se*/appearance.

Further layered references focus on the idea of the "reed" in the phrase "tuning the reed" (*tiao huang* 調簧). *Huang* refers to reed instruments, or to the reeds used in such instruments. In its metaphorical usages, however, including its appearance in compounds, it tends to refer figuratively to the process of making the unreal real. For example, *huang kou* 簧口 (a reed-like mouth), *huang she* 簧舌 (reed-like tongue), and *huang yan* 簧言 (reed-like words) refer to powers of eloquence that stir and shape the listeners' emotions and thoughts, while *huanghuo* 簧惑 (delusion of the reed), *huanggu* 簧鼓 (drumming up of emotions as by a reed), *huangyou* 簧誘 (seductiveness as of a reed), and *huanggu* 簧蠱 (bewitchment as by a reed) all refer to the ability of such crafty eloquence to manipulate, mislead, and enchant listeners, causing them to lose touch with reality. The phrase *tiaohuang* 調簧 thus refers not only to a novel world of musical performance but also to the bewitching world of illusion conjured forth by the crafty manipulation of sounds and images.

The title and frontispiece illustration thus seem quite well integrated, as both raise, in complementary ways, invitations to the seductions of music and desire, especially erotic desire, along with veiled ridicule or admonition concerning the illusory nature of those seductive charms. Looking further to see how this cover page relates to the book as a whole, we see another intriguing technique of doubling or reversal at work: the printed pages show clear signs that this title page, and the title itself, were added as part of a fairly minimal adaptation of a previously existing set of blocks that had earlier been used to produce a different book. Both figures 3.4 and 3.5, for example, convey hints that the title *Yugu xinhuang* was, in fact, added on after scraping off an earlier title. Figure 3.4 shows where part of the old title has been planed off, but the new title has not been inserted, while figure 3.5 shows how the old title, *Yuzhen jinsheng*

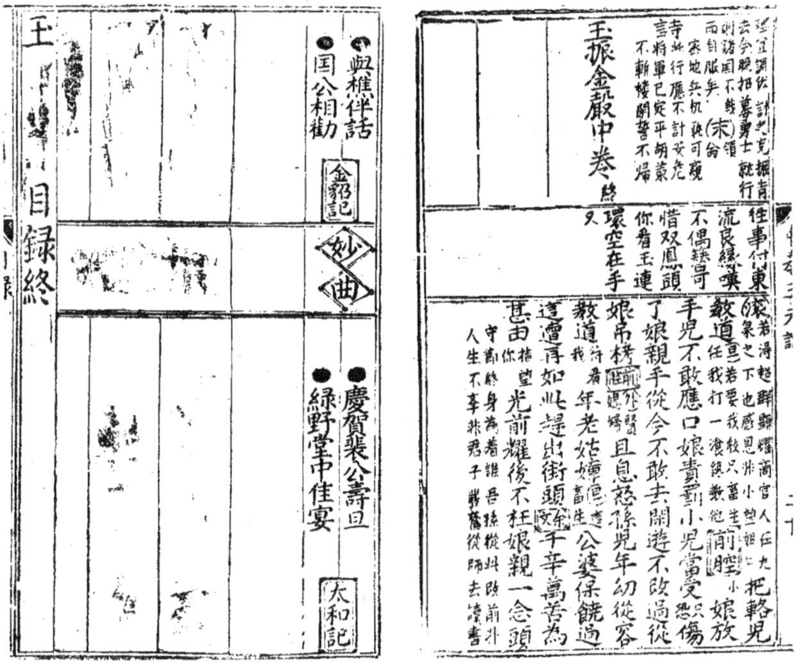

Figs. 3.4 and 3.5. In the leftmost column seen in figure 3.4, the old title of "Yu..."/玉... is shown partially scraped away. In the leftmost column of the top register seen in figure 3.5, the old title of "Yu zhen jin sheng"/玉振金聲 is shown intact. From *SBXQCK*, vol. 2, pp. 9, 110.

玉振金聲 (Chimes of jade and tones of bronze), survived the process of adaptation.

Clearly then, the book entitled *Yugu xinhuang* was created through the minimal adaptation of an earlier set of blocks. The phrase *yu zhen jin sheng*, referring to the ancient ritual music characterized by the tones of lithophones and bronze bells, appears in early texts in association with music as part of a sagely legacy,[7] where music is treated in terms of correspondences between sounds of musical instruments and a larger ethical and cosmological order. The use of this sort of classical and lofty-sounding title for a collection of popular songs or dramatic literature was an established tradition in Ming and later song and drama anthologies.[8] Some readers might have sensed tensions or double meanings in the discursive gaps between such a lofty-sounding title and the often sensual and risqué lyrics contained in the anthology proper. But by exchanging the earlier high-sounding title for one that more emphatically points in the direction of the world of the ravine of desire, this particular instance of the recycling of an old set of blocks shifts the entire text into the world of the *se* (sensuality of desire, lust, and pleasure), and brings those fluid and ambiguous doublings of meaning closer to the surface. The new title *Yugu xinhuang*, with its new cover illustration containing the words *Yugu tiaohuang*, points toward the possibility of slippage between "straight" and "reversed" readings and, as an opportunistic editorial intervention in the reissuing of a previously cut set of blocks, is itself an instance of such slippage.

Judging from the style of calligraphy and carving of the distinct layers of production reflected in the *Yugu xinhuang* imprint, the compiler's name, Liu Ciquan, appears to have been added on along with the new title and illustration. Liu Ciquan thus seems to be the reissuer of the new title rather than the compiler of the earlier *Yuzhen jinsheng* anthology. Liu, as discussed in the previous chapter, is known mainly as a skilled engraver of woodblock illustrations, but here in the *Yugu xinhuang* we see evidence that he also worked as publisher.[9] Though no name is signed as the maker and designer of the frontispiece, it is not unlikely that Liu Ciquan had a hand in it, judging from other known works of his. In any event, Liu's production of the *Yugu xinhuang* was largely a matter of repackaging the preexisting *Yuzhen jinsheng*, while for his strategy as a marketer and illustrator he was able to draw more generally on a broad understanding of the fashions and trends of the contemporary world of woodblock imprints.

Comic One-Upmanship: Illustrations in the Miaojin wanbao quanshu

For many producers of Ming woodblock printed books, it was desirable to recycle or adapt extant material, both to keep production costs low and to take advantage of the most popular and proven material in circulation. At the same time, as the above example of the adaptation of the *Yuzhen jinsheng* into the "new" *Yugu xinhuang* illustrates, producers also exercised great ingenuity in imparting a sense of freshness and up-to-date appeal in each new imprint. One of the main ways they achieved this was through updating or adding illustrations.

As suggested by the example of the *Yugu xinhuang*, frontispiece illustrations were a particularly effective tool in "repackaging" material in circulation. Within encyclopedias or other compendium formats, the illustrations that introduced each new section or category could serve a similar purpose in reframing recycled material, presenting a fresh and inviting gateway to entice readers, and providing hints as to the textual attractions to follow. Just as urban shops or eating establishments might hire touts to stand at the doorway to urge passers-by to come inside, these title-page and chapter-heading texts and illustrations are the places where book producers competed most sharply to persuade readers of the appeal and currency of their particular book. In the discussion below I will examine some examples of the use of illustrations in such reframing or repackaging, focusing on the category of banter and banqueting games. As noted in previous chapters, these texts form a relatively stable category, displaying a high level of reuse and close adaptation from one imprint and one format to another. Along with specialized anthologies of "laughing matters" such as the *Boxiao zhuji*, these materials typically appear as subcategories within two other compendium forms: the drama miscellany and the daily-use encyclopedia. I will focus on the daily-use encyclopedia entitled *Miaojin wanbao quanshu* 妙錦萬寶全書 (A wondrous brocade: the complete book of myriad treasures).

Liu Ciquan, whom we encountered above as the artist-publisher of the *Yugu xinhuang*, also carved the frontispiece illustration for the division entitled *Zalan* 雜覽 (Miscellaneous items for browsing) in the *Miaojin wanbao quanshu* (fig. 3.6).[10] This division is composed of lantern riddles and other riddle-like games.[11] The central feature depicted in the illustration is a *dengpeng* (lantern awning), or Aoshan, a structure of lanterns and puppet figures that was often the most anticipated spectacle in the metropolis during the annual Lantern Festival. Liu Ciquan's illustration draws on two strands in conventional representations of this festival. The first is to represent the Lantern Festival as urban spectacle and imperial extravaganza, as seen, for example, in the *Xianzong xingle tu* 憲宗行樂圖 (Merrymaking in the palace of Emperor Xianzong, fig. 3.7) and the *Nandu fanhui tu* 南都繁會圖 (Prosperous celebration in the southern metropolis, fig. 3.8). Another is to represent this festival in terms of elegant leisure and material comfort, as depicted in the Song dynasty painting entitled *Guan deng tu* 觀燈圖 (Viewing lanterns, fig. 3.9). These paintings also share common elements such as children and their toys.

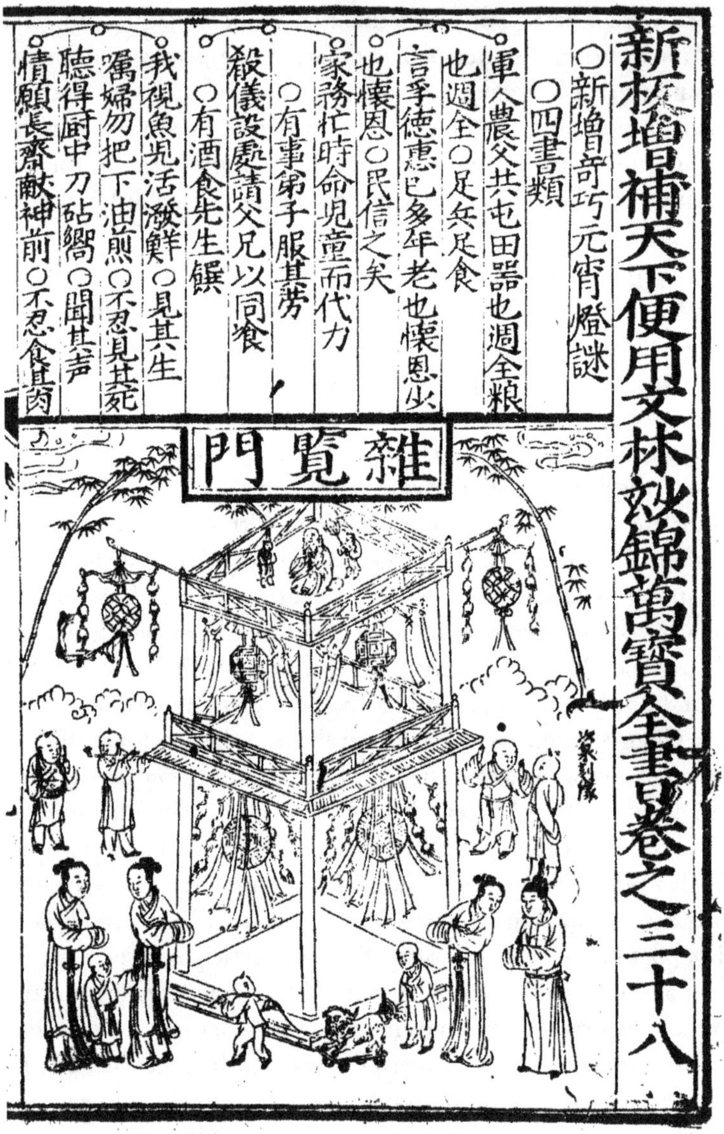

Fig. 3.6. Frontispiece to "Miscellaneous Items" 雜覽 division. The words "Ciquan kexiang" 次泉刻像 (picture engraved by Ciquan) appear on the right side of the illustration. From *CNRS*, vol. 14, p. 421.

Fig. 3.7. *Xianzong xingle tu* (detail). From *Zhongguo guojia bowuguan guancang wenwu yanjiu congshu*, vol. 8, pt. 1, p. 40.

Fig. 3.8. *Nandu fanhui tu* (detail). From *Zhongguo lishi bowuguan*, pl. 184.

Liu's illustration, while referencing both traditional approaches to this type of image, also mixes them and incorporates them into a close-up view of the urban commoner's moment of participation in the festivity. It also highlights the mingling of genders, a theme that seems to have been particularly fascinating to Liu Ciquan, and also an aspect of the Lantern Festival quite familiar to seventeenth-century readers of vernacular literary works such as Ruan Dacheng's 阮大鋮 (1587–1646) play *Chundeng mi* 春燈謎 (Spring lantern riddles), in which riddle-solving on the night of the Lantern Festival sets in motion a romance between riddle solvers that is fraught with interruptions and misidentifications. Liu's illustration here again links the texts with a vision of *se*: the new urban life in the late Ming and its allure made manifest through musical, acoustic, visual, and verbal sleight-of-hand.

Fig. 3.9. *Guan deng tu (detail),* attr. Li Song 李嵩 (Song dynasty). From *Shinü hua zhi mei*, p. 25.

The first page of the division entitled "Banqueting Aids" (*you shang* 侑觴) (fig. 3.10) in the *Miaojin wanbao quanshu* sheds further light on the ways Ming illustrators and designers drew on and adapted visual and literary conventions. The allusion in this illustration is hard to miss: it is the gathering at the Orchid Pavilion, the iconic fourth-century event in which a group of cultural giants of the age gathered beside a stream for a springtime purification ceremony, where they banqueted and composed poems. It had since become the locus classicus for elegant gatherings in both literary and visual traditions. The illustration, appearing at the head of a section composed of drinking games and dice games, thus places and promotes these games as part of a long-standing elite cultural tradition.

The Orchid Pavilion gathering had long been a popular visual topos in Ming art, reflected in records of and poems on paintings as well as in numerous extant paintings from the period. It also appears in painting manuals, a flourishing print genre in the late Ming that presented a digest of motifs from pictorial traditions and provided blueprints for further reproductions in books and other media.[12] In creating a new version of this common pictorial exercise, the *Miaojin wanbao quanshu* woodblock illustrator emphasizes the informality and naturalness of the scene, depicting it as an event that might happen in his readers' own lifetimes, unlike the more "classical" renderings with their elegant pavilions, controlled atmosphere, and decorous gestures (fig. 3.11).[13] Note, also, that the division-head illustrations in the *Miaojin wanbao quanshu* are largely consistent in their view distance, indicating that another factor in the book's design is the consistency of style and perspective throughout the book itself.

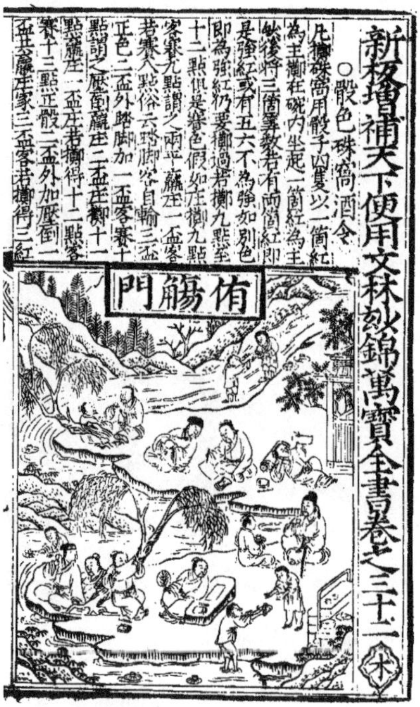

Fig. 3.10. Frontispiece to the "Banqueting Aids" 侑觴 division. From *CNRS*, vol. 14, p. 251.

Fig. 3.11. "Purification Ceremony at the Orchid Pavilion" *Lanting xiuxi tu* 蘭亭脩禊圖 (detail), Yongle reign, stone carving after Li Gonglin 李公麟 of the Song. From *Zhongguo meishu quanji*, vol. 19, p. 88.

The *Miaojin wanbao quanshu* division entitled "Laughing and Joking" (*Xiaotan men*) is an assemblage of jokes, humorous verbal games, and witty expressions. The heading illustration for this division (fig. 3.12) depicts three people: a Confucian scholar, a Buddhist monk, and a Daoist priest gesturing and laughing together, and alludes to the traditional episode designated by the phrase "three persons laughing at Tiger Creek" (*huxi san xiao*), involving the renowned medieval cultural figures Tao Yuanming 陶淵明 (364–427) the Confucian scholar, Lu Xiujing 陸脩靜 (406–77) the Daoist priest, and Huiyuan 慧遠 (334–416) the Buddhist monk.

This cultural anecdote enjoyed a rich pictorial life in the Ming.[14] One of the most distinctive and imaginative variants on the theme is an odd cartoon-like image of a triple-headed round figure, titled *Yituan heqi tu* 一團和氣圖 (One mass of cordial feeling), and attributed to the Chenghua emperor (r. 1465–87). The emperor's colophon relates the anecdote and a pictorial depiction of it called *Sanxiao tu* 三笑圖 (Three laughing ones):

> 朕聞晉陶淵明乃儒門之秀，陆脩静亦隱居學道之良，而惠遠法師則释氏之翹楚者也。法師居廬山，送客不過虎溪。一日，陶、陸二人訪之，與語道合，不覺送過虎溪，因相與大笑。世傳爲《三笑图》此豈非一團和氣所自邪？…　豈無斯人，輔予盛治。披圖以觀，有概予志。聊援筆以寫懷，庶以警俗而勵世。成化元年六月初一日。

> We have heard it said that, in the Jin, Tao Yuanming was the most excellent of the *Ru* school, Lu Xiujing the finest among recluses and learners of the Dao, and Master Huiyuan the supreme among Buddhists. Master Huiyuan dwelt on Mount Lu, and never crossed Tiger Creek when sending off guests. One day, Tao and Lu came to visit. On conversing with them Huiyuan found their ways accorded, so much so that when sending them off he crossed Tiger Creek without knowing it. They laughed heartily together at this. (The story) is transmitted in *The Picture of Three Laughing Ones*. Isn't this where "One Mass of Cordial Feeling" comes from? . . . Is there truly not such a person to assist me in achieving prosperous governance? As I spread out the painting to gaze on it, it stirs my deepest aspirations. For the moment, I take up brush to give vent to what I feel—perhaps this might serve to admonish common customs, and urge this age to higher things. Year One of the Era of Accomplished Transformation [Chenghua], first day of the sixth month (June 24, 1465).[15]

The emperor's painting was incorporated into woodblock publications such as the book *Qunxian ji* 群仙集 (A book of all immortals); a replica was also made as a stone carving in the Shaolin temple in Henan. The *Miaojin wanbao quanshu* illustration here again draws on this legacy of pictorial precedents to endorse the texts it accompanies as the continuation of a cultural tradition, as it re-enacts the heightened exercise in the illustrator's own trade of drawing. The illustration thereby opens up the reading of "Laughter and Banter" texts to a field of associations in cultural anecdote, transmitted images, imperial life, court politics,

Fig. 3.12. Frontispiece to the "Laughing and Joking" 笑談 division. From *CNRS*, vol. 14, p. 277.

and religious teachings. The "Three Laughing Ones" (*sanxiao tu* 三笑圖) became a favored conventional subject for woodblock prints, as seen, for example, in a version of the theme included in the block-printed book *Shishi yuanliu* 釋氏源流 (Spiritual descendants of the Buddha). The artists of these *Miaojin wanbao quanshu* illustrations, whether Liu Ciquan or others working within a similar style, composed their images by drawing on a repertoire of cultural traditions and visual practices of the era, and consistently related the matter of each of the encyclopedia's sections with iconic moments in the shared cultural history of Ming Chinese. The illustration of the lantern festival, further, displays a still closer connection with contemporary urban life and, together with the *Yugu xinhuang* cover page illustration, showcases Liu Ciquan's grasp of contemporary scenes in an urban setting.

Pictorial Variation in Drinking Scenes

As the above examples have begun to show, the complex webs of interrelation constituting the fields of medium and genre for woodblock illustrations mean that to read one illustration is always to read it against other illustrations and/or other visual or textual reference points. As suggested, for example, by the above example of the pictorial traditions surrounding the Orchid Pavilion gathering, the adaptation of extant visual traditions by woodblock illustrators may be viewed as the opportunistic recycling of extant visual compositions, or as drawing on images already familiar to the audience as a way of appealing to established tradition. At the same time, however, such adaptation may be seen as creatively tailoring classical models to the needs and sensibilities of a latter-day audience, or even as suggesting layers of ironic meaning in the gaps between such culturally significant moments and the often irreverent and lowbrow comic material that made up the substance of the divisions introduced by these images. We see a vivid example of visual meaning as difference, and of the ways in which shared visual composition and iconography could be adjusted "up" or "down" in tone by illustrators, in the comparison of a pair of Ming illustrations of drinking scenes.

The first example, "Farmer's Joy" (fig. 3.13), is from the *Bianmin tuzuan* 便民圖纂 (Illustrated compendium for the convenience of commoners) and the second, "A Picture of Joyful Drinking" (fig. 3.14), from the "Agriculture and Sericulture" (*Nong sang men* 農桑門) division

Fig. 3.13. "Farmer's Joy" (*tianjia le* 田家樂) from Kuang Fan's 鄺璠 (fl. mid-Ming dynasty) *Bianmin tuzuan* 便民圖纂, printed by Yu Yongqing 于永清, 1593. From *Xinbian Zhongguo banhua shi tulu*, vol. 6, p. 215.

of the *Miaojin wanbao quanshu*. The two illustrations are clearly versions of a shared type: in both pictures, amidst the chaos of intoxication, tilted wine jars, and flailing arms, the most noticeable detail is a person vomiting at the lower left corner. More interesting still is the skinny dog sniffing the vomit. The figure of the dog, while echoing the ancient idyllic vision from the *Laozi* of a peaceful agrarian society where "the crowing of cocks and barking of dogs can be heard, yet the people there grow old and die without ever visiting one another," reveals a particular brand of rural vulgarity (*cunsu* 村俗) in these visions of "Farmers' Joy" that contrasts with depictions of more fashionable celebrations and gatherings in urban settings.

Though they are clearly versions of the same basic design, these two illustrations differ in significant ways. Specifically, in figure 3.14, the revelers are adorned more neatly and appear somewhat less boisterous. The background has also been changed to an exquisite ornamental screen. The person who was sick has been promoted to a member of the rural gentry—there is a boy servant comforting him—and seems less hopelessly intoxicated. The whole picture celebrates the connection between a good harvest and a contented life. As for the dog, it is now obscured behind the vomiting person, consistent with the more controlled atmosphere of the whole scene. This picture reduces the air of country vulgarity (*cunsu*) and promotes in exchange an air of the village gentry (*xiangshen* 鄉紳); however, this joyful drinking still borders on being laughable. This picture itself hints at the idea of a comical spectacle: the two figures in the upper right corner are poking one another and calling each other's attention to the vomiting person. Their gaze signals to readers a self-consciousness about the act of looking in on or interpreting a scene, and an awareness of the boundary between the rural naiveté of those depicted in the scene versus the sophistication of those who observe and appreciate it.

These illustrations stimulate simultaneous and contradictory directions for reading. They package their books as cultural goods for circulation and project an ideal viewer who is urbane, knowledgeable, and playful. Illustrations bring new dimensions to the activity of reading and open up the relational space among illustration, text, and brush painting, decipherable in the context of networks of textual and pictorial conventions and reference points not at all limited to those of the texts

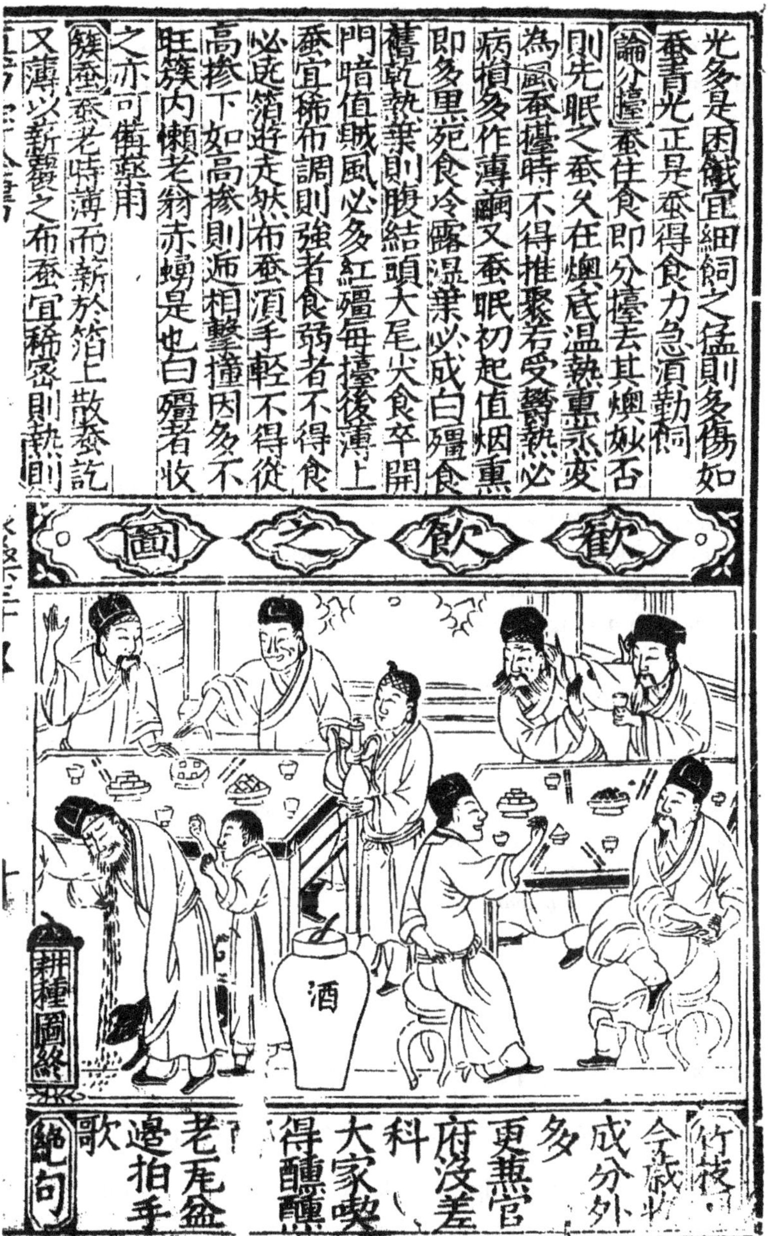

Fig. 3.14. "A Picture of Joyful Drinking" (*huanyin zhi tu* 歡飲之圖), in "Division of Agriculture and Sericulture" (農桑門), *Miaojin wanbao quanshu*. From *CNRS*, vol. 14, p. 213.

that the illustrations accompany. David Rolston has aptly observed that the close connection between the developments of vernacular fiction and commentary cultivated in readers a desire to join in a competition of wits with the authors and commentators to decode the meaning of the text.[16] In drawing from and translating between textual, verbal, and pictorial conventions, Ming woodblock illustrations seem to be taking part in the same process, opening up new imaginative spaces for readers to exercise their interpretive competence.

Popular Songs: Visual Variation and the Space of Performance

Visual variations in woodblock imprints were not limited to illustrations alone. Page layout and various techniques of xylographical composition could give new twists to circulating textual materials as well, with different xylographic realizations of the same written texts amounting to a kind of "printed performance." To see the dynamics of this process, let us begin with a song, circulated as lyrics to the tune named "Luojiang yuan" 羅江怨 (Luo River lament), that appears in the drama miscellanies *Baneng zoujin*, *Cilin yizhi*, and *Zhaijin qiyin*. The following passages are transcriptions of the texts as they appear in these three sources (see also figs. 3.15a–3.15c):

> 紗窗外　月正圓　淨手焚香禱告天　對天發下洪誓願　一不爲 自己身單　二不爲少吃無穿　三來不爲家不辦　爲只爲妙人兒　我的心肝　阻隔在萬水千山　千山萬水　難得見　告蒼天　早賜一陣神風　把冤家吹到眼前　那時方顯神明現[17] (*Baneng zoujin*, fig. 3.15a)

> 紗窗外，月正圓，洗手焚香禱告天，對天發下洪誓願。一不爲自己身單；二不爲少吃無穿；三來不爲家不辦。爲只爲妙人兒，我的心肝，阻隔在萬水千山，千山萬水難得見。告蒼天，早賜一陣神風，把冤家吹到跟前。那時方顯神明現。[18] (*Cilin yizhi*, fig. 3.15b)

> 紗窗外月兒圓洗手焚香禱告天對天發下紅誓ㄟㄟ[19]願一不爲自己身單二不爲少吃無穿三來不爲家不辦爲只爲玅人心肝阻隔在萬水千山千山萬水難得ㄟㄟ見望蒼天早賜順風把冤家吹到跟前那時方顯神明ㄟㄟ現[20] (*Zhaijin qiyin*, fig. 3.15c)

These texts are transcriptions of the same song, with only slight variations. The song is translated below:

> Outside the gauze window, the moon is just at the full,
> Cleaning my hands to burn incense, I pray to Heaven,
> To Heaven I swear this overflowing oath:

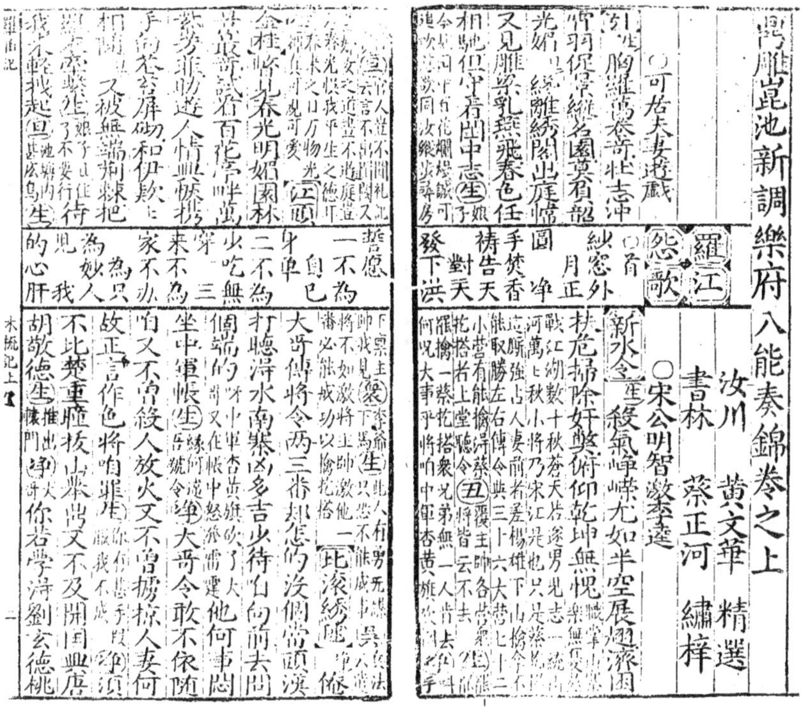
鼎雕崑池新調樂府八能奏錦卷之上

汝川　黃文華　精選

書林　蔡正河　繡梓

羅江怨歌

Fig. 3.15a. Two pages from *Baneng zoujin*. The song is seen in the middle register. From *SBXQCK*, vol. 5, pp. 10–11.

> First, it's not because of living alone by myself,
> Second, it's not because of lack of food or clothes,
> Third, it's not because my household is neglected—
> It's only because of a fine young man, my sweetheart,
> Blocked from me by ten thousand waters and a thousand mountains,
> A thousand mountains and ten thousand waters,
> So hard to see.
> I cry to you blue heaven, send me a gust of divine wind,
> To blow my lover back before my eyes,
> Once that happens, your divinity will be clearly seen!

The most obvious visual difference between these song transcriptions is their printing formats: *Baneng zoujin* uses empty spaces to indicate pauses, *Cilin yizhi* uses punctuation, and *Zhaijin qiyin* provides neither punctuation nor spacing, thus completely leaving it up to the reader to punctuate the song while making his or her way through the text.

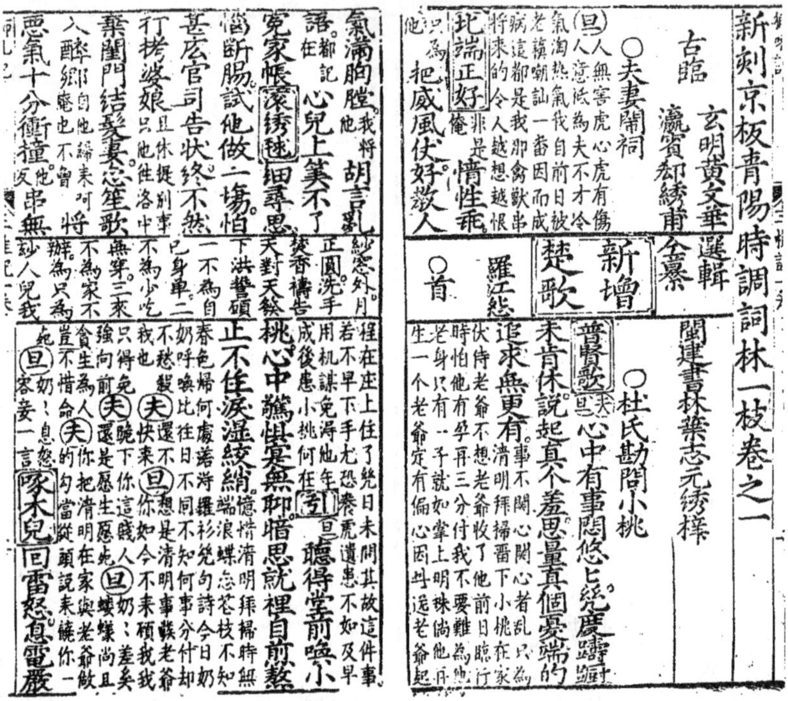

Fig. 3.15b. Two pages from *Cilin yizhi*. The song is seen in the middle register. From *SBXQCK*, vol. 4, pp. 8–9.

Printers' decisions about how to present their texts varied,[21] and the differently formatted pages they created led to varied reading experiences for buyers of these books.

While punctuated text is easy for any reasonably competent reader, non-punctuated text renders the process of reading a process of differentiation: those with enough knowledge or memory of the song would have been able to read through the text smoothly, while less competent readers would have had to read back and forth to figure out where the lines should break. In fact, the *Zhaijin qiyin* text, though it does not indicate pauses or line breaks by spaces or punctuation, is alone in designating the two-word phrases that are to be repeated toward the end of each of the three sections of the song simply as part of the musical rendering. In this sense the version that is graphically the least forthcoming about metrical structure might be the most explicit prompt text for a reader who knows the tune and wants to use the text as an aid to sing-

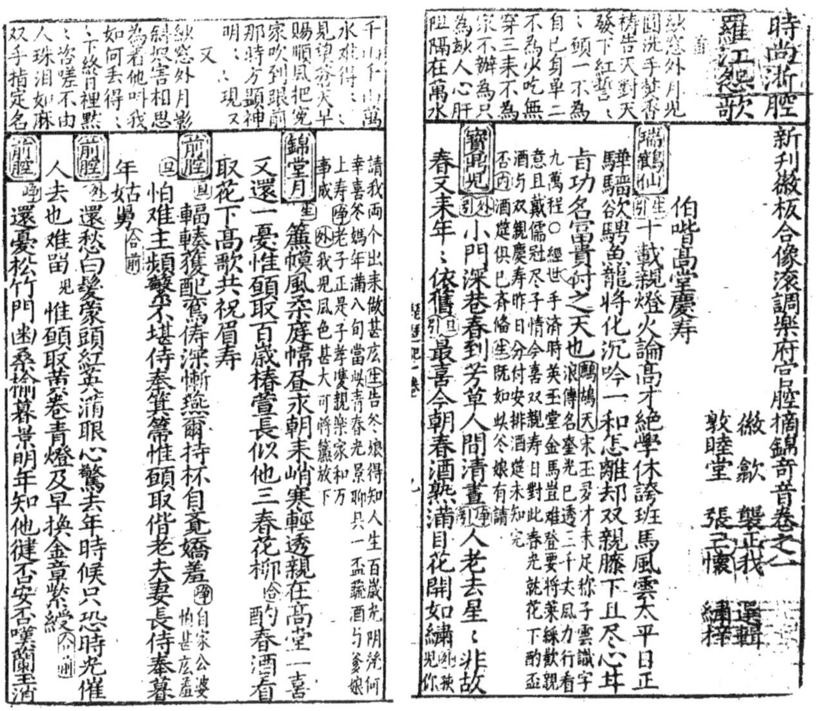

Fig. 3.15c. Two pages from *Zhaijin qiyin*. The song is seen in the top register. From *SBXQCK*, vol. 3, pp. 11, 14.

ing the lyrics. Thus different ways of formatting the text demand from readers varying degrees of familiarity with the milieu of songs that were popular at the time, and further differentiate among readers in terms of which books will be accessible to which audiences. Such freedom in the graphic realization of the "same" material means that the producers of drama miscellanies were unconcerned with adhering to orthographic standardization or editorial regularization. As a result, drama miscellanies claimed and created a space in printing culture vis-à-vis other models of editing etiquette, especially the norms governing the printing of orthodox works, which center on the fixity and proper presentation of written texts and aim to rigidly control those texts' social meaning.

Based on an implicit linkage between textual policing and moral order, overseers of orthodox printing projects held to exacting standards about proper print formulae relating to the proper employment of punctuation, to page format, and to the correct graphic forms of characters and their arrangement on the page.[22] Printing technology itself brings such questions of unified standards to the fore in a pointed way, and the idea that print reproduction without strict controls over format might bring about pernicious social or moral effects is familiar in other historical contexts as well. For instance, in recounting the effects of the introduction of layout conventions related to paragraphing of text in the sixteenth to eighteenth centuries in Europe, Roger Chartier observes, "The effects of breaking up Scripture in this manner were disastrous: it authorized every religious sect or party to found its legitimacy on the scriptural passages that seemed to support its views."[23] In China, the hastily produced and notoriously bad Jianyang imprints created to assist examinees in coping with the examination system triggered outrage among elite literati and government officials and led to censorship and punishment of those involved. Lucile Chia has compiled a list of government-issued pronouncements relating to the printing of texts connected with the examination system in the Song dynasty.[24] To quote just one exemplary record from this list, an education official named Su Yue requested in 1108 that "commercial editions of examination essays that are printed merely for profit and do not conform to the Way of the kings of antiquity be replaced by well-edited government editions."[25]

If the Jianyang commercial publishers' daring endeavor in the Song dynasty to benefit from the official "industry" of the examinations encountered harsh responses from the government, however, their ventures in the late Ming to cash in on the social desire for musical performance provoked little official concern. Thus drama miscellanies from the Ming convey a culture of printing given over to the whims of oral performance or performance in general, which features adaptability instead of fixity. Just as in the experience with oral performance, where the same song is sung differently each time, the formatting of the song varies each time when engraved onto a woodblock. In other words, the unstandardized textual and layout practices of these popular Ming song texts create a visual experience that may be viewed as a transference of the inherent variability of oral song performance into text. Such variations in textual "performances" of the song cited above appear not only in the xylographic presentation and page layout but also in the text itself. Note that "to clean hands to burn incense" is transcribed differently in *Baneng zoujin* and *Cilin yizhi*, as *jingshou fenxiang* (淨手焚香) and *xishou fenxiang* (洗手焚香), respectively. Similarly, the phrase "before one's eyes" is also transcribed differently—as *genqian* 跟前 in *Cilin yizhi* and *Zhaijin qiyin*, but *yanqian* 眼前 in *Baneng zoujin*. This transcribed indeterminacy presents to readers the lack of a strict "verbatim" in each repeated performance, even if the performer or narrator sincerely believes (s)he is giving a verbatim recitation.[26] The example of Li Mengyang 李夢陽 (1472–1530), the leading poet of the day and one of the Former Seven Masters, illustrates this point: when asked by a disciple about the songs he recommended using as a model, responded, "I cannot recall (the songs) completely. Just stroll around the streets and markets; there is sure to be someone singing them" 不能悉記也, 只在街市上閑行, 必有唱之者.[27] Memory (recollection) of oral text is never as fixed and sure as written text, which one can always glance back at and check against. For "they are sounds, you might 'call' them back—'recall' them. But there is nowhere to 'look' for them."[28] Specifically, memory does not reproduce song text in perfect completion but reproduces it with ellipses, add-ons, and changes. To transcribe the same song with slight variations can, therefore, present and evoke the experience and memory of oral performance to its readers.

The analogy with oral cultures of performance and memory may also shed light on the prevalence in drama miscellanies of so-called *baizi* 白字. By definition, the term *baizi* (lit. pale characters) refers to "wrong" characters that are used as homophonic prompts for the "correct" written character. In practice, in *baizi* the sound value of the character overtakes its significance as a written sign. For example, the *hongshi* (overflowing oath) is transcribed with the correct graph in both *Baneng zoujin* and *Cilin yizhi* as 洪誓—literally, a "flooding oath." However, *Zhaijin qiyin* uses its homophone *hong* 紅 (red) instead of the "correct" *hong* (flooding). Similarly, both *shunfeng* 順風 (in *Zhaijin qiyin*) and *shenfeng* 神風 (in *Baneng zoujin* and *Cilin yizhi*) are used in transcribing the sounds in the same position of the same line. *Shunfeng* (favoring wind), though it makes sense to certain extent, is most likely a dialect-based mis-transcription of *shenfeng* (magical breeze). *Baizi* become primarily aural prompts to a meaning that is unrelated to the significance of the written symbol; the dark characters on the page fade off into the colorless world of sounds.[29]

This is not to say that song texts in drama miscellanies faithfully recorded any particular real-time performance. The books are joint products of performance culture and printing practice. The fact that the particular "Luo River Lament" song under discussion appears as the first song text in all three collections is indicative of the printing reorganization that occurs in the process of committing songs to the printed page. Although it is possible that this song was the first song of some performance sequence, it seems more likely that printing it first simply evolved into a standard practice within a printing culture marked by pervasive recycling and imitation. Nevertheless, in this printing culture, the fluidity and immediacy often associated with orality is not erased, but transposed to an alternative medium between the covers of the book.

Student Zhang Jumps over the Wall: Generic Crossing and Transgression

Both the illustrations and the song texts examined above show that the meanings generated by woodblock texts are inseparable from the webs of reference, repetition, and variation that link them to other popular forms, which in turn shaped the reading possibilities for their readers. In other words, the recycling and recasting of extant material that woodblock book producers engaged in was not limited to the world of woodblock texts but was part of a larger network of other genres and media. Perhaps no case better illustrates the complexity of this network than the rich history of reproduction and rereading surrounding the famous episode from *The Story of the Western Wing* that came to be designated "Student Zhang Jumps over the Wall" (*Zhang sheng tiao qiang* 張生跳墻).

This episode, which was to provide the point of reference for innumerable reinterpretations and rereadings, itself hinges on reading and interpretation. Having received a poem from Yingying 鶯鶯, the beautiful daughter of a deceased chancellor, delivered by her maidservant, Hongniang 紅娘, Student Zhang both correctly and incorrectly interprets the text as an encrypted invitation to a romantic tryst. The poem is as follows:

待月西廂下	I await the moon beneath the western wing;
迎風户半開	receiving breeze, the door half-opens.
隔墻花影動	From across the wall, flowers' shadows stir;
疑是玉人來	I suspect that the jade one has arrived.[30]

Student Zhang naturally interprets "the jade one" as referring to himself, and "from across the wall, flowers' shadows stir" as an invitation for him to jump over the wall into the flower garden for a meeting with Yingying. Acting on his skills in poetic interpretation, Student Zhang leaps over the wall into the flower garden, thinking that the prophecy of the poem's suggestive lyrics will be fulfilled. What he does not anticipate is that Yingying will then claim that her poem, while she had indeed intended for Student Zhang to read and respond to it just as he has, had been simply a ruse to give her an opportunity to berate him for his presumption in seeking a liaison, particularly since he has become Yingying's sworn brother and therefore the protector of Yingying and her mother. Student Zhang leaves the garden, discomfited. The ambiguity of the poem and this scene is enhanced, however, when later in the play Yingying again uses another poem to indicate her intent and then arrives in Student Zhang's bedroom in the middle of the night, and they consummate their relationship. Both in itself and in its position within the drama as a whole, then, the episode of the poem and Student Zhang's first ill-fated nighttime outing is a signal instance in which text, author, and reader engage in a sustained struggle to produce a meaning that is always in flux.

As mentioned in chapter 1, the number of reprintings of *The Story of the Western Wing* dramatically increased in the late Ming, both reflecting and cementing the play's status as a household standard. An astonishing number of complete editions, more than sixty, of the *The Story of the Western Wing* are documented as having been produced in the late Ming.[31] Meanwhile, many drama anthologies excerpted highlights from the play. Their selections indicate that certain episodes enjoyed more popularity than others, and the episode referred to as "Student Zhang Jumps over the Wall," or "Student Zhang Jumps over the Whitewashed Wall" (*Zhangsheng tiao fenqiang* 張生跳粉墻), was among the most frequently reprinted. By the Wanli reign, representations of this episode, so pregnant with comic potential in its dramatization of thwarted desire, became increasingly rich, tantalizing, and torturing, both within the story for Student Zhang and for consumers of performance and text. Narrative details were varied, often quite ingeniously, and illustrations added to elaborate upon or heighten this dramatic moment. For example, the southern adaptation of *The Story of the Western Wing* (the

Nan Xixiang 南西廂, ca. 1522), often attributed to Li Rihua 李日華 (fl. sixteenth century), adds a scene in which Yingying and Hongniang play *wei qi* 圍棋, the board game also known as *go*, before student Zhang's leap over the wall.[32] Yingying and Hongniang engage in a conversation in which whatever they say about their game can also be understood as a double entendre referring to the romantic battle between Yingying and Student Zhang. The term *wei qi,* after all, is a long-established pun for "failing to honor an appointed rendezvous" (*wei qi* 違期).

Another example of variation is found in an excerpt from the *Zhaijin qiyin*, which is believed to closely reflect the stage practice of the time, entitled "Student Zhang Jumps over the Wall but Misses Out on a Tryst" (*Zhang sheng tiao qiang shi yue* 張生跳墻失約). In this excerpt, the act of "jumping" is agonizingly prolonged by the mischievous Hongniang. She frightens the timid, anxious, and insecure student Zhang into a panic by falsely reporting the approach of Yingying's mother, and makes Student Zhang walk along the wall to allow his anxiety to build while she claims to be searching for the perfect spot for him to jump down. When the earnest and unsuspicious student raises the question, "How can I jump over with my boots on?" Hongniang suggests he take them off and hold them in his mouth. When he has done that, Hongniang immediately calls out, "Mr. Zhang!" Student Zhang answers, "Yes!"—and the boots, of course, drop. When he is finally ready to jump and asks about the perfect spot, Hongniang informs him that it is right next to the privy.[33] The dramatic elements of the wall and the jump are more fully exploited in this version for potential to generate situational gags, with the boots and the privy being newly introduced elements that are particularly effective.

Variation in these editions and selections is not only a matter of reworking the dramatic material, but in some instances also involves contested interpretations of the meaning of the original text. For example, an enigmatic line in this episode sung by Hongniang, "when your fingers report back from duty worn out" (*shou zhi'er gao le xiao fa* 手指兒告了消乏),[34] seems to be bawdy teasing of how Student Zhang whiles away the time as he yearns for a tryst with Yingying. The Hongzhi edition of 1498 has no comment on this line, but the *Zhaijin qiyin* goes out of its way to supply dialogue that provides context for the line in the song, with the aim of diffusing any appearance of indecency and suggesting that Hongniang's expression refers to Student Zhang "calculating with his fingers":

[紅白：]張先生，我想軍圍普救之時，你下工夫筆尖下寫着那封書也，則費力來。爭奈夫人賺你，小姐卻留你，我想你只把指頭掐算，巴不得有今日呵。[唱]你指頭兒告了消乏。

[Hongniang speaks:] Mr. Zhang, I remember that when the (rebel) army surrounded the (Temple of) Universal Salvation, with great care and effort you wrote that letter under the tip of your brush—how strenuous! How difficult it is that the Madame set a trap for you, but our young missy makes you linger, I fancy that you count with your fingers all the time, you can't wait for a day like today. [Hongniang sings:] Your fingers report back from duty worn out.[35]

This interpretation was certainly not convincing for Wang Jide, who specifically notes in his commentary to this scene that "fingers report back from duty worn out" is an "indecent expression" (*xie ci* 褻詞).[36]

In addition to frequently featuring in new imprints of dramatic literature and in new stage performances, the "wall-jumping" episode also became a focal point for other forms of representation, including illustrations, popular songs, riddles, drinking games, and witticisms. Figures 3.16a–3.16f show a series of illustrations sampling the impact that visual art had come to exert on late Ming knowledge and memory surrounding this scene. These illustrations can be roughly divided into two groups in terms of the moments they capture, with some focusing on the moment just after the jump (figs. 3.16a, e, and f) and others focusing on the process of jumping, when we see student Zhang crawling on top of the wall.

Dated to 1498, figure 3.16a is the earliest known illustration of the wall-jumping scene. Here it seems as though Student Zhang need not have jumped but could just as easily have simply stepped over into the flower garden. However, this first impression has to be qualified by a survey of all the illustrations in this edition as a whole, where the height of the wall is consistent with the perspective of the rest of the illustrations in the book, which together occupy the book's entire top register. Figure 3.16b was made by the famous Huancui tang (see also chapter 2). The wall is now conspicuously higher, and student Zhang is awkwardly perched on top. This illustration suggests the increasing importance that the wall takes on in representations of the episode, a development that can be traced in both textual and pictorial sources. The following two figures are close in composition to this illustration, showcasing again the modeling, borrowing, and adaptation involved in the production of such materials. What is unique about the last two figures in this group is that they depict a theatrical pose similar to what the actors would

Fig. 3.16a. The earliest known illustration of the wall-jumping moment from *Xinkan qimiao quanxiang zhushi Xixiang ji* 新刊奇妙全相註釋西廂記. Beijing, 1498. The caption says, "Student Zhang Embraces Crimson by Mistake" (張生誤摟紅娘). The wall's height is insignificant. From *Guben xiqu congkan chuji*, vol. 2, 104B.

Fig. 3.16b. *Huancui tang yuefu Xixiang ji* 環翠堂樂府西廂記. Jinling 金陵, Wanli reign. Edited by Wang Tingne; illustrations cut by Chen Pinzhou et al. About a hundred years after the appearance of the illustration in figure 3.16a, the wall has obviously become an obstacle, indicating its rising visibility and significance in this narrative moment. From *Guben xiqu banhua tulu*, vol. 2, p. 170.

Fig 3.16c. *Chongjiao bei Xixiang ji* 重校北西廂記. Jizhi zhai 繼志齋, Jinling 金陵, Wanli reign. Note the very close connection with figure 3.16b. From *Guben xiqu banhua tulu*, vol. 2, p. 36.

Fig. 3.16d. *Zhaijin qiyin* of 1611. Another version showing elements common to figures 3.16b and 3.16c. From *SBXQCK*, vol. 3, p. 81.

Fig. 3.16e. *Xinke chuxiang yinzhu Li Rihua nan Xixiang ji* 新刻出像音註李日華西廂記. Fuchun tang 富春堂, Jinling, Wanli reign. This illustration, deviating from usual practice, represents a theatrical pose. The caption reads, "Student Zhang jumps over the whitewashed wall to join in playing chess." From *Guben xiqu congkan chuji*, vol. 33, *xiajuan* 下卷, 7B.

Fig. 3.16f. *Chongke Yuan ben tiping yinshi Xixiang ji* 重刻元本題評音釋西廂記. Liu Longtian's 劉龍田 Qiaoshan tang 喬山堂, Wanli reign. This figure is strikingly similar to figure 3.16e. The couplet reads: "Don't say his literary talent is as deep as the sea, he still cannot guess the real meaning of a four-line poem; no one would have expected that a courage of lust as big as heaven would make it easy to jump over a hundred-foot wall." The horizontal caption reads, "Jumping over the wall at night." From *Guben xiqu congkan chuji*, vol. 4, 1A.

Fig. 3.17. "Jumping over the Wall." Colored woodblock illustration. Min Qiji edition. From *Ming Min Qiji huike Xixiang ji caitu* 明閔齊伋繪刻西廂記彩圖.

have assumed on stage. Such direct mirroring of stage acting is quite rare in Chinese drama illustrations.[37] Each individual picture-maker finds in this narrative moment an opportunity to give rein to his own interpretive whimsy, the best example perhaps being Min Qiji's 閔齊伋 (1580–after 1661) rendering of the scene in his exquisite set of *Story of the Western Wing* illustrations (fig. 3.17), which circulated separately from the text of the play. His illustration depicts three Student Zhangs in all: one perched on top of the wall, his reflection in the water, and his shadow on the ground.[38]

The wall-jumping episode from *The Story of the Western Wing* also became a favorite topic in Ming popular songs. Here I will consider three such songs, the first to the tune name "Gua zhen'er" 掛眞兒,[39] and the other two under the tune name "Luo River Lament." The first song reads:

西廂記

張君瑞跳過月墻内,
崔鶯鶯問紅娘,
太湖石上站的是誰?

紅娘道姐姐，是張君瑞，
黃夜入人家，
非姦做賊拿.
姐妹們的相交，
ヒヒヒヒ
哥，豈有這個理？

"The Story of the Western Wing"

Zhang Junrui jumps across the moon-shaped wall;
Cui Yingying asks Hongniang who is standing on the Taihu rock.
Hongniang says sister that is Zhang Junrui,
having broken and entered in the dead of night.
If it was not for fornication, then it was for theft.
In the relations between brother and sister,[40]
In the relations between brother and sister,
Brother, Where is this permitted?[41]

The lyrics to the second song read:

時尚浙腔羅江怨歌

紗窗外，月影昏，
鶯鶯紅娘后花園內等。
一等等得更闌盡。
粉墻外站立張生，
太湖石倚着鶯鶯。
紅娘寄柬傳書傳書信，
那張生跳過墻來，
雙手接抱著鶯鶯。
輕言細語低聲兒問：
我爲你死裡逃生，
你緣何不下顧學生？
學生爲你憂成憂成病。[42]

Popular Tune from Zhejiang, A Song of "Luo River Lament"

Outside the gauze window
the moonlight is dim.
Yingying and Hongniang wait in the back flower garden,
they wait and wait until past midnight.
Outside the whitewashed wall stands the student Zhang,
against the Taihu rock leans Yingying.
Hongniang has delivered the letter and transmitted a message,
so that student Zhang jumps over the wall,
and with both arms he embraces Yingying.

In low and tender tone he asks:
Because of you, I have been tortured between life and death—
Why don't you descend to take care of me?
Because of you, I am sick with anxiety.

The third song is quite similar to the second in a way that suggests the operation of orally transmitted literature, where it is common for similar but not completely identical works to constantly emerge:

楚歌羅江怨

紗窗外，月正明，
張生月下等鶯鶯，
一等等得更闌靜。
粉墻外，站立張生，
太湖石，斜倚鶯鶯。
紅娘遞柬傳書信，
那張生跳過墻來，
雙手兒摟抱鶯鶯，
輕言細語低聲問：
肯不肯見憐小生？
我爲你死裡逃生，
生生死死憂成病。[43]

A song of the Chu region, "Luo River Lament"

Outside the gauze window
the moonlight is bright.
Student Zhang under the moonlight waits for Yingying.
He waits and waits until past midnight.
Standing outside the whitewashed wall is Student Zhang;
inclined against the Taihu rock leans Yingying.
Hongniang has delivered the letter and transmitted a message,
so Student Zhang jumps over the wall.
With both hands he takes Yingying to his arms,
in low and tender tone he asks:
Won't you take pity on me, this student?
Because of you, I have been tortured between life and death;
Between life and death I am sick with anxiety.

Songs and illustrations like these both draw on and reinforce a vocabulary of the visual-textual associations, for example, the link alluded to in the preceding chapter between the Taihu rock and the clandestine tryst. They also build on a memory of the play and relate to the play in several ways: descriptive narration, direct quotation, and paraphrase.

Descriptive narration recounts the story or actions. Take the first song as an example: the beginning of this song, "Zhang Junrui jumps across the moon-shaped wall," opens the memory of the episode. Following these lines is a direct quotation from the play: "Having broken and entered in the dead of night/if it was not for fornication, then it was for theft." The original aria from the play is sung by Hongniang:

> 誰著你賫夜入人家，
> 非奸做賊拿。
> 你本是個折桂客，
> 做了偷花漢；
> 不想去跳龍門，
> 學騙馬。
>
> Who had you *break and enter in the dead of night?*
> *If it was not for fornication, then it was for theft!*
> You are a cassia-plucking man
> Who's turned into a flower-filching lout!
> You don't want to jump across the dragon's gate
> But do want to learn how to mount a mare.[44]

A third mode of the song-play relation is paraphrase, which opens the possibility for the song to depart from the play and makes independent use of the dramatic material. In the play, Yingying scolds Student Zhang by saying:

> 張生雖有活人之恩，恩則云報。既爲兄妹，何生此心？…若更爲之，與足下決無干休。
>
> Although you, sir, have done the favor of saving my life—and a favor should be repaid—how, since we have become sworn brother and sister, could you have this thought? . . . If you ever do this again, I will not let you off so easily. (Hongzhi edition, 106B)

The words in the play *Jiwei xiongmei, hesheng cixin* (Since we have become brother and sister, how could you have this thought?) become in the song *Xiongmeimen de xiangjiao, qiyou zhe ge li* (In the interaction between brother and sister, where is this permitted?) One subtle change is from the vague *jiwei* (since we have become . . .) to the action-replete *xiang jiao* (relation or interaction), which leads the memory to the actual exchange of passion and desire between Student Zhang and Yingying. Since *xiang jiao* was often used in Ming popular songs for romantic courting, the very use of this phrase also tinted the line with an air of illicit sentiment. In this way, the song creates an intimate bond with its audience by evoking the unspoken secret of desire.

In the late Ming, popular songs like these were performed most often at private gatherings when singsong girls or courtesans were summoned to entertain a private party in a banquet. Sometimes, male guests themselves might also join the singing and performing. In the context of their typical performance setting, songs were most effective socially when they cultivated a sense of intimacy and a special bond, one whose allure draws from the way it may hover on the boundary between fantasy and reality.[45] In this way, these late Ming songs are laden with romantic and erotic sentiments.

The songs' typical structure also contributes to their effectiveness in this performance setting. The "Gua zhen'er" lyric, for example, begins with a third-person narrator relating "Zhang Junrui jumps across the moon-shaped wall" but soon slips into direct speech ("Hongniang says") in which the singer assumes the voice of Hongniang: "Sister, that is Zhang Junrui." At the lyric's close, the impersonation of Hongniang is taken a step further as the singer, in the voice of Hongniang or possibly Yingying, addresses a plea to her listener: "Brother, where is this permitted?" All three of these songs end with this sort of direct address to the listener. In the other two songs, a narrator steps into the role of Student Zhang and begs for Yingying's care and pity. One says, "Why don't you descend to take care of me?" And the other closes with the appeal, "Won't you take pity on me, this student?" Such appeals can be read both within the frame of the drama *and* as reaching beyond the frame, to address and involve the listener—perhaps even to address the listener as a Student Zhang. After all, the pleasure of flirtatious banter with female performers is part of the explicit program of banqueting in good fashion.

Late Ming popular publications also circulated riddles based on the wall-jumping episode:

果名

相國行祠遇解張
良緣配合托紅娘
海棠花下傳書札
約我佳期到粉墻
(梅杏)

[A Riddle on] Fruit Names

At the temporary shrine of the Chancellor, Yingying meets Student Zhang,
a good romance is brought about all because of Hongniang.

Below the crabapple flowers she has delivered the letter,
and invited me to the whitewashed wall for a romantic tryst.[46]
(*Answer*: "plum and apricot")

The answer is 梅杏 *meixing* (plum and apricot), a homophone for *meixing* 沒興 ("no good mood" or "disappointment"), which the answerer of the riddle is to call to mind by remembering the disappointing outcome of Student Zhang's leap into the garden. In addition, one may find drinking-game verses based on the wall-jumping episode:

鶯鶯後園燒夜香。甚麼時候?一更盡，二更初。　勾引張生跳粉墻。墻有多少高?四丈少，三尺餘。 一股金釵爲表記有多少重?五錢六分七釐八毫九絲十忽。 夫人聞知打紅娘。打了多少?打了十十一十二。

[A Verse of Drinking Game]

Yingying burns incense at the back flower garden, What time? The end of the first watch, the beginning of the second. She entices student Zhang to jump over the whitewashed wall. How high is the wall? Lower than four *zhang*, higher than three *chi*. A piece of gold hairpin presented as token, what does it weigh? Five *qian* six *fen* seven *li* eight *hao* nine *si* ten *hu*. The Madame discovers it and beats Hongniang. How many times? Ten, eleven, twelve.[47]

The verse is chanted to accompany dice throwing. Each throw is accompanied by one line. For example, a player would throw the dice and chant, "Yingying burns incense at the back flower garden,/ What time?/ The end of the first watch, the beginning of the second." If the dice-throw matches the numbers being recited, then the player drinks. Afterwards, the turn would pass on to the next participant, who would chant the second line and throw the dice.[48]

This episode is also captured in "winsome sayings" like the following one cited in chapter 1:

張生跳粉墻—偷花賊[49]

Student Zhang jumps over the whitewashed wall—a "flower thief" [i.e., a womanizer].

The different genres through which the scene is recounted all function within the memory of the episode, but they also contribute to the openness of the memory by bringing changes and variations in their own generic language. For example, the excerpt from *Zhaijin qiyin* indicates how stage performance differs from the shared dramatic text and develops the comic potential of that text. In the drinking game, the verse retells the episode of "Student Zhang jumps over the wall," but also adds new detail—the gold hairpin—by way of tailoring the narrative to suit the requirements of the dice game that the chanted words incorporate numbers from five to ten.

Although the texts, pictures, and games inventoried above are far from an exhaustive survey of late Ming retellings and representations of "Student Zhang jumps over the wall,"[50] they are sufficient to demonstrate an intense energy in cross-generic reproduction that appears almost obsessive. As concrete reproductions of this scene proliferated across a wide range of popular forms such as written texts, visual images, oral performances, and party games, the interweaving of aesthetic experience and daily pleasure filtered back and forth between genres and from old renderings to new ones, constituting a mode of reading that fuses the textual and visual. Texts and pictures were displayed, related, and explicitly and implicitly embedded within each other in such a way that the reading of one text or picture evokes and implicates a range of others.[51] Meanwhile, the circulation of these texts also made possible the reproduction of social relations, whether it be between a singer and her audience, or among players of a game, fellow banqueters, or drama connoisseurs. With all their apparent arbitrariness, such entwined relations of borrowing and cross-fertilization are instrumental to the process of establishing meaning, a process that also involves the negotiation of social relationships within the play as well as among the audience members who interpret it and put it to their own uses.

The dense stratigraphy of accumulated textual and visual renderings of this emblematic dramatic and psychological moment offers many possible registers of memory, with each genre bringing its own languages and conventions. What happened in the original episode becomes open to modification to suit each genre's own particular needs and to satisfy the whims of each successive text- or picture-maker. Each genre recalls the old layer of memory when adding new layers. In the end, the memory of this episode becomes informed by a (con)fusion of genres, with sometimes conforming and sometimes conflicting messages. In other words, as the narrative moment of the "wall-jumping" becomes obsessively reproducible, any single reliable version of events or any single textual authority disappears. Instead, the visual pleasure, the play of oral reperformance (as manifested by the popular songs), and wit (as manifested by the riddle and "winsome saying") shape the fluid transformation of this iconic scene. In the center of this (con)fusion, there forms an accumulative, cross-generic, and conflicted collective memory of the "same" episode, whose suggestive power is heightened rather than weakened by the impossibility of definitively pinning it down.

It is within this field of reproduction that "Student Zhang jumps over the wall," beginning as a moment that is narrated within a text, becomes an expression that narrates a complex range of situations outside the text. The mere mention of the phrase recalls one's reading, seeing, and experiencing of the episode, a moment in which the recaller-reader becomes the co-author of this episode. It is also through this reproduction that "wall-jumping" became part of the common vocabulary of everyday life. This is quite clearly demonstrated in the "winsome saying" example, where the conclusion can be left unspoken on the basis that everybody knows what "Student Zhang jumps over the wall" means. In the end, the phrase *Zhangsheng tiaoqiang* became deeply implanted into the collective and enduring cultural memory of Ming readers, in functioning as a mobilizing reference to a wide variety of texts, pictures, and practices. In this process we glimpse the formation and operation of cultural references in Ming China, when a reference is socially valuable and viable not necessarily for its connection to an established authorial voice, but because of its openness to a large field of cultural reproduction.[52]

Texts, Charts, and Pictures of the Foreign Tribute Ceremony

The range and variety in the circulation and variation of the wall-jumping episode point to the oft-noted centrality of dramatic culture in the formation of late Ming identity and sensibility.[53] The question of how Ming Chinese reflected on their collective identity, however, emerges more clearly in texts reflecting the period's imagination of imperial spectacle, particularly in its relations with the world beyond. The imagination of exotic worlds beyond the Ming empire will be taken up for discussion in the following chapter. Here, as a final example of the way texts and meanings are recycled and reshaped in circulation within the culture of Ming woodblock imprints, I will examine a series of representations of one of the most significant imperial spectacles in defining the

Ming imperium in relation to regions beyond: the ceremony for court appearances and tribute submission by foreign kings.

Imperial rituals like that conducted for receiving foreign kings are complex subjects in part because these rituals themselves are a kind of representation, ideally intended to manifest and give ritual articulation to relations of power and deference within a broader cosmic order. Such rituals would also themselves have been part of a performance tradition that was derived largely from texts. That is, performance of such rites was the fruition of a meticulous procedure of interpretation of traditional texts of ritual and court protocol. Learning to stage, perform, and comprehend such ritual acts and their scripts was an important dimension of the imperial project of education aimed at forming a competent class of administrative elites.[54]

Others, including not only foreigners but also non-elite Ming subjects, however, might find this punctilious ritual language impenetrable. Sui Jingchen's 睢景臣 (ca. 1273–1320) song suite entitled "Gaozu Returns to His Home" includes an aria that plays up the comic potential in a rustic villager's inability to decipher the symbolic language of an imperial procession: he misreads all the imperial symbols in terms of his own quotidian experience, seeing the banner of the flying phoenix, for example, as a chicken learning to dance, and the banner of the flying tiger as a dog growing two wings.[55] We might assume the point of such comedy to be to poke fun at the villager for his ignorance, but the song suite builds up to a moment of recognition when the villager realizes the central figure in all this outlandish display is his own former fellow townsperson—one, moreover, who used to cheat in his everyday dealings and refuse to repay his debts. Upon this realization of the "true" identity of the newly minted Han emperor, the villager-viewer now wants to settle scores with him: "I say [your name is] Liu the Third [*Liu san* 劉三]!—someone grab him—why in the world did you change your family and given names and now call yourself Han Gaozu?" The villager here takes the imperial title of "Emperor Gaozu of the Han dynasty" as simply a change of name to Han (surname), Gaozu (given name).[56] Clearly, the portrayal of imperial pageantry as something that became mere bewildering spectacle held some subversive potential.

Court Norms and Ritual Manuals

The Ming, from the time of its founder, had adopted a policy of promulgating texts from the emperor and more generally texts reflecting court protocols and court norms and standards as part of a program of propaganda designed to develop a motivated and informed citizenry.[57] In the case of the rituals for receiving foreign kings, textual accounts and representations run a wide gamut. On one end are texts that directly reflect the terminology, norms of expression, and perspectives of the ritual experts who were involved, or might potentially become involved, in actually staging such ceremonies. These approximate or partially duplicate the formal protocol documents that would have not simply described but prescribed how the rite was to be performed. At the other end were texts and images reflecting a vernacular imagination of how such moments "ought" to look, drawing on the vocabularies of other social milieus and of other widely disparate sorts of texts in circulation that provided useful vocabularies for imagining such moments. Taken as a whole, these examples provide yet another illustration of the ways in which the producers of texts and the associated practical and representational conventions played an active role in the shaping and dissemination of knowledge about the world, and particularly the formation of a view of the world that was capable of being assimilated to the horizons of the householder, or commoner reader of books.

As two major expressions of the Ming imperial house, of the Ming state, and Ming society, the *Da Ming huidian* and *Da Ming jili* 大明集禮 (Collected rites of the grand Ming) went through several revisions and reprintings throughout the Ming. In both of these texts, the sections on *fan guo li* 蕃國禮 (rites for foreign/tribute states) form a significant proportion of the whole. Among the rites for foreign states, the *fan wang laichao yi* 蕃王來朝儀 (deportment protocols for court appearances by foreign kings) is a centrally important site for prescribing the ritual reception of foreign tribute missions and for imagining the relations between the Ming sovereign and foreign powers.[58] In a real sense, the proper performance and recording of these rituals is both a representation and a symbolic enactment of a Ming cosmic order, and even if the substance of the ritual is directed towards the assertion of Ming preeminence over foreign rulers, the real impact and significance of such rites and their multilayered networks of representation lay in the way they presented a vision of ritual and political meaning and collective identity for domestic audiences.

The following text is a page from the *Da Ming huidian* entry on the "deportment protocols for court appearances by foreign kings" (fig. 3.18). Very close in its language to ritual manuals, in its appearance on the page the text also adheres to ritualistic protocols for respecting and reinforcing imperial prestige and authority. When terms directly related to the emperor appear, they always begin a new line at the very highest position on the page. Second in stature are imperial buildings, which always start a new line, from a position one space lower than the very top. Lines that merely continue from the preceding line in ordinary sequence begin from a default position three spaces below the top of the page. To convey something of the sense of this graphic hierarchy, the translation below places these "privileged" terms at the beginnings of lines as well, with the highest-level terms in boldface and the second-highest in italics:

> (禮部告示侍儀司，以)蕃王及其從官具服於天界寺，習儀三日，擇日朝見。前一日，内使監陳設御座香案於奉天殿，尚寶司設寶案於御座前。侍儀司設蕃王與其從官次於午門外。蕃王拜位於丹墀中道稍西，及御座之南。其從官拜位，於蕃王丹墀拜位之後，俱北向。設方物案於丹墀之北中道東西，方物狀案於御前及丹墀中。受方物官位於方物案之東西，知班二人位於蕃王拜位之北，引蕃王舍人二人位於蕃王之北。引蕃王從官舍人二人位於蕃王從官之北，俱東西相向。餘如朝會儀。是日鼓初嚴，禮部陳方物於午門外，舉案者就案；次嚴，執事官俱入就位，接伴舍人、引班舍人引蕃王及其從官立俟於午門外；三嚴，文武官具朝服，入就俟立位。執事者舉方物案，蕃王等從其後，由西門入奉天西門，至殿前丹墀西俟立。侍從奉迎皇帝具禮服御輿以出。大樂鼓吹振作，陞座，樂止，捲簾，鳴鞭，報時訖。

> (The Ministry of Rites sends a proclamation to the Bureau of Deportment that the)[59] foreign king and his attending officers are to prepare their regalia at Tianjie temple, where they are to practice their deportment for three days, after which a day shall be chosen for their audience. On the day before the audience, palace attendants are to array the
> **Imperial Seat** and offering tables in
> *Fengtian Hall*; the Bureau of Treasures is to array the Treasure Table before the
> **Imperial Seat**; the Bureau of Deportment arranges the positions for the foreign king and his attending officers outside the
> *Meridian Gate*. The position for the foreign king to make obeisance is by the central pathway of the crimson stair, slightly to the west, and to the south of the
> **Imperial Seat**. The positions for the obeisance of his attendant officers are behind the foreign king's position for obeisance beside the crimson stair. All face northwards. The tables for the regional offerings are arrayed to the north of the crimson stair, to the east and west of the central pathway, and tables bearing registers of the regional products, before the

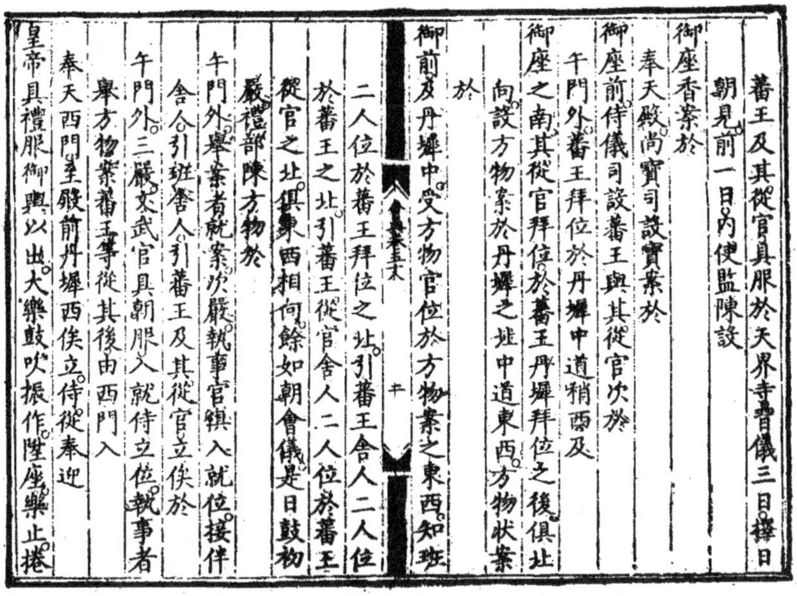

蕃王及其從官具服於天界寺習儀三日擇日
朝見前一日內使監陳設
御座香案於
奉天殿尚寶司設寶案於
御座前侍儀司設蕃王與其從官次於
午門外蕃王拜位於丹墀中道稍西及
御座之南其從官拜位於蕃王丹墀拜位之後俱北
向設方物案於丹墀之北中道東西方物狀案
於
御前及丹墀中受方物官位於方物案之東西知班
二人位於蕃王拜位之北引蕃王舍人二人位
於蕃王之北引蕃王從官舍人二人位於蕃王
從官之北俱東西相向餘如朝會儀是日鼓初
嚴禮部陳方物於
午門外舉案者就案次嚴執事官俱入就位接伴
舍人引班舍人引蕃王及其從官立俟於
午門外三嚴文武官具朝服入就侍立位執事者
舉方物案蕃王等從其後由西門入
奉天西門至殿前丹墀西俟立侍從奉迎
皇帝具禮服御輿以出大樂鼓吹振作陞座樂止捲

Fig. 3.18. "Deportment protocols for court appearances by foreign kings." From *Da Ming huidian*, p. 1001.

Imperial Seat in the middle of the crimson stair. Officials receiving the regional offerings are positioned to the east and west of the tables for regional offerings, and two ritual attendants are positioned to the north of the position for the obeisance of the foreign king. Two court men-in-waiting charged with leading in the foreign king take positions to the north of the foreign king: two court men-in-waiting charged with leading in the foreign king's attendant officers take positions to the north of the foreign king's attendant officers to the east and west, facing one another. The remaining details follow the protocol for court audiences. On the day itself, when the first drumming has sounded, the Ministry of Rites lays out the regional products outside the

Meridian Gate, and those charged with bearing the table take their places by the table. At the second drumming, the attending officials all enter and take their positions, while the receiving court men-in-waiting and the escort of court men-in-waiting guide the foreign king and his attendant officers to wait outside the

Meridian Gate. At the third drumming, the civil and military officials take up their places in their court regalia. Those in attendance bear the table for regional products, and the foreign king and the rest of them follow after, entering from the west gate to the west gate of the

Fengtian compound and standing in waiting before the hall to the west of the crimson stair. The attendants and retinue, in full court regalia, receive the

Emperor in his ceremonial garments as he emerges upon the imperial litter.

> Grand Music begins; and when the rise to the imperial seat is complete, it ceases. The curtain is pulled back, and the whip cracked, announcing the hour.

The passage continues with the prescription for the performance of the tribute submission ritual:

> 蕃王及其從官各就拜位。執事者以方物案置蕃王拜位前。贊拜。樂作。蕃王及其從官皆四拜。樂止。引班導蕃王陞殿，宣方物官取方物狀從行。俱由西陛。樂作，從殿西門入。内贊接引蕃王至御前，樂止，贊拜。蕃王再拜，跪，稱茲遇某節，欽詣皇帝陛下稱賀。致詞訖，宣方物官跪於御前西宣狀，承制官跪承制詣蕃王前立，宣制訖，贊拜，蕃王俯伏，興，再拜，蕃王及宣方物狀官俱由西門出。樂作。復位。樂止。贊拜。樂作。蕃王及其從官皆四拜。樂止。禮畢。鳴鞭。皇帝興，樂作，至謹身殿，樂止。引班導蕃王及其從官俱出見皇太子。
>
> The foreign king and his attendant officials all assume their positions for making obeisance. The attendants place the tables of regional products before the position for the foreign king's obeisance. The call is issued to perform obeisance; the music begins. When the foreign king and his attendant officials have bowed four times, the music ceases. The escorts lead the foreign king to ascend into the hall, and the official in charge of announcing the regional products takes up the register of regional products and follows them. They all mount from the west side. The music begins, and they enter through the west door of the hall. The ritual majordomo receives the foreign king and leads him before the imperial seat. The music stops, and the call is issued to perform obeisance. The foreign king bows twice, and, kneeling, says that on such and such an occasion he has the honor of presenting himself before the throne of the emperor to offer his congratulations. When he has finished his speech, the official charged with announcing the regional products kneels before the imperial seat, to the west side, and reads the register; the official charged with bearing the imperial command kneels to receive the command and goes before the foreign king, where he stands to read the command. When the reading is finished, the call is issued to perform obeisance. The foreign king prostrates himself, then rises, and bows twice. The foreign king and the official charged with announcing the register of regional products all go out through the west door. The music begins, and they return to their original positions. The music ceases. The call is issued to perform obeisance. The music begins. The foreign king and his attendant officials all bow four times. The music stops. The rite is complete. The whip is cracked. The emperor rises, and the music begins; when he has arrived at Jinshen Hall, the music ceases. The escort leads the foreign king and his attendant officials together to have an audience with the imperial heir.

Here the orderliness of ceremony is mirrored by the orderliness of text. The laying in readiness of every accoutrement of the ceremony, signaled by the word *she* 設, is related in scrupulous detail, and most of the participants are designated by phrases that serve both as dignified ritual titles and as functional statements of their roles in the ritual (as, e.g., with the term "ring-bearer" in some modern Western wedding ceremonies): the table-bearers, the escorts, the readers of the register of offerings and of the imperial command, and so on. The orderly flow of time is carefully punctuated, first by the three days the foreigners will spend learning the proper execution of the ritual, by the time set aside the day before for the advance preparations, and then by a strict choreography of the final predawn assembly, the sequence of three drum warnings, and finally the crack of the whip that announces the start of the ceremony proper. The presentation of the offerings and the foreign king's court appearance unfold in a time of ritual, punctuated by music.

Another account of this ceremony appears in the *Da Ming jili*. In addition to offering an even more detailed textual record of the ceremony, the *Da Ming jili* account differs from that of the *Da Ming huidian* in that it provides a visual representation of the ceremony. Appropriately, as one might imagine when trying to keep track of the intricate spatial arrangements in the scripts for the rite, this visual representation takes the form not of a picture but of a chart (*tu* 圖) (fig. 3.19).[60]

Text and chart center the position of the emperor in different ways. The text, while intermittently specifying the positional and hierarchical relations that govern the ceremony, and reinforcing the sense of the centrality and prestige of the emperor in the ceremony by its system of raised line-beginnings, for the most part follows a single chronological sequence from beginning to end. The chart, by contrast, draws heightened attention to the two crucial moments in this sequence when the foreign king bows down, marked on the chart by the "position for the obeisance of the foreign king" (*fanwang baiwei* 藩王拜位). More so than the text, the chart highlights the "obeisance of the foreign king" as the primary spectacle of the whole ritual.[61]

Both *Da Ming jili* and *Da Ming huidian* were printed as instruction manuals for the inner and outer courts (*zhongwai* 中外), as the imperial preface states: "(This is) to serve as models and rules for ten thousand generations, and for our sons and grandsons to guard for generations and to obey, practice, and continuously implement" (允爲萬世之法程，子孫之所世守而遵行推衍之也).[62] Their purported purpose of prescription as the *dian* 典 (norms) helped, however, to make the complex visual code of the imperial equipage and imperial visuality intelligible to a broad readership, as the general reader would be able to purchase a set of *Da*

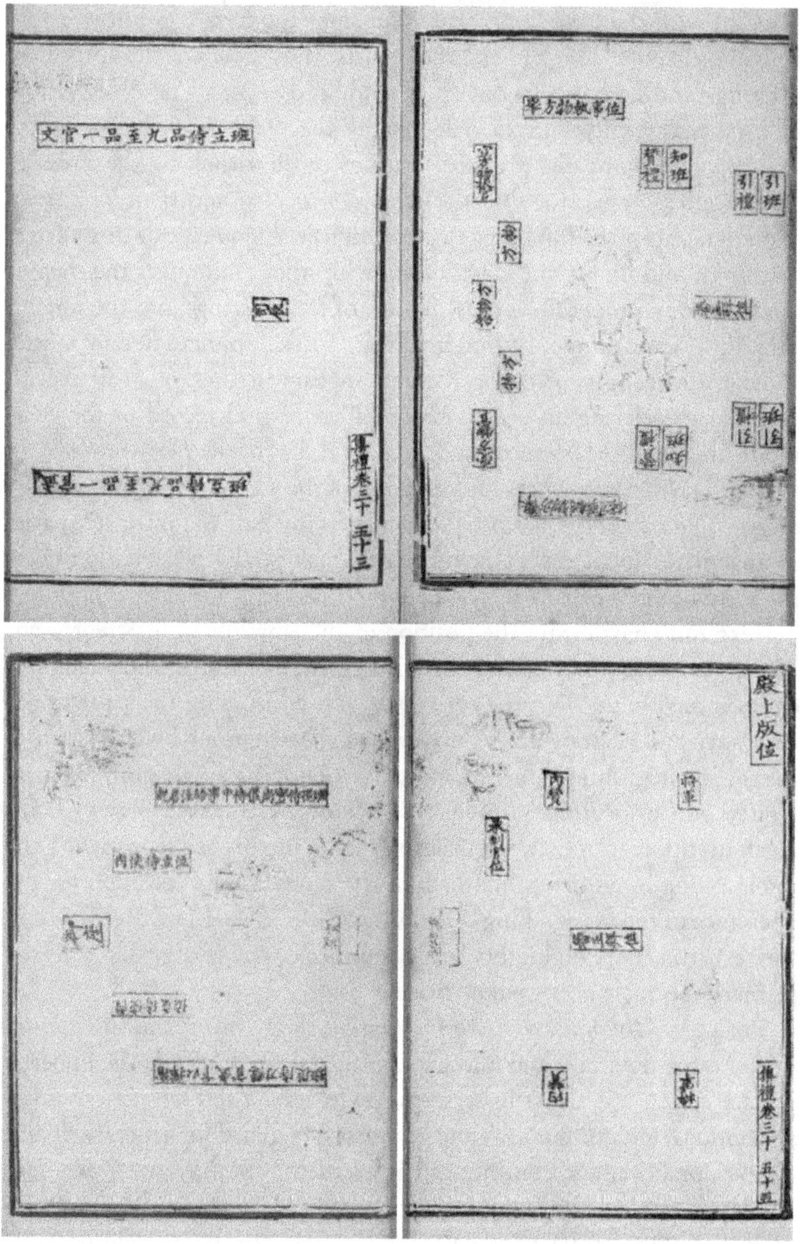

Fig. 3.19. Two moments in the chart of "Ritual for the Foreign Kings," in the *Da Ming jili* (printed in the Jiajing reign), highlighting the "position for the obeisance of the foreign king" as the primary spectacle of the whole ritual procession. Photo courtesy of the C. V. Starr East Asian Library, University of California, Berkeley.

Ming huidian in a bookstore.[63] Further, books such as *Sancai tuhui* that gained great popularity as household encyclopedias and that served not to prescribe but to display, share, and promote knowledge also included both the text and chart. In their own ways, each of these books fostered visual literacy, particularly literacy in the symbolism of imperial spectacle, which contributed to the formation of good Ming citizens. They also provided a system of reference and a symbolic language for the visual representations of appearances by foreign dignitaries at the Ming court in daily-use encyclopedias, which I will discuss in the following section.

Illustrating the Coming of the Barbarians

Along with the imperially sanctioned imprints like those discussed above, a number of texts with more popular and market-driven impulses intervened in forming the popular imagination of these spectacles of foreign dignitaries' appearances at the Ming court. A unique representative of the commonplace books' use and depiction of this theme is seen in the division devoted to "Various Foreigners" in daily-use encyclopedias. This division, divided into top and bottom registers following the usual format of these encyclopedias, features a list of "strange beings of mountains and seas" in the top register, and a list of barbarians of various lands in the bottom, both in the form of a gallery of pictures with captions. Chapter 4 discusses the details of the compilation and circulation of these pictures and textual descriptions. In the context of the present discussion, I will here first take a preliminary look at two of the frontispiece illustrations for these encyclopedic divisions, which take this very ceremony of the tribute-offering as their reference point in creating visual emblems to introduce the textual world of lore about foreigners compiled within. The first noticeable feature of these illustrations is that, in keeping with the content and format of the encyclopedic division, these illustrations are *hua* (pictures) instead of *tu* (charts), and their compositions reveal a great deal about how the vernacular woodblock illustrations intervened in the circulation of knowledge about, and images of, the Ming imperial spectacle as directed outward toward foreigners.

Let us first look at the compositions themselves (figs. 3.20 and 3.21). These illustrations, which are from two daily-use encyclopedias, appear at the heads of divisions with the rubric "Various Barbarian Lands." Both

Figs. 3.20 and 3.21. Illustrations in *Wanshu yuanhai* 萬書淵海 (1610, Fujian) and *Wanyong zhengzong buqiuren* 萬用正宗不求人 (1609, Fujian). From *CNRS*, vol. 6, p. 185; vol. 10, p. 455.

illustrations bring readers directly into the interior space of the imperial court and depict what, as seen in the ritual texts discussed above, was perceived as the most spectacular moment of the whole ritual process, namely the moment when "foreigners present tribute" (*Fan jin gong* 番進貢)—the very words appearing on the booklet that the dignitary is holding in fig. 3.21. In this ceremonial spectacle, as outlined in both the *Da Ming huidian* and *Da Ming jili* accounts, tables are laid out to display the foreign products being presented, while dignitaries in exotic indigenous costume appear before the emperor.

The two pictures are largely similar. Both depict one foreigner and three Chinese officials, of whom the middle one could be read as the emperor within the convention of woodblock illustrations in late Ming commonplace books.[64] The differences between the two illustrations are more subtle. In the upper halves of the two pictures, figure 3.21 appears to be a fine-tuned version of figure 3.20: the landscape painting is more carefully rendered, and the brocade desk covering is drawn in finer detail. In the lower halves, the version in fig. 3.21 displays more elements. In general, the latter version differs from the simpler version through its careful composition and clearly realized groupings of objects: a tripartite screen with a landscape painting, a desk, a cart, a display table, and the booklet in the foreign chief's hands. These objects and the human figures together weave a complex relational web, mapped out in the way they occupy the space of the page.

The upper half of the picture is the space marked as "ours" for the Ming viewer: two officials and the emperor dressed uniformly in court clothes with benevolent facial expression and composed bodily posture. They are surrounded by objects that signify culture and civilization: a screen with a landscape painting, a desk covered by ornamented brocades on which are set an inkstone and brushes, and the *hu*-tablet 笏 held by ministers during audiences with the emperor.[65] This group of figures, through whom the Ming viewer is invited to project his or her own group identity, is represented as both civilized and civilizing.

Noticeably, the "things" used in the upper space are not among the things deemed significant as ceremonial props in *Da Ming huidian* or *Da Ming jili*. In fact, most of them (e.g., brush, ink-stone, screen) do not appear in the imperial ritual text at all. Rather, these "things" had been established as signs of domestic respectability in Ming visualizations of elegant living and connoisseurship, markers of cultured daily life.[66] Thus in this illustration we see the visual vernacular that took shape around depictions of elegant domesticity being put to work in translating and rendering intelligible for its readership an imperial spectacle that would otherwise have remained inaccessible and incomprehensible.

The lower half of figure 3.21 is the "them" space. It depicts a single barbarian in what was stereotypically understood to be *the* "barbarian" indigenous costume: feathered hat and animal-skin clothes. He is holding a memorial with the characters "Foreigners Present Tribute." His equipage, in contrast with that displayed in the upper space, includes only a single cart (actually, one corner of a single cart), presumably what he used to transport his tribute, and a display table for the tribute objects, which include items such as coral and a rhinoceros-horn cup. This lower space is exotic, material, and numerically disadvantaged.

At the border of the upper and lower space of this picture is the third official, accepting the memorial submitted with the tribute objects. He mediates the relation between the upper and lower spaces of the picture and guarantees the propriety of the ceremonial relationship by ensuring that interactions between the foreign emissaries and the emperor do not involve direct confrontation or contact. The spatial relation between the upper and lower halves of the picture is also coded in two different visual languages. The upper half is metaphorical, representing China with all its lands and waters, its sophisticated culture and civilizing influence. The lower part is synecdochic: just as the partial cart pictorially represents the whole cart, the single display table represents all the display tables, the four emblems on the table represent all the treasures from lands and waters outside China, and the single foreigner represents all the tribute countries outside China.

What these two visual languages reveal is the suturing of two visual moments (the upper and lower halves of the picture) so that the two are juxtaposed in two distinct sets of visual convention. The upper half of the picture, as discussed above, transposes the sign system representing domestic respectability marked by furniture, architecture, and things of good taste and refinement to the imagination of the imperial spectacle. This transposition, however, is not done simply by these two illustrations but rather reflects a larger visual convention in depicting court scenes.

In this connection we may compare the illustration of figure 3.22 with figure 3.21. Figure 3.22 is almost identical with the upper half of figure 3.21, and they both appear in the same daily-use encyclopedia. Apparently, figure 3.21 simply lifts figure 3.22 and transposes it onto the upper half of its own composition. This "lifting" is certainly a technique of efficiency, yet another case of the sort of re-appropriation of ready-at-hand materials that characterized Ming commercial imprints in general. However, it also places upon figure 3.21 the burden of differentiating itself from figure 3.22 and other court scenes like it, and to convey clearly the specificity of its pictured event. The illustrator uses the lower half to turn this burden into novelty, and he achieves this by adding a few crucial things. Further, in adding these things he draws directly on the imperial ritual texts, as for example in the case of the display table (*fang wu an* 方物案) depicted here. That is, while the upper half strays from the ritual text due to its use of conventional block illustrations of court

Fig. 3.22. A division-head illustration, that of the chapter of "Heavenly Patterns" 天文門, in *Wanyong zhengzong buqiuren*. From *CNRS*, vol. 10, p. 17.

scenes, the lower half draws itself closer to the ritual text. In this way the lower half not only becomes more text-based but also conveys more of an "inside" view of the spectacle—"inside" in its confessed connection to the authority of written texts, particularly the official imprints of imperial ordinances.

What reveals this textual derivation most clearly is the booklet and the writing on it—*fan jin gong*. In comparing figure 3.20 and figure 3.21, we note that figure 3.21 replaces the treasure boat in the foreign chief's hand with this booklet, signaling the more important role of text in this picture. The booklet and its writing are key in several ways: first, they distinguish this moment from other similar court scenes (e.g., fig. 3.22) in the clearest possible way: in black characters on white paper. Second, they point to the importance of textual declaration (*biao* 表) in this ritual moment, when the foreign chief declares his purpose (*jingong*, paying tribute) and loyalty to the Ming emperor. Although the booklet is held and supposedly written by the foreign chief, it is lifted from the Chinese ritual prescription, and spoken here in the picture in the voice of the Chinese (as signaled by the word *fan*/foreign) and for the comfort of a Chinese book consumer. The booklet thus helps to wedge and suture the upper half that strays from the imperial ritual text with the lower half that translates and transposes the ritual text into its visual composition. To read the picture as a whole, a generic court scene on the top is effectively commented on by the bottom as the specific spectacle of "foreigner presents tribute." Also noticeable in this spatial mapping is how the side and front panels of the tripartite screen form an angle of pivots that accommodates the reader's viewing. Along this line, in both division-head illustrations the foreign dignitaries face the direction of reading towards the viewer. Their three-quarter view conveniently accommodates a triangular relation among the foreign dignitary(ies), the court, and the viewer. Both the emperor and the barbarian have become part of a court drama, arranged to suit both the visual orientation and visual imagination of ordinary late Ming readers.

All this is achieved under an overarching transposition—of the emperor and the imperial palace (*dian* 殿) to a typified respectable residence hall (*ting* 廳) within the ambit of common experience. This is highly consistent with the visual system of signs of the day, where the hall and the screen become immediately legible signs for cultural respectability and elegant comfort. The popular books, driven by the market, did not just popularize or spread knowledge. Rather, in their own novel visual and verbal language, they also used, translated, and remade both the knowledge and the imaginative spaces within which that knowledge was conceived. In the next chapter, I will look at how the poetics of error, of straying away and making anew, worked to shape one of the bestselling books of the day, the *Luochong lu*.

CHAPTER FOUR

The Book and the Barbarian: A History of the Luochong lu

In a text entitled *Record of Grand Lessons to Wake the Errant* (*Da yi jue mi lu* 大義覺迷錄), the Yongzheng emperor (r. 1723–36) of the Manchu Qing dynasty argued that the Chinese word *yi* 夷 (commonly translated as "foreign" or "barbarian") was merely an archaic equivalent of the latter-day word for "birthplace" and thus ought not be thought insulting to Manchu sensibilities. The practice of some early Qing authors, who had self-censored their writings by avoiding the term, however, suggests that they indeed had felt its connotations to be problematic.[1] Whatever the success of Yongzheng's attempt to lay to rest the unease about *yi*, this eighteenth-century dispute over its connotations invites us to consider the specific history of use of the term, and the circulation of related bodies of knowledge, during the centuries preceding Yongzheng's pronouncement. How might this history have inclined Qing writers to self-censor, or alternatively how might it have supported Yongzheng's claim that the term *yi* should be thought inoffensive? Pursuing these questions may lead to a better understanding of the complex and lively world of descriptions, opinions, and fantasies concerning the outside world and its inhabitants in early modern China.

A Ming book entitled *Luochong lu* 臝蟲錄 (Record of naked creatures), a text that was in its heyday one of the definitive sourcebooks for knowledge of the foreign, is the perfect place to begin searching for answers to this question. It provides a unique window on Ming ideas of

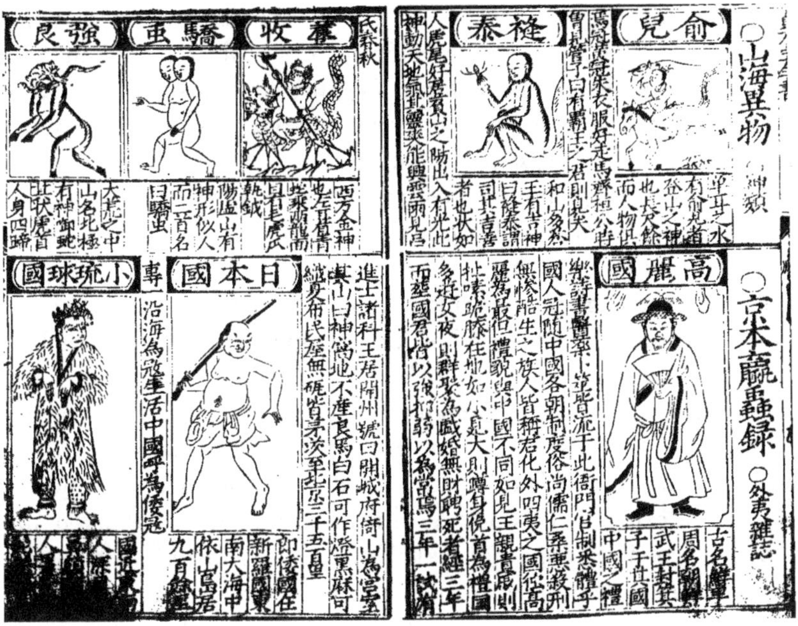

Fig. 4.1. The *Luochong lu* as encyclopedia division, seen in the bottom register of the daily-use encyclopedia *Miaojin wanbao quanshu*, along with its typical companion text drawn from the *Shanhai jing* (here titled *Shanhai yiwu* 山海異物) in the upper register. 1612. Published by Liu Shuangsong 劉雙松 of Anzheng tang 安正堂. From *CNRS*, vol. 12, pp. 210–11.

the world at large at a historical moment when the unprecedented expansion of global trade and political networks were beginning to reconfigure traditional visions of the world. Just as importantly, this text and its history of dissemination sheds light on the processes through which ideas about the larger world were adapted, articulated, circulated, and read.

The *Luochong lu* (fig. 4.1) is a block-printed text that assembles images and descriptions of over a hundred types of *luochong* 蠃蟲 (literally, naked creatures), otherwise known as *yi* 夷 (barbarians, foreigners).[2] Its entries, organized under headings for various *guo* 國 (states, countries, or polities), cover regions all across Asia and the Indian Ocean, the Middle East (e.g., Dashi Wusili 大食勿斯離, present-day Mosul in northern Iraq), Africa (e.g., Mojiala 默伽臘, present-day Morocco), and Europe (e.g., Sijialiye 思伽里野, Sicily).[3] The main focus of the text is on "outside foreigners" (*waiyi* 外夷) beyond the territory of the "central states" (*zhongguo* 中國), but it also includes ethnic groups within that territory, as well as legendary countries originally recorded in early Chinese texts such as the *Shanhai jing* 山海經 (Classic of mountains and seas). Like that text, with which it was often paired in the Ming, moreover, the *Luochong lu* places emphasis not only on written accounts of exotic peoples but also on often correspondingly exotic illustrations.[4]

The *Luochong lu* is a classic instance of the "hucksterish" mode of knowledge production that became associated with the Ming, and it is thus not surprising that the work has, since the eighteenth century or so, fallen into neglect, only in recent times beginning to attract scholarly interest.[5] As this chapter will recount, however, in the Ming this text was produced again and again over an extended period by a diverse range of publishers. Many of these editions are rife with errors and variants, and they seem on the whole to reflect a rather casual attitude toward collation, to the extent that it would be difficult to point to one edition or to a group of "good" editions that could be viewed as standard. Nonetheless, as this chapter sets out to demonstrate, the *Luochong lu* was a wildly popular text (or cluster of texts) that was reproduced, marketed, and consumed with great gusto by Ming publishers and readers.

The Ming, whose increased maritime activities led to a rise in direct contacts between peoples from various continents, generated numerous writings on the foreign.[6] The *Luochong lu* stands out among these works in several ways. First, it is a pictorial, and thus it is closely linked to the flourishing industry of block-printed illustrations (*banhua* 版畫) in the Ming. Second, it stands out for its aim at comprehensiveness, covering countries and polities of both continental and maritime worlds. Most significantly, as the following discussion shows, it enjoyed wide circulation and popularity with a large and diverse readership, so it can shed light on a world of Ming reading that includes, but is by no means limited to, the elite discourses of formal scholarship and state policy. Through close reading of texts and pictures from the work as well as an examination of its history of circulation, promotion, and use, this chapter traces the history of the *Luochong lu*, including its various editions, makers, and intended audience, as well as how it was circulated and read across time and space. Through this tracing, I hope to gain a sense of not only what the text says but how it came to say it, and how the readers of the time heard it.

At the outset, the term *luochong* itself merits some explanation. It belongs to a zoological schema from the classical tradition of dividing creatures into five groups: the scaled 鱗蟲, feathered 羽蟲, haired 毛蟲, shelled 介蟲, and naked 蠃蟲 (*luo* 蠃 is also written *luo* 倮 or *luo* 裸). A typical formulary of this schema appears in the *Kongzi jia yu* 孔子家語 (Family sayings of Confucius):[7]

> 羽蟲三百有六十而鳳爲之長， 毛蟲三百有六十而麟爲之長， 甲蟲三百有六十而龜爲之長， 鱗蟲三百有六十而龍爲之長， 倮蟲三百有六十而人爲之長。
>
> Of feathered creatures there are 360, and the phoenix is their leader; of haired creatures there are 360, and the *qilin* is their leader; of shelled creatures there are 360, and the tortoise is their leader; of scaled creatures there are 360, and the dragon is their leader; of naked creatures there are 360, and the human is their leader.[8]

The human being, in this five-class system, is the leader of the "naked creatures." Although this system and variants of it do appear in pre-Ming writings,[9] it seems to have been the Ming book market that brought the concept "*luochong*" back to the attention of a wide readership. Ming writers played rather uninhibitedly for humorous effect on this notion of labeling human beings as *chong* 蟲, meaning variously bugs, worms, insects, reptiles, with colloquial and playful connotations somewhat like those of the word "critters." The peculiar choice of the title *Luochong lu* not only (re)introduced to the broad Chinese reading public the notion of *luochong*, but also set the tone for the Ming popular imagination about the foreign and exotic. While the word *yi* 夷, as seen above, became a focal point for elite cultural and diplomatic disputes over notions of ethnicity and foreignness, the term *luochong* makes its reappearance in the Ming book world in association with a less highbrow mode of representation that is marked by humor, informality, and unabashed exoticism. Thus although the term *luochong* has classical antecedents, we may also think of it in this latter incarnation as something of a Ming neologism, a reinvented notion meant to help create an expectation of novel and amusing information about the inhabitants of foreign lands.

The Journey to the West, the fantastic sixteenth-century novel about the pilgrimage to the west of the Monk Tripitaka and his four disciples (most famously Monkey, or Sun Wukong),[10] provides another window into the growing fascination in sixteenth century China with collecting and classifying all creatures that can be known, especially exotic species and beings, including the special category of the *luochong*. This novel and *Luochong lu* are two remarkable expressions of the cultural imagination of the exotic and foreign of their time; both assemble relevant information in a comprehensive panorama and present readers with an overarching system or framework—in the form of an episodic quest narrative in the case of the novel and, in the case of the *Luochong lu*, a picture gallery. The novel's deployment of the classical five-creature schema is particularly revealing. This system of classification appears several times in the narrative of the *Journey to the West*, involving in each instance confrontations between the monkey protagonist Sun Wukong and the five-class schema.[11]

In chapter 3 of the novel, Monkey's quest for immortality leads him to disrupt the archive of the infernal bureaucracy. Believing that he has obtained the Way and transcended the boundary between life and death, Monkey is shocked and offended when two ghosts come to fetch him to the underworld. He runs riot there and demands to check the *Shengsi buzi* 生死簿子 (Register of lives and deaths):

> The [infernal] judge . . . brought out five or six books of documents and the ledgers of ten classes. He [i.e., Sun Wukong] went through them one by one—naked creatures, haired creatures, feathered creatures, crawling creatures, and scaled creatures—but he did not find his own name. He then proceeded to the file on the monkey category. You see, though the monkey resembles a human being, he is not listed under the names of humans; though he resembles the naked creatures, he does not dwell in any country (*guo*); though he resembles running creatures, he is not subject to the *qilin*; though he resembles flying creatures, he is not governed by the phoenix. He has a separate ledger, which Wukong examined himself. Under the heading "Soul 1350" he found the name Sun Wukong recorded, with the description: "Heaven-born Stone Monkey. Age: 342 years. A good end." Wukong said, "I really don't remember my age. All I want is to erase my name. Bring me a brush" . . . Wukong took the ledger on monkeys and crossed out all the names he could find in it."[12]

The *Shengsi buzi*, an exhaustive list arranged according to a hierarchy of creatures, appears here as an ultimate authority of the cosmological order. The "naked creatures" are further divided according to geopolitical entities called *guo* (states), just as in the presentation of the *Luochong lu*. An equally key point of comparison between the ethnographical fantasies of these two Ming works is Sun Wukong's anarchic refusal to submit to the written discipline of the register, and his erasure of its claim to set boundaries around his identity or existence. As I will show below, the reception history of the *Luochong lu* also affords examples of such play between archival authority and ludic subversion.

The five-class schema of creatures reappears in chapter 58 of *Journey to the West*, when Sun Wukong's identity is contested by a double who is indistinguishable from the real monkey hero. Sun returns once more to the Region of Darkness to check the documentation of all beings and their proper lots—however, his search in the volume "Haired Creatures" (*maochong*) proves futile since, as we recall, he himself had crossed out the whole class of monkeys back in chapter 3. At this point a beast by the name of "Investigative Hearing" (*di ting* 諦聽) rises to the occasion. Though he usually reclines beneath the desk of Bodhisattva Ksitigarbha (*Dizang pusa*), he is able to crawl on the ground and instantly "perceive the true and false, the virtuous and the wicked among all naked creatures, scaled creatures, haired creatures, feathered creatures, and crawling creatures. He also has the ability to distinguish among the celestial immortals, the earthly immortals, the divine immortals, the human immortals, and the spirit immortals resident in all the cave heavens and blessed lands; as well as among shrines, rivers, and mountains of the Four Great Continents."[13] Thus "Investigative Hearing" is depicted as a superior sort of geo-ethnographer whose judgment does not rely on texts. But the task of subduing the demon double is left to the all-mighty Tathāgata Buddha, who effortlessly contains the spirit—but not before smilingly delivering the following cosmo-ethnographic sermon to a vast assembly of beings that includes the Four Great Bodhisattvas, the Eight Great Diamond Kings, the five hundred *arhats*, the three thousand guardians of the faith, the mendicant nuns and the mendicant monks, the *upādakas* and the *upasikas*:

> Though all of you possess vast dharma power and are able to observe the events of the whole universe, you cannot know all the things therein, nor do you have the knowledge of all the species . . . There are five kinds of immortals in the universe, and they are the celestial, the earthly, the divine, the human, and the spirit. There are also five kinds of creatures, and they are the naked, the scaled, the haired, the feathered, and the crawling.[14]

Finally, Tathāgata announces that the false Monkey is the six-eared macaque (*liu er mihou* 六耳彌猴) and confines it under his alms bowl. However, Monkey impulsively raises his rod and kills it with one blow. Hence, we are told by the storyteller, "to this day this species [of six-eared macaque] is extinct" (至今絕此一種).

These excerpts from *Journey to the West* not only point to a Ming fascination with gathering and classifying all that is fantastic and exotic, but also deliver ironic—and, in some particulars, satirical—reflections on issues of identity, knowledge, and power. In their humorous effect, they express an appreciation of the incommensurability of an orderly taxonomy based on systematic similarities and distinctions (*leibie* 類別) with anomalous phenomena and beings that resist categorization. These *Journey to the West* excerpts are notable in part because they corroborate the resurgence during the Ming of the old five-class taxonomy and its most intriguing and problematic category, the *luochong*. This chapter's investigation of the *Luochong lu* itself will further reveal how that system and that category formed part of the Ming imaginary landscape within which readers could conceive of biological, ethnic, geographical, and political identity. While the term *luochong* and the work *Luochong lu* thus occupied, to a degree, a space of playful fantasy, this space also served as a venue for working out contradictions and anxieties about how to understand cultural or geographical others in an increasingly complex global reality.

From Yiyu tuzhi *to* Luochong lu

The text that became the *Luochong lu* once circulated under the alternative title *Yiyu tuzhi* 異域圖志 (Illustrated record of foreign lands). The editors of the eighteenth-century *Siku quanshu* compendium do not mention the *Luochong lu*, but do note the *Yiyu tuzhi* in their coverage of the section of historical works dealing with geography. Their notes on the *Yiyu tuzhi* appear in the *cun mu* 存目 category, that is, among those texts whose existence is noted but which are not deemed worthy of inclusion in the *Siku* compendium. Their short and dismissive comments on this title give a forceful and concise statement of the attitudes and rationale for the Qing rejection of the *Luochong lu*:

> 不著撰人名氏。後有明廣信府知府金銑序，謂宋亦有應天府，疑是宋書。然書中載明初封元梁王子於耽羅，則爲明人所作無疑。其書摭拾諸史及諸小説而成，頗多疏舛，如占城役屬於安南，乃云安南爲占城役屬，殊不足據，其他敘述，亦太寥寥。
>
> No author is named. In an appended postface, Jin Xian, prefect of Guangxin Prefecture of the Ming, says that there was a Yingtian Prefecture in the Song as well, and that he suspects this is a Song book. This book, however, records the

> investiture of the son of Prince Liang of the Yuan in Danluo, leaving no doubt that this is the work of a Ming author. The book itself is composed of cobbled-together fragments of the various histories along with various collections of apocryphal tales *(xiaoshuo)*, and is quite full of oversights and inconsistencies, as, for example, when it says that Annam is an administrative subdivision of Zhancheng, though Zhancheng is really an administrative subdivision of Annam—such a text is decidedly not to be relied on as a source of information. In other instances its relation of events is also too cursory.[15]

These comments, which were quoted in the epigraph to the introduction, provide several grounds for discounting the merit of the *Yiyu tuzhi*, which would naturally apply as well to the book under its later title *Luochong lu*. The first area of complaint has to do with the book's pedigree, or lack thereof: it has no clearly attributed author, and its history, from the perspective of this late eighteenth-century editor, is filled with false claims that tend to make it appear more ancient than it really is. Second, it is composed of snippets of other works from different bibliographical categories, not only reflecting a careless and haphazard approach to compilation, but also tending, by the disparity in the sorts of sources it draws on, to blur the proper distinctions between official history and the fabulations of *xiaoshuo* texts. Finally, the text is found wanting in regard to factual accuracy and consistency. Amid such criticisms, readers of the eighteenth century and later would certainly have been justified in their neglect and disesteem for the *Luochong lu*.[16] For our purposes, however, these criticisms serve as a way of framing another set of questions. Given that the *Luochong lu* was wildly popular and influential in the late Ming, in what ways did its readers approach the work from a different perspective and with different purposes from those assumed as normative and correct in the above critique?

The origins of the *Luochong lu* are somewhat murky.[17] According to the available bibliographical evidence, between 1392 and 1430 a text by the title *Yiyu tuzhi* was commissioned, possibly by the Ming prince and polymath Zhu Quan 朱權 (1378–1448). Whether Zhu Quan himself produced printed editions of this text is unknown, but in 1489 Jin Xian 金銑, the prefect of Guangxin 廣信 prefecture in Jiangxi (where Zhu Quan and his descendents resided), commissioned a woodblock edition.[18] A comparison of these texts confirms that the *Yiyu tuzhi* and the *Luochong lu* are variants of the same book. The earlier title *Yi yu tuzhi* had a more restrained and classical-sounding tone, while subsequent productions of the text as *Luochong lu* tended to highlight the potential in the material for humor and sensationalism. This latter title seems to have essentially replaced the title *Yiyu tuzhi* in the early sixteenth century, and it remained the predominant designation by which the text was known to Ming readers.

Throughout the Ming there appear to have been three distinct types of editions of the *Luochong lu*. The first, the fifteenth-century form circulating under the title *Yiyu tuzhi*, exists in an exemplar of an imprint now housed in the Cambridge University Library. The second type comprises imprints under the later and more widespread title *Luochong lu*, the form in which the text became widely known and eventually a bestseller in the sixteenth and seventeenth centuries, as the Wanli era commercial publisher Zhuang Rujing 莊汝敬 notes in his preface to a 1593 reprint of the text: "This book, the *Luochong lu*, has been in circulation for a long time, and there has been a profusion of editions." A copy of this 1593 imprint, included in Hu Wenhuan's 胡文煥 (fl. Wanli reign) massive *Gezhi congshu* 格致叢書 (Compendium of books inquiring into and extending knowledge), is now housed in the Beijing Capital Library.[19] Another copy of a different edition dated to 1550 is found in the Seikidō collection in Japan.[20] The third type comprises the numerous reprintings of the *Luochong lu* as a chapter in encyclopedias, a publication genre whose popularity mushroomed in the late Ming.[21] We have abundant extant copies of this final type, including the famed *Sancai tuhui* and dozens of other titles. In the end, the *Luochong lu* circulated not in one "correct" version, but in a range of versions that shared a common origin and were modeled after each other, albeit with various editorial changes.

The *Luochong lu* drew textual material from an impressive range of previous works, such as *Lingwai daida* 嶺外代答 (Proxy answers concerning what is beyond the ranges),[22] *Shanhai jing*, *Shilin guangji*,[23] *Youyang zazu* 酉陽雜俎 (Miscellaneous morsels from Youyang),[24] *Bowu zhi* 博物志 (Treatise on broad learning of things),[25] and the *Yuan chao mishi* 元朝秘史 (The secret history of the Yuan), in addition to official dynastic histories. Further, its conception of producing pictures for all known exotic peoples treated is ambitious, if not visionary.[26] Such a compilation project is reminiscent of the work of an archival collector, drawing from sources inaccessible to most readers to assemble a gallery of rarities in the form of exotic human and human-like beings.

To summarize, the sixteenth century was the period in which the *Luochong lu* rose to popularity. Two significant changes took place during this span of time: first, whatever its precise origins, the text had by then become fully commercialized, picked up and printed by numerous publishers for marketing to a broad and diverse readership. In the process it became accessible to a broader audience, carrying with it the cachet of rarity and novelty as a textual cabinet of curiosities. A second change occurred in the late sixteenth century, when the *Luochong lu* was appropriated wholesale as the text for one of the chapters conventionally included in the daily-use encyclopedias under the "Various Barbarian Lands" (*si yi* 四夷 or *zhu yi* 諸夷) rubric.[27] That the *Luochong lu* was chosen to fill out this encyclopedic category is attributable to two distinctive qualities: the comprehensiveness of its listings, and the fact that it accorded significant space to pictures. In other words, what made the *Luochong lu* re-packageable and re-salable was its quality as a portable "museum," and this attractiveness stemmed not only from the rarity of some of its textual sources but also from the appeal of its visual depictions of exotic curiosities. Of course, by the late sixteenth century, the text had accumulated a long-standing reputation, which must have added to its appeal both for encyclopedia publishers and for their readerships. It was through the daily-use encyclopedia that the *Luochong lu* consolidated its place in the Ming knowledge system.

"The Country of Koryŏ," "The Country of Japan," and the "Xiongnu"

Both the content and composition of specific entries within the *Luochong lu* yield clues as to how the text was compiled. The text reveals itself as a hybrid in many ways. For example, older classical or classical-sounding rubrics are employed in classifying and labeling the entries, but the entries themselves reveal extensive ad hoc modifications to incorporate a range of later and often more colloquial-sounding material. This textual heterogeneity, characteristic not only of the *Luochong lu* but also of a wide range of popular Ming woodblock imprints, worked not as a failing but as an attraction in the Ming world of reading. Here I will examine three entries that reflect the sort of heterogeneity we find in the *Luochong lu*, first in the geographical and ethnographical information compiled under its entries for various *guo* (countries), and second in terms of the jumbling of different written styles and linguistic registers that occurs throughout the text.

In terms of the first aspect, consider the entry on "The Country of Koryŏ" (fig. 4.2):

高麗國

商名鮮卑，周名朝鮮，武王封箕子于其國。中國之禮樂詩書醫藥卜筮皆流于此。衙門官制悉體中國，衣冠隨中國各朝制度。俗尚儒，人（仁）柔惡殺，刑無殘酷。[28]王之族人皆稱君。化外四夷之國，獨高麗爲最。但禮貌與中國有差。如見王親貴戚，則扯嗦跪膝在地；如小見大，則蹲身俛首爲禮。如中國人見賊寇不敢仰視之類。此夷狄之風俗，習以爲常焉。地不產良馬。白石可作燈具；黑麻可織夏布。其國君皆是以強抑弱，而王國治東西二千里，南北千五百里。王居開州，號曰開城府。依山爲宮，名其山曰神窩。民居多茅茨，少陶瓦。以樂浪爲東京，百濟金州爲西京。西京最盛，有郡百十八，縣鎮三百九十，洲島三千，郡邑小者，或止百家，西北接契丹，以鴨綠江爲固。江廣三百步，海水至高麗機清，入登州，經千里沙即濁。東南望明州數日，水皆絕碧，至洋中則黑海，人謂此無底之谷也。

"Gaoli guo" (The Country of Koryŏ)

Its Shang dynasty name was Xianbei; its Zhou dynasty name, Chaoxian (Chosŏn). King Wu enfeoffed Jizi in this county. The rituals and music, poetry and writing, medicine and divination from China (*zhongguo*) were all transmitted to this country. (Koryŏ's) offices and institutions all follow those of the Chinese people, and in norms of robes and hats they follow those of Chinese dynasties. Their customs esteem Confucianism; they are benevolent and gentle, dislike killing, and their penal codes lack cruel punishments. The clansmen of a king are all called lords. Of all four barbarians outside the sphere of transformation, Koryŏ is the most civilized.[29] But their rituals are still different from those of China: when they see members of the royal family and aristocracy, they pull up their lower garment and kneel;[30] when the younger meet the older, they squat and lower their heads in respect—as when Chinese people encounter bandits and dare not look up. These are barbarian customs to which they have grown accustomed as norms. Its land does not produce top-quality horses. Its white slate can be used to make lanterns; its black hemp can be woven into cloth for the summer. Though with their kings it is all a matter of the stronger suppressing the weaker, the kingdom's domain covers two thousand *li* from east to west, and a thousand and five hundred *li* from north to south. The king lives in Kaizhou (Kaechu), in a residence called the Kaicheng (Kaesŏng) Compound. Their palaces are built on mountain slopes; and the mountain is called "the nest of divine beings."[31] Its common dwellings do not have roof-tiles, but all use thatch. It takes Lelang (Nangnang) as its Eastern Capital, Baiji (Paekche) of Jinzhou (*Kŭmchu*) as its Western Capital.[32] The Western Capital is the most prosperous.

Fig. 4.2. A picture to accompany the description of the "Country of Koryŏ" in *Yiyu tuzhi*. Courtesy of the Cambridge University Library.

> It has 118 prefectures, 390 counties and townships, and three thousand islands. Its small prefectures have no more than a hundred households. In the northwest, it connects with Qidan, with [the river] Yalujiang as its fort. The river is three hundred paces wide. The ocean reaching Koryŏ is extremely clear. After a thousand *li* into Dengzhou, the sand makes the water muddy. Its southeast reaches Mingzhou in several days, the water is all extremely blue. But when it reaches the ocean it becomes deeply dark, which people call the bottomless ravine.[33]

This entry traces the beginning of Koryŏ history to a Chinese founder and describes its foundational institutions and social beliefs as based on Confucian ritualism and Chinese technologies of medicine and divination. It also introduces Korean local products, architecture, and general geography. In several respects—the linguistic register, the gestures towards historical chronicle, and the range of subjects covered—this record on Koryŏ falls in line with the form used for writing official histories. In fact, this entry draws heavily from the official account appearing in the *Song shi*. Many editions of *Luochong lu* begin with Koryŏ, the gateway piece for the throng of foreign peoples to come. The reason is made specific in the entry itself: "Of all four barbarians outside the sphere of transformation, Koryŏ is the most civilized." Still, readers are told, Koryŏ has its own customs distinct from China's, thereby balancing Koryŏ's institutional sinification with customary indigenousness.

This entry would have been outdated for readers from the fifteenth century and onward, since by then the Chosŏn 朝鮮 dynasty (1392–1910) had replaced the Koryŏ dynasty 高麗 (918–1392), and its capital had moved from Kaesŏng to Hansŏng. Although editors of the many editions of the *Luochong lu* did not show concern with updating the text to reflect this, they did exhibit great enthusiasm for another kind of "updating," in the form of going back to ancient records for supplementary information. In addition to the *Song shi*, they favored *Bei shi* 北史 as a source,[34] and they also occasionally tapped *Hou Han shu* 後漢書 for supplementary information.[35] Their editorial energy was focused on a process of textual archeology, and the entry served as a place holder to accumulate and rehearse ancient received wisdom. No doubt the motivations of various editors for specific additions varied, but any reader would be impressed and delighted, for example, by the new line about "roving girls" that appears in the *Miaojin wanbao quanshu* recension of the text: "This country has a lot of roving girls, who gather to live together at night and play around" 國多遊女, 夜則群居爲戲.[36] For readers of active imagination (or, in the language of Ming cultural observers, *haoshi zhe* 好事者),[37] this somewhat enigmatic line would have shifted the tone of an entry otherwise largely in the style of official history towards the realm of *chuanqi* tales of mysterious and alluring women (who often turn out not to be human, or to be only partly human) and their unpredictable sexual availability, thus enhancing the flavor of exoticism in the *Luochong lu*.

A second example is the entry on "The Country of Japan":

日本國

> 即倭國。在新羅國東南大海中。依山島居九百餘里，專一沿海盜寇爲生。[中]國呼爲倭寇。[38]

"Riben guo" (The Country of Japan)

> That is, "Dwarf Land." It is located in the ocean southeast to the country of Silla. [People of this country] dwell on a nine hundred *li* stretch along the mountainous islands, and their exclusive way of making a living is to work as bandits. China (*Zhongguo*) calls them "wokou" ("the dwarf bandits").

This short entry is complex in the ways it references the three main East Asian geopolitical entities we now know as China, Korea, and Japan. Silla (57 BCE–935 CE)[39] was one of the three powers during the Korean Three Kingdoms period, which by the Ming had long since become ancient history. The reference to this medieval kingdom thus evokes an earlier frame of reference. At any rate, its use here in the *Luochong lu* involves a past designation being used as a spatial marker for mapping Ming-era East Asia. Here, the archaic terminology recalls the ancient Silla kingdom's enormously important role in the medieval history of regional relations during what has been termed "the greatest period of maritime activity in Korean history."[40] Not only did Silla have a great impact in medieval East Asian interstate affairs, and act as the conduit in Chinese cultural transfer to Japan (not to ignore the fact that Japan itself had direct and active interaction with China), but Silla's merchants and shipping played a dominant role in trade among the three regions by the ninth century.[41]

What is the textual origin of this frame of reference? A survey of historical documents shows that referencing Japan (referred to in early Chinese texts as Wo 倭) via a locale on the Korean peninsula is typical and formulaic in early Chinese histories.[42] A decisive change in documenting Japan was seen in the tenth-century *Jiu Tang shu* 舊唐書, which still gives an individual entry for Wo 倭 but introduces the designation Riben 日本 as a replacement. It is also in *Jiu Tang shu* that one finds the exact language used in the *Luochong lu* entry: "The country of the Wo . . . is located in the ocean southeast of Silla; [People of this country] dwell along mountainous islands."[43] The conjecture that the *Luochong lu* entry is extracted from the *Jiu Tang shu* is confirmed, first, by the disappearance of this exact language in the *Xin Tang shu* 新唐書 and, further, by the discontinuation altogether in the *Song shi* of referring to Japan's location via the Korean peninsula.[44]

The above survey shows that the compilers of the *Luochong lu* chose a medieval frame of reference that bears witness to the stage when Japan was still mapped as remote and removed, as a periphery of a periphery. The fact that the name Silla remained well-known in Ming China— due to the popularity of the legend of Xue Rengui 薛仁貴 (614–83), a Tang dynasty general who waged military campaigns in the Korean peninsula—contributed to the legibility of the reference and may have been one more reason for retaining this reference in the *Luochong lu*. After quoting the *Jiu Tang shu*, the entry snaps readers back to the border crisis current to the Ming: pirate incursions along the coasts. In this entry's mapping of East Asian triangular power, "Japan," "Silla," and "China" (lit. the Central States) are terms with divergent constellations of spatial, chronological, and cultural connotations. While "Silla" perpetuates the memory of a past world order, and "Central States" suggests an entity that transcends time and trans-regional change, "Woguo" (Land of Dwarves) consigns Japan to seemingly perpetual and congenital liminality. Against the range of tone of these terms is staged the Ming dynasty's actual pressing border issue, that of the "pirate" incursions on the southeast seaboard—not to mention the specter of full-scale conquest that arose in the final decade of the 16th century.

As the "Country of Japan" entry suggests, the entries were composed based on or excerpted from prior documents, with a nod to the world of contemporary readers. Once put together, the individual entries seem generally to have remained stable throughout roughly two centuries of circulation. Changes were occasionally made, however, and these changes are very often revealing of the dynamics of the text's reception and circulation. "The Country of Japan" is, again, a case in point. As discussed above, the suturing of historical documentation bearing witness to the medieval world order together with current reports of border troubles reveals a textual tension—one that views Japan as being peripheral and at the same time as posing a serious military threat, so much so that military aggression is described as Japan's sole purpose. This textual tension between dominance and affliction, between the self-image of a civilizing center and an awareness of territorial threat, is made still more manifest by the changes made in the entry's accompanying illustration. While the fifteenth-century *Yiyu tuzhi* and some later imitators portray the people of Japan as amiable and appropriately robed, with ceremonially proper-looking deportment (fig. 4.3), some of the other editions depict a half-naked figure wearing a *fundoshi* lower garment and brandishing an unsheathed sword threateningly and carelessly at his shoulder, ready to attack (fig. 4.4). The entry, especially when accompanied by the depiction of a bandit, added a dimension of contemporary

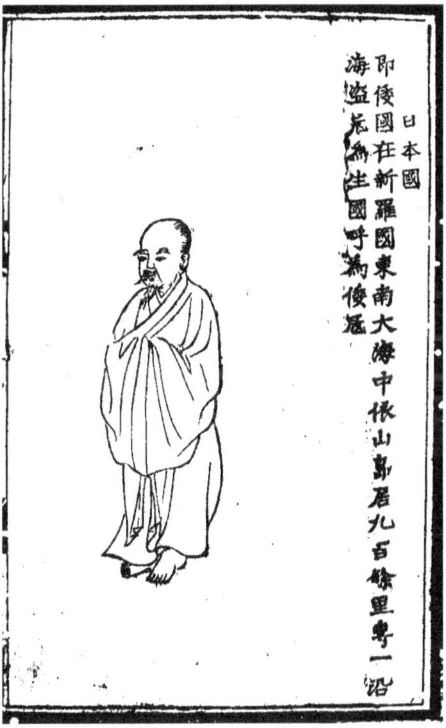

Fig. 4.3. "The Country of Japan" in *Yiyu tuzhi*. Courtesy of the Cambridge University Library.

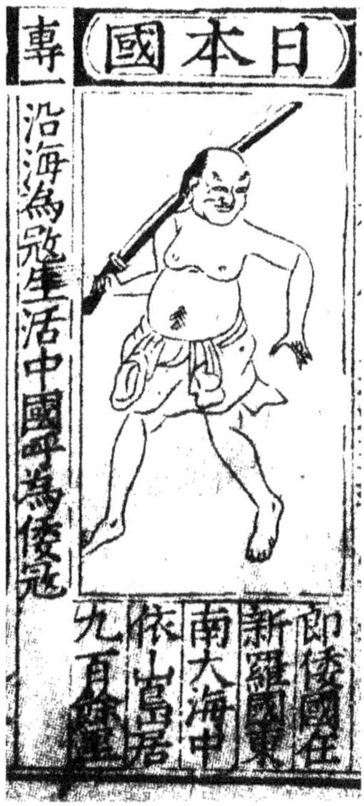

Fig. 4.4. "The Country of Japan" in *Miaojin wanbao quanshu*. From *CNRS*, vol. 12, p. 211.

commentary to what was, in many ways, a very traditional account.[45] As recent scholarship has shown, the actual pirates came from various regions of the Pacific coast, by no means limited to or even primarily centered in Japan. What we see here, then, is an example of Ming pictorial propaganda making the border crisis solely foreign, and pirates solely external. Such a propagandistic tone might have been further incited by the massive war involving Japan, Korea, China, and other nations over the course of the 1590s, fueled by a series of abortive attempts by the Japanese imperial regent and military commander Toyotomi Hideyoshi to invade Ming China via Korea—in what has been termed "the single largest conflict in the world during the sixteenth century."[46]

The entry on Japan is revealing of the construction of the *Luochong lu* entries in general. Each entry heading serves as a placeholder for a descriptive summary and a picture of the country under discussion, heavily drawing on previous documents but also mindful of more recent developments. As also attested by the entry on Japan, later editors, through a process that reveals much about the spectrum of attitudes and sentiments towards various foreigners at the time, made modifications as they saw fit.

The third example, the entry for "Xiongnu" 匈奴 (fig. 4.5),[47] is a good illustration of how the mixing of traditional and newly incorporated elements in the *Luochong lu* is reflected at the level of style and language:

匈奴

其種有五色。一種黄毛者，乃山鬼與牸牛所生。一種短項矮胖者，乃玃猳與野猪所生。一種黑髮白身者，乃漢李陵兵遺種也。一種名突厥，其先乃射摩，舌利海神女與金角白鹿交感而生。射摩因手斬阿吙首領，金以人祭纛。俗尚射殺，事妖神，無祠廟，刻氈爲形，盛於毛袋，行動之處以脂蘇塗之。或繫竿上，四時祀之。一種乃塔巴赤罕之祖。《元朝秘史》云：蒼白狼與慘白鹿所生。二十五世生帖木眞，是稱大蒙古部長，僭號皇帝。世居沙漠東北六千里。後居山陰。號韃靼。地產羊馬，無城池房舍，隨水草所居。俗尚射獵，食羊馬野鹿。衣皮革。帖木眞四世孫忽必烈僭居中國稱帝。

"Xiongnu"

This breed comprises five types. One, with yellow hair, was born from a mountain ghost and a cow. One, short-necked, stout, and fat, was born of the *juejia*-ape and a wild hog. One, with black hair and white body, is the remaining offspring of the troops of Li Ling of the Han. One is called Tujue; their ancestor was Shemo, who was born from a union of the female divinity of the Sheli Ocean

Fig. 4.5. A picture to accompany the description of the Xiongnu in *Yiyu tuzhi*. Courtesy of the Cambridge University Library.

> and the golden-horned white deer.[48] Since Shemo killed the chief of the A'nuo tribe with his own hands, to this day they perform human sacrifice to their banner.[49] Their customs set great store in archery and killing. They worship the Zoroastrian god and do not maintain ancestral temples.[50] They carve felt into icons and put these onto fur bags.[51] Whenever they take actions, they smear the icons with butter. Sometimes they tie the icons to a pole, and they worship them in all four seasons. Another tribe is of the ancestry of the Tabachi Khan. *The Secret History of the Yuan* says:[52] this line was born of the grey wolf and pale deer. Its twenty-fifth generation gave birth to Tiemuzhen, who was called the Ruler from Great Mongolia (Genghis Khan) and who was illegitimately granted the title of "emperor." For generations they lived six thousand *li* northeast in the desert. Later they moved to the north of the mountains. They are called the Tatars. Their land produces sheep and horses, with no cities, moats, and houses. They set up their dwellings wherever the water and grass are. Their customs set great store in archery and hunting, and they eat animals such as sheep, horses, and wild deer. They clothe themselves in leather and skins. Tiemuzhen's fourth generation grandson Kublai Khan usurped the empire of China (*zhongguo*) and called himself emperor.[53]

This entry is a recklessly simplified sampling of notations about peoples of the northern regions covering an enormous span of time, from an unspecific mythical era down to the Mongol Yuan dynasty (1279–1368). It is framed by the notion of *zhong* 種, which can mean "kind," "race," or "breed." The sense of "breed" is amplified throughout the entry, which lists five sub-breeds, all born, except for one group descended from Han Chinese ancestors, by cross-breeding with animal species.[54] Instead of weaving together citations from official histories, this entry, in its language and in its choice of sources, bears clear marks of "unofficial history" (*ye shi* 野史, a designation that itself refers both to a type of document and to a mode of storytelling). It uses a peculiar language that mixes the vernacular and the literary. The source for some of the information on the Mongols is stated explicitly in the entry itself: *The Secret History of the Yuan* (hereafter *Secret History*). The rest of the entry, whose source is not mentioned, is based on the *Youyang zazu*, a Tang dynasty compendium of curiosities.[55]

The entry's reference to the *Secret History* is crucial for a number of reasons. This text was composed as a Mongolian text in Uighur script, and that from the time of its completion sometime in the mid-thirteenth century it was carefully guarded by the Yuan imperial house,[56] who took significant precautions to prevent it from being transmitted to outsiders. When it fell into the hands of the Ming court, it became a document of great interest to court scholars of Yuan history and a key text for training state translators in the Translators' Institute (*Siyi guan* 四夷館). It was also consulted in the Hongwu era (1368–98) during the compilation of the linguistic treatise *Huayi yiyu* 華夷譯語 (Chinese and foreign languages: translation and transliteration). Within this context of locating, studying, and drawing on Yuan documents in the early Ming, the *Secret History* was translated by court scholars into a peculiar kind of Chinese vernacular that aimed to retain some of the linguistic features of the original, a style of translation referred to as *yingyi* 硬譯 (rigid translation).[57] The early Ming imperial house made a print edition of the translation and later included the translation in the *Yongle dadian*. The *Secret History* thus appears to have been well-known in Ming court circles, but there is still no evidence that it circulated among a broader public. By referencing this Mongol text, the *Luochong lu* advertises to its readers that they are getting a unique glimpse of esoteric Mongolian lore. It also plays into the impact of dynastic change on the meaning of the text, as mythical tales of the origins of the Mongolian ruling lineages could now be read as a confession and evidence of their uncivilized and animal origins. References in the *Luochong lu* entry to Mongol emperors having "usurped" the title of emperor of course do not reproduce the voice of the *Secret History* as far as Yuan legitimacy is concerned, and such adjustments to the source text allow the entry's Ming narrator to reassert an authentic and orthodox lineage (*zhengtong* 正統) of "Chinese" rule over the central kingdom while playing on the allure of the secret and exotic source.

What kind of voice, then, is projected by the Ming narrator? The rest of the entry gives more cues. As mentioned above, another source for the entry is *Youyang zazu*, and the description of the fourth sub-breed, the Tujue, is a verbatim excerpt from that source. The description of the third sub-breed, that of the Chinese descendants, alters the *Youyang zazu* slightly, yet significantly:

> 其髭髯俱黑者，漢將李陵及其兵眾之胤也。
>
> Those whose mustaches and sideburns alike are black are the descendants of Li Ling, the Han general, and his forces.[58] (*Youyang zazu*)
>
> 一種黑髮白身者，乃漢李陵兵遺種也。
>
> There is one breed with black hair and white body—these are the remaining offspring of the troops of Li Ling of the Han. (*Luochong lu*)

The most obvious change is from *qi* (those) to *yizhong* (one kind/breed) so as to fit the line into the overall narrative of "five breeds." The descriptions of the first two sub-breeds diverge more from those in *Youyang zazu*, but traces of textual connection still appear:

(帝女子澤，性妒，有從婢散逐四山…) 北通玃猳，所育爲傖。

(The God on High's daughter, Zize, was jealous by nature and had her maidservants banished into the four mountains . . .) In the north, [the maidservant] mated with the *juejia*-ape.[59] The resulting offspring is called the *cang*.[60] (*Youyang zazu*)

一種短項矮胖者，乃玃猳與野豬所生。

There is one breed with short necks, stout and fat—these were born of the *juejia*-ape and a wild hog. (*Luochong lu*)

The texts agree as to the cardinal direction in which the breeding took place. Further, the recurrence of the term *juejia* marks a link between the *Youyang zazu* account and the *Luochong lu* account, as prior to the *Luochong lu* this rare animal name seems only to have appeared in *Youyang zazu*. Now, regarding the first sub-species in the entry:

堅昆部落非狼種。其先所生之窟在曲漫山北。自謂上代有神與牸牛交於此窟。其人髮黃目綠赤髭髯。

The tribe of Jiankun is not descended from the wolf. The cave where their ancestor was born was at the north of Mount Quman. They themselves say that in early antiquity a god and a cow mated in this cave. The members of the tribe have yellow hair, green eyes, and red beards.[61] (*Youyang zazu*)

一種黃毛者，乃山鬼與牸牛所生。

One, with yellow hair, was born from the mountain ghost and a cow. (*Luochong lu*)

The mating between a spirit and a cow (*ziniu* 牸牛) and the color of their descendants' hair (yellow) are two details shared by the corresponding *Youyang zazu* and *Luochong lu* accounts. It appears that the *Luochong lu* descriptions of the first two sub-breeds are creative paraphrasings of those in the *Youyang zazu*. Even if the *Youyang zazu* was not the immediate source text, these parallel passages nonetheless provide a useful system of comparison with the *Luochong lu* in terms of tone and register, revealing the sorts of changes taking place between the classical text and the Ming rewriting. Below are some comparisons:

Youyang zazu	*Luochong lu*
胤 *yin*	遺種 *yizhong*
髮黄 *fahuang*	黄毛 *huangmao*
髭髯俱黑 *ziran ju hei*	黑髮白身 *heifa baishen*
（山）神 *shanshen*	山鬼 *shangui*
	短項 *duanxiang*
	矮胖 *aipang*

The *Luochong lu* entry consistently transposes literary Chinese into a vernacular register. In place of literary wordings such as *yin* and *fahuang* to mean "descendants" and "yellow hair," respectively, *Luochong lu* uses the colloquial-sounding *yizhong* and *huangmao*. The formal *ziran ju hei* (the mustache and sideburns are both black), along with being written in classical Chinese, is also more technical, suggestive of a classicist's punctiliousness about taxonomy, whereas *heifa* (black hair) falls in the realm of simple and straightforward description, as does *baishen* (white body), both of which are intended to expose the naked truth of the subject's lineage. Mirroring the rhetorical effect of this lowering of register, the entry also vulgarizes the story, as the mating between a mountain god and ape is told as the mating between a mountain ghost and ape.[62] Further, the *Luochong lu* entry also introduces a distinctly colloquial-sounding register with the expressions *duanxiang* 短項 ("short neck," an attribute commonly associated with pigs) and *aipang* 矮胖 (stout and fat), neither of which, strikingly, had ever appeared in any of the official dynastic histories at the time the *Luochong lu* was compiled. By using all these linguistic cues, the entry distances itself from the formality and norms of official and classical documentation to access the alternate authority and novelty of the vernacular voice.

Further, the theory that the Xiongnu are subdivided into five "kinds," in the absence of any evidence to the contrary, appears to have been concocted by the *Luochong lu* compilers themselves through selective excerpting of a range of sources. This theory of five kinds, in its crowd-pleasing simplicity and boldness, is reminiscent of the voice of the storyteller in vernacular fiction, a figure often given to digressions and asides to the audience to supply them with little known facts, etymologies, historical trivia, and particularly any amusing or useful information taking the form of a numbered list. Such features of the *Luochong lu* remind us of the text's intriguing hybridity, as it interweaves classical citations and vernacular turns of phrase. Three interlocking modes of vernacular discourse are present in this entry: first, the vernacular as the voice of the storyteller, then as oral versus literary linguistic register, and lastly as a technique of translation, including, in the instance of the translations from the *Secret History*, drawing on non-standard or colloquial registers to mark the otherness of a text originally written in a foreign language.

Several of the daily-use encyclopedia recensions of the *Luochong lu* cap off this cumulative process of rewriting by coining a new title for this entry, through the whimsical creation of a wholly factitious ethnographic epithet—"Xiongnu Dada guo" 匈奴韃靼國 (The country of Xiongnu and Tatars). The classification of peoples of north and central Asia has long been a thorny issue for historians, who often must attempt to parse overlapping and conflicting terms for tribes, peoples, and confederations that are hopelessly enmeshed in misinformation and competing claims.[63] This Ming coinage "Xiongnu Dada," with its wanton melding of two epithets with quite different chronological and political origins in Chinese documents, seems oblivious to such problems of historical accuracy. Viewed purely as part of the project of voicing the text to address the concerns and frame of reference of the *Luochong lu*'s readers, however, the coinage reveals a certain logic. The designation "Dada" (Tatars) gives a sense of contemporary relevance, since this term was pointedly revived in the Ming after the Yuan ruling house had suppressed its use due to its perceived derogatory tone, while "Xiongnu" activates associations with a storied and ancient—and culturally and territorially expansionist—period of Chinese history, particularly the Western Han (206 BCE–23 CE). All this reminds us as well that the notion of *guo* was very loosely applied in the *Luochong lu*, often more as as a unit of distinctive fashioning of a cultural or ethnic other than as any recognizable political or geographical entity of the past or present. The coinage of the epithet "Xiongnu Dada" invents a kind of historical continuity about the northern border, making it an easily manageable concept, at least textually. In the end, such Ming dynasty ethnographic fabulation draws on the same sort of imagination that in earlier eras had created countries such as the "Country of [Men with] Holes in their Chests" recorded in the *Shanhai jing*.

In its ease in paraphrasing and inventing not only details but historical visions, the *Luochong lu* mingles the scholarly mode of historical writing with bold verbal and narrative imagination, interweaving the textual modes of *shi* 史 and *xiaoshuo* 小說. The Siku editors' dismissive comments on the *Yiyu tuzhi* cited above point to this hybrid sourcing, bridging and blurring the categories of *shi* and *xiaoshuo*, as a defect, but it may well be that just such textual interweaving, along with the interplay between text and picture that distinguished the *Luochong lu*, were also key to the attraction the text held for Ming readers.

This vernacular flair and exuberance of invention, however, did become a source of unease among later readers. As noted above, the *Luochong lu* was incorporated as a chapter in the famed *Sancai tuhui*, first printed around 1609. When the 1609 blocks were used to run another printing some years later, most likely in the Qing dynasty, the new publisher decided to alter some of the blocks. One of these alterations was to plane away the entire text for the entry on the Xiongnu, leaving an empty page to accompany the picture; the empty page, however, betrays clear traces of scraping (fig. 4.6).[64] Scholars under the new Manchu regime were conventionally dismissive of the sloppiness of Ming scholarship and book culture, and when derisive depictions of "northern barbarians" were involved the

Fig. 4.6. Pages from a reprinting of *Sancai tuhui*, showing traces of block scraping for the text on Xiongnu. Photo courtesy of the C. V. Starr East Asian Library, University of California, Berkeley.

response was, naturally, doubly intolerant. In the scraping of the block containing the *Luochong lu* "Xiongnu" entry, we see an analogue to the anxiety and self-censorship that prompted the Qing authors to remove the character *yi* from their writing.

Early Reception of the Luochong lu

How was the *Luochong lu* read, and how did it circulate, during the Ming? Through unearthing and interpreting contemporary records on this text, we can chronicle episodes of the book's impact on a range of reading communities and better understand its status vis-à-vis other contemporary works as well as among various groups of readers. A recorded conversation from the Jiajing reign between Wang Duanxi 王端溪 (cognomen of Wang Chongqing 崇慶, 1484–1565) and one of the leading intellectuals of the period, Lü Nan 吕柟 (1479–1542), is an early testament to the prominence of this text in sixteenth-century reading culture:

> 問《倮蟲錄》不如《山海經》；《山海經》不如《博物志》；《博物志》不如《爾雅》；《爾雅》不如《詩》。故曰："小子何莫學夫詩。"曰：詩非止優於《爾雅》、《博物》、《山海》、《倮蟲》也；《爾雅》等書止明物，《詩》則即物以明人耳。
>
> [Duanxi] inquired, "*The Luochong lu* is not as good as *The Classic of Mountains and Seas*; *The Classic of Mountains and Seas* is not as good as *A Treatise on Broad Learning of Things*; *A Treatise on Broad Learning of Things* is not as good as *Approaching Elegance*; *Approaching Elegance* is not as good as *The Odes*. Hence Confucius says: "Little ones, why do you not study *The Odes*?"
>
> [Lü Nan] replied, "*The Odes* is not simply superior to *Approaching Elegance*, *On Broad Learning of Things*, *Mountains and Seas*, and *Naked Creatures*. Books like *Approaching Elegance* only illuminate things; *The Odes* take things as an occasion for illuminating the human." [65]

This conversation took place between 1524 and 1527, when Lü Nan was establishing the Hailiang Academy 解梁書院 in Shanxi and promoting his own curriculum and philosophy of learning. The questioner Wang Duanxi was another influential scholar-official of the time whose writings include studies on the *Yijing* and local history. Both men passed the *jinshi* examination in 1508, with Lü Nan taking the top honors in that year. By the time of this conversation, they had already become prominent public figures in official and scholarly circles. Lü Nan was particularly influential, with an enormous number of followers; his impact on the world of learning was said to rival that of the contemporary iconic figure Wang Yangming.[66] This conversation appears in *Duanxi wenda* 端溪問答 (Questions and answers with Duanxi), compiled by Lü Nan's disciples in the tradition of *yulu* (recorded sayings) and modeled on, for example, Zhu Xi's famous *Zhuzi yulei* 朱子語類 (Master Zhu's sayings, recorded and categorized). These were all ultimately patterned after the Confucian *Analects*, in a textual genre presenting itself as the verbatim transcript of the speaking voice of a figure of great cultural authority. Even though both Wang Duanxi and Lü Nan treat the *Luochong lu* dismissively in the above exchange, the choice of this text as the baseline reference among contemporary texts of this category reflects its prevalence as a familiar point of reference during this era.

In his proposition, Wang Duanxi gives a list of relevant texts in order, each new text superior to the last, and concludes with Confucius' famous advice on learning, which served as the *locus classicus* for traditionalist study of *mingwu* (names and things)—that the *Odes* is the preeminent text through which one may come to know the world. The *Luochong lu* is treated here as a representative of the latest stage in the gradual decline of orthodox learning. Despite the view of the relative merits of these texts reflected in this conversation, however, Wang Duanxi would go on to produce one of the better editions of *Shanhai jing*, accompanying that text with his own commentary. Interestingly, moreover, the *Shanhai jing* and *Luochong lu* later became cousin texts in the Ming publishing world. They were frequently cross-referenced, even appearing together on the same page, as, for example, in the pages shown in figure 4.1, where the top register is drawn from the *Shanhai jing* and the bottom from the *Luochong lu*. Thus Lü Nan and Wang Duanxi's conversation, though it allots a relatively low status to the *Luochong lu*, nonetheless attests to the fact that that text had achieved wide currency in the Jiajing world of learning; it reflects not only the book's rising popularity in this period but also the bibliographical context in which it most typically came to be referenced and reproduced—that is, in conjunction with the *Shanhai jing*.

The Luochong lu *and Ming Diplomacy*

Lü Nan's comments suggest that the status of the *Luochong lu* as an object of serious study was questionable. As it happens, the dubious factual reliability of the text, along with its widespread currency, also led to problems for Jiajing-era statesmen and diplomats. Zheng Kaiyang

鄭開陽 (1503–70), a scholar, military strategist, and cartographer, gives an account of one such complication in his *Liuqiu tushuo* 琉球圖説 (Illustrations and descriptions of Liuqiu):

> 嘉靖十一年，尚眞卒，子尚清請嗣，遣科臣陳侃、行人高澄弔祭，封清嗣王，賜王及妃冠服錦綺。使臣至其國，尚清拜曰：天朝詔敕，藏金匱者八葉於茲矣。請留爲鎮國之寶。比還，遣其王親寧吉長史蔡瀚奉表入謝，幷言：《一統志》中，載琉球有落漈，王居壁下聚髑髏，非實事。《杜氏通典》、《集事淵海》、《嬴蟲錄》、《星槎勝覽》所述，亦皆傳聞之妄。乞下史館。從之。蓋海外荒服，欽承王化，漸革故習，君臣父子間彬彬有禮，文物之盛，迥殊他邦矣。
>
> In the eleventh year of the Jiajing reign [1532], [King] Shang Zhen died. His son Shang Qing requested to succeed to the kingship. Civil official Chen Kan and Ambassador Gao Cheng were dispatched to offer condolence and sacrifices, to enfeoff Qing as the new king, and to present the king and his consort with hats, clothes, and fine fabrics. When the embassy arrived at that country, Shang Qing bowed and said: "The imperial commands now stored in gold caskets here in this country number eight. I request to retain this edict as a national treasure." When the embassy returned, the king sent Ning Ji[67] of the royal family and Senior Scribe Cai Huan to deliver a memorial to express his gratitude, and to say, "In the *Gazetteer of the Unified Empire* [*Yitong zhi*],[68] it is documented that Liuqiu has a *luoji*-maelstrom[69] and that skulls are piled beneath the walls of the king's residence. This is untrue. Moreover, the things recounted in Master Du's *Comprehensive Canons* [*Tongdian*],[70] in the *Deep Ocean of Collected Matters* [*Ji shi yuan hai*],[71] in the *Luochong lu*, and in *Spectacles of the Starry Rafts* [*Xing cha sheng lan*][72] are all erroneous reports. I humbly request that this matter be submitted to the Office of History." This request was granted.
>
> [Zheng Kaiyang's comment:] This is a matter of wild regions beyond the seas reverently submitting to kingly transformation, and thereby gradually changing their former practices, until relations between lord and subject, father and son are now all ceremonious and proper. The splendor of civilization there is far different from other states.[73]

Zheng Kaiyang here singles out a moment in Ming-Liuqiu relations when Liuqiu officials protested the distorted mythical accounts of the dangers and primitiveness of their kingdom in almost all the primary records in Ming China, including the *Luochong lu*. Ming ambassadors shared this sentiment—Chen Kan 陳侃, who is mentioned in the above passage as one of the Jiajing-era envoys to Liuqiu, himself also submitted a memorial on the unreliability of documents on Liuqiu. When preparing for his mission to Liuqiu, Chen had been struck by the utter lack of practical and reliable documents to consult. To improve this situation, he composed *Shi Liuqiu lu* 使琉球錄 (Records of a mission to Liuqiu, preface dated 1534) after his return. In a section of this document entitled

"Verifying Doubtful Points in the Various Books" 群書質異, he evaluates the merits of records extracted from the following books:

Da Ming yitong zhi 大明一統志
Gazetteer of the Unified Grand Ming

Luochong lu 蠃蟲錄
Record of Naked Creatures

Xing cha sheng lan 星槎勝覽
Spectacles of the Starry Rafts

Ji shi yuanhai 集事淵海
Deep Ocean of Collected Matters

Du shi tong dian 杜氏通典
Master Du's Comprehensive Canons

Shi zhi yao wu 使職要務
Guidelines for Dignitaries

Da Ming huidian 大明會典
The Collected Statutes of the Grand Ming

Note that many of these books are also mentioned in the reported Liuqiu memorial.[74] Zheng Kaiyang, however, takes a different perspective on these records. While Chen attempts to correct them for practical reasons of statecraft, Zheng Kaiyang views the discrepancy between written record and current reality as reflecting the progressive success of Liuqiu's sinification. The early records, in Zheng Kaiyang's view, are important not because they contain unreliable and fanciful mythography, but rather because they reflect an earlier primitive state of Liuqiu civilization. In other words, even though the records are no longer accurate, the Liuqiu requests for corrections reflect not the faultiness of these records themselves but rather the laudable progress made by Liuqiu in becoming more civilized under Chinese influence.

After Chen Kan, it became conventional for Ming dignitaries to Liuqiu to compile their own *Records of a Mission to Liuqiu* (hereafter *Records*). In these later *Records*, Chen Kan's "Resolving Doubtful Points in the Various Books" section remains virtually intact, while new comments are appended.[75] "Resolving Doubtful Points in the Various Books" in effect became a routine exercise in bureaucratic archiving, a marker of reliable *Records* (*lu*). It eventually influenced how Qing scholar-official Xu Baoguang 徐葆光 (?–1723) critiqued Ming records on Liuqiu in his much-acclaimed *Zhongshan chuanxin lu* 中山傳信錄 (Account of a mission to Zhongshan), compiled 1718–20.[76]

Private Readers and Stories of the Extraordinary

Despite these persistent queries by diplomats, the *Luochong lu* circulated continuously without any alteration to its record of Liuqiu. For private readers, the text was the latest product in the long history of books on extraordinary phenomena, and as such it drew much of its appeal precisely from the outlandishness of its accounts of distant places. Lang Ying 郎瑛 (1487–1566) presents the following musings in his *Qixiu leigao* 七修類稿 (Manuscript in seven categories), offering a glimpse into the mentality of the Ming book culture that welcomed and sought out texts like the *Luochong lu*:

> 元詩人陳孚，出使安南，有紀事之詩曰：“鼻飲如瓴甋，頭飛似轆轤。”蓋言土人能鼻飲者，有頭能夜飛於海食魚，曉復歸身者。予見《蠃蟲集》中所載：“老撾國人，鼻飲水漿，頭飛食魚。”近汪海雲亦能鼻飲。頭飛則怪也。昨見《星槎勝覽》亦言：“占城國人，有頭飛者，乃婦人也。夜飛食人糞尖。知而固封其項。或移其身則死矣。”作書者自云目擊其事。予又考占城正接安南之南，而老撾正接安南西北。信陳詩之不誣也。
>
> The Yuan dynasty poet Chen Fu went on a diplomatic mission to Annam. One of his poems on events includes the lines, “Noses that drink like water jars; / heads that fly like windlasses.” This describes the locals who are able to drink through their noses, and those who have heads that can fly to the sea to eat fish at night and return to their bodies again at dawn. I saw the account in the *Luochong* collection that states, “People of the country of Laos drink liquids with their noses; their heads fly and eat fish.” In recent times, Wang Haiyun could also drink with his nose. As for flying heads, that is truly strange. Recently I saw that *The Spectacles of the Starry Rafts* also says, “Among the people of the country of Zhancheng, there are people with flying heads—they are women. Their heads fly at night to eat the tips of human excrement. When such persons are discovered, if they have their necks firmly secured, or if the body is moved, they die.” The person who composed this book said that he witnessed this himself. I have further investigated the matter and found that Zhancheng is adjacent to Annam to the south, and Laos is adjacent to Annam to the northwest. Indeed, Chen's poem was no fabrication.[77]

This short essay is placed in the chapter on “the strange and the humorous” (*qixue* 奇謔) in Lang's book. Lang's perspective differs from that of defenders of classicist orthodoxy such as Lü Nan, as well as from that of court officials concerned with the reliability of information available to civil servants. For Lang, the *Luochong lu* is one of a range of recent books that can be mined for new and amusing information. Such books provided him with a bibliographical field to track down cross-references and to formulate his own equally "strange and humorous" ideas. Lang Ying is first and foremost a bibliophile, and what he does here is quote books of his time to comment on a poem from a previous dynasty. His comment on these exotic reports begins and ends in the moments of reading: the Yuan poem provides a pretext for him to recall what he saw in the *Luochong lu* first, then in *The Spectacles of the Starry Rafts* "recently." The essay develops a narrative of discovery, of encountering and realizing (*jian* 見) through accumulative reading, and reports a breakthrough moment when several textual encounters are linked together to shed new light on abstruse and exotic questions. In light of this narrative, his conclusion—"Indeed, Chen's poem was no fabrication"—expresses a kind of bibliographical pride. This essay projects a reader self who indulges in explorations of the boundary between fantastic tales and actual geopolitical reports. Bibliographical inquiries allow him to display a form of erudition and wit that separates one's private world of letters from bureaucratic writing and public discussions of state matters. If Lang Ying's reasoning—in its close attention to the "thing" (a poem's depiction) under investigation, in its parsing of the patterns embedded in the "thing," and in its final arrival at an interpretation—appears to follow the philosopher Zhu Xi's script of "investigating things" (*gewu* 格物), what is noteworthy is that for Lang Ying the process is carried out entirely within a network of books.

This mode of reception that promotes bibliographical expertise is also seen later in Xu Yingqiu's 徐應秋 (*jinshi* 1616) *Yuzhi tang tanhui* 玉芝堂談薈 (Miscellany of conversation from Jade Mushroom Hall), compiled in the Wanli era. By gathering records from various books, Xu cataloged a curious species of human being: "The *Man*-Barbarians of Flying Heads" 飛頭蠻:[78]

飛頭蠻

桓譚《新論》:"荆州有鼻飲之蠻,南城有頭飛之夷"。《搜神記》:"晋朱桓一婢,其頭夜飛。或從天窗出入,以耳爲翼,將曉復還……"。《北户錄》:嶺南溪洞中，往往有飛頭者……《星槎勝覽》：“占城國婦人有頭飛者，人知而封固其項，及移其身，則死。”《羸蟲集》：“老撾國鼻飲水漿，頭飛食魚。”《瀛州勝覽》：占城有尸頭蠻，但眼無瞳……《拾遺記》：漢武時因墀國言南方有解形之民，能使頭飛南海……

"The *Man*-Barbarians of Flying Heads"

Huan Tan's *New Treatise*: "In Jingzhou, there are *man*-barbarians who drink with their noses; in Nancheng, there are yi-barbarians of flying heads." *Records of the Search for Spirits*: "Zhu Huan of the Jin had a maid whose head flew at night. Sometimes she flew in and out of the high window, using her ears as wings. She always came back at dawn. . . ." *Record of the Beihu*: "In the caves and creeks south of the five peaks, there are often those whose heads can fly . . ."[79] *The Spectacles of the Starry Rafts*: "Among the women of the country of Zhancheng, there were those whose heads could fly. When those who detect this seal the neck, or move the body, then they die." *Compendium of Naked Creatures*: "People of the country of Laos drink liquids with their noses; their heads fly and eat fish." *Spectacles of "Immortals' Isles"*: "There are corpse-head barbarians in Zhancheng, who have only eyes, with no pupils . . ."[80] *Record of Lost Accounts*:[81] "At the time of Emperor Wu of the Han dynasty, the country of Yinchi reported that there were people whose bodies can disassemble. They could make their heads fly to the south sea . . ."[82]

To Xu Yingqiu, the *Luochong lu* is to be mined for fantastic accounts of zoological anomalies and denizens of outlandish regions. It was one of the source books for extracting ethnographical information on an evidently universally known species: barbarians with flying heads. Driving Xu's aggregation of related tales from a broad range of books is a reading culture that avidly sought out unique and rare books, as testified by Xu's own words at the very beginning of his preface to *Yuzhi tang tanhui*: "Master Yuzhi has no other obsessions, but delights in reading books that he has not before seen, earnestly admires displays of erudition and comprehensive knowledge, and delights to speak of unusual matters."[83]

After this confession of an appetite for books and curiosities, Xu Yingqiu offers his view on those records that seem to shock people with their bizarre and unbelievable tales. The problem, according to Xu, lies not with the records themselves, but rather with their readers. He cites the commonplace expression that "those who have seen very little are shocked by much" 少見多怪 to explain the reactions of such readers.[84] For Xu the issue is not whether the account of the strange is truthful, but whether the reader is qualified to read it. The key is to cultivate the right reading subject, what Xu calls "a comprehending man of wide reading" 弘覽之通人. As his account of "Barbarians of Flying Heads" shows, the usefulness of recent books on foreign countries is brought to light when these are placed alongside classical tales of the strange and rare. A qualified reader, for Xu, would be one with sufficient book knowledge and bibliographical sophistication, including the proper repertoire of genre-specific modes of reading.

The Popularity and Influence of the Luochong lu

The *Luochong lu* also inspired new works, chief among them *Dongyi tushuo* 東夷圖說 (Pictures and descriptions of eastern barbarians), commissioned in 1586 by the Provincial Administration Vice Commissioner of Guangdong province Cai Ruxian 蔡汝賢 (*jinshi* degree 1568).[85] Cai's book contains twenty pictures—some copied from the *Luochong lu*, such as the one for Java 爪哇, and others newly added, such as the one for Folangji 佛朗機, that is, the Portuguese (fig. 4.7).[86]

Fig. 4.7. Illustrations from the *Dongyi tushuo*. 1586. The left-hand side shows the illustration for "Folangji," and the right, for Java. From *SKCM*, *shibu* 史部, vol. 255, p. 415.

Guangdong was one of the most active regions in global trade at the time, and Cai Ruxian, in his official capacity, had opportunities to receive tribute bearers and merchants from overseas. His pictorial was prompted by and based on direct contact with these peoples. Cai's book is oriented toward *shi* 實 (the real); his narrative stresses current situations and real-time observation. In this regard he is similar to the Jiajing-era diplomat Chen Kan, who was also concerned with pragmatism and accuracy. What differentiates Cai from Chen is that besides the concerns he raised about matters of statecraft, Cai recognized the value of popular and fanciful books such as the *Luochong lu*. Here is what he wrote in his preface to his own pictorial:

> 或曰："……東南夷該此乎？"曰："未也。雜見於杜氏《通典》、《集事淵海》、《星槎勝覽》、《蠃蟲錄》、《吾學編》諸書，蕃乎夥矣。存而弗論可也。"
>
> Someone asked, ". . . Are all the Southeastern barbarians collected here?" I answered, "No. The accounts seen in all those books such as Master Du's *Comprehensive Canons*, the *Deep Ocean of Collected Matters*, the *Spectacles of the Starry Rafts*, the *Luochong lu*, and the *My Studies Compilation* are truly numerous. With such things it is acceptable to simply preserve them without opining about them."[87]

Books such as Master Du's *Comprehensive Canons*, the *Deep Ocean of Collected Matters*, *Spectacles of the Starry Rafts*, and the *Luochong lu*—all of which, we recall, were also cited in "Resolving Doubtful Points in the Various Books"[88]—were given legitimacy: "With such things it is acceptable to simply preserve them without opining about them." Cai seemed to have no trouble balancing his recognition (if not appreciation) for popular books with his own endeavor to produce factually reliable pictures. One wonders if he possessed a personal quality that a rising class of people dealing with foreign issues (later called *yangwu* 洋務) cultivated in themselves, namely *kaiming* 開明 (enlightened, or worldly-wise), as his preface continues:

> [或曰：]"……所圖狀貌習尚審乎？"曰："千里殊風，百里異俗，中國且然，矧夷乎？彼此互見，論而弗膠可也。"
>
> [Someone asked,] ". . . As for the appearances and habits pictured, are they accurate?" I answered, "'Ways of life differ within a thousand miles; customs vary within a hundred miles.' This is true even within the central states—how much the more must it be so in the case of barbarians? Such things appear through reciprocal comparison—with such things we may opine about them without being inflexible about literal accuracy."[89]

Here he expresses a worldly understanding of the inter-referentiality between "us" and "them": foreign appearances and customs are to be understood with reference to domestic analogues, and vice versa.

The popularity of the *Luochong lu* remained high through the late Ming, as the text enjoyed a remarkable number of reprints and was appropriated to fill a category in daily-use encyclopedias. Since numerous publishers rushed to print their own editions of more or less the same daily-use encyclopedia during this period, this resulted in dozens of reprintings of the *Luochong lu* in encyclopedias alone.[90] Thus the text does seem to have enjoyed very widespread currency in the late sixteenth century. The 1607 Buddhist treatise *Fajie anli tu* 法界安立圖 (Maps of the configuration of dharmadhātu) refers to the *Luochong lu* as a supplementary lay source text for information about the human realm, the continent known in Buddhist cosmology as Jambudvīpa: "The layman's book *Luochong lu* records various countries with a diverse range of human forms. These are perhaps the various small islands in the ocean" 俗書《臝蟲錄》載諸國人形各異，或是海中諸小洲也.[91] Private bibliophiles of the Ming and early Qing also recorded this title in their catalogs, showing that many of the most illustrious book collectors of the time did not shun the *Luochong lu*. These private library catalogs include the *Chao shi Baowen tang shumu* 晁氏寶文堂書目 (Bibliography of the Chao family's Studio of Treasured Texts) compiled during the Jiajing reign, the *Dansheng tang shumu* 澹生堂書目 (Bibliography of the Studio of Detached Life) of the Wanli reign, and later the *Qianqing tang shumu* 千頃堂書目 (Bibliography of the Thousand-Acre Studio) compiled in the early Qing.[92]

The above reconstruction of various episodes related to the social influence of the *Luochong lu* in the Ming suggests that the *Luochong lu* was read or known broadly—by literati, religious practitioners,[93] common readers, officials, and foreigners.[94] It appears to have been the most prominent—if not the only—pictorial document offering an exhaustive inventory of foreign peoples as they were known in Ming China. It became a much-utilized source book and reference book—the bibliographical category that most effectively shaped the collective consciousness of readers of this period. In the following section I return to consider some of the specific features of the text as it circulated within Ming daily-use encyclopedias, as their packaging of the *Luochong lu* provides a unique window into how the *Luochong lu* was viewed in relation to the broader Ming social order.

Packaging the Luochong lu*: Prefaces and Illustrations in Encyclopedia Editions*

The many reprintings of the *Luochong lu* as a chapter in late Ming daily-use encyclopedias provide rich material for examining how publishers shaped their texts to make them appealing and marketable, as well as what kinds of readers and ways of reading they envisioned. Here I will focus on two sorts of supplements that often appear in such reprintings, namely, prefaces and division-head illustrations.

As figure 4.1 shows, the "Various Barbarian Lands" chapters packaged the *Luochong lu* together with a listing of "Strange Beings of Mountains and Seas" 山海異物 largely drawn from the *Shanhai jing* in a double-register format. The double-register layout is characteristic of the encyclopedia as a whole, but this particular juxtaposition gave apt expression to Ming readers' already well-established association between the *Luochong lu* and the *Shanhai jing*.[95] In these encyclopedias, a preface explains the origin of the term "Luochong" and the association between foreigners in the lower register and fabulous animals in the upper register:

贏蟲錄序

鱗蟲三百六十而龍爲之長，羽蟲三百六十而鳳爲之長，毛蟲三百六十而麟爲之長，介蟲三百六十而龜爲之長，贏蟲三百六十而人爲之長。贏蟲者，四方化外之夷是也。何則以人爲贏蟲之長？書曰：生居中國，故得天地之正氣者爲人；生居化外，不得天地之正氣者爲禽爲獸，故曰"贏蟲"。孔子曰："治夷狄如治禽獸。"其説有自矣。原其無倫理綱常，尚戰斗輕生樂死，虎狼之性也；貪貨利好淫僻，麀鹿之行也，故與人之性情實遼矣。

Preface to the *Record of Naked Creatures*

Of scaled creatures there are 360, and the dragon is their leader. Of feathered creatures there are 360, and the phoenix is their leader. Of haired creatures there are 360, and the *qilin* is their leader. Of shelled creatures there are 360, and the tortoise is their leader. Of naked creatures there are 360, and the human is their leader. "Naked creatures" refers to the barbarians of all four directions outside the sphere of transformation. Why, then, is it said "humans are the leader of the naked creatures"? The book says: those born and residing in the middle kingdom, who receive the correct and proper *qi* of heaven and earth, are human;

> those born outside the sphere of transformation, who do not receive the correct and proper *qi* of heaven and earth, are animals, and are therefore called "naked creatures." Confucius says, "Governing the *yi*-barbarians and the *di*-barbarians is like governing animals"—thus we see that this explanation is of long standing and authority. Because they do not have ethical principles, love war and battles, take life lightly and delight in death, they share the nature of tigers and wolves. Because they hanker for material gain and are fond of licentiousness, just like the behavior of incestuous deer, their nature and disposition are truly distant from the human.[96]

This preface has two notable formal attributes. First, it is structured by the familiar steps of *qi-cheng-zhuan-he* 起承轉合 (beginning, elucidation, turning, and closing), a basic compositional principle engrained in the minds of examination candidates and students of prose in general in late imperial China. Second, it features an elevated proportion of quotation.

Specifically, the preface opens (*qi*) its discussion by quoting, though without specifically saying so, from *The Family Sayings of Confucius* and the like, before moving on to an elucidation (*cheng*) of its key concept *luochong*. Though some earlier scholars had believed that the *luochong* were a class of short-haired animals such as tigers and leopards,[97] these earlier philological inquiries are beyond the concern of our anonymous author, who resolves to simply assert that *luochong* means "barbarians." The author continues by posing a question (*zhuan*) that is rhetorical in nature: "Why, then, is it said 'humans are the leader of the naked creatures'?" and answers with yet another quote, this time from an anonymous "book" (*shu*): "those born and residing in the middle kingdom, who receive the correct and proper *qi* of heaven and earth are human; those born outside the sphere of transformation, who do not receive the correct and proper *qi* of heaven and earth, are animals." Thus, to the author, barbarians are those "naked creatures" whose endowment makes them in some way less than fully human. Finally, the author concludes with a third quote, this time from none other than Confucius, stating that "governing the *yi*-barbarians and the *di*-barbarians is like governing animals," and continues this thought with a quick-tempo portrayal of these barbarians' beastly attributes: "Because they hanker for material gain and are fond of licentiousness, just like the behavior of incestuous deer, their nature and disposition are truly distant from the human." In this preface, the *yi* is glossed as and "proven" to refer to an animalistic or subhuman sort of creature.[98] It is easy to imagine how text like this might have prompted Qing writers to suppress the use of the term *yi* 夷 in a regime that was ruled by, according to these texts, just such creatures.

Compared to other prefaces and comments on the *Luochong lu*, what this preface does *not* do is philosophize or historicize the relation between China and barbarians. Instead, it quotes. It quotes from the most familiar and authoritative stock phrases, first the familiar enumeration of the five-family system of living beings, which had appeared in medieval texts such as the *Family Sayings of Confucius*, then with a declared quotation from an anonymous book, and finally with the ultra-authoritative Confucius—though this particular quotation is not found in received texts clearly attributed to him but rather is a recurrent idea in early classical writings such as *Han shu* 漢書 and *Guo yu* 國語. "Confucius" is invoked here as a label for authoritative wisdom rather than as the author of a definite text.

The familiarity of the overall structure and the dependence on commonplaces make the preface a great piece of comfort reading that confirms a set of conventional assumptions. To be sure, the preface is a pastiche of the most common clichés and stereotypes when it comes to the representation of foreigners, particularly in its strong reliance on animal analogies. Seen across time and space in world history, the animal motif is undoubtedly played up in this preface, enhanced by the juxtaposition of the exotic peoples and the fantastical animals. This is not to say, however, that some readers of the Ming would not recognize the preface as a clever text intending to evoke laughter, albeit at the expense of the foreigners discussed. The point is that while the dissemination of the *Luochong lu* no doubt expanded readers' knowledge and awareness of the world, it also perpetuated and solidified certain prejudice against the Other. However, it should be noted that text alone does not complete meaning, which can only be actualized by a reader, and, as seen above, readers employed diverse ways of reading the *Luochong lu*. Prejudice and enlightenment can come out of the same text, and the marketplace spreads knowledge that can be used and read in different and, at times, opposing ways.

Prefaces aside, publishers of encyclopedias put even more effort into producing division-head illustrations that would promote their own products and accommodate and guide readers' viewing experiences. Chapter

3 presented two such illustrations, and below I will consider another pair from two other daily-use encyclopedias that draw on visual conventions different from those discussed in the previous chapter. Both illustrations are embedded within the specific pictorial subject of *zhigong* 職貢 (submission of foreign tribute). *Zhigong* had long been established as a pictorial genre in court painting (one painting of this type is attributed to Emperor Yuan of the Liang [552–55]). State offices (such as the Bureaus of Reception 主客司 of the Tang and Song dynasties) also produced likenesses of foreigners as part of the empire's ethnographic documentation. Painters outside court circles produced versions of this pictorial topic as well; the sixteenth-century painter Qiu Ying 仇英, for example, is credited with one of the most acclaimed such paintings.

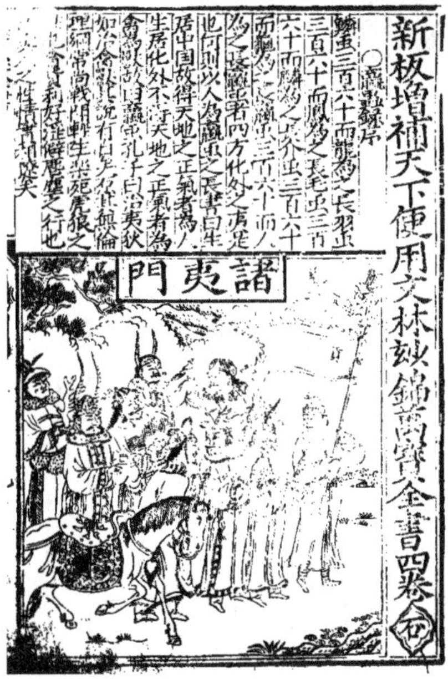

Fig. 4.8. Division-head illustration in *Miaojin wanbao quanshu*. From *CNRS*, vol. 12, p. 209.

The division-head illustration in *Miaojin wanbao quanshu* (fig. 4.8), possibly engraved by Liu Ciquan, is reminiscent of Qiu Ying's "Picture of Tribute Bearers," where the tribute bearers are depicted in groups rather than as individuals. There are other obvious borrowings from established visual convention—the bird, for example, is commonly seen in *zhigong* paintings. The overall tone of this picture is one founded on the ideal of *renao* (lively and loud), which differs from the solemnity often seen in iconic court paintings. What is presented to readers is a group of happy, chatty, festive people dressed in exotic costumes on their way to the Chinese court.

The attention to detail and clear reference to iconic paintings are far less prominent in the division-head illustration in *Wuche wanbao quanshu* 五車萬寶全書 (Complete book of myriad treasures from five carriages of books) (fig. 4.9).[99] While it could be viewed as rather sloppily

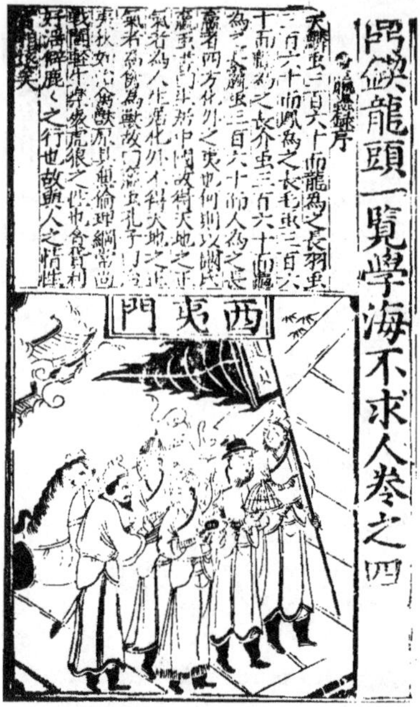

Fig. 4.9. Title page of the chapter on "Western [sic] Barbarians" from *Wuche wanbao quanshu*. Wanli reign. Jianyang imprint. From *CNRS*, vol. 8, p. 125. "Western" (*xi* 西) in the chapter title is almost certainly a transcription error for *si* 四 (four), referring to all four cardinal directions.

produced, it does take an economical approach that favors significant features over minor details.[100] These features include the steepness of the steps and the palace top surrounded by auspicious clouds, which serve as visual cues to convey the sense of Ming China being the "Heavenly Country" (*tianguo* 天國) or the "Supreme Country" (*shangguo* 上國).

The history of circulation and evaluation of the *Luochong lu* from the fifteenth century through the end of the Ming shows that regardless of occasional doubts about its factual reliability, it served in the minds of a wide range of readers as a basic reference point for shaping their vision of the broader world of regions and peoples outside the Ming empire. The choice of the tribute procession as the representative pictorial image of foreigners to introduce the *Luochong lu* in these daily use encyclopedia illustrations provides further clues as to how this text was received and made use of by its readers. Just as in the case of the illustrations of court audiences with foreign dignitaries discussed in the preceding chapter, such images remind us of the important role of imperial spectacle as a lens through which readers could understand their own relationship to the foreign Other, even if the real ritual and diplomatic world of the court was far removed from their own daily experience. The space of wonder and fantasy about the exotic thus became a fruitful field for articulating a personal and domesticated sense of Ming identity.

The Luochong lu *and Global Exchange*

Perhaps the most telling sign of the *Luochong lu*'s fame and authority—which had been acquired due to its popularity in the book market, rather than through the sanction of the state or of scholarly orthodoxy—may be seen in how it was referenced and appropriated in the new Manchu dynasty. The prestigious imperial *Kangxi Dictionary* 康熙字典 (completed 1716) quotes it in its definition of the character *ge* 虼: "*Gelu* 虼魯, a name of a country. 'To go from there to the Jiangnan region by horse takes seven months.' Seen in *Luochong lu*."[101] Another example of its continued but now somewhat less public influence was the fact that the *Gujin tushu ji cheng* 古今圖書集成 (Complete collections of illustrations and writings from the earliest to current times), compiled under the auspices of Prince Yinzhi 胤祉 (1677–1732) and the Kangxi emperor (r. 1662–1723), ultimately based its pictorial section about foreigners on the *Luochong lu*.[102] Official disapproval of the text did not come until the Qianlong period (1736–96), when the *Siku* scholars dismissed it, saying "such a text is most decidedly not to be relied on as a source of information."[103] From this point on, the *Luochong lu* began its descent into prolonged obscurity.

It did not, however, die out entirely. First, Ming imprints remained in the hands of book collectors and could be accessed and read. More to the point, the daily-use encyclopedias printed in the Qing retained the "Barbarians of Various Lands" chapter, where the Ming preface to the *Luochong lu* discussed in the previous session remained virtually intact. And this is the preface that, we may recall, contained the statement "Confucius says, 'governing the *yi*-barbarians and the *di*-barbarians is like governing animals.'" However, the evidence available to me suggests that the title *Luochong lu* had gradually faded away, as this chapter in at least some Qing daily-use encyclopedias was now called, more generically, "Pictures of Foreign Peoples and their Local Products" 外夷土產人民圖.[104] In other words, what had been known as the *Luochong lu* during the Ming was still in circulation in Qing popular encyclopedias, but it had become disassociated from its former title. Another important factor to note is that although the Yongzheng emperor redefined *yi* to mean the equivalent of "birthplace," thereby removing any insult to Qing sovereignty, the word *yi* continued to be imbued with slighting connotations in popular books, which seem to have exempted themselves from imperial vision and/or self-imposed censorship. The popular discourse and elite and court discourse do not agree but compete with each other—all the more reason, perhaps, for the court and court scholars to be nervous.

Beyond China, the *Luochong lu* had quite a colorful life: In early Edo Japan (1600–1868), it was recast in a popular pictorial and narrative genre of the day, that of the "Nara picture book" (Nara *ehon* 奈良繪本), under the title *Ikoku monogatari* 異國物語 (The tale of foreign countries), with illustrations rendered delicately in vivid and elegant colors. Not surprisingly, in this new hand-copied album, the illustration accompanying the entry for "Great Japan" (*Dai Nihon koku*, fig. 4.10) depicts an elegant interior scene of lavishly dressed figures. This contrasts quite markedly with the original Chinese depictions (figs. 4.3 and 4.4).[105] Still, in this Japanese rendition, the Chinese perspective remains loosely apparent, as Japan is still ranked among the "foreign countries" (*ikoku*). While the circulation of *Ikoku monogatari* suggests a shared East Asian view of the "world" shaped by common texts and images,[106] it also brings to light the complex process through which the entity called "Great Japan" (Dai Nihon) came to be understood in Edo Japan vis-à-vis China and the world, a process by which the reworking of Chinese books and frames of reference became a crucial and contested issue.[107]

The *Luochong lu* circulated in other parts of the world as well. An edition dated to 1550 now preserved in Japan was obtained from Korea, attesting to its circulation there.[108] The encyclopedias that incorporated the *Luochong lu* were brought to Korea, Japan, and Europe,[109] bringing the *Luochong lu* into the orbit of the global circulation of books and ideas. For example, *Luochong lu* passages are excerpted in Han Ch'i-yun's 韓致奫 (1765–1814) *History of Korea* (Haedong yŏksa 海東繹史). In this book, Han Ch'i-yun cites from the *Luochong lu* entry on Koryŏ: "People in charge of poetry and writing, rituals and music, medicine and divination all followed (Jizi from the Central States) to Chosŏn. (This country's) offices and institutions, and norms of clothes all follow those of the Central States."[110]

Conclusion

The *Luochong lu* and its spinoffs proved to be remarkably mercurial and adaptable. It easily survived and circulated in whole or in partial or changed forms. Its contribution to the burgeoning discussion surrounding the notion of the foreigner in the Ming and beyond is not just in its subject matter as such, but in the ways that it selected its source material, reached readers, and realized its social impact as a book or part of a

Fig. 4.10. A new picture to accompany "The Country of Great Japan." In *Ikoku monogatari* 異國物語 (aka *Kara monogatari* 唐物語), Edo period. From *Ikoku monogatari*, p. 10.

book. The breadth of the reading public it reached and its involvement in the realms of diplomatic relations, reading activities, and book culture in the early modern era form a stark contrast with the text's oblivion in later cultural memory. It is in the coming together of the subject matter of the barbarian and the social process of the creation and use of books that the *Luochong lu* offers a unique window into the history of early modern China.

CONCLUSION

Home and the World: Editing Ming China

Figure C.1 is a typical frontispiece illustration for a division in a daily-use encyclopedia: it presents a lively image designed to entice the reader, drawing on a visual language whose conventional associations suggest the space of circulation and use of the texts to appear within. The central figure is an itinerant peddler, one of the sorts of cultural intermediaries who have been the heroes of this study. This peddler is seen selling poem-fans (*shishan* 詩扇) to a group of three women. Holding a brush poised to write in one hand, he is depicted in the act of inscribing a poem or couplet on a fan, in response to his female customer's particular request, as she is gesturing theatrically before him to convey what she wants. Two other women, each holding a newly purchased and inscribed fan, read and discuss their own inscriptions and their fans—one a "round fan" (*tuanshan* 團扇) and the other a "folding fan" (*zheshan* 摺扇).

The motif of distance is key in this picture. The basic visual layout is of a type known in painting manuals as "level distance" (*pingyuan* 平遠) composition: the viewing perspective is from an elevated spot in the foreground, looking out toward mountains in the distance.[1] The suggestion is of a distant place outside the hurly-burly of the cosmopolitan center. With the four treasures of a literary study (*wenfang sibao* 文房四寶)—brush, ink, paper, ink-stone—as the tools of his trade, the peddler brings cultural goods to this remote yet elegant site. The elegance is signaled by

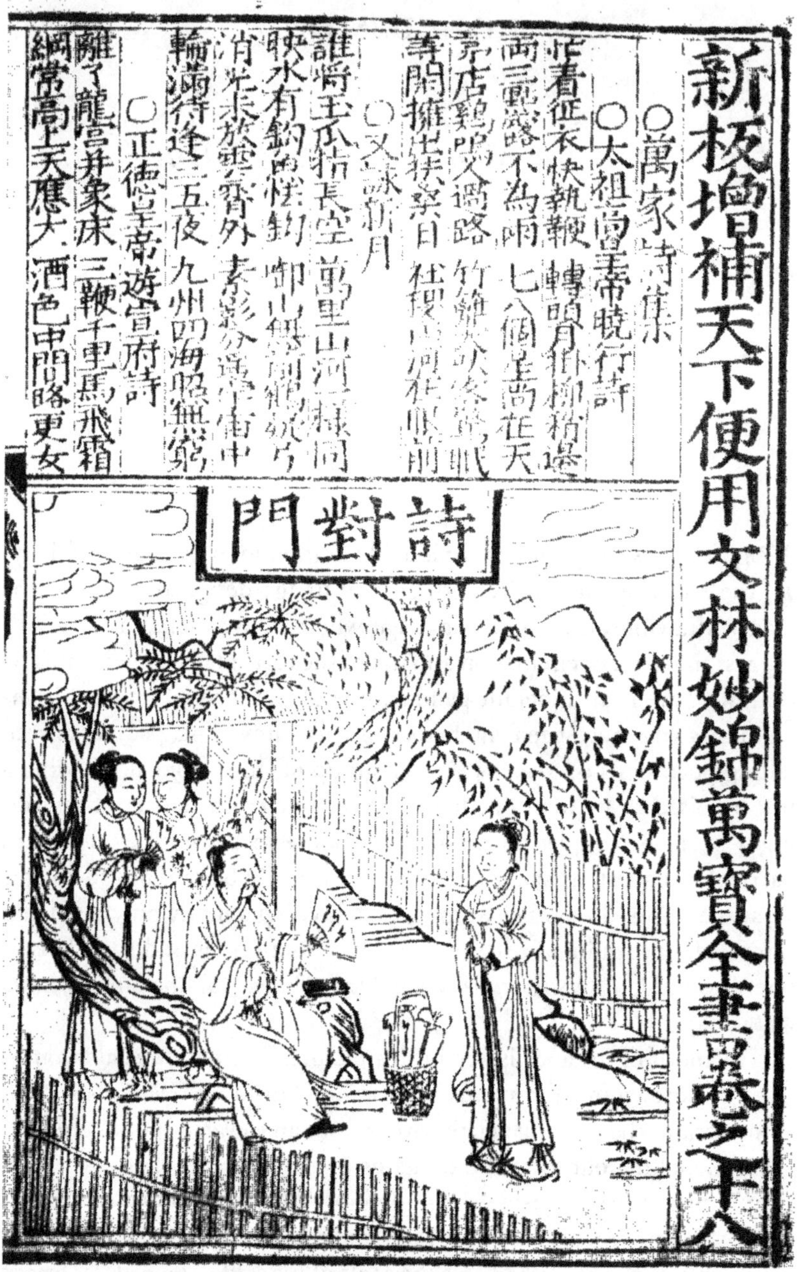

Fig. C.1. Frontispiece illustration to the "Poems and Couplets" division, *Miaojin wanbao quanshu*. From *CNRS*, vol. 13, p. 175.

the pastoral landscape, the bamboo branches, and the little pavilion—and the peddler himself contributes an element of cultural refinement by bringing both writing and material artifacts with cultural cachet, namely, fans. His clientele in this remote location is further marked by another sort of distance from the political, economic, and cultural center: its female gender. The figure of the woman, in the meantime, symbolizes new classes of art and print consumers. In this connection, the idea of distance also doubles as the idea of the new, specifically the new market forces that seek to stake a claim in the cultural fashions of the day.[2] The peddler, the last link in a network of transmission and adaptation of cultural goods, recycles and markets his wares, adapting them to suit the needs and whims of an ever broader circle of reader-consumers, for as we clearly see, his basket has yet more to offer.[3]

It was the fan peddler and other cultural intermediaries like him, including the publishers, printers, editors, and text- and picture-makers discussed in this study, who presided over and enabled the circulation of texts and images among diverse social circles.[4] They, along with various reading groups such as the women shown above, made use of, interpreted, and appropriated a repertoire of cultural forms in a range of categories including *guwen*, poetry, theater, and geography. These cultural intermediaries, like the peddler in the illustration who inscribes the fan in response to a particular customer's request, had highly developed skills in tailoring these widespread and prestigious cultural forms to the local and particular desires of their clienteles. On the other hand, that repertoire of forms itself was, in turn, constantly reshaped due not least to their editing and intervention—as we see in the illustration, the fan-peddler's brush is yet to settle on the fan.

What remains of these moments of adaptation and accommodation are the material traces of the work of these cultural intermediaries—fans in this picture, and blocks, pages, and books elsewhere in this study. The enclosing fences and the female gender of the residents in the illustration also mark the space in which the fan-peddler and the women interact, bridging the gap between home and the world. In the moment frozen in time by this illustration, desirable cultural goods of cosmopolitan and empire-wide ambit are converted to personal possessions for home consumption. Both customers and the cultural intermediary participate in the remaking of the exchanged goods and, in the end, create new cultural forms. In the domestic retailing of poetry in this picture, and in the general commerce of books, it is the dimension of *use*—how texts matter to their readers, and how objects matter to their owners—that counts the most.

In a textual universe centered on use and re-use, it was in this adaptation to domestic use that Ming editors excelled, rather than in staking and maintaining authorial claims or in guarding textual pedigrees. The pattern of circulation and adaptation that came to be referred to disparagingly as "hucksterish" editorial practice was, in its own terms, a set of strategies evolving out of market-driven imperatives to both reproduce and differentiate, imperatives that provided the driving force behind novel fashions and new cultural forms. Blocks, pages, texts, and images were all objects for re-use and editing, and making small changes to an established model offered an expedient way to serve new purposes, convey new meanings, and reach new audiences. In the process, a new system of visual signs was established. Through these new repertoires of composition, and the corresponding skills readers had to draw on to decode them, there emerged a new and distinctive world of reading. As one book title states, readers were offered "the myriad phenomena made fresh" (*wanxiang xin* 萬象新).

As captured in the picture, the poetic inscriptions and the fans that serve as their material medium are equally fundamental components of the cultural product. Customers value the inscriptions, but also have to know what to do with the fans. Thus the fan serves as an apt reminder of the sort of know-how (or "book conversancy" beyond mere literacy per se) that emerges from many of our case studies of Ming book culture: conversancy with the form of a page, the type of a book, the intent of a compiler, or the importance of reading or owning a book as a marker of social distinction. This notion of conversancy renders obsolete the dichotomy between form and content, and compels us to set aside in our own study of Ming book history some of the conventional divisions of labor, such as that between the study of text and the study of images, or between the study of drama and the study of poetry, and to follow the lead of "hucksterish" Ming learning to remain open to the interpenetrations among genres and registers. Whether through texts, images, books, or woodblocks, the effort in this study has been to approach these in terms not of the academic discipline governing each category, but rather in terms of the use of the material by early reader/consumers.

Editing Ming China

Many of the books examined in this study are imprints from the period conventionally known as the late Ming (1570s to 1650s), an era known for its distinctive social fashions, its rapid economic development, and its cosmopolitan attitudes and tastes. In book history, this era saw the production and circulation of woodblock-printed texts reach an unprecedented height. Looking closely at a selected set of exemplars from this era, this study tries to understand the place of these books in the cultural life of the time in general, and the ways of reading that were specific to this period. Further, by tracing the pre-history of late Ming books and alluding to their afterlives both within and beyond China, this study suggests ways in which late Ming books are part of a history of a longer duration and a space of broader extent. Within Ming history itself, in their appropriation and accumulation of earlier materials, these late Ming books also serve to re-present and edit what Ming China was.

To return to the frontispiece illustration from the *Miaojin wanbao quanshu* "Poems and Couplets" section, it would be fruitful to consider, given that the illustration offers itself as an emblem for the texts to be presented in the chapter to follow, how those texts themselves are presented, and how the encyclopedia editor has re-worked his material to suit its local use in its new setting. This "Poems and Couplets" section comprises a top register occupied by a poetic anthology, and a bottom register presenting a collection of antithetical couplets tailored to various occasions and sites. The anthology in the upper register shows pervasive evidence of mutual borrowing with the *Huang Ming shixuan* discussed in chapter 1, both in the poems selected and in the order of presentation: both start with "Taizu Sets Out at Dawn" and follow with "The Zhengde Emperor Dallies at Xuanfu."[5] The encyclopedia, however, uses a different title for its poetry anthologylet, *Wanjia shiji* 萬家詩集 (A collection of poems of ten thousand masters), suggesting an ambition to rival the popular poetry primer *Qian jia shi*, and signaling the representativeness and comprehensiveness of the voices collected in it.

In terms of the overall composition of the two compilations, then, the *Huang Ming shixuan* and the *Wanjia shiji* may be viewed as two editions, versions, or realizations of what is, in some sense, the same small anthology. We do not know the direction of adaptation, and in fact it is quite likely they could both have been derived from another shared source text or texts. For narrative convenience, and to suit the order in which they have appeared in this study, the following comparison will treat the *Wanjia shiji* as derived from the *Huang Ming shixuan*.

One prominent editorial difference between the two cognate realizations of the anthologylet is in their treatments of Han Yong. As discussed in chapter 1, the *Huang Ming shixuan* took rhetorical revenge on Han Yong from the viewpoint of Jiangxi commoner poets with the satirical poem "Han Du's Poem on the Oriole (An Allegory for Himself)." That poem is nowhere to be found in the *Wanjia shiji*. Instead, we find three entirely different poems involving Han Yong: "Han Du chuzheng ouxing" 韓都出征偶興 (Chief Han's chance thoughts when departing on a military campaign), "Shang Han Dutang" 上韓都堂 (Submitted to Chief Han), and "Han Du ji zhong guanyuan" 韓都譏眾官員 (Chief Han ridiculing the many officials).[6] All these poems contrast sharply with the tone of satire in "Han Du's Poem on the Oriole." The first poem, "Chief Han's Chance Thoughts," conveys a scene that could have been taken from a political drama, when the general (here Han Yong) is given command of an imperial army to suppress rebels on the distant southwest frontier:

殿閣雲南草寇興	To the palace comes news that rustic bandits have arisen in Yunnan;
皇恩差我出巡征	imperial grace delegates me to go out on a pacification campaign.
殿前親賜三杯酒	In front of the hall, three cups of wine bestowed by his Majesty's own hand;
馬上忙登十里程	on horseback I rush through ten-*li* post stages.
斬草除根諸鬼伏	In cutting grass, tear out the roots: all the demons submit.
推山塞海一般平	toppling mountains to fill the seas, and make all even land.
安民待詔回頭日	When the masses are pacified, I await the imperial summons,
一統乾坤屬大明	when one unity of heaven and earth belongs to our Glorious Ming!

Han Yong as depicted here is perfectly pious, and the whole poem ends with a rousing slogan of Ming jingoistic sentiment. The other two Han Yong poems in this anthologylet also portray him as righteous, standing out among a group of corrupt officials and ready to prosecute them. The regional subversion in the *Huang Ming shixuan* of Han Yong's image into one of hubris and self-delusion is reversed here to restore an imperial order of worthy agents and protectors of both the empire's borders and its administrative order.

Further, to the particular editor(s) of the *Wanjia shiji*, the anthology would not be complete without poems on the foreign, especially Japan, the state that epitomized the Ming's troublesome relationship with the wider world. Two poems on "Wo," the derogatory name for Japan, are included: "He daxun zheng Wo desheng" 賀大巡征倭得勝 (Celebrating a triumphant return from an imperial military campaign against the Wo) and "Wu Xun'an shang Wo luan" 吳巡按傷倭亂 (Inspector Wu lamenting the turmoil caused by the Wo). The former celebrates Taizu and his court officials' successful military campaign that has restored the proper order: "Spring now returns to Min and Zhe, and all the commoners rejoice; / Ruler and subjects of one mind, between Earth and Heaven" 閩浙春回黎庶樂，君臣道合地天間. The latter is a scene of bleak war-torn misery: "Speak not of grass by palace walls besmirched with gore; / From afar one hears, from villages by the seaboard, weeping in the wilds" 腥汙不論宮墻草，野哭遙聞海岸村. The concern over Japan in this compilation replaces the distinct regional voice of Jiangxi with that of Fujian ("Min" in the poem), the native place of the editor and publisher of this encyclopedia, as well as the region most afflicted by incursions of seafaring pirates. Thus another compilation of the anthology presents another configuration of home and the world, with home as Fujian, and a world encompassing both the Ming empire itself and its fraught relations with lands beyond.[7]

The concern over the Ming empire's place in a trans-regional context is shared by many editors of the daily-use encyclopedias. The "Poetry and Couplets" division of *Wuche bajin* includes the following poem, well-suited to reassure readers' anxieties about the Ming's relations with Japan:

日本使者答聖上問風俗 *An Envoy from Japan's Reply to an Imperial Query about the Customs of His Land*

國本中原國 Our state is modeled on the Central States,
人如上國人 its people like the people of this esteemed state.
衣冠唐制度 Our robes and caps follow the Tang model;
禮樂漢君臣 in rites and music we act as Han ruler and ministers.
銀甕漉新酒 In silver ewers we filter the newly brewed wine;
金刀剖細麟 our metal knives carve the fine-scaled fish.
年年二三月 Each year in the second and third months
桃李一般春 our peaches and plums are alike in springtime blossom.

This poem edits away any anxiety over Japan's presence or the incursions of Japanese bandits, real and supposed, that are expressed in the two poems above into a simple refrain of imitation and copying: Japan is a copy of the Central States in its origins, customs, and ritual and political institutions. The poem's language is simple, miming the earnest attempt by a Japanese envoy to copy Chinese forms. The gore and weeping witnessed or envisioned by Inspector Wu is replaced by "newly made wine," a sign of celebration, harmonious living, and even good hospitality, while the knife is not a weapon but rather an accoutrement of a refined (albeit exotic) banquet; the spring, which needs to be restored by military force in the previous poem celebrating the campaign against the Wo, is here presented as forever changeless (*yiban* 一般, the same, and *niannian* 年年, every year).[8] Thus a cursory comparison of these two variants of essentially the same anthology reveals how editorial adaptation can shape radically different spaces of imagination and appeal to quite different concerns and moods in its readership.

As touched upon in chapter 4, the Ming editors' textual constructions of home in the world themselves went into circulation in the broader world, becoming part of a global market of cultural goods.

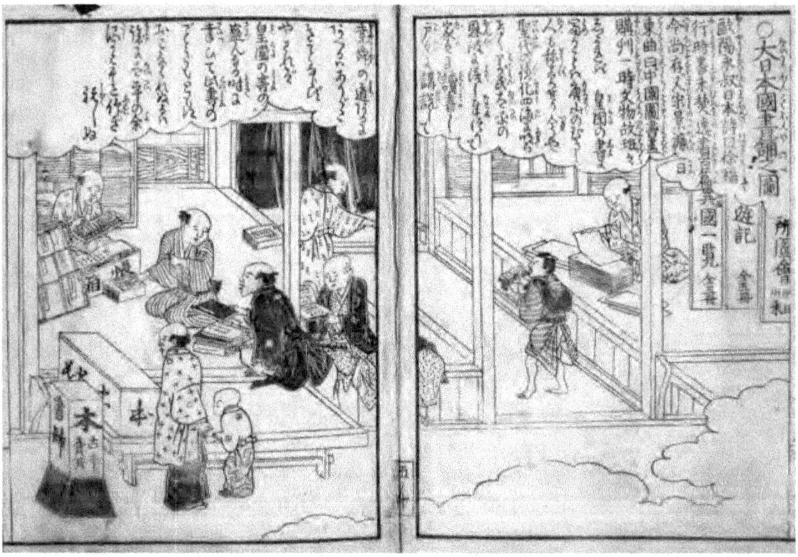

Fig. C.2. "A Bookstore of Great Japan," in *Ikoku ichiran*, 1799. Courtesy of Wasada University Library.

The *Luochong lu* was made into both a hand-drawn picture book and a block-printed text in early Edo Japan, and continued to circulate in various forms for centuries to come. One of the later outgrowths of this text in Japan, called *Ikoku ichiran* 異國一覽 (Foreign countries at one glance), includes an illustration of "A Bookstore of Great Japan" where *Journey to the West* and *Foreign Countries at One Glance* are prominently displayed (fig. C.2).[9] Though this picture depicts a route of circulation of books and ideas that are commercially manageable and profitable, the notion of the foreign would become fiercely contentious in an age of diplomacy backed up with military prowess at the dawn of a new era of colonial acquisition. The home and the world of the Ming commercial publishers were to be severely challenged in this new era.[10]

The Figure of the Fan

The choice of goods in the "Poems and Couplets" frontispiece illustration is significant in terms of this larger history of circulation as well. The fan became a central emblem in the Ming world of cultural fashions and their display. Though the importation of folding fans (known under such diverse designations as *zhe shan* 摺扇, *zhedie shan* 折疊扇, *jutou shan* 聚頭扇, *zhezi shan* 摺子扇, or *Wo shan* 倭扇) from both Korea and Japan can be traced to Song China if not earlier, Ming people themselves viewed the rise to popularity of Japanese folding fans as having begun in the Yongle reign, and this type of fan was given further impetus as an item of prestige consumption by its appearance in tribute offerings from Korea and Japan.[11] Ming-made folding fans quickly gained their own market share and were even exported to Japan. Fans, as modern scholarship has shown, would soon go on to become a truly global cultural fashion.[12]

Thus when our peddler brings folding fans to this distant place, he brings a popular cultural commodity. It is particularly significant, moreover, that he brings both "round fans" (*tuan shan*) and folding fans. In the late Ming, *tuan shan* were also known as *gu shan*, or "ancient-style" fans, and although women of the Jiangnan region could still be seen using the "round fans," Ming cultural observers noted a sharp decline in their popularity, which they attributed to the fad of the folding fan.[13] Thus when the peddler comes equipped with both types of fans, he is mobilizing his reader-customers' agency in exercising control over a range of options: something ancient and of Chinese origin, increasingly rare in use and a marker of traditionalist tastes, or something in the current vogue, both exotic in origin and yet popular in use, a sign of up-to-date fashion—or both. Furthermore, as both Liu Yuanqing 劉元卿 (1544–1609) and the *Sancai tuhui* note, it used to be that proper women in the south all used "round fans" and only courtesans used folding fans; but in recent years women from good families had also adopted the use of folding fans.[14] In this light, the peddler figures as a facilitator, allowing fashions in one social realm (the brothel) to be copied in another social realm (respectable homes). The combination of types lends the peddler market advantage (recall the mixture of *guwen* and *suyu* in riddles, jokes, and games of the same period), and provides his customers the opportunity to show their discernment and expertise as consumers and collectors.

As the author or transcriber of inscriptions on the fans he sells, the peddler also participates in an intricate culture of reproduction, copying, and differentiation. As fans increasingly became desired commodities, those painted or inscribed by famous painters, calligraphers, and authors became highly sought-after objects, and a class of specialist craftsmen also emerged to cultural renown.[15] Either famous scholars or such renowned craftsmen would have earned the qualifications to become *ming ren* 名人, renowned persons—or more simply, and also more precisely, persons whose names are known. It was figures like our anonymous peddler, however, who made it possible for the fame, fashions, and prestige of that rarefied stratum to circulate among wider audiences and to shape the broader culture. Thus the renowned cultural elite and the anonymous peddler become partners in a network of business and cultural ventures. As the picture shows, he is the enabler of a cultural sphere that links the distant place with the cosmopolitan center, and responds to the quotidian tastes and desires of his reader-customers in a reshaping of the cultural forms at his disposal. In the process, he enables his reader-customers to make the patterns and fashions of that exalted cosmopolitan sphere their own domestic possessions.

APPENDIX ONE

Other Known Titles by Makers of Drama Miscellanies[1]

Yu Shaoya (aka Yu Liangmu), printer for *Yuefu yushu ying*, is also credited with having printed:

Tongjian zuanyao chao hubai 通鑒纂要抄狐白. 1573.
(White fox furs: Copies of selected essentials of *The Comprehensive Mirror*)

Shiji cuibao pinglin 史記萃寶評林. 1590.
(Critical forest of treasures in *The Records of the Historian*)

Xuke Wenling si taishi pingxuan gujin mingwen zhuji 續刻溫陵四太史評選古今名文珠璣. 1595.
(A continuation: Precious pearls of well-known writings ancient and modern, commented on and selected by the four grand historians of Wenling)

Ke zhushi Lunxue cang'er 刻註釋論學藏耳. 1598.
(Treasured record, annotations on discourses on learning)

Xu wenzhang guifan baijia piping zhushi 續文章軌範百家批評註釋. 1599.
(A continuation: Principles of writing, critique and annotations of a hundred masters)

Dingjuan Jinling san huiyuan hexuan pingzhu Shiji hubai 鼎鐫金陵三會元合選評註史記狐白. 1600.
(White fox furs: Newly cut, commentaries on *The Records of the Historian*, collectively selected by the Three Metropolitan Principals of Jinling)

Xinjuan Zhang zhuangyuan linji pinglin Qin Han hubai 新鐫張狀元遴輯評林秦漢狐白. 1605.
(White fox furs of the Qin and Han: Newly cut, forest of critiques compiled by Valedictorian Zhang)

Dingjuan Jinling Tang huiyuan pingshi Hanshu hubai 鼎鐫金陵湯會元評釋漢書狐白. 1608.
(White fox furs of *The Book of Han*: Newly cut, with critical commentaries by Metropolitan Principal Tang of Jinling)

Jingxuan juye qieyao Shu Shi cuiyan fenlei pinglin zhuzi hubai 精選舉業切要書史粹言分類評林諸子狐白. 1614.
(Meticulously selected, essentials of the civil examinations, essential words from *The Documents* and *The Records of the Historian*, categorized forest of critiques, and white fox furs of the pre-Han masters)

Dingjuan Huang zhuangyuan pixuan Meishan san Su wen hubai 鼎鐫黃狀元批選眉山三蘇文狐白. *Wanli reign.*
(White fox furs: Newly cut, selections and critiques of the three Sus of Meishan, by Valedictorian Huang)

Guan Yan chunqiu baijia pinglin 管晏春秋百家評林. *Wanli reign.*
(A Forest of critiques by a hundred people on Master Guan and Master Yan's Spring and Autumn Annals)

Jingxuan juye qieyao zhuzi cuiyan fenlei pinglin wenyuan zonghai 精選舉業切要諸子粹言分類評林文源宗海. *No date.*
(Meticulously selected, essentials of the civil examinations, essential words of various masters, categories of the forests of commentaries, the sources and seas of literatures)

Heke Li Du erjia chaoping 合刻李杜二家鈔評. *No date.*
(Combined copies of commentaries on the two poets Li Bai and Du Fu)

Liu Ciquan, printer for *Yugu xinhuang*, also served as the woodblock engraver for the illustrations in:

Tang shi huapu 唐詩畫譜. *Jiya zhai* 集雅齋. 1620s.
(Pictorial album to accompany Tang poems)

Tang Hairuo xiansheng piping Pipa ji 湯海若先生批評琵琶記. *Wanli reign.*[2]
(Mr. Tang [Xianzu] Hairuo's commentaries on *The Story of the Lute*)

Dingjuan Xixiang ji 鼎鐫西廂記. *Shijian tang* 師儉堂. *Wanli reign.*
(Newly cut, the story of the western wing)

Hongfu ji 紅拂記. *Shijian tang. Wanli reign.*
(The story of Hongfu)

Wuxian lingguan dadi huguang tianwang zhuan 五顯靈官大帝華光天王傳. *Changyuan tang* 昌遠堂, *Jianyang.* 1571.
(Hagiography of the Heavenly King Huaguang, the Great Emperor of the Five Manifestations)[3]

Xinjuan quanxiang nanhai guanshiyin pusa chushen xiuxing zhuan 新鐫全相南海觀世音菩薩出身修行傳. *Huanwen tang* 煥文堂, *Jianyang. Wanli reign.*
(Newly cut, completely illustrated, the hagiography of the Bodhisattva Guanyin of the Southern Sea)

Xinke yinshi pangxun pinglin yanyi Sanguo zhi zhuan 新刻音釋旁訓評林演義三國志傳. *Jianyi shulin* 建邑書林. *No date.*
(Newly cut, with phonetic explanations and side elucidations, the forest of critique of the historical romance of tales from the *Record of the Three Kingdoms*)

Ke xinban zengbu tianxia bianyong wenlin miaojin wanbao quanshu 刻新板增補天下便用文林妙錦萬寶全書. *Anzheng tang* 安正堂. 1612.
(Reedition from newly carved blocks, expanded and supplemented—for ready use throughout the sub-celestial realm, wondrous brocades from the forest of letters: complete book of myriad treasures)

Liu Ciquan also printed:

Jingxuan baijia jinxiu lian 精選百家錦繡聯. *Chongzhen reign.*
(Refined selection of lavishly crafted couplets by a hundred masters)

Sizhi guan (fl. Jiajing–Tianqi reigns), the print shop for *Shidiao Qing Kun*, also printed:[4]

Danxi xinfa fuyu 丹溪心法附餘. *Jiajing reign.*
([Zhu] Danxi's methods of actualizing the mind, with appendices)

Su Wenzhong gong jixuan 蘇文忠公集選. *Wanli reign.*
(Selected collections of Master Su [Shi] Wenzhong)

Sanke taiyiyuan buzhu furen liangfang 三刻太醫院補註婦人良方. *Wanli reign.*
(Third cutting, effective prescriptions for women, supplemented with annotations, from the Court of Imperial Physicians)

Wujing tongjian 武經通鑿. *Wanli reign.*
(A comprehensive mirror of the military classics)

Yingtong baiwen 嬰童百問. *Wanli reign.*
(A hundred questions on infants and children)

Jiezi zhanshu 揭子戰書. *Wanli reign.*
(Master Jie's [Xuan] book on war)

Bingjing baipian 兵經百篇. *Wanli reign.*
(Military classics in a hundred passages)

Xingjun jishan lu 行軍積善錄. *Wanli reign.*
(Records of accumulating good deeds during military campaigns)

Xinqie Jingban gongshi diaozhuo zhengshi Lu Ban jing jiang jia jing 新鍥京版工師雕斫正式魯班經匠家鏡. *Wanli reign.*
(Newly cut, capital edition, carved by skilled masters, the official classic of Lu Ban and the mirror of a craftsmen's family[5])

Xingshui bian 醒睡編. *Wanli reign.*
(The text of waking from sleep)

Xinqie Shenfeng Zhang xiansheng tongkao bimiu mingli zhengzong daquan 新鍥神峰張先生通考辟謬命理正宗大全. *Wanli reign.*
(Newly cut, comprehensively examined and corrected by Mr. Zhang [Nan] of Shenfeng, complete book on life and reason)

Zhou Dunxuan xiansheng wenji 周鈍軒先生文集. *Wanli reign.*
(A collection of Mr. Zhou [Fu] Dunxuan)

Zhong Bojing xiansheng piping Shuihu zhuan 鍾伯敬先生批評水滸傳. *Tianqi reign.*
(The story of the *Water Margin*, with evaluative annotations by Zhong [Xing] Bojing)

Chen Pinzhou (fl. Wanli reign), woodblock illustration engraver for *Cilin yizhi*, also engraved illustrations in:

Dangui ji 丹桂記. *Baozhu tang* 寶珠堂. *Tianqi reign.*[6]
(The story of cinnabar osmanthus)

Huancui tang Yuefu Xixiang ji 環翠堂樂府西廂記. *Huancui tang* 環翠堂. *Wanli reign.*
(The story of the western wing of the music bureau, by Huancui tang)

Dingqie Chen Meigong xiansheng piping Xixiang ji 鼎鍥陳眉公先生批評西廂記. *Shijian tang. Wanli reign.*
(Newly cut, the story of the western wing, critique by Master Chen Meigong)

Xiuru ji 繡襦記. *Shijian tang. Wanli reign.*
(The story of the embroidered jacket)

Xinke sasa pian 新刻灑灑篇. *Cuiqing tang* 萃慶堂. *Tianqi reign.*
(Newly cut, a compilation of desultory ramblings)

Zhu Dingchen (style name Chonghuai, fl. Wanli reign), who compiled *Da Ming chun*, also compiled or edited:

Dingqie quan xiang Tang Sanzang xi you zhuan 鼎鍥全像唐三藏西遊傳. *No date.*
(Newly cut, with complete illustrations, the romance of the journey to the West of Monk Tripitaka of the Tang)

Xinqie quan xiang Nanhai Guanshiyin pusa chushen xiuxing zhuan 新鍥全像南海觀世音菩薩出身修行傳. *Huanwen tang. No date.*
(Newly cut, with complete illustrations, the hagiography of the Bodhisattva Guanshiyin of the Southern Sea)

Xinke yinshi pangxun pinglin yanyi Sanguo zhi zhuan 新刻音釋旁訓評林演義三國志傳. *Jianyi shufang. No date.*
(Newly cut, with phonetic explanations and side elucidations, the forest of critique of the historical romance of tales from the *Record of the Three Kingdoms*)

Xinke yejia xincai wanbao quanshu 新刻鄴架新裁万寳全書. *By Xiong Duishan* 熊對山, *Jianyang, Fujian. Preface* 1614.

(Newly engraved, newly selected from the library shelves of Duke Ye: *The Complete Book of Ten Thousand Treasures*)

Bolan quanshu 博覽全書. *By the Xiong family printshop, Tanyi* 潭邑, *Fujian. Wanli reign.*
(A broad survey of all books)

Longtou yilan xuehai buqiuren 龍頭一覽學海不求人. *By the Xiong family printshop of Tanyi* 潭邑, *Fujian. No date.*
(Dragon head at a glance, the sea of learning—seek no further)

APPENDIX TWO

The "Classic of Whoring": Demimonde Fantasy and the Formation of the Ming Vernacular

"Piao jing" 嫖經 (Classic of whoring) is a title often applied to any of a family of texts (some illustrated) that circulated in the late Ming purporting to provide advice for visitors and courtesans, insider knowledge, and lore of the bewildering world of the brothel.[1] These brothel treatises circulated as individual volumes as well as within larger collections, such as the daily-use encyclopedias (fig. A.1) and drama miscellanies discussed in this study.[2] This appendix examines and translates parts of such a late Ming "Piao jing" in a book called *Piao du jiguan* 嫖賭機關 (Tricks and traps in whoring and gambling), not just to journey into the late Ming urban milieu as a cultural tourist—as many Ming readers themselves might have done—but also to examine the mode of urban vernacular writing that made such textual tourism possible and profitable. This text shows an intense interest in linguistic novelty, in exuberant rhetorical effects (especially parody), and in the reappropriation and subversion of canonical texts along with their system of value and social respectability. Reflecting late Ming fashions in writing on urban life, especially the vices of whoring, money, and sensual indulgence, it takes up a unique discursive position between the romanticized inwardness of *qing* 情 (feeling/sentiment) and the problematic yet seemingly tangible practicality in the exchange of money and sex.[3]

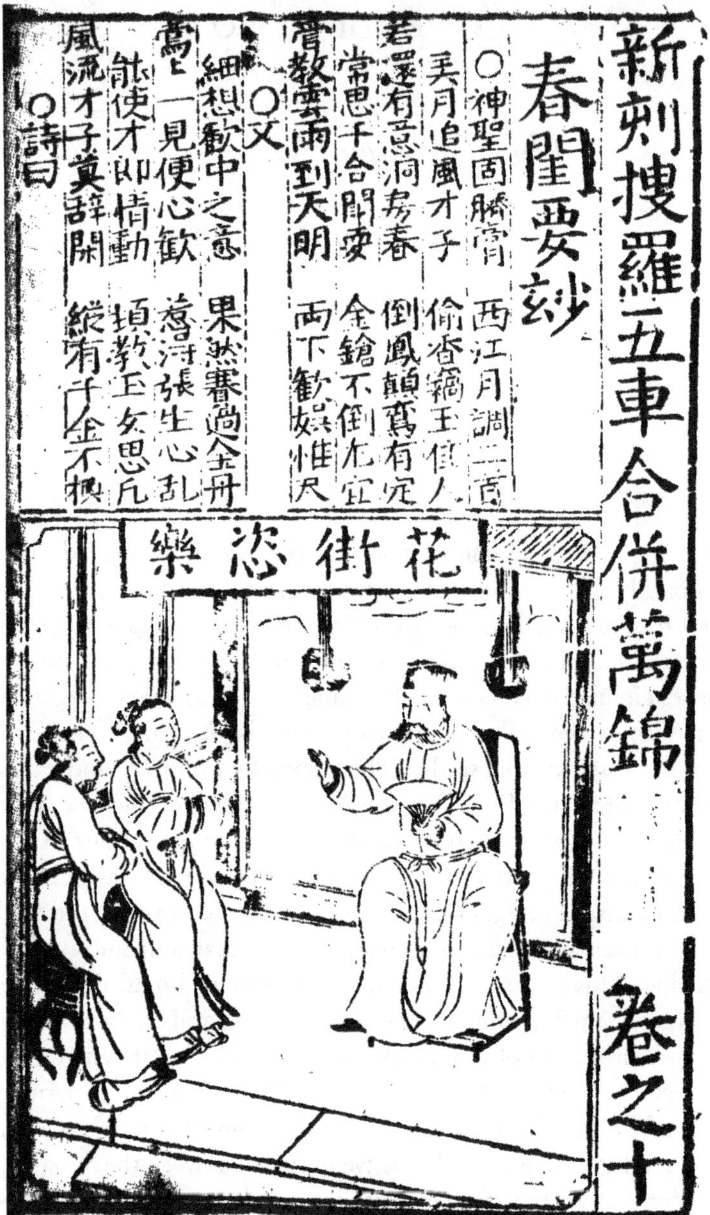

Fig. A.1. Brothel instructions, seen in the lower register, in the late Ming daily-use encyclopedia *Wuche wanbao quanshu*. The upper register is a list of recipes for aphrodisiacs and other drugs to enhance sexual function. From *CNRC*, vol. 8, p. 249.

One Ought to Whore!

The *Piaodu jiguan* opens with a poem entitled "An Argument in Favor of Whoring":

論人該嫖

世事渾如春夢、韶光真似浮雲、人生聚散有何憑、瞬息青年可敬、若論賞心樂事、無過月夕花晨、從來柳陌勝蓬瀛、自古高人親近。

An Argument in Favor of Whoring

Events of the world are just like spring dreams;
splendid times truly resemble floating clouds.
Amid life's meetings and partings, on what can one depend?
The brief moment of youth is to be revered.
And as for the "appreciative mind meeting delightful events,"
nothing can compare with moonlit evenings and dawns among flowers.
The willow lanes surpass the immortal isles—it has always been so;
from antiquity, wise men have held them dear.[4]

The poem meditates glibly on the transience of the world, time, life, and youth, and lingers on the interiority of the mind, its pleasures, and its fondness of the company of the moonlight in the evening and flowers at dawn—two symbols of romantic and carnal pleasure best embodied, according to the author, in the willow lanes, the common metaphor for brothels. The poem assembles a catalog of perspectives—space, time, life, youth, the mind, and wisdom from history—all leading to the conclusion that the brothel is the ideal site for human fulfillment. One might add that this vision of human desire and fulfillment bears the imprint of a late Ming urban ideal of humanity. The milieu of the brothel showcases not only bodies and their desires but also the skills and specialized knowledge needed to operate in a tricky and sophisticated world of commerce and sentiment in the rapidly evolving urban culture of the time.

This book's author, Shen Hongyu 沈弘宇, whose style name is Yuanfu 元甫, is likely the opera performer and brothel denizen Shen Yuanfu mentioned in Yu Huai's 余懷 (1616–96) *Banqiao zaji* 板橋雜記. The book presents itself as a manual on how to prepare for and behave in and around brothels in bodily, financial, social, and cultural terms, and directs its advice to both brothel frequenters and courtesans. It highlights the temper of the time, reflecting the sorts of skills and wisdom in the management of sexual, economic, and social assets that were considered essential for up-to-date urban men and women in sixteenth- to seventeenth-century China.

Shen was not the only late Ming author to write brothel manuals; nor was his text, or the many others like it from the period, intended for the private enjoyment of a small circle of friends. Rather, such works were printed by commercial publishing houses and sold to an ever-growing reading public. As seen in chapter 2, the immensely popular daily-use encyclopedias that emerged in the late sixteenth century included a section under the heading of brothel instructions. All these brothel manuals helped to shape the public knowledge of the day and signaled the heightened importance of relations founded in commercial exchange (here specifically the trade of sex and romance) as an effective form of social organization, when the hurly-burly of these marketplace transactions caused much anxiety and spoke to a need for rules, protections, and guidebooks.

Whoring Is Hard!

In his manual, which provides a taxonomy of brothel matters, Shen Hongyu organizes his topics by numbered categories, a form of textual organization that mirrored the fondness for numbered lists found in a wide range of "how-to" texts in popular publications. For example, his first topic is on the general rules on "whoring":

嫖有五要三不可

一要會溫存，二要會念作，三要有功夫，四要有本事，五要用錢俏。一不可跳槽、二不可訕臉、三不可揚風。

In Whoring There Are Five Do's and Three Mustn't's

One, be caring; two, be eloquent; three, take time; four, have skills; five, spend money handsomely.

One, one mustn't switch troughs (i.e., change partners); two, one mustn't squabble; three, one mustn't boast.[5]

Shen makes clear the important role of sex skills in his fourth rule in "whoring":

四要有本事：

婦性淫，都喜幹，十個常有九個賤；果然潑戰遂他心，這好休把尋常看。

Four, Have Skills:

Women are lascivious by nature, and all love doing it; of every ten women, nine are degenerates. If you really go at it the way she likes it—the pleasure obtained will be far from ordinary.[6]

Whoring is no easy business. To succeed, one has to be prepared through study and native talent. Shen elaborates this point in a section called "On the Seven Ways in Which Lads Are Fine":

論子弟有七俏

一風度俏、二學問俏、三談吐俏、四曲藝俏、五服飾俏、六飲食俏、七乖狡俏
風度俏：人飄逸、性溫柔、磊落春風、絶無寒氣、姊妹愛之
學問俏：多問學、廣音韻、詩詞歌賦、無不通曉、姊妹敬之
談吐俏：長應對、善説詞、談吐詼諧、悉皆中節、姊妹聽之
曲藝俏：能壺馬、諳絲竹、風塵六藝、件件精通、姊妹奇之
服飾俏：冠履精、裳服潔、一塵不染、精致瀟然、姊妹重之
飲食俏：不茹葷、不飲酒、燒香品茶、蘇氣逼人、姊妹親之
乖狡俏：會討好、慣弄乖、聰明伶俐、圓融小巧、姊妹喜之

On the Seven Ways in Which Lads Are Fine

1, Fine in demeanor; 2, Fine in knowledge; 3, Fine in conversation; 4, Fine in musicianship and games; 5, Fine in attire; 6, Fine in food and drink; 7, Fine in flirtation.

Fine in demeanor: Light and airy in their persons; warm and yielding in nature; unaffected as a spring breeze, without the least taint of cheap narrowness. The girls prefer this type.

Fine in knowledge: Widely inquisitive; broadly versed in prosodic arts; in poems, lyrics, ditties, or verse disquisitions, there is nothing in which they are not fluently at ease. The girls revere this type.

Fine in conversation: Good at ingenious replies; skilled in oral persuasion; witty and elegant in conversation, striking the right note in every situation. The girls attend to this type.

Fine in musicianship and games: Capable in toss-pot and the *dama* (lit. driving horses) board game; versed in the stringed and wind instruments; in all six arts of the demimonde, fully expert in every one. The girls are astonished by this type.

Fine in attire: Cap and shoes exquisite; robes and vestments natty; with no trace of sloppiness, a complaisant image of refinement. The girls respect this type.

> Fine in food and drink: Refraining from meats, abstaining from wine, burning incense and sampling teas, full of that unmistakable Suzhou style. The girls feel close to this type.
>
> Fine in flirtation: Adept at currying favor; well-versed in coyness; clever and winsome, full of ingratiating wiles. The girls like this type.[7]

In short, one "merely" needs to be winsome, healthy, charming, scholarly, and witty. More than once, Shen reminds whoring aspirants that one has to weigh one's looks, sex appeal or lack thereof, social status, financial qualifications, literary talent, and emotional sophistication to set realistic expectations about one's prospects in the brothel world.

Shen's book is not a one-sided manual to prepare men for their entrance into the dangerous and alluring pleasures and the complicated transactions in the brothel; he also addresses requirements for the women to be successful. Shen fondly reveals the ten perfections of the girls:

觀姐妹之十全

一文雅、二脱俗、三翰墨、四技藝、五歌唱、六絲竹、七涇渭、八風情、九停當、十蘇樣

The Ten Perfections to Be Observed in Girls

1, Refined elegance; 2, Freedom from vulgarity; 3, Writing and drawing; 4, Skills and arts; 5, Singing; 6, Stringed and wind instruments; 7, Clear observance of social distinctions; 8, Romantic sentiment; 9, Politic behavior; 10, Suzhou style.[8]

How and why should a girl be good at poetry and drawing? Shen elaborates:

三翰墨

朱樓内詩詞難得、曲檻中寫畫爲高、翰墨流香、芳名遠著、文人墨士、莫不車馳馬驟、愚夫俗子、不過仰望豐采、縱家寒貌醜、此亦不足以限之。

3, Writing and Drawing

Poetry is hard to come across in the "vermillion halls"; amid the curved balustrades, drawing and painting are considered best. Traces of the brush emit a fine scent, and a fragrant name is manifest from afar—writers and adherents of the brush will all arrive at a headlong gallop, while idiots and the vulgar will merely be awed by such dazzling beauties. Even if her family is poor and her looks are ugly, such defects will not limit her appeal.[9]

A girl's bedroom manner and sexual charms and skills are designated by the term *fengqing*, passions of wind/breeze, drawing on the association of wind both with romantic scenery and with subtle influence and persuasion:

八風情

姊妹要穩重、又要飄颻、要沉潛、又要活潑、槁木瓠瓜、人都惡其死石、若枕席間、被窩中、此正歡娛之際、尤當操弄風騷、勾引子弟迷戀、不然、一宿再宿而已、依依不舍能幾何？

8, Romantic Sentiment

Girls need to be dignified, yet mercurial; restrained and understated, yet also lively. With dried out wood or ladle-gourds, people all detest their inert hardness. As for the space of pillow and mat, inside the quilts, this is where delight and pleasure are to be felt, and in these places it is especially important to give free rein to seductive charms, to seduce the boys to love her. Otherwise it will be a matter of one or two nights—how long could they feel lingering affection?[10]

Further, the book's emphasis on managerial skills and business instinct is expressed in its extolling of the girl's judicious behavior:

九停當

處得意時、樽節而不奢華、當落剝日、勉強而不狼狽、廣結要路、以備雀鼠、買好巨室、以防匱乏、用意周密、做人停分、家業自是崢嶸、氣象昂然光彩

9, Judicious Behavior

When in favor, she adheres to the proper measure without extravagance; on the day of dejection, she makes an effort to avoid seeming discomposed. She widely forges alliances with those in power as a precaution against sparrows and mice; she trades for alliance with mighty families as a protection from want. In planning, she is comprehensive and minute; in behavior, she shows due regard for proper station; her fortune is lofty of itself, her aura exalted and brilliant.[11]

It is evident from this passage that her fortune relies on her dignified and studied responses to adversaries and opportunities, her social skills, and her social vision.

Chen also makes sure that both men and women strive to conform to the new fashions in urban living, called the "Suzhou style" (*suyang* 蘇樣). Suzhou was the capital of Chinese metropolitan fashions in the late Ming. In #10, Chen prescribes:

十蘇様

房中葺理精致、几上陳列玩好、多蓄異香、廣貯細茶、遇清客、一爐煙、一壺茶、坐談笑語、窮日徹夜、並不以鄙事縈心、亦不以俗話出口、這段高雅風味、不啻桃源形境。

10, Suzhou Style

Her interior decor is refined and elegant; on her sideboard are displayed a variety of objets d'art. She lays in store much exotic incense and widely collects fine teas. Encountering a high-minded client, with a censer of smoke, a pot of tea, she sits and converses with lighthearted banter, all day and through the night, with no vulgar concern crossing her mind, nor any common talk emerging from her lips. A dose such as this of the flavor of lofty elegance exceeds the charms of the realm of the Peach Blossom Spring.[12]

Peach Blossom Spring is the Chinese utopian land beyond the constraints of historical time and social structures depicted in the medieval poet Tao Yuanming's 陶淵明 (364–427) renowned essay "The Story of the Peach Blossom Spring." Here, if done right, the brothel would be the gateway to such a utopian land.

At the end of his book, Shen lists 108 pieces of advice and observations for brothel patrons; the following sentences are some representative examples:

會飲酒留量，能謳不可先。

Those who know how to drink keep capacity in reserve; those good at singing know better than to perform first.

寢未安處求雲雨，不以急乎？事方畢復求再合，失於俗矣。

To seek sex before one's properly settled in bed—is this not too pressing? To seek another round just after finishing—this is to commit a vulgar error.

情正濃而遽別，後會如故。意寢衰而後離，復見如讎。

When parting comes suddenly just when feelings are most tender, the subsequent meeting will be as between old friends; If separation occurs only after sentiments have gradually cooled, the reencounter will be like that between sworn enemies.

衾被重薰，今夜斷然清客。門窗早閉，此宵定是村夫。

If quilts and bedcovers are repeatedly infused with incense—tonight's guest is definitely a high-minded man; when the doors and windows are closed early—this evening's arrival is certainly a bumpkin.

凡觀枕上之歡慍，遂知心中之愛惡。

In general, observation of her delights and ill temper on the pillow will allow one to know her mind's likes and dislikes.

廣席上就位附耳，殊欠冠冕；稠人中視有若無，才爲雅致。

In a big banquet, he goes to her seat and whispers in her ear—this indicates a gross lack of breeding; amidst a crowd, he looks at her as though she's not there—now *this* is elegance and refinement.

無情強苦挾，雖槃桓而非高懷；得趣便抽身，縱乖狡而亦薄倖。

When she lacks passion he still entreats plaintively—such is one who lingers and paces and yet not a man of lofty sentiment; one who absconds as soon as he's satisfied—though he have charm, he remains a scoundrel.

見名妓而不流暢，定受禁持；遇俗儕而不尊重，反遭譏訕。

One who seems ill at ease in the presence of a renowned courtesan will in the end be constrained; one who shows no respect when encountering the common crowd will in the end be the subject of mockery.

之乎也者，省此；鄉談土語，少說。

"Yea, verily, forsooth"—less of this; country talk, rustic sayings—use them sparingly.

好話兒只説一遍，趣事兒只幹一遭。

Only say clever things once; only pull clever pranks one time.[13]

Throughout the book, Shen reminds his readers that the most important thing in the business of brothels is to be able to tell genuine passion from fake, and to manage money accordingly. Chen lists twenty-four ways of playing with the heart of a lad, tricking him into emotional and monetary devotion. Many things are desired in a relationship between the patron and the courtesan: money, sex, emotional and intellectual companionship, and the opportunity to get married. Money and gifts become tricky, for they can either be a token of genuine interest or just the means to buy a good service. Though the ideal seems to be genuine passion, other elements such as money and sex supplementing and enhancing each other nicely, the brothel operates within tricks and traps that make it one of the hardest places to discern truth from falsehood, for both the lads and girls. In the following examples, Chen warns the girls of the emotional cruelty that is an unavoidable part of their business:

子弟有二丟閃

一才好就丟，二正好就閃

Lads have two situations in which they drop a girl:

1, Dropping when things have just got going; 2, Dropping just as things are going well.[14]

一才好就丢

子弟與姊妹初會、百般念作、萬種謀為、說我兩個生死相靠、半步不離。婦人水性、信以為實。枕席歡情、俱已承奉、風月趣事、靡不盡為。你圖他山高水遠、他做了日出露稀。方纔到手、血心就昧；並無繾綣之情，亦無留戀之意。為姊妹安能驅之使來？怎得縛之不去？追悔何及？悶坐長吁，天丢得他、思一回、怨一回、暗地偷垂。

1, Dropping When Things Have Just Got Going

When a lad meets a girl for the first time, he coins all manner of fine phrases, concocts ten thousand stratagems, saying, "Let's stay together in life and death, without parting a half a step." The woman with her fickle nature believes this all as truth. In all the delights of pillow and mat she's done her best; of all the charming acts of romance there remains not one she hasn't done. Her expectations of him are "high as mountains, extensive as seas," and what he does is "evaporate like a dewdrop at sunrise." Just when he's got what he wants, the blood of his heart becomes darkened; he has neither lingering affection, nor a feeling of reluctance to part. A girl in this situation, how can she compel him so as to make him come? How can she restrain him so as to prevent him from leaving? She reflects with regret, but all too late; sitting despondently and sighing deeply. Heavens! To be dropped like this . . . she longs for a while, feels resentment for a while, and secretly she sheds tears.[15]

The brothel became one of the trickiest marketplaces in that it purported to produce and consume a special "good": sex and romance. Its whoring program commends not only good managerial skills in regard to one's body, sexual availability, and money, but more fundamentally, good managerial skills in relation to human warmth and cruelty.

Urban Vernacular Writing

Though Shen's book purports to be instructional, most readers likely consumed it as a fantastic novelty text rather than for practical advice. Shen himself admits that his own knowledge of the realms of whoring and gambling is through hearsay, though perhaps he's being overly humble. The Ming brothel manual holds a special place in the book culture of its time. The flourishing book trade reshaped the social expectations as to what one should read and possess, and these brothel instructions, like other sorts of book in the literary marketplace, were a commodity to be owned, consumed, and displayed, not necessarily for practical purposes in actual brothel visits, but in order to qualify, in one's own mind as well as in the minds of others, as cosmopolitan and up-to-date with the latest fashions. The language and form of the book embodies a distinctive linguistic and literary fashion in this period, a kind of writing that had grown charming, desirable, and profitable. Late Ming urban vernacular writing was a complex field of linguistic performance that drew inspiration from the long history of storytelling, translation, and regional speech patterns. This form of vernacular is less a matter of the marking of a relatively unprivileged mode of social identity than it is a matter of giving voice to a body of tastes, styles, and values emerging from the growing urban society of the period, and represented most centrally in Shen's book by the supralocal commercial splendor of the Suzhou region.

Writers like Shen, along with other players in the book industry, developed a lively and highly profitable textual system of new slang, genres, modes of speech, and fashionable styles of writing that was received with enthusiasm and traveled far and wide via the pan-empire book market. This was a mode of writing that came into competition with literary writing. High literacy in the vernacular writing style was not necessarily easier to obtain than in the literary style, partially because the literary was the language form used in formal education.[16] Now, along with the literary, the vernacular became a language that an author could choose to work in. Shen made such a choice. By inventing and accessing the alternative authority and novelty of the vernacular voice, Shen's text mirrors and enhances the air of freshness and exoticness of its subject matter.

Urban vernacular writing devised and favored certain rhetorical contours, tonality, and textual rhythm. Parody and satire were practiced with gleeful abandon. Shen Hongyu, for example, appropriates and parodies several well-established genres of writing such as *jiaxun* (family instructions) and *jiali* 家禮 (family rites), the most famous examples of which are the sixth-century *Yanshi jiaxun* 顏氏家訓 (Yan family instructions) and the *Zhu zi jiali* 朱子家禮 (Master Zhu's family rites) from the Southern Song. The latter became in the Ming a fundamental document on cultivating ethical decorum.[17] Also noteworthy is his parody of exegetical conventions of the classical tradition, such as the interlinear commentary on the classical texts, in which the commentator expands on the implicit meanings of the text. This exegetical convention is observed in Shen's 108 items of advice and warning:

之乎也者，省些；鄉談土語，少說。

"Yea, verily, forsooth"—less of this;
country talk, local sayings—use them sparingly.

The line is followed by the following commentary:

邪語太多，他說你不脫俗；之乎重疊，他笑你欠斯文。

When there's too much slang and innuendo, she'll say you're not free of vulgarity; when "yea" and "verily" pile up, she'll laugh at you for lacking style.

In a way, this advice to the brothel patron mirrors the writing of Shen's book itself. The high-sounding language Shen warns against is indicated by the common function words *zhi*, *hu*, *ye*, and *zhe* that are characteristic of the literary writing style to which the civil examinees and bureaucrats were restricted. On the other hand, "country talk and local sayings" are not desirable alternative vocabulary, either. The desirable way of speaking transcends the parochial but does not fall pedantically in line with the traditional and literary. Shen here reveals the linguistic enterprise of urban writers in creating a new stylistic model in a vernacular mode that is not defined as the language of any undifferentiated local or class group, but rather succeeds in striking a balance among a variety of registers—including more bookish classical-sounding ones as well as a range of colloquial, dialect, and argot modes of speech—among which one shifts freely. Shen truly had a talent for speaking differently, for using, even making, new words. Local idioms were, in fact, a major source of inspiration in Shen's style, but he chose the ones that could easily be understood. As Shen's preface states, "In this work I take what I have learned (about the brothels) and, forming it into outlandish and absurd phrases, submit it to young scholars and women as a resource for their idle amusement. My writing is an uneven mix of the bookish and the vulgar, so I dare not attempt to embellish it with fine turns of phrase; my understanding is common and pedestrian, so that I am deeply shamed by its crude and shallow tone."[18] Shen was fully aware that he was carrying out a textual experiment, and beneath the self-deprecation about his lack of literary refinement one can sense that the odd hybrid style he concocts in the book is central to the sort of mark he wants to make on readers' minds and on the fashion of the age. As chapters of this book have persistently shown, the authority or prestige of the up-to-date and cosmopolitan authors and speakers exists in a relationship of creative tension and subversive repurposing of scholarly and ethical canons. In this sense it is perhaps fitting that Shen closes his preface with an enigmatic echo of Confucius's supposed attitude towards his own authorship of the *Chunqiu* 春秋 (Spring and autumn annals): "As for whether I am to be understood or blamed as a result of writing in this way, I can only await the world's verdict. You readers of lofty mind—what do you think of this?"[19]

NOTES

Introduction

1. *General Catalog to the Complete Library of the Four Treasuries* 四庫全書總目, *juan* 78, history category, geography sub-category, title 7. See Yong Rong et al., eds., *Siku quanshu zongmu*, p. 678.

2. The former statement is found in Lu Xinyuan's 陸心源 (1834–94) *Yigu tang tiba* 儀顧堂題跋, 1.19B. The latter is seen in Ye Dehui's 葉德輝 (1864–1927) *Shulin qing hua* 書林清話, p. 150, with contemporary references in, e.g., Zhou Caiquan's preface to Du Xinfu's authoritative *Mingdai banke zonglu*. Although contemporary use of these traditional bywords does not necessarily imply full agreement with the sentiment they express, even such half-conscious echoing of this traditional phraseology reflects how deeply rooted it has become over the centuries as part of the specialized idiom of bibliographical studies.

3. Scholars have explored various aspects of the cultural transformation from the late Ming to the high Qing. For example, Benjamin Elman's *From Philosophy to Philology* grounds the transformation in a study of both discursive and institutional revolution of knowledge making and shows how norms of acceptable knowledge were decisively changed. Kent Guy's *The Emperor's Four Treasuries* provides an illuminating account of the complex unfolding of the *Siku* project, a process that involved constant rebalancing among the interests of the emperor, bureaucrats, and scholars. As Guy shows, the idea of superseding a predecessor, particularly a Ming predecessor, was of paramount importance to the Qianlong emperor (r. 1736–95), and an anti-Ming bias pervades the whole *Siku* collection. Finally, in *The Rise of Confucian Ritualism in Late Imperial China*, Kai-wing Chow demonstrates how the Qing scholars' classical studies evolved in connection with a ritualist ethics and a vision of a new social order.

4. For a summary of *Siku* bibliographical comments on Ming encyclopedias, see Sakai Tadao, "Mindai no nichiyō ruisho to shomin kyōiku," 29–38.

5. Critical reassessment of the judgments and perspectives of the *Siku* scholars has been a notable trend in recent scholarship, and works by Chinese print historians have provided a much more balanced and historically grounded account of the development of commercial printing in late imperial China, and of the social impact of block-printed books in particular. Significant works in English on Chinese Ming-Qing printing history include Hegel, *Reading Illustrated Fiction in Late Imperial China*; Chia, *Printing for Profit*; Chow, *Publishing, Culture, and Power in Early Modern China*; Brokaw and Chow, *Printing and Book Culture in Late Imperial China*; McDermott, *A Social History of the Chinese Book*; and Brokaw, *Commerce in Culture*. A substantial portion of Dorothy Ko's *Teachers of the Inner Chambers* also examines the printing culture of the seventeenth century. For review articles on recent work in Ming-Qing book history, see Meyer-Fong, "The Printed World"; and Brokaw, "Book History in Premodern China."

6. Craig Clunas has prominently applied the term "early modern China" to the period, in, e.g., his *Pictures and Visuality in Early Modern China* and *Superfluous Things*.

Clunas's preface to the 2004 paperback edition of the latter work touches on the debate around questions of the appropriateness, and rhetorical impact, of the term so applied.

7. Wang points out that "those who are skilled at compiling encyclopedias" (*shan lei zhe* 善類者) "are like those skilled in peddling and trading" (*huozhi* 貨殖). See Wang's preface to Zheng Ruoyong's 鄭若庸 (fl. 16th c.) *Lei juan* 類雋, p. 225.

8. See Deng Guangming 鄧廣銘 (1907–98), "Lun *Siku quanshu cunmu congshu* buyi kanxing." Emphasizing that *Siku* scholars' evidential studies of texts remain important for judging a book's value, Deng called upon scholars to distinguish between those books that are "national treasures" (*guobao* 國寶) and those that are "national dross" (*guozha* 國渣). This late twentieth-century debate surrounding the project of reissuing works that had been rejected by the eighteenth-century *Siku* editors involved a number of top state leaders and departments of the central government. For a summary, see Du Zexun, "*Siku quanshu cunmu congshu* chengshu shimo."

9. In the historical experience of "modernization of text"—the collation and publication of traditional texts in modern format (often in the form of a "*biaodian ben*"/punctuated version, marked clearly by the application of modern and partially imported punctuation marks) as part of the process of modernizing humanistic studies and disciplines—different authorial attributions and textual variations more often than not are treated as mistakes rather than as windows into how these textual factors came into play in the reading culture of a given historical time. Here I draw the notion of "modernization of text" from Philip Gaskell's *From Writer to Reader*, where he states that "the deliberate modernization of the spelling, punctuation, etc., of an early text is undesirable since it suggests that the modern meaning of the words of the text is what the author meant by them . . . because it causes the editor to choose where the author was ambiguous; and *because it deprives the work of the quality of belonging to its own period*" (italics mine), p. 8. In this study, authorial attributions and variations are viewed as factors shaping the meaning of the text for its original readers, rather than as facts to be verified or repudiated.

10. See Darnton, "What Is the History of Books"; and Chartier, "Communities of Readers," in *The Order of Books*, pp. 1–23. The field of the history of books has exploded in the past two decades or so. For a convenient overview of the field in general, see Finkelstein and McCleery, *The Book History Reader.*

11. In fact, the early history of the *Shanhai jing* is complicated; the earliest attested edition appearing in the fourth century CE purports to represent much older traditions. On the early sources, see Fracasso, "*Shan hai jing.*" For modern readers, a representative "authoritative" text would be, e.g., Yuan Ke, Shanhai jing *jiaozhu* 山海經校注.

12. The ancient fourth-century *Shanhai jing* recension was itself accompanied by illustrations, but these had long since been lost by the Ming, and the illustrations in Ming editions had, and made, no claims to authenticity in regard to the ancient text. On this cluster of illustrated *Shanhai jing* texts, see Ma Changyi, *Guben* Shanhai jing *tushuo*, and *Quan xiang* Shanhai jing *tu bijiao*. For a recent study and English translation of selections from a 1597 illustrated edition of *Shanhai jing*, see Strassberg, *A Chinese Bestiary.*

13. de Magalhães, *A New History of China,* p. 61.

14. Such a critique leveled at the Jesuits is considered, e.g., in Wu Liwei, "Ming Qing chuanjiaoshi dui *Shanhai jing* de jiedu."

15. On material culture and its representation in early modern China, see Clunas, *Superfluous Things.*

Chapter 1

1. By block edition, I refer to each time a new or newly modified set of blocks was used to produce a run of imprints. The internal evidence of a poem celebrating the reign of the Jiajing emperor gives a terminus post quem of at least the mid-1520s for this text (or at least for versions containing this poem). A comparison of copies of this text in the Shanghai library and in Zheng Zhenduo's 鄭振鐸 (1898–1958) collection indicates that they were printed from separate sets of blocks. The Shanghai library copy is in four *juan*. A copy preserved in the National Library in Beijing contains a further fifth *juan*. From these examples it is clear that the *Boxiao zhuji* was modified over the course of its printing and circulation history.

2. See Du Xinfu and Du Tongshu, *Quan Ming fensheng fenxian keshu kao.* The Zhongde tang of the Xiong family started to print books in the Yuan dynasty. Xiong Chongyu is the fifth-generation grandson of Xiong Zongli 熊宗立 (1409–82).

3. Wu Xiaoling recorded that the two copies of this text in Fu Xihua's 傅惜華 (1907–70) collection were both printed by Wende tang. See Ma Wenda and Wang Zhijun, *Wu Xiaoling xiansheng zhencang gu banhua quanbian*, 316. According to Du Xinfu and Du Tongshu, Wende tang was a commercial printer in Wu xian 吳縣, Jiangsu 江蘇, during the Tianqi reign (1621–28). See Du Xinfu and Du Tongshu, *Quan Ming fensheng fenxian keshu kao*, vol. 2, "Jiangsu sheng shulin juan" 江蘇省書林卷, 30B.

4. This copy is now preserved in the Shanghai library.

5. As mentioned above, a five-volume version of *Boxiao zhuji* was in circulation in the Ming as well. The further fifth volume comprised brothel instructions and popular songs.

6. "Winsome sayings" in Ming publications are what is known today as *xiehouyu* 歇後語 (phrases omitting the end), a form of word-play centered on creating witty riddling alternatives to familiar words and phrases. For further discussion of this genre, see chapter 2.

7. The abbreviated form of this alternate title, *Tanxiao jiuling* 談笑酒令, is also used by bibliographers, but following Zhou Yubo, Chen Shulu, and others, I will continue to refer to it as *Boxiao zhuji.* See Zhou Yubo and Chen Shulu, *Ming dai min'ge ji*, p. 208. As this book demonstrates, titling was handled rather fluidly in the Ming, and a book's title may appear in several places in a Chinese woodblock imprint apart from the title page itself, e.g., in the first column of the first beginning leaf/page (頁 or 葉) of each *juan*, or the center of the page (called the "block center" 版心). These titles serve different purposes and are often of varied lengths even when they refer to the same text. On conventions relating to book titles, see also chap. 2, note 11, below. For an illustration of a leaf in a block-printed Chinese book, see, e.g., Chia, *Printing for Profit*, p. 43.

8. *Boxiao zhuji* (hereafter *BXZJ*) 1.2B–3A. Judging from the examples given for this game and consulting another edition of the text, the phrase 比名 in the rule stipulations

is a mistranscription for 地名, and my translation reflects this conclusion. It is also possible that this is simply a variant graphic form current in the Ming. The tune title 雙聲子 is treated as if written 雙生子 (twin kids), and the word "moth" in the title "lamp-plunging moth" is written with the homophonic character for goose (鵝).

9. On the discourse and cultural attitudes towards "things" in early modern China, see, e.g., Brook, *The Confusions of Pleasure*; and Clunas, *Superfluous Things*.

10. *BXZJ* 1.8A.

11. *Jingchai ji*, scene 2. See Yu Weimin, ed., *Song Yuan sida xiwen duben*, pp. 12–17. On scenes related to civil service examinations in Chinese drama, see Xu Xuefeng, "Keju changmian yu xiju xiaoguo."

12. For an interesting point of comparison (though on a less worldly register) for such fantasies of personal contact with Zhu Xi as emblematic of mastery of tradition, compare the recent discussion of Wu Yubi's 吳與弼 (1391–1469) dream encounter with Zhu Xi in Bol, *Neo-Confucianism in History*, pp. 149–50.

13. See Brokaw and Chou, *Printing and Book Culture in Late Imperial China*, particularly Joseph McDermott's essay "The Ascendance of the Imprint in China."

14. China had a lively and long-standing tradition of drinking games taking classicist texts as ingredients—see, e.g., Harper, "The *Analects* Jade Candle." On drinking games and literary culture in the Tang dynasty in general, see Wang Xiaodun, *Tangdai jiuling yishu*.

15. *BXZJ* 2.2B.

16. "Thimble phrasing" (*dingzhen* 頂針) is a pattern in which the beginning of one line repeats the end of the preceding line.

17. *Analects* 1.10.

18. *Analects* 16.8. The full passage reads: Confucius said, "The gentleman has three things he fears: he fears the will of heaven; he fears the great person; he fears the words of a sage" (孔子曰: 君子有三畏。畏天命。畏大人。畏聖人之言).

19. The first sentence in this solution is quoted from *Mencius* 7A.20: Mencius said, "A gentleman has three delights, and ruling over the world is not among them. That his parents are both living, and that his elder and younger brothers are without mishap—this is one delight. That on looking upward he is without shame in regard to heaven, and that turning his gaze below he is without shame before men—this is his second delight. To obtain the flowering talents of the world and instruct and form them—this is his third delight. The superior person has three delights, and ruling over the world is not among them" (孟子曰:"君子有三樂,而王天下不與存焉。父母俱存,兄弟無故,一樂也;仰不愧於天,俯不怍於人,二樂也;得天下英才而教育之,三樂也。君子有三樂,而王天下不與存焉). The second sentence is quoted from the *Analects* 16.5: Confucius said, "There are three delights of a beneficial sort, and three delights of a deleterious sort. Delight in the due ordering of ritual and music, delight in speaking of others' fine qualities, and delight in having many worthy friends—these are beneficial. Delight in unrestrained pleasures, delight in roaming excursions, and delight in banquet entertainments—these are deleterious" (孔子曰:益者三樂,損者三樂。樂節禮樂,樂道人之善,樂多賢友,益矣。樂驕樂,樂佚遊,樂宴樂,損矣).

20. In another late Ming book, the game rule is corrected as "一令要四書二句." See Xi Zhengwo, *Zhaijin qiyin* 5.12A, rpt. p. 273.

21. For a list of Qing scholars' criticism of Ming books, especially those printed in the late Ming, see Zhang Xiumin and Han Qi, *Zhongguo yinshua shi*, pp. 375–76.

22. See note 19 above.
23. *BXZJ* 2.5A.
24. *BXZJ* 2.4B.
25. *BXZJ* 1.9A.
26. *BXZJ* 1.25A.
27. *BXZJ* 1.1B.
28. *BXZJ* 1.3A.
29. *BXZJ* 1.18A.
30. *BXZJ* 1.24B.
31. For English translation accompanied by an introduction to this text, see Jiang Yonglin, *The Great Ming Code/Da Ming lü*.
32. For the textual histories of some of these works, see Zhang Zhigong, *Chuantong yuwen jiaoyu jiaocai lun*; and Yuming He, "Productive Space," pp. 246–54.
33. *BXZJ* 1.19B–20A.
34. This is a line from Su Shi's 蘇軾 (1037–1101) poem "Chun xiao" 春宵 (Spring night). See *Qian jia shi*, 2A (this page appears in fig. IN.2 in this book). In the *BXZJ*, "*chun xiao*" is mistakenly written as "*chun ri*" (spring day, or springtime). This is just one example of the copious scribal errors in a book such as the *BXZJ*.
35. *Shijia* 時價 "current price" is related to *shigu* 時沽 "current estimation," which refers to a market system in which the government at each level estimates the current prices for goods and services. These prices then are used in the transactions between the government and the public. "To raise" 高抬 or "to lower" 少估 the current price unduly is an offense. For specific regulations, see the "*Shigu*" entry in the Wanli edition of the *Da Ming huidian*, rpt. p. 698. For scholarship on "current estimation," see , e.g., Qiu Pengsheng, "*You shichang lüli yanbian kan Ming Qing zhengfu dui shichang de falü guifan*."
36. This line is from Zhang Ji 張繼 (fl. mid-8th c.), "Feng qiao ye bo" 楓橋夜泊 (Night mooring at Maple Bridge).
37. "*Si yue mao du guanjin*" 私越冒度關津 is an item in *The Ming Code*, *juan* 15: Those who secretly pass checkpoints or ferry crossings without a traveling document—beat them eighty times with the stick. As for passing a checkpoint not through a gate or passing a ferry crossing not through a station—beat them ninety times with the stick. As for circumventing checkpoints along the borders—beat them a hundred times with the stick and send them into three-year penal servitude. Those who thereupon go outside the borders, garrote them" 凡無文引私度關津者，杖八十。若關不由門，津不由渡而越度者，杖九十。若越度緣邊關塞者，杖一百，徒三年。因而出外境者，絞. See Huai Xiaofeng, *Da Ming lü*, p. 117.
38. This is from Bai Juyi's 白居易 (772–846) poem, "Zhi Zhongshu sheng" 直中書省 (On duty in the Secretariat).
39. This is from "Tong xing weihun" 同姓爲婚, an item in *The Ming Code*, *juan* 6: "Those who marry bearers of the same surname should be beaten sixty times with a stick and ordered to divorce" 同姓爲婚者，杖六十，離異. See Huai Xiaofeng, *Da Ming lü*, p. 62.
40. The high demand for *Da Ming lü* in the book market is also connected to a policy that punished officials who could not master the Ming codes and provided incentives for commoners to read and understand them—in fact this policy of promoting broad

study and promulgation of the code appears in the *Da Ming lü* itself. See Huai Xiaofeng, *Da Ming lü*, p. 36.

41. For example, the *Juan Da Ming longtou biandu bangxun lüfa quanshu* 鐫大明龍頭便讀傍訓律法全書 (New edition: complete book of legal codes of the Great Ming, for valedictorians, in an easy-to-read format with explanatory comments), printed by Liu Shuangsong 劉雙松 (fl. Wanli reign) of Anzheng Tang 安正堂, Jianyang, Fujian, opens its first *juan* with a rhymed mnemonic (*gejue* 歌訣) entitled "Liu lü zong kuo" 六律總括 in the middle register of the page.

42. Zhu Xi, *Yuding xiaoxue jizhu* 御定小學集註, *juan* 2. *SKQS*. In this example, as in several others in the *Boxiao zhuji*, the answer is given first and the riddle afterward.

43. *BXZJ* 2.5B.

44. *BXZJ* 2.5A.

45. *BXZJ* 2.6A–6B.

46. This is a line from "Youyuan bu zhi" 游園不值 (On an outing to the garden, failing to meet my companion) by the Southern Song dynasty (1127–1279) poet Ye Shaoweng 葉紹翁 (fl. first half of the 13th c.).

47. This is from a poem by Li Bai entitled "Yu Shi langzhong Qin ting Huanghe lou shang chuidi" 與史郎中欽聽黃鶴樓上吹笛 (Listening to flute-playing atop Yellow Crane tower with palace gentleman Shi Qin).

48. This is a line from a Cheng Hao 程顥 (1032–85) poem entitled "Ti Huainan Si" 題淮南寺 (Inscribed on Huainan temple). Received texts of Cheng Hao's works read *wan shan* 晚山 (evening hills) instead of *wan feng* 晚風 (evening breezes) for this line.

49. *BXZJ* 2.12A–12B.

50. Although theater-going and theatrical performance played a central role in the literary culture of the Ming, as attested in the careers of Xu Wei 徐渭 (1521–93), Tang Xianzu 湯顯祖 (1550–1616), Zang Maoxun 臧懋循 (1550–1620), and Feng Menglong 馮夢龍 (1574–1646), other scholar-officials viewed theater as morally dangerous in its licentious display of both romantic stories and female performers, as expressed by Chen Longzheng 陳龍正 and cited in Wang Liqi, *Yuan Ming Qing sandai jinhui xiaoshuo xiqu shiliao*, p. 171. There are many records on treating drama and drama performance as dangerous in Wang Liqi's compilation; it seems that as the fashion of private theater became widespread, so did criticism of private theater as a force corrupting the order of domestic life and personal integrity. On private theater, see chapter 2.

51. Although this game seems to indicate again the necessity of a fairly comprehensive grasp of drama knowledge, further examination shows that not every aspect of knowledge about drama is needed to put on a good performance in gaming. What emerges in these game texts as the most important category of knowledge about drama is tune names.

52. Huang Lin, "*Xixiang ji*, *Pipa ji*, *Mudan ting* huiping shulue," p. 3. On *Xixiang ji* editions, see also works by Jiang Xingyu 蔣星煜, e.g., *Ming kan ben Xixiang ji yanjiu*.

53. As pointed out by Stephen West and Wilt Idema in the introduction to their translation of *The Story of the Western Wing* (p. 7), no other work of vernacular literature can boast a comparable number of editions.

54. *BXZJ* 2.7A–7B. In the place of the character 見 (to meet) in solution #2 was written 爻 (交?) in *BXZJ*.

55. In scenes 5, 24, and 12, respectively.

56. Xu Wei, *Nanci xu lu*, p. 240.

57. *Pipa ji* also enjoyed a great number of printings, totaling over 70 editions by 1597. See Zhang Xiumin and Han Qi, *Zhongguo yinshua shi*, p. 240. On materials that shed light on the printing, reception, and popularity of *Pipa ji* in the Ming dynasty, see Hou Baipeng, Pipa ji *ziliao huibian*.

58. *BXZJ* 1.22B.

59. *BXZJ* 2.11A–11B.

60. *BXZJ* 1.20A–20B.

61. On dating this text, see Kang Chan-soo, "Zhongguo keben *Guwen zhenbao*"; and Huang Jian, *Xiangshuo Guwen zhenbao daquan*.

62. The three answers from the first example are from the following poems: Huang Tingjian, "Zizhan zhe Hainan" 子瞻謫海南; Li Bai, "Song Zhang sheren zhi Jiangdong" 送張舍人之江東; and Li Bai, "Su Wu" 蘇武. The three answers from the second example are from the following poems: Su Shi, "Bobo jiu" 薄薄酒; Wu Rong, "Hua shanshui ge" 畫山水歌; and Li He, "Qiang jinjiu" 將進酒. The lines from the third example are from Han Yu, "Fu dushu chengnan" 符讀書城南, though the order of lines in the answer is not the same as in Han Yu's original poem.

63. For studies on the Former and Latter Seven Masters and Ming *guwen* movements, see, e.g., Chen Shulu, *Mingdai qianhou qizi yanjiu*; Liao Kebin, *Mingdai wenxue fugu yundong yanjiu*; Zhang Weibao, *Mingdai wenxue "fugu yu gexin" yantaohui lunwen ji*. On the distinction between the "Masters'" notion of *guwen* and that reflected in the *Guwen zhenbao*, see Kang Chan-soo, "Zhongguo keben *Guwen zhenbao*," p. 112.

64. Preface to the imperial edition of the *Guwen zhenbao*. Quoted in Wang Zhongmin, *Guohui tushuguan cang Zhongguo shanben shu lu*, p. 1076. As discussed below, this preface and others like it would have been composed by court literati in the voice of the emperor rather than being personally drafted by the emperor. The point remains, however, that the association of the *Guwen zhenbao* with the voice and prestige of the emperor was deemed natural as well as politically and culturally advantageous.

65. For Yuan-Ming editions of *Guwen zhenbao*, see Xiong Lihui, "*Guwen zhenbao* de bianzhe, banben yanbian jiqi zai Hanguo, Riben de chuanbo," pp. 9–11.

66. For commercial publishers in Fujian, see Chia, *Printing for Profit*; Xie Shuishun and Li Ting, *Fujian gudai keshu*.

67. See *Sanshan lunxue* 三山論學, by Aleni, in Zheng Ande and Lou Yulie, eds., *Mingmo Qingchu Yesuhui sixiang wenxian huibian*, vol. 7; see also Cui Laiting, *Haiguo gusheng*. Ye Xianggao was also the chief editor of *Guangzong Zhen huangdi shilu* 光宗貞皇帝實錄.

68. In light of the widespread use of spurious authorial attribution as a marketing strategy, the attribution of the editorship of this text to Ye Xianggao would seem questionable. So far, however, I have not found evidence to overturn this attribution, which has been accepted by all past and current bibliophiles who have mentioned this text.

69. *Ming shilu*, 136.2529.

70. *Ming shilu*, 138.2569.

71. See Timothy Brook, "Edifying Knowledge."

72. Recent scholarship bears this out; see for example Chia, *Printing for Profit*, pp. 6–7.

73. For further discussion on this point, see the next chapter.

74. Here my use of the notions of canonization and popularization is inspired by Haruo Shirane, who explains, "A careful distinction is made between popularity, which implies increased accessibility and wider audiences, and canonicity, which implies authority (often related, in the case of the *Genji*, to the emperor or imperial court), privilege, and pedigree (such as association with the aristocracy) . . . In contrast to canonization, which has tended to emphasize the reading, interpretation, and transmission of the written or printed text, popularization typically transforms or dramatically alters the text, making it accessible to new audience, frequently through or with the assistance of new media and visual technology." See Shirane, "*The Tale of Genji* and the Dynamics of Cultural Production," in *Envisioning* The Tale of Genji, p. 2.

75. See *Siku quanshu zongmu*, p. 1697, on *Song wen jian*; Ma Maojun, "*Song wen jian* yu *Song wen hai*."

76. Such an instance is the *Juan Da Ming longtou biandu bangxun lüfa quanshu* 鐫大明龍頭便讀傍訓律法全書, discussed in note 41 above.

77. Jiang Mian, "*Cao cibu ji* xu" 曹祠部集序 (dated 1528), in Cao Ye, *Cao cibu ji*. *SKQS*.

78. Sun Xu, *Shaxi ji*, *juan* 13. *SKQS*.

79. Wu Kuan became an iconic figure in the Ming. The book *Zhuangyuan tukao* 狀元圖攷 (An illustrated study of valedictorians), published in 1643, includes an entry on him. See Clunas, *The Empire of Great Brightness*, p. 133.

80. Pan Fu'en, *Lü Zuqian pingzhuan*, esp. chap. 1, "Jiashi, shengping, ji xueshu huodong" 家世，生平及學術活動.

81. This phrase is from *Shi ji* 6:48.1952, where it was uttered by the soon-to-be rebel leader Chen Sheng 陳勝 (?–208 BCE) to agitate his fellow soldiers to overthrow the rule of the Qin. Interestingly, this phrase was changed by later publishers to "九重春色醉仙桃" (Hues of springtime in the ninth heaven make drunk the fairy peaches), signaling a shift of emphasis in conceptions of the text's usefulness from social mobility to leisurely and sensual pleasure.

82. The dating of the *Guwen zhenbao* has been debated. The fact that it incorporates Xie Fangde's commentaries indicates an earliest possible date that is close to or during the Yuan, since Xie lived during the Song-Yuan transition.

83. I base this conclusion on my comparison of commentaries in the *Guwen zhenbao* and the other three anthologies.

84. Quoted in Kang Chan-soo, "Zhongguo keben *Guwen zhenbao*," p. 2.

85. Hu Shi famously remarked that Jin Shengtan's critique on the *Shuihu zhuan* was "the view of a popular anthologizer-commentator" (選家評文的眼光) who had butchered the *Shuihu zhuan* into a vernacular version of seventeenth-century model prose. See Hu Shi, "Shuihu zhuan kaozheng," in *Hu Shi wencun*, vol. 1, pp. 363–64. Hu Shi meant to criticize the influence of traditional *guwen* commentary in Jin Shengtan, but his remark also shows how the commentarial styles of earlier commentated *guwen* anthologies had shaped Jin Shengtan's *xiaoshuo* commentary. On how commentarial genres connected to classical literary writing and examination composition served as sources for *xiaoshuo* criticism, see Rolston, "Sources of Traditional Chinese Fiction Criticism," pp. 17–29; On *guwen* anthologies as source

materials for *xiaoshuo pingdian*, see Tan Fan, *Zhongguo xiaoshuo pingdian yanjiu*, pp. 10–11; as source materials for *xiqu pingdian*, see Zhu Wanshu, *Mingdai xiqu pingdian yanjiu*, pp. 8–11.

86. Huang Yuji, *Qianqing tang shumu*, p. 758. Huang lists the *Guwen zhenbao* as one of the titles in the *zongji lei* 總集類 (category of collective anthologies) of the Ming dynasty. He might be criticized for failing to observe the pre-Ming origins of the text; at the same time, his categorization may be seen as a reflection of Ming readers' own sense that this was one of "their" essential texts.

87. To paraphrase the general point, the *Guwen zhenbao* and these *guwen* anthologies shaped what Pierre Bourdieu called the "habitus" of the readers, the "durable, transposable dispositions, structured structures predisposed to function as structuring structures." See Bourdieu, *The Logic of Practice*, p. 53.

88. For example, based on his evaluation of the *Guwen zhenbao*, Liu Ruoyu 劉若愚 (fl. Wanli and Chongzhen [1628–44] reigns) called its compiler an "old erudite" 老學究, a rather flattering appellation. Liu Ruoyu, *Zhuo zhong zhi*, p. 157.

89. *Qinding Tianlu linlang shumu*, *juan* 10. *SKQS*.

90. For example, according to the Korean bibliography *Sŏngam mun'go mongnok* (Bibliography of old books in Sung-am collection), the *Guwen zhenbao* enjoyed 53 editions during the Chosŏn dynasty (1392–1910). See Zhang Bowei, "Xuanben yu yuwai Han wenxue."

91. Park Sam-soo, "Shilun Hanguo ban *Guwen zhenbao*"; Zhang Bowei, "Yuwai Hanji yu Zhongguo wenxue yanjiu"; Kang Chan-soo, "Zhongguo keben *Guwen zhenbao*"; Huang Jian and Xiong Lihui, *Xiangshuo Guwen zhenbao da quan*.

92. The *Tang wencui* was compiled by Yao Xuan 姚鉉 (968–1020) of the Song dynasty. In including poems, the *Guwen zhenbao* distinguishes itself from the other Song dynasty commented anthologies of *guwen*. On the notion of "guwen" embodied in the *Tang wencui*, see Bing Jieyong, "Lun *Tang wencui* 'guwen' lei de wenti xingzhi yuqi daibiao yiyi."

93. *Suyu* has been a subject of fascination and study from ancient times to the present. On contemporary studies of *suyu*, see Wen Duanzheng and Zhou Jian, *Ershi shiji de Hanyu suyu yanjiu*.

94. The character that I read as *ao* 拗 here is indistinct. Another Ming book uses *xiangfan* 相反 instead of *aoshuo* 拗說. See *Miaojin wanbao quanshu*, vol. 3, p. 271.

95. From a poem by Zhao Shixiu 趙師秀 of the Song entitled "Yue ke" 約客 (Inviting a guest).

96. Zeng Ji 曾幾 of the Song, "Sanqu dao zhong" 三衢道中 (On the road to Sanqu).

97. Dai Min 戴敏 of the Song, "Chuxia you Zhangyuan" 初夏遊張園 (An early summer excursion to Zhang garden).

98. Lu Meipo 盧梅坡 of the Song, "Xue mei" 雪梅 (Snowy plums).

99. Ibid.

100. Xie Fangde 謝枋得 of the Song, "Canfu yin" 蠶婦吟 (Song of the silkworm-tending woman).

101. Cui Tu 崔塗 of the Tang, "Lü huai" 旅懷 (Journey thoughts).

102. Wang Ling 王令 of the Song, "Song chun" 送春 (Sending off spring).

103. *BXZJ* 2.8a– 2.8b.

104. *BXZJ* 1.18b.

105. *BXZJ* 1.19B.

106. *BXZJ* 1.6B–1.7A. The character *kai* 開 is omitted in the *BXZJ* and supplied here for coherence; the expression is still current in modern Chinese. The application of this saying to the preceding character rhyme seems a bit strange in modern Mandarin. However, *yang* (ocean) and *liang* (grain) are homophones in the Jiangxi dialect in the Yiyang region. See Sun Yizhi, "Jiangxi Yiyang fangyan de yinyun tedian." This may be further evidence of the connection between the *Boxiao zhuji* and Jiangxi. See the discussion of the *Huang Ming shixuan* in the final section of this chapter.

107. It could also mean that adding even a small amount of extra food or income is always a good idea; adding another mouth to feed will create trouble. The meaning of this saying may be region specific.

108. *BXZJ* 1.20A.

109. *BXZJ* 1.18B. The conundrum (*mi mian* 謎面) references the story of the old man with a thornwood staff (*qingli* 青藜) who visits the bibliophile and scholar Liu Xiang 劉向 (ca. 77 BCE–6 BCE) in his study. To be able to resolve the riddle requires mastery both of the classical reference and of current slang.

110. On the rise of the "hoodlum" class in Ming cities, see Han Dacheng, *Mingdai chengshi yanjiu*, pp. 341–74. "Winsome sayings" seems to be the urban dwellers' sharp tool for satirical depiction of the ways of the world.

111. Riddles on "ancient persons" or "circumstances relating to an ancient person" are drawn from a body of books such as *Riji gushi* 日記故事 on model personages in history and their deeds.

112. *BXZJ* 2.6A.

113. *BXZJ* 1.25B–1.26A.

114. This is a truncated phrase from *Analects* 16.7: "There are three things in which the superior person must be warned: in youth, when the blood and vital energies are not settled, the warning concerns sex; when he attains his prime, and the blood and vital energies are at their firmest, the warning concerns fighting; when he is old, and the blood and vital energies are in decline, the warning concerns acquisitiveness."

115. This is a skewed quotation from *Analects* 10.27.

116. *BXZJ* 2.7B–2.8A. The final example involves a punning misquotation of *Analects* 6.25, with *gu* 孤 "orphan" replacing the original text's reading of *gu* 觚, the name of an ancient bronze ritual drinking vessel.

117. An important *jie jing* endeavor worth mentioning here are the vernacular Chinese texts created during the Yuan dynasty for a Mongolian readership using a kind of plain language that itself was developed under the influence of Mongolian and other languages.

118. Tang Xianzu, *The Peony Pavilion*, scene 7, "The Girls' Schoolroom." For example, in this scene, the opening line of the first poem in the *Shijing*, "(Guanguan cries the osprey,) in the island in the river" (zai he zhi zhou) is interpreted by Chunxiang's mishearing of the homophonic as "at the home of the Prefect He" (zai He zhizhou). For discussion of this scene, see Owen, *An Anthology of Chinese Literature*, pp. 71–76; and Volpp, "Texts, Tutors, and Fathers." Tang Xianzu created striking and novel effect in his own plays by mixing elements and styles from both popular theater and classical texts.

119. On this text and the print genre of the "drama miscellany" to which it belongs, see the discussion in chapter 2.

120. Xi Zhengwo, *Zhaijin qiyin*, p. 316.

121. Translation adapted from Legge, *The Four Books*, pp. 279–80.

122. In this regard we may consider as well the following example: *Ju shang bu kuan*: A husband and a wife are having sex. The husband dislikes his wife's vagina being so wide. His wife says, "That's not hard. Put me on top and it will be tight." The husband asks, "Why is that?" The wife says, "*Ju shang bu kuan* (Being on top but without generosity/On top it won't be loose)." 居上不寬：夫妻交媾。夫嫌其妻陰寬。妻曰：不難。放我上便緊。夫曰:何也？妻曰:居上不寬。 In Yin Qisheng, *Yao tian yue*, pp. 8–9. The joke hinges on a skewed reference to *Analects* 3.26: The master said, "Ruling (lit. being on top) without generosity (*ju shang bu kuan*); performing ritual without reverence; mourning without sorrow—how should I contemplate such ways?" Here again wit comes from the contrast between the officially sanctioned correct reading and the intentionally incorrect reading in a lower register.

123. The topic is a recurrent one in Ming jokes and bawdy humor (see, e.g., the joke appearing in the lower register of the *Boxiao zhuji* page presented in fig. 1.4 below). The most renowned such instance is that underlying the storied romance between Emperor Xuanzong and Yang Guifei of the Tang (Guifei having entered the palace as a junior consort of Xuanzong's son Prince Shou). Another well-known case is the incestuous relation between Jia She and Qin Keqing, which is strongly hinted at in the *Story of the Stone*.

124. This is the first phrase of, and in traditional discourse functionally names, *Analects* 5.10. See the discussion below.

125. Yin Qisheng, *Yao tian yue*, 9–11.

126. This passage can be seen in Legge, *The Four Books*, p. 53.

127. The editors of the *Siku* catalog do note a Ming text entitled exactly *Suyu*. However, no extant copy of this text is known. See Yong Rong et al., *Siku quanshu zongmu*, *juan* 126.

128. Printed either in the Wanli reign or the Tianqi reign, all these reference works were included in Kikuya Nagasawa, *Min Shin zokugo jisho shūsei*, a five-volume photo facsimile reproduction of Ming-Qing reference works on *suyu*. This collection was reissued by Shanghai guji chubanshe in 1989. For dictionaries on *suyu* from Ming-Qing China, see Liu Yeqiu, *Zhongguo zidian shilue*, pp. 174–99. Liu views these dictionaries as continuing the tradition of Yang Xiong's 揚雄 (53 BCE–18 BCE) *Fang yan* 方言.

129. This work is included in *Meiguo Hafo daxue Hafo Yenching tushuguan cang Zhongwen shanben huikan*, vol. 32.

130. For an overview of this subject, see Liu Yeqiu, *Zhongguo zidian shilüe*.

131. To "make use of lechery in putting a stop to lechery" is part of the title of the first chapter of *The Carnal Prayer Mat*: "Make use of lechery in putting a stop to lechery, Start off with sex in treating the subject of sex."

132. Translation from Legge, *The Four Books*, pp. 488–89, with minor changes.

133. Zhao Qi and Sun Shi, *Mengzi zhushu jiejing* 孟子註疏解經, 19A–20B.

134. Translation from Hanan, *The Carnal Prayer Mat*, pp. 10–11, with minor changes.

135. These are the dates for Li Wen's life span given in most sources. A recent argument for 1607 as Li's birth date, however, seems plausible. See Yao Rong, "Li Wen shengnian bianzheng."

136. An argument for 1617 as the year for Song Zhengyu's birth is proposed by

Lu Yongqiang. See Lu Yongqiang, "Song Maocheng shengzu nian kaobian ji qita," p. 140.

137. See Hou Rongchuan, "Ming chao Zhu Zhifan, Zhu Mengzhen, Pan Zhiheng shengzu nian kao," p. 122.

138. Chen Zhenghong and Zhu Bangwei, "Mingshi zongji biankan shilue—Mingdai pian (shang)"; Ma Hanqin, *Ming dai shige zongji yu xuanji yanjiu.*

139. See the following poems in the *Huang Ming shixuan*: "Taizu xiaoxing" 太祖曉行, "Ke zhong faliang" 客中乏糧, "Gui gelao songyou" 桂閣老送友, "Meiren chunshui" 美人春睡, "Shu zhuangyuan youchun" 舒狀元遊春, and "Ti jiang zhong shi" 題江中屍.

140. On the Wanli era *Yuzhi wenji* and this poem, see *Quan Ming shi* bianzuan weiyuanhui, *Quan Ming shi*, vol. 1, pp. 47–50.

141. On Zhengde emperor's use of *jiali* 家裏, see Shen Defu, *Wanli yehuo bian*, pp. 544–45; *Ming shi* 26:307.7887.

142. Exemplary traditions of *daiyan ti* include that of male literati poetry in the voice of women, as well as the notion of "speaking on behalf of the sages and worthies" (*dai shengxian liyan* 代聖賢立言), which was the guiding rationale of the "eight-legged" examination essay.

143. This poem has to be understood within the context of tales and dramas on the Zhengde emperor's un-emperor-like conduct that became widespread in the Ming, especially through the play *Zhengde ji* 正德記 (also known as *Zhengde piaoyuan* 正德嫖院). Though the original survives only in fragments, Pu Songling's 蒲松齡 (1640–1715) play *Zengbu Xing yun qu* 增補幸雲曲, a reworking of the Ming play, provides revealing details. See *Pu Songling ji*, pp. 1542–1669. This Ming play itself also became the subject of popular songs in the Ming; see Yuming He, "Productive Space," p. 180; *Yuefu yushu ying*, pp. 52–53; *Da Ming chun*, pp. 152–53; and Xi Zhengwo, *Zhaijin qiyin*, pp. 302–8.

144. Ming cultural observers also pointed out analogies between the Zhengde emperor and Huizong of the Song. See, e.g., Shen Defu, *Wanli yehuo bian*, p. 544.

145. Both "peach-blossom waves" and "cassia flowers" are conventional references to success in the spring and fall civil service examinations. These references and the phraseology itself are ubiquitous in theatrical depictions of young scholars.

146. "Green coin selection" refers to the selection of talented persons on the basis of their literary compositions in the civil service examinations. The line as a whole thus refers to the successful candidate standing next to the stone tortoise carved on the steps in the imperial palace.

147. Here again, sequencing matters, as the first poem in the voice of Prince Ning in the *Huang Ming shixuan* comes after two poems in the voice of the Jiajing emperor, depicting that emperor's vigilance in guarding the empire: one "Jiajing Emperor at the Pavilion of 'Observing the Plough,'" the other "To Mao Baowen" (Mao being a general of the Ming). The sequencing of the Prince Ning poem immediately after these Jiajing poems creates an effect analogous to that of the Xuande emperor poem that immediately follows the anthology's opening poem in the voice of the Hongwu emperor. Note another small yet revealing connection between Wang Shouren and the textual universe of the *Boxiao zhuji*: Wang wrote a preface for Xie Fangde's *Wenzhang guifan*. See Rolston, "Sources of Traditional Chinese Fiction Criticism," p. 25.

148. This poem, like the one in the voice of the Zhengde emperor discussed above, needs to be understood within the context of the proliferation of tales and dramas on

contemporaneous events in the Ming. For instance, a southern drama called "Ning wang" (The Prince of Ning) was circulated in the song and drama anthology *Fengyue jinnang* 風月錦囊 (Brocade bag of breezes and moonlight) of the Jiajing reign. See Sun Chongtao, Fengyue jinnang *kaoshi*, p. 12; Sun Chongtao and Huang Shizhong, Fengyue jinnang *jianjiao*, pp. 31–33. Xu Wei's *Nanci xu lu* also records a play called *Wang Yangming ping ni ji* 王陽明平逆記 (Story of Wang Yangming's suppression of rebellion).

149. See *Ming shi* 1: 1.11–12.

150. See Jiangxi native Yin Zhi's 尹直 (*jinshi* 1454) *Jian zhai suozhui lu* 謇齋瑣綴錄, *juan* 8. Yin Zhi recorded three poems by Liu Chonghua: "Ten Grand Secretaries from the Ji Prefect" 吉郡十閣老, "Nine Ministers" 九尚書, and "Ten Valedictorians" 十狀元.

151. To bring up just one example, the earliest known anthology of dramatic excerpts and songs, the *Fengyue jinnang*, was compiled by a Jiangxi editor named Xu Wenzhao 徐文昭 during the Jiajing reign, and it featured texts with Jiangxi connections. Jiangxi was also known for producing high-quality paper called Guanyin zhi 觀音紙 in the Ming. This gave the region another advantage in the printing industry.

152. The "du" in "Han du" is an abbreviation of "dutang" 都堂 or "du yu shi" 都御史, two designations for the post of Censor-in-Chief. Further poetic reflections on Han Yong are discussed in the conclusion.

153. *Ming shi*, 14: 161.4388.

154. Chen Zhenghong and Zhu Bangwei, "Ming shi zongji biankan shilüe," pp. 110–12.

155. From a preface by Han Yang 韓陽, *Huang Ming Xijiang shixuan*, 2B. This editorial policy aims to continue the legacy of an early Ming style of poetry that came to be called Taige ti 臺閣體 (lit. cabinet style) due to the high court rank of its main practitioners. See Wang Wentai, "Mingdai ren bianxuan Mingdai shige zongji yanjiu," pp. 9–11. The chasm between the literary communities led by official-scholars, or poets of high social status and the literary communities of commoners is seen in Xu Wei's indignation over Li Panlong 李攀龍 and Wang Shizhen's 王士貞 marginalization of Xie Zhen 謝榛, a commoner 布衣, in their poetry club "The Club of the Seven," aka the "Latter Seven Masters." Li eventually severed his interaction with Xie. On the Seven Masters, see also discussion on *Guwen zhenbao* above. Xu Wei in turn refused to join the group led by Wang and Li. *Ming shi*, 24: 288.7388.

156. On using poetry to criticize officials, the *Ming shilu, Longqing shilu* has the following record, in Frederic Wakeman's rendition: "Recently mores have become quarrelsome and superficial drivel. People are much more contemptuous. They use young students to assault and berate prefects. They use licentiates to attack and accuse civil officials. They revile their [educational] superintendents by displaying couplets on every street corner. Their popular ballads, full of vengeance, hatred, and envy, are engraved on printing blocks." See Wakeman Jr., "The Price of Autonomy," p. 145.

157. On Ming commoners' literary activities, see, e.g., Fang Zhiyuan, *Mingdai chengshi yu shimin wenxue.*

158. On the organization and social hierarchy of local society, see, e.g., Wang Rigen, *Ming Qing minjian shehui de zhixu.*

159. Xie Jin was one such esteemed court official from Jiangxi. On Jiangxi elites and Ming court politics, see Zheng Kesheng, "Mingdai ganxi zhongfu yu Jiangxi shidafu."

160. I am grateful to Richard von Glahn for pointing out Xu Zhenjun's Jiangxi connections.

161. Jiang Yikui, *Yao shantang waiji*, p. 492. The phrase "cong zhong xing" 從終興 has also been construed as the name for the Japanese poet.

162. Poems by Japanese visitors were collected and circulated in various records in the Ming. For example, a poetry anthology compiled by Mu Ang 沐昂 (1379–1445), called *Canghai yizhu* 滄海遺珠, collected poems by twenty-one poets who sojourned in Yunnan, among whom eighteen were Chinese officials and three were Japanese monks. See Ma Hanqin, *Mingdai shige zongji yu xuanji yanjiu*, pp. 22–24.

Chapter 2

1. For a comparison of the material in the *Boxiao zhuji* and two other Ming books, the *Wenlin jubao* 文林聚寶 and *Guang xiaofu* 廣笑府, see Ogawa Yōichi, *Nichiyō ruisho ni yoru Min Shin shōsetsu no kenkyū*, pp. 51–56. Note that Ogawa refers to the *Boxiao zhuji* by its alternate title *Tanxiao jiuling* 談笑酒令. Ogawa also discusses the connection between Ming drinking games and riddles and the Qing novel *Story of the Stone.*

2. For a summary of early scholarship on this type of book and another similar type called the fiction miscellany, see Richard Wang, "Creating Artifacts," pp. 26–29. For extensive discussion of drama miscellanies in relation to Ming popular songs, see Lowry, *The Tapestry of Popular Songs in 16th- and 17th-Century China.*

3. As Lang Ying 郎瑛 (1487–1566) records, "The folk phrase for things incomplete in excellence is 'three-pawed cat.' During the Jiajing reign, the Daoist master Yuan Suju at the Shenle Temple in Nanjing had a cat with three paws, who was quite good at capturing mice but could not walk in proper steps." *Qixiu leigao*, p. 541. Later in this chapter, Wang Jide 王冀德 (1542?–1623) uses this slang to refer to the know-it-all of the theater who unwittingly reveals himself to be a mere poseur.

4. Tang Laihe, *Neixing zhai wenji* 內省齋文集, cited in Han Dacheng, *Mingdai chengshi yanjiu*, p. 479.

5. "Liangtou mang" here may be what is called "Liangtou man" 兩頭蠻 (two-headed barbarian) in other Ming-Qing documents. It refers to either a tune title or a style of operatic singing that mixes different styles. See Ban Youshu, "'Liangtouman' bianxi"; Deng Wei and Deng Xiangyun, "Zai lun 'liangtouman'."

6. This title is difficult to make out in the *Yuefu yushu ying* text. The transcription is based in part on the close analogy in both title name and title sequencing between the *Yuefu yushu ying* and another drama miscellany entitled *Yuefu wanxiang xin*. See p. 257 in the photoreprint edition of the latter text for the parallel listings.

7. "Xishang shengfeng" is a kind of drinking game that involves referencing things or persons at the banquet.

8. The *Zhaijin qiyin* reflects the double register layout. More discussion of this text follows below.

9. For more on the *Fengyue jinnang*, see chap. 1, note 148.

10. In a paper entitled "Materiality and Text Organization in Early and Medieval Chinese Manuscripts," Jean-Pierre Drège proposed the function of "tabulation"—in the sense of the creation of spatial relationships within the grid field of the page, as opposed to linear flow of a single text—as the distinctive function of woodblock printing as compared to manuscript textual reproduction.

11. Like the material of the books themselves, titling tended to be handled quite fluidly by Ming book producers and readers. The longer titles given here are generally the titles that would have appeared as the first column of text in each *juan* of the book; the shorter titles might have appeared on the title page in oversize print as a design element, and also served as abbreviated forms for easy reference (for example, in prefaces). Note that some of the short titles in the above list were formulated by later bibliographers in imitation of Ming practice. On the general conventions for form and placement of titles in such texts, see the discussion throughout this chapter, along with chap. 1, note 7. For another list of Ming drama miscellanies, see Lowry, *The Tapestry of Popular Songs in 16th- and 17th-Century China*, pp. 377–81. Note that Lowry's list is more inclusive than the one given here, since it considers as drama miscellany a number of books composed entirely of *qu* 曲 (dramatic excerpts and songs). I am reserving the term "drama miscellany" for texts displaying the distinctive juxtaposition of drama excerpts and the miscellaneous middle-register materials under discussion here, excluding such homogeneous anthologies of *qu*.

12. The translation of *gundiao* as rapid recitative is Piet van der Loon's. See his *The Classical Theatre and Art Song of South Fukien*, p. 42.

13. Given how few examples of the Ming drama miscellany survive, it is surprising that such central figures in modern Chinese drama studies as Fu Yunzi 傅芸子 (1902–48), Wang Gulu 王古魯 (1901–58), Ye Dejun 葉德均 (1911–56), and Zhao Jingshen 趙景深 (1902–85), to mention only a few of the most prominent names, drew so heavily on these sources in their accounts of Chinese theater history, and that they continue down to the present to be core primary sources. This apparent disparity between the small number of these texts and their impact in modern scholarship may in part be explained by their very ephemeral nature: the very fact that they were products of a relatively fleeting moment in publishing fashion (and indeed seem never to have been highly esteemed by Chinese bibliophiles, often surviving only in copies that circulated abroad and thereby gained value as exotica) gives them something of the status of archaeological relics of the popular culture of their time. On the modern rediscovery of these drama miscellanies and the scholarship they generated, see appendix 1 in Yuming He, "Productive Space," pp. 283–88.

14. On recent scholarship on *gundiao*, see Ban Youshu, "Qingyang '*gundiao*' yuanqi xin lun"; Li Diankui, "'*Gundiao*' zai tan." The term *gun* can still be found in Cantonese opera, which has a tune name *gwanfa* 滾花. According to Bell Yung ("Model Opera as Model," pp. 153–54), gwanfa "does not conform to any fixed meter or beat but is rhythmically rather free."

15. In his preface to the *Yuefu yushu ying*, the editor Huang Wenhua compares his compilation to the "precious trees in heaven's courtyard" (*tianting baoshu* 天庭寶樹). In *HWSZ*, p. 2.

16. This is seen, for example, in the Ming painting "Nandu fanhui tu" 南都繁會圖 held in the National Museum of China.

17. This is the case with *Yugu xinhuang*; the next chapter will discuss this text in further detail. *Yao tian yue* has also been identified as a title added in the course of another such minimal adaptation of blocks for an earlier title. See Yao Shuyi, Wang Yongkuan, and Gao Mingluan, *Xiju tongdian*, p. 260.

18. For criticism of Ming commercial books, see chap. 1, note 21.

19. I adapt the term "xylographic dignity" from Roger Chartier's phrase "typographic

dignity" to describe how formal or ornamental aspects of the presentation of a text can create implicit claims about the canonicity or classic status of the work in question. See his *Order of Books*, pp. 10–11. Ming cultural observers were keenly aware of the rampant use of "vulgar characters" 俗字, that is, non-standard graphs. Jiao Hong's 焦竑 (1540–1620) treatise *Sushu kanwu* 俗書刊誤 collects and corrects these graphs. But his treatise is also a testimony to the wide currency of these graph forms and their influence. Such "vulgar characters" themselves provide a unique window into the social processes through which they became both legible and acceptable. On this topic, see Chen Wuyun, *Cong xin shijiao kan Hanzi*, esp. pp. 160–74.

20. For lists of studies and new editions of these books, see appendix 1 in Yuming He, "Productive Space," pp. 283–88; along with Miao Huaiming, *Ershi shiji xiqu wenxian xue shulue*, pp. 25–33. These books are reproduced in Wang Ch'iu-kuei et al., *Shanben xiqu congkan*, and Li Fuqing and Li Ping, *Haiwai guben wan Ming xiju xuanji sanzhong.*

21. For primary scholarship on drama materials in these books, see Fu Yunzi, *Baichuan ji*; Wang Gulu, *Mingdai Huidiao xiqu sanchu jiyi*; Ye Dejun, "*Qiu ye yue* zhong hanjian juming kao," in *Xiqu xiaoshuo congkao*, pp. 371–81; and Zhu Chongzhi, *Zhongguo gudai xiqu xuanben yanjiu.* In recent years scholars have been increasingly interested in the middle registers. Representing this interest in these sources are Lowry, *The Tapestry of Popular Songs in 16th- and 17th-Century China*; Richard Wang, "Creating Cultural Artifacts" and "The Publishing of the Ming Novellas"; and Shang Wei, "*Jin Ping Mei* and Late Ming Print Culture." On the related issue of Ming elite editors' rewriting of early sources in the process of producing imprints of theatrical texts, see Sieber, *Theater of Desire.*

22. By "community of interpretation," I refer to book-makers and users, as both partake in the collective process of making sense of a book, a text, or a picture. See also the introduction, p. 8.

23. Jiangxi is separated from Fujian by only the Wuyi Mountains. The routes between the two provinces had long been established by, among other migrating peoples, merchants and migrant workers who came across the mountains in the Song-Yuan period. See Gardella, "Fukien's Tea Industry and Trade in Ch'ing and Republican China," and idem., *Harvesting Mountains.* For regional migration in the economic and social organization of the publishing industry in late imperial China, see Brokaw, "Commercial Publishing in Late Imperial China."

24. Sun Chongtao, Fengyue jinnang *kaoshi*, p. 12.

25. "Shulin" refers to the part of the town or city where printshops, bookstores, booksellers, and buyers gathered and traded, and the term appears to have been favored by Fujian printers. On Nanjing publishers who marked their printshops as those of Shulin, see Chia, "Of Three Mountain Street," esp. pp. 113–23. Chinese rare book experts disagree on whether particular occurences of the the term "Shulin" in these drama miscellanies designate a printer in Fujian or Anhui. See Zhou Xinhui, "Zhongguo gudai xiqu banhua kaolüe," p. 8; Du Xinfu and Du Tongshu, *Quan Ming fensheng fenxian keshu kao*, Anhui volume, 10B. On the deciphering of Jianyang printers' designations for places of printing, see, e.g., Xiao Dongfa, "Jianyang Yu shi keshu kaolue"; Fang Yanshou, "Songdai 'Jianben' diming kaoshi"; and Chen Duo, "Guanyu 'Jianben' yu 'Jian'an banhua' yanjiu zhong jige diming de wujie." On some of the Jiangxi compilers of drama miscellanies, see Li Ping, "Liuluo Ouzhou de sanzhong wan Ming xiju sanchu xuanji de faxian," pp. 17–19.

26. The idea of niche marketing is examined in relation to fiction printing in Hegel, "Niche Marketing for Late Imperial Fiction."

27. During their history of circulation, these two books were put together under the single title *Qiu ye yue* 秋夜月. On this work, see Ye Dejun, *Xiqu xiaoshuo congkao*, pp. 371–81; and Zhao Jingshen, "*Qiu ye yue*."

28. On illustrations by Shijian tang, see, e.g., Zhu Chongshou, *Zhongguo chatu yishu shihua*, pp. 81–82.

29. On the importance of this pictorial album and Ming illustrated texts in general, see Hegel, *Reading Illustrated Fiction in Late Imperial China*, pp. 164–250, especially p. 197. For further discussion of Liu Ciquan and his work, including a more detailed look at the production of the *Yugu xinhuang*, see the following chapter.

30. On the Yu family, see, e.g., Chia, *Printing for Profit*, pp. 87–93; Xiao Dongfa, "Jianyang Yu shi keshu kaolue."

31. See appendix 1 for a list of these other works.

32. "Seated reclusion" is a kenning for *wei qi* playing, and "Master Seated Reclusion," as noted here, is a cognomen of Wang Tingne, whose Huancui Tang, or "Emerald-encircled Hall," was both a publishing house and an elaborate garden complex. On Wang Tingne's publishing activities and his social milieu, see Berliner, "Wang Tingna and Illustrated Book Publishing in Huizhou," Carlitz, "Printing as Performance," and Hegel, "Niche Marketing for Late Imperial Fiction," pp. 252–53.

33. Yu Wentai, *Ke quanxiang wuxian lingguan dadi Huaguang tianwang zhuan* 刻全相五顯靈官大帝華光天王傳. Yu Wentai is considered by many scholars to be the most important Jianyang commercial publisher. On his life and career, see, e.g., Chia, *Printing for Profit*, pp. 156–60; Xie Shuishun and Li Ting, *Fujian gudai keshu*, pp. 241–49.

34. This is one early recension of the material best known to us as the *Romance of the Three Kindoms*. Some scholars also refer to Zhu's recension as the *Sanguo zhi shizhuan* 三國志史傳. See Zhang Zhihe, "Zhu Dingchen ben *Sanguo zhi shizhuan* tankao."

35. For a brief overview of the specific titles and types of these miscellaneous texts, see the summary in Yuming He, "Productive Space," pp. 91–96.

36. The phrase "*fangqing miyu*" is seen in Yu Wentai, *Santai wanyong zhengzong*, vol. 3, p. 591. In *Yuefu yushu ying*, *Da Ming tianxia chun*, and *Da Ming chun*, the category is referred to as *jianghu fangyu*.

37. On a modern overview on the history of this kind of coded diction and a representative collection, see Qian Nanyang, "Shi yu huichao" 市語彙鈔 and "Cong fengren ti dao qiaopi hua" 從風人體到俏皮話, in *Han shang yi wencun*, pp. 117–87.

38. These are seen in *Da Ming tianxia chun*, pp. 579–80; also in Cheng Wanli and Zhu Dingchen, *Da Ming chun*, pp. 10–12.

39. *BXZJ* 1.9A–9B.

40. In *Da Ming chun*, a group of *qiaoyu* are labeled as *jianghu fangyu*; in *Santai wanyong zhengzong*, the so-called *zidi qiaoyu* 子弟俏語 are actually "local expressions." See Cheng Wanli and Zhu Dingchen, *Da Ming chun*, p. 214; Yu Wentai, *Santai wanyong zhengzong*, vol. 3, p. 599. See also the discussion of *qiaoyu* in connection with "common speech" within the *Boxiao zhuji* in Chapter 1.

41. *Da Ming tianxia chun*, p. 616.

42. *Da Ming tianxia chun*, pp. 597–609.

43. Yu Wentai, *Santai wanyong zhengzong*, vol. 3, pp. 591–99.

44. The two drama miscellanies that list this brothel treatise in their tables of contents have not survived intact, and in their extant forms they lack the text of the treatise itself. Versions of the treatise, however, appear in other late Ming publications, such as daily-use encyclopedias. The text given here is that which appears in the daily-use encyclopedia *Santai wanyong zhengzong*. For a Japanese translation and annotation of this text, with useful cross-references to a broad range of related Ming and Qing literary texts, see Ogawa Yōichi, *Mindai no yūkaku jijō: Fūgetsu kikan* and *Fūgetsu kikan to Min Shin bungaku*.

45. "To taste vinegar" is to be jealous, therefore, "don't be jealous over little matters."

46. Yu Wentai, *Santai wanyong zhengzong*, vol. 2, pp. 294–98.

47. Yu Wentai, *Santai wanyong zhengzong*, vol. 2, p. 296.

48. See appendix 2 for more on the brothel treatise.

49. Another way to refer to these books is with the phrase *buqiuren* 不求人, literally, "not asking help of others," meaning that the book promised to resolve any questions of knowledge or social or cultural know-how for which the prospective buyer might otherwise need to seek help from others. Where the phrase appears as the name of a publication genre in titles below, I translate it as "seek no further."

50. The "shelves of the Marquis of Ye" is a proverbial expression for a vast collection of books.

51. "Dragon's head" refers to the first place candidate in the *jinshi* examination.

52. Wu Huifang, *Wan Bao quan shu: Ming Qing shiqi de minjian shenghuo shilu*, pp. 649, 651, 658.

53. For an annotated bibliography of Chinese *leishu*, starting from the *Huang lan* 皇覽, which was compiled under the auspices of Emperor Wen of the Wei dynasty, Cao Pi 曹丕 (187–226), to the current *Zhonghua dadian* 中華大典, which was directly supported by the State Council of China, see Zhao Hankun, *Zhongguo leishu*.

54. See the summary in Sakade Yoshinobu, "Kaisetsu—Mindai nichiyō ruisho ni tsuite." Important works on the daily-use encyclopedia have emerged in the past several decades, for example, Sakai Tadao, "Mindai no nichiyō ruisho to shomin kyōiku"; and Wu Huifang, *Wanbao quanshu*. For a comprehensive survey of works on Ming daily-use encyclopedias, see Shang Wei, "*Jin Ping Mei* and Late Ming Print Culture," pp. 222–23. For a critical reflection on studies of daily-use encyclopedia, see Wang Zhenghua, "Shenghuo, zhishi yu wenhua shangpin," pp. 2–14.

55. Examples of early (i.e., before the late Ming) comprehensive daily-use encyclopedias include, along with the *Shilin guangji* discussed above, the *Gujin hebi shilei beiyao* 古今合璧事類備要 and *Jujia biyong shilei quanji* 居家必用事類全集. For comparisons of these books and late Ming daily-use encyclopedias of Jianyang in recent studies, see, e.g., Wang Zhenghua, ibid, pp. 14–22; Xu Huilin, "Chaogong de xiangxiang," pp. 172–178; and Wu Huifang, *Ming Qing yilai minjin shenghuo zhishi de jiangou yu chuandi*, pp. 11–54.

56. Titles and publishing dates are based on Sakade Yoshinobu, "Kaisetsu—Mindai nichiyō ruisho ni tsuite," pp. 18–23; and Wu Huifang, *Wanbao quanshu*, pp. 641–59.

57. The phrase "wuche" (five carriages) is a proverbial expression for a great volume of texts or great breadth of knowledge. "Simin" (four peoples) refers to *shi* (scholars), *nong* (peasants), *gong* (craftsmen), and *shang* (merchants).

58. Meigong is the cognomen of the eminent Ming poet and calligrapher Chen Jiru 陳繼儒 (1558–1639).

59. On commoners and their cultural life as reflected in popular books, see Wang Ermin, *Ming Qing shidai shumin wenhua shenghuo*. Wang Zhenghua also distinguishes these Fujian daily-use encyclopedias from other types of daily-use encyclopedias that she terms "scholar-type daily use encyclopedias" (*shiren xing riyong leishu* 士人型日用類書). See Wang Zhenghua, "Shenghuo, zhishi yu wenhua shangpin," p. 20.

60. On how these encyclopedias contributed to the creation of new common knowledge for public consumption, particularly in answering the needs of merchants and the individual's welfare and in relation to the novel *Jin Ping Mei*, see Shang Wei, "The Making of the Everyday World." On the connection between these encyclopedias, urban culture, and new social space, see Wang Zhenghua, "Shenghuo, zhishi yu wenhua shangpin."

61. On this novel, see Nienhauser, *The Indiana Companion to Traditional Chinese Literature*, vol. 2, pp. 53–58. For English scholarship, see, e.g., Yenna Wu, *Ameliorative Satire and Seventeenth-Century Chinese Novel*; Epstein, *Competing Discourses*, pp. 120–49; Berg, *Carnival in China*; Martin W. Huang, *Desire and Fictional Narrative in Late Imperial China*, pp. 137–75; Dudbridge, *Books, Tales and Vernacular Culture*, pp. 275–302. For a survey and review of scholarship on this novel, see Robert Hegel's review article on Berg's *Carnival in China*.

62. On this novel, see Charles R. Stone, *The Fountainhead of Chinese Erotica: The Lord of Perfect Satisfaction (Ruyijun zhuan) with a Translation and Critical Edition*.

63. These episodes are depicted in chapters 1 and 2 in the novel. See Xizhou sheng, *Xingshi yinyuan zhuan*, pp. 2, 24, and 27. Ogawa Yōichi, *Nichiyō ruisho ni yoru Min Shin shōsetsu no kenkyū*, pp. 43–44, and Wang Zhenghua, "Shenghuo, zhishi yu wenhua shangpin," p. 23, also discuss these passages in connection with the phenomenon of the Ming daily-use encyclopedia.

64. For discussion of the new developments in the late Ming daily use encyclopedia, see Sakai Tadao, "Confucianism and Popular Educational Works" and "Mindai no nichiyō ruisho to shomin kyōiku"; as well as Sakade Yoshinobu, "Kaisetsu—Mindai nichiyō ruisho ni tsuite." See also note 55 above.

65. For the textual history of the *Complete Collection of Matters Necessary for Household Use*, see Sakai Tadao, "Mindai no nichiyō ruisho to shomin kyōiku," pp. 133–36.

66. *Jujia biyong shilei quanji*, p. 393.

67. Ibid., pp. 393–94.

68. The thematic allocations of the literature discussed may vary only slightly from encyclopedia to encyclopedia. For example, brothel treatises, which appear in "Shanglü men" in *Santai wanyong zhengzong*, appear in the "Fengyue men" (Division on breezes and moonlight) in other compilations.

69. The lists differ in areas such as printing format, order of the localities, and scribal variations. Possible reasons for the differences include the editor's native place and the regionality of the targeted audience. Though these are important variations that led to different reading experience, here my focus is on how the list was circulated and remade in various publishing genres.

70. The fascination with mapping the whole empire in drama miscellanies can also be seen in the inclusion of a list of "Rhymed Verses on Local Products of the Two

Capitals and Thirteen Provinces" 兩京十三省土產歌 and a list of "Rhymed Verses on Offices and Officials, both Civil and Military, in the Two Capitals of the North and South and the Thirteen Provinces in the Sub-Celestial World" 南北兩京天下十三省文武官員衙門歌 in *Shi diao Qing Kun*.

71. Brook, "Introduction," in *Geographical Sources of Ming-Qing History*, p. 3.

72. Wang Zhideng, *Ke Yue zhilue* 客越志略. Cited in Brook, "Introduction," p. 4.

73. For scholarship and reproduction, see Chen Xuewen, *Ming Qing shiqi shangye shu ji shangren shu zhi yanjiu*; Brook, *Geographical Sources of Ming-Qing History*; Yang Zhengtai, *Tianxia shuilu lucheng*.

74. Compiled by Tao Chengqing 陶承慶 (fl. Wanli era) of Xinyu, Jiangxi, and published by Jianyang publisher Liu Dayi.

75. Chen Xuewen, *Ming Qing shiqi shangye shu ji shangren shu zhi yanjiu*, p. 242.

76. This is an incomplete text whose compiler and publisher are unknown. For an introduction and partial reproduction, see Lai Xinxia and Gao Weiguo, *Za zi*.

77. For scholarship, see Rawski, *Education and Popular Literacy in Ch'ing China*, pp. 128–39; Lai Xinxia and Gao Weiguo, *Za zi*. In her *Ming Qing yilai minjian shenghuo zhishi de jiangou yu chuandi*, Wu Huifang provides an extensive survey and study of Ming-Qing character books.

78. The phenomenon of "*liuwen*" 留文, or "lingering phrases," referring to the free appropriation of stock lines and descriptive or narrative passages by writers in premodern fiction and drama, is just one example. Such *liuwen* reflect a form of textual transmission and recycling beyond what can be readily accommodated within a model of an "original" and subsequent "borrowings" or "variations." For a useful discussion of *liuwen*, see Liu Hui, *Xiaoshuo xiqu lunji*, pp. 42–54.

79. See Yong Rong et al., *Siku quanshu zongmu*, pp. 596–97.

80. *Da Ming yitong zhi*, printed in the Qing by Jixiu tang 積秀堂 from a modified set of woodblocks by Wanshou tang 萬壽堂 of the Ming. Held in the collection of C. V. Starr East Asian Library at the University of California, Berkeley. Recorded in Chen Xianxiang and Guo Lixuan, *Bokelai Jiazhou daxue Dongya tushuguan guji shanben shuzhi*, p. 79.

81. See "Shao zhanshi Ke gong zhuan" 少詹事柯公傳, in *Ming mingchen wanyan xulu* 明名臣琬琰續錄, *juan* 13. Ke Qian is the *zhuangyuan* of the year 1451.

82. The original text mistakenly repeats the temple name of the Hongwu emperor, Taizu, where clearly it is the Yongle emperor, with the temple name Taizong, who is the intended referent.

83. The Wanli emperor's preface to the *Guwen zhenbao*, discussed in chapter 1, is another example of such imperial prefaces.

84. Li Dongyang, *Huailu tang ji*, *juan* 38.

85. Ming court intrigues were also enmeshed with book-making and book-reading. See, e.g., Fan Shuzhi, *Wan Ming shi*, pp. 520–34.

86. *Da Ming huidian*, pp. 2–3.

87. Yu Xian, *Sheng Ming baijia shi*, p. 672.

88. As recorded in *Qi Zhongmin gong riji* 祁忠敏公日記, Qi Biaojia 祁彪佳 (1602–45) on a leisure day went to a temple market, ran into a friend at a bookstore, and bought *Da Ming huidian* and several memorials to the emperor by court officials. See Qi Biaojia, "She bei cheng yan" 涉北程言, in *Qi Zhongmin gong riji*, 12A.

89. *Da Ming huidian*, pp. 6–7.

90. On "*haoshi zhe*" as the maker and ideal reader of *xiaoshuo*, see Mclaren,

"Constructing New Reading Publics," pp. 163–67. "Haoshi zhe" are often differentiated from "shangjian jia"賞鑒家 (connoisseurs) in the late Ming, as seen in books such as Wen Zhenheng's 文震亨 *Zhangwu zhi* 長物志, Xie Zhaozhe's 謝肇淛 *Wu za zu* 五雜組, and Shen Defu's 沈德符 *Wanli yehuo bian* 萬曆野獲編. For discussions on this distinction, see Clunas, *Superfluous Things*, pp. 86–87; Wang Zhenghua, "Shenghuo, zhishi yu wenhua shangpin," pp. 37–38.

91. Cited in Brook, *Geographical Sources of Ming-Qing History*, p. 16. Brook's introduction to this volume, pp. 3–25, provides a useful overview of Ming route books that conveys the significance of Huang Bian's work.

92. Heijdra, book review of *Geographical Sources of Ming-Qing History*, p. 68.

93. Chartier, *The Order of Books*, p. viii.

94. Only one preface to a drama miscellany survives, composed by Huang Wenhua for *Yuefu yushu ying*. For a translation and discussion of that preface, see Yuming He, "Productive Space," pp. 223–25.

95. In the Qing novel *Rulin waishi*, to place one's name on the cover page of a book as the editor or printer is an art called "standing on the cover page" (zhan fengmian 站封面) by Mr. Ma Er, an anthologizer of examination essays. According to Mr. Ma Er, there are two ways of "zhan fengmian," "duzhan" (standing alone) and "hezhan" (standing together with someone else); the latter is a particularly tricky business in terms of negotiating the fame and financial gain between the co-editors. See Wu Jingzi, *Rulin waishi*, p. 137. In relation to this *Rulin waishi* example, we may observe that Ye Zhiyuan's "standing" on the cover page is tied to his pronounced authority on the genre of song anthologies, and to the community of cultural life spun by music as the cover page design reveals (see discussion below).

96. This statement may be a clue that the phrase "tapestry of a thousand kinds" served as a Ming designation for the bibliographical category we now refer to as the "drama miscellany."

97. Dorothy Ko discusses the image of the portable stove and picnic box (fig. 2.11) in *Teachers of the Inner Chambers*, pp. 45–47.

98. *Xidan* is called "handbook on plays" (*xiwen shouben* 戲文手本) or "disclosing-notes on plot prompts" (*guanmu jietie* 關目揭帖) in chapters 43 and 64 of the *Jin Ping Mei cihua*.

99. *Xinke xiuxiang piping Jin Ping Mei* 新刻繡像批評金瓶梅, chap. 1, "Ximen Qing with great enthusiasm forms the brotherhood of ten; Wu Erlang is met with coldness when meeting his real brother and sister-in-law" 西門慶熱結十弟兄, 武二郎冷遇親哥嫂. Note that this edition of the novel differs from Xiaoxiaosheng's 笑笑生 *Jin Ping Mei cihua*.

100. For a history of Chinese theater, see Liao Ben, *Zhongguo gudai juchang shi*; Wang Qiang, *Huiguan xitai yu xiju*; Zhou Huabin and Zhu Lianqun, *Zhongguo juchang shi lun*.

101. He Liangjun, *Si you zhai congshuo*, p. 109.

102. Gu Qiyuan (1565–1628), *Kezuo zhuiyu*, p. 303; He Liangjun, *Si you zhai congshuo*, p. 109.

103. This social fashion of private performance was typified by the practice of raising one's own family performing troupe (called *jiaban* 家班 or *jiayue* 家樂) that became prevalent in the Wanli reign. Though maintaining household musicians and

performers was an elite tradition with a long history in China, the efflorescence of this fashion in the Wanli era appears to have been of unprecedented scale and impact. Private performances paralleled other venues of performance in late Ming—temples, outdoor stages, festival gatherings, etc. For example, Tanaka Issei has argued in his *Ming Qing de xiqu* that Ming-Qing drama served as an expression for the clan society in the Jiangnan region. Theatrical desire certainly is transportable between public and private space, and this phenomenon of transportability could make a research topic on its own. However, as a spatial practice, private performance served in the late Ming as a marker of status, fashion, and sociality that public performance could not duplicate. For recent work on family performing troupes in the history of Chinese theater, see Zhang Faying, *Zhongguo jiayue xiban* and *Zhongguo xiban shi*; Liu Shuiyun, *Ming Qing jiayue yanjiu*; Yang Huiling, *Xiqu banshe yanjiu*.

104. Tao'an is one of Zhang Dai's cognomens. For English scholarship on Zhang Dai and his *Tao'an mengyi*, see Kafalas, *In Limpid Dream*; and Spence, *Return to Dragon Mountain*.

105. Shi Jilun, whose name is Chong 崇, was a wealthy official of the Jin dynasty (265–420). Song Zijing, whose name is Qi 祁, was a literatus-official of the Northern Song (960–1127). Both of them allowed their maids or family performers to meet and entertain guests.

106. Zhang Dai, "Bao Hansuo," *Tao'an mengyi*, p. 53.

107. This refers to the chapter number in Wang's whole treatise.

108. This refers to the Song dynasty author Qiu Jun 丘濬 and his treatise entitled "Mudan rongru zhi" 牡丹榮辱志 (Record of the peony's honor and shame).

109. Wang Jide, *Qulü*, pp. 274–75.

110. Chartier, *The Order of Books*.

111. *Yugu xinhuang*, pp. 11–34.

112. *Da Ming tianxia chun*, pp. 544–68. *Da Ming tianxia chun* does not claim these songs as specifically commenting on prostitutes, but the girls and lads in these songs are as desirous and available.

113. For productions of pictorial materials in Ming China and their socio-cultural connotations, see Clunas, *Pictures and Visuality in Early Modern China*.

Chapter 3

1. The analogy between the medieval scribal culture he describes and the world of Ming books is in many ways a distant one, but Bernard Cerquiglini's oft-cited formula, "l'écriture médiévale ne contient pas des variantes; elle est variance" is worth recalling here. See his *Eloge de la Variante*, p. 111. Donald Harper's recent work on medieval manuscript culture also reveals patterns of text-making and circulation within which variations reveal significant information on how text and picture were made relevant and meaningful to readers' real and perceived needs in daily life. See, e.g., "The Textual Form of Knowledge."

2. Wang Jide, "Lun jufa" 論句法, in *Qulü*. See Guo Shaoyu and Wang Wensheng, *Zhongguo lidai wenlun xuan*, p. 269.

3. The study of Ming block-printed illustrations has been developing various perspectives and focuses. The titles of the following works give an indication of the range of recent English scholarship: Hegel, *Reading Illustrated Fiction in Late Imperial China*; Li-chiang Lin, "The Proliferation of Images"; Chia, "Text and Tu in Context"; Murray, "Didactic Illustrations in Printed Books." Murray's *Mirror of Morality* also has substantial discussions on illustrations in woodblock-printed books, as do Craig Clunas' works on Ming material and visual culture.

4. Other common reasons for modifying woodblocks include shifts in political sensibilities and taboos. I will discuss one such instance in the following chapter.

5. For an earlier reading of this illustration, see Yuming He, "Productive Space," pp. 139–40, 143–44.

6. One emblematic early statement appears in *Xunzi*'s "Discourse on Music": "Music is joy" 樂者, 樂也.

7. See, for example, *Mencius* 5B.1, where the phrases "jade chiming" and "tones of bells" are used metaphorically to describe Confucius's teaching.

8. For example, in Zhu Quan's preface to his *Taihe zhengyin pu*, an aria register, he used a variation of "yu zheng jin sheng," "keng jin jia yu" 鏗金戛玉 (making the metallic and jade sounds), to describe the virtues of musical instruments as the moral instrument of the state; Feng Menglong, in his preface to his song collection *Mountain Songs* (Shan'ge 山歌), also cites Confucius' anthologizing of the "Airs of the States" as a model act of collecting popular songs. On Ming representation of its musical culture, see Lam, "Ming Music and Music History."

9. Liu Ciquan is also credited as the publisher of the *Jingxuan baijia jinxiu lian* 精選百家錦繡聯 (Refined selection of lavishly crafted couplets by a hundred masters). See Qu Mianliang, *Zhongguo guji banke cidian*, p. 162.

10. The practice in producing illustrations in Ming publications sometimes involved separate artists doing the design itself and the carving of the block. We cannot say with absolute certainty that Liu Ciquan designed the illustration as well as carving it, but for simplicity the following discussion will treat the image as a whole as Liu's work.

11. Lantern riddles are a traditional part of nighttime festivities during the Lantern Festival on the night of the fifteenth day of the first lunar month: riddling verses were written on or affixed to hanging lanterns, with prizes often being offered to those who could correctly guess the answers.

12. On Ming painting manuals, see Park, *Art by the Book*. Park discusses the motif of the Orchid Pavilion banquet in particular on pp. 158–65.

13. One can also compare the illustration discussed here with another block-printed illustration from *Master Cheng's Ink-Stick Collection* (1606) to see how the former brings the scene of the gathering closer to Ming life. As a matter of fact, parties emulating the Orchid Pavilion gathering became a social vogue and part of the program of leisurely and cultured life in the Ming. On this point and a reproduction of the image from *Master Cheng's Ink-Stick Colleciton*, see Park, *Art by the Book*, pp. 158–65.

14. This story also enjoyed a wide circulation in Japanese paintings; see Rosenfield, "The Unity of the Three Creeds."

15. Cited in Wang Yucheng, *Mingdai caihui Quanzhen zongzu tu yanjiu*, p. 7.

16. Rolston, "Traditional Fiction Commentary," p. 940.

17. *Baneng zoujin*, 10–13.

18. *Cilin yizhi*, 9–10.

19. A shorthand mark indicating the repetition of word or phrase immediately before it.

20. *Zhaijin qiyin*, pp. 11, 14.

21. One factor in the editorial decision of not using space nor punctuation in the *Zhaijin qiyin* may be the overall design of a self-conscious Anhui style of block engraving, which features orderly refinement, among other things. While Anhui-style block engraving has been largely discussed within the context of woodblock illustrations, it seems that the design of the page in general is also an important factor contributing to the styling of the engraving. On Anhui style woodblock illustrations, see, e.g., Bussotti, *Gravures de Hui*; Zhou Wu, *Huipai banhua shi lunji*; Zhou Xinhui, *Zhongguo gu banhua tongshi*, pp. 153–71.

22. I will present one example of such a "heavily policed" text in the final section of this chapter.

23. Chartier, *The Order of Books*, pp. 11–12.

24. Chia, *Printing for Profit*, pp. 121–23.

25. Quoted in Chia, *Printing for Profit*, p. 121.

26. On oral performance and textual variation, see Ong, *Orality and Literacy*, pp. 20–21.

27. Lu Jiye, *Ci xue*, p. 13. Many attribute the *Ci xue* to Li Kaixian 李開先 (1502–68).

28. Ong, *Orality and Literacy*, p. 31.

29. Actually, the word *bai* 白 in the expression *baizi*, according to Gu Yanwu 顧炎武 (1613–82), is itself a *baizi*. Gu points out "what people nowadays call *baizi* ("white" or "pale" characters) is a phonetic transformation of the term *biezi* (alternate or substitute characters)" 今人謂之白字, 乃別音之轉. See Gu Yanwu, *Ri zhi lu*, pp. 99–100.

30. Wang Shifu, *Xixiang ji*. Translated in West and Idema, *The Story of the Western Wing*, p. 205.

31. See Jiang Xingyu, *Ming kan ben Xixiang ji yanjiu*, p. 16.

32. The *Nan Xixiang* (Southern-style *Story of the Western Wing*) is only one example in what seems to be a long history of the circulation of a *wei qi* scene. As early as the Hongzhi edition, the earliest edition of the complete play of the *Story of the Western Wing* known to us, a song suite in the mode of Nanlü 南呂 on a *wei qi* scene, was already included in a group of miscellaneous texts leading to the play itself. For an introduction and translation of the Hongzhi edition of the play, see West and Idema, *The Story of the West Wing.*

33. Xi Zhengwo, *Zhaijin qiyin*, pp. 80–88.

34. West and Idema, *The Story of the West Wing*, p. 89.

35. Xi Zhengwo, *Zhaijin qiyin*, p. 84.

36. See Wang Jide, *Xin jiaozhu guben Xixiang ji*, 3.29A.

37. Although it is rare to see this kind of direct mirroring, Li-ling Hsiao has argued for many dimensions of connection between Ming drama illustrations and theatrical practice. See Hsiao, *The Eternal Present of the Past.*

38. I am grateful to Wu Hung for calling my attention to these aspects of this illustration. On how Min Qiji's set of block print illustrations to the *Story of the Western Wing* serve as "metapictures," see Wu Hung, *The Double Screen*, pp. 237–59.

39. This song is one of a few dozen songs called "Personages Ancient and Modern"

(*gujin renwu* 古今人物), on personages from Chinese drama. For a list of these songs and the social relations they produce, see Yuming He, "Productive Space," pp. 177–200.

40. 姐妹 "elder and younger sisters" in this line is a mistranscription of 兄妹. The translation reflects the correct reading, which appears in, e.g., *Zhaijin qiyin*, p. 140.

41. Cheng Wanli and Zhu Dingchen, *Da Ming chun*, pp. 142–43. The "匕" is a repetition mark used in the original Chinese text.

42. Xi Zhengwo, *Zhaijin qiyin*, pp. 34–35.

43. *Cilin yizhi*, pp. 22–23, 25.

44. West and Idema, *The Story of the Western Wing*, p. 213.

45. In this social function of popular songs in the late Ming, we see a parallel to the social function of *ci*-lyrics in the early stages of the development of that form. See Owen, "Meaning the Words."

46. Xi Zhengwo, *Zhaijin qiyin*, p. 330.

47. Yu Wentai, *Santai wanyong zhengzong*, vol. 2, p. 251.

48. There might be slightly varied ways of playing this game. For ways of playing, see Yu Wentai, *Saitai wanyong zhengzong*, vol. 2, pp. 248–49, and Ma Guojun and Ma Shuyun, *Zhongguo jiuling daguan*, p. 153.

49. *Da Ming tianxia chun*, p. 609.

50. There are numerous works on *Story of the Western Wing* illustrations; for recent works aiming to comprehensively study these illustrations, see Dong Jie, *Ming Qing kan* Xixiang ji *banhua kaoxi*; Meng-ching Ma, "Fragmentation and Framing of the Text."

51. Some scholars have used the concept of "iconotext" to capture the fusion of text and image. See, e.g., Wagner, *Reading Iconotexts*. The late Ming world of reading is particularly rich in the ways that text and picture interrelate and interpenetrate. A detailed study of this aspect of reading culture in the Ming is beyond the scope of this study, but I would like to point out that text and image often serve as substitutes for one another. This mechanism is apparent in the composition and organization of texts as well. For example, the *Huang Ming shixuan* discussed in chapter 1 mimics the unfolding of a painted scroll, with emblematic scenes of Ming society revealed one after another.

52. Another example of this type of reference is "Emperor Ming (i.e., Xuanzong) of the Tang goes to the moon-palace" 唐明皇遊月宮, seen in pictures, verses, and theatrical performances (sometimes with special stage effects) in the Ming. The opening page of the *Boxiao zhuji* features such a block illustration.

53. The centrality of problems of identity in this "wall-jumping" episode is most poetically shown in Min Qiji's pictorial rendering of the moment (fig. 3.17), where student Zhang's actual form is almost completely obscured, and his figure becomes distinctly "legible" only in the reflection on one side of the wall and the shadow cast on the other.

54. In this connection we might recall Li Dongyang's characteristic insistence, in his examination question cited in chap. 2 above at note 84, that even textual mastery in such fields as history or geography only becomes complete and meaningful if students "embody it in themselves" (*ti zhu shen* 體諸身). Since ritual texts are those that most centrally foreground the issue of embodying textual meaning in real action, mastery of such texts may be considered the most emblematic sort of textual mastery for orthodox thought.

55. "Gaozu huan xiang" 高祖還鄉, in *Quan Yuan sanqu jianbian*, ed. by Sui Shusen, pp. 214–15.

56. A character mishearing a title or a name based only on its aural associations is also used in the *Peony Pavilion* as a way to subvert the orthodox establishment of meaning. See chap. 1, note 118.

57. See, e.g., Miao Yonghe, *Mingdai chuban shigao*, pp. 48–57, 133–48.

58. Note that the offering of "tribute" is treated as the core ritual act underlying all court appearances by foreign dignitaries.

59. The words in parentheses are supplied from the end of the preceding page of the original for continuity.

60. Although the terms *tu* and *hua* could at times be used interchangeably, here the word *tu* carries its more particular sense of explanatory or instructional diagram.

61. As is often recounted this very spectacle was to generate a crisis in Sino-British relations when, in 1793, Macartney refused to kowtow to the Qianlong emperor. On the Macartney mission to China, see Hevia, *Cherishing Men from Afar*.

62. This passage is from the imperial preface by the Jiajing emperor to the *Da Ming jili*. See *Da Ming jili*, 1B.

63. Chap. 2, note 88.

64. In Ming woodblock illustrations, sages and emperors are at times represented with visual formulae that do not clearly distinguish them from common officials or even commoners, the identification being left to captions or accompanying text. Still, the question of how to "read" the central figure seems open.

65. This is a long narrow tablet, made of various materials, that was used as a writing surface and ritual prop when having an audience with the royal court.

66. Clunas, *Superfluous Things*.

Chapter 4

1. For discussion of this text in relation to eighteenth-century and later disputes over the term *yi*, see Lydia Liu, *The Clash of Empires*, chap. 3, esp. pp. 81–88 (note that Liu renders the title as "Awakening to Supreme Justice"). See also pp. 31–107 for a discussion of the clashes over the word *yi* in the Anglo-Chinese Treaty of Tianjin signed in 1858, where 夷 was banned from use in reference to "the Government or subjects of Her Britannic Majesty in any Chinese official document issued by the Chinese Authorities either in the Capital or in the Province."

2. Specific counts of entries vary from edition to edition. The *Miaojin wanbao quanshu* edition (see fig. 4.1) has 139; this edition has been reproduced in *CNRS*.

3. The identification of the countries and regions recorded in the *Luochong lu* is based on *Yiyu zhi*, annot. Lu Junling.

4. The Ming book market also favored illustrated versions of the *Shanhai jing*. See note 12 in the introduction.

5. A photo facsimile reproduction of this text was published by Xueyuan chubanshe in Beijing in 2001. For works that note this text or versions of it, see, e.g., Zhou Xinhui, *Zhongguo gu banhua tongshi*, p. 179; *Zhongguo banhua shi conggao*, p. 241; Bai Qianshen,

Fu Shan's World, pp. 17–18; Laura Hostetler, *Qing Colonial Enterprise*, pp. 92–96. For recent studies on one particular version of the *Luochong lu*, the chapter on foreigners in the late Ming daily-use encyclopedia, see, e.g., Xu Huilin, "Chaogong de xiangxiang"; Miura Kunio, "'Banpō zensho' shoimon shōron." The latter also discusses some of the connections between the encyclopedia division and the *Luochong lu* as a self-contained work.

6. For a sample of important Ming works on the foreign, see the *Zhongwai jiaotong shi ji congkan* by Zhonghua shuju in Beijing. For studies on Ming interactions with foreigners, see, e.g., Ptak, *China, The Portuguese, and the Nanyang* and *China and the Asia Seas*.

7. This zoological schema also appears in such early texts as the *Da Dai Li ji* 大戴禮記, *Lun heng* 論衡, *Guanyinzi* 關尹子, *Guanzi* 管子, and *Huangdi neijing* 黃帝內經.

8. See Chen Shike, *Kongzi jiayu shuzheng*, p. 168.

9. What exactly *luochong* signified was debated from time to time. Many early and medieval Chinese scholars used *luochong* to refer to "barbarians," but some disagreed. For example, Lin Xiyi 林希逸 of the Song dynasty explained that *luo* (naked) means "short hair" (*qianmao*), referring to a zoological class that includes tigers (*hu*) and leopards (*bao*). See Lin Xiyi, *Kaogong ji jie* 考工記解, 2.27B.

10. The earliest extant dated edition of the novel was printed in 1592. On the sources and process of formation of the novel, see Dudbridge, *The Hsi-yu chi*.

11. The articulation of the five-classification system in the *Journey to the West* is slightly different from that of *Kongzi jiayu*.

12. From Anthony Yu's translation of Wu Cheng'en, *The Journey to the West*, vol. 1, p. 111, with slight modifications.

13. Ibid., vol. 3, p. 127, with slight modifications.

14. Ibid, vol. 3, pp. 130–31.

15. Yong Rong et al., eds., *Siku quanshu zongmu*, p. 678.

16. The exclusion of the *Luochong lu* (or *Yiyu tuzhi*) from the Siku compilation was likely a major reason for the subsequent disappearance of this text from our collective memory of Ming book history. Other factors contributed to this, such as the Qing court's own monumental compendium of illustrated accounts of foreign lands, the *Huang Qing zhigong tu* 皇清職貢圖, which eclipsed and replaced the unique position in the book market that *Luochong lu* had enjoyed for over two centuries. Finally, the *Luochong lu* itself, in the process of circulation of over two centuries, gradually became disassociated from its title when being incorporated into high-profile encyclopedic chapters on foreigners in later reproductions, such as in the *Sancai tuhui* 三才圖會 and later in the *Tushu jicheng* 圖書集成.

17. For example, one unresolved question is the relation between the pictorial *Luochong lu* and a text called *Yiyu zhi* 異域志, reputed to be written in the Yuan by a Zhou Zhizhong 周致中. The texts in these two books overlap.

18. Moule, "An Introduction to the *I yü t'u chih*."

19. Regarding Hu Wenhuan's *Gezhi congshu*, records of the number of works included in Hu's compendium range from 46 to 346; the number 346 is the most widely accepted. It appears that Hu would update the list of works while printing. See Wang Baoping, "Hu Wenhuan congshu kaobian"; Du Lei and Zhu Chongzhi, "Hu Wenhuan he *Qunyin leixuan*"; and Elman, *On Their Own Terms*, pp. 34–60, and "Collecting and Classifying."

20. See Sohō sensei koki shukuga kinen kankōkai, *Seikidō zenpon shomoku*, p. 334.

21. On the late Ming daily-use encyclopedia, see also chapter 2.

22. Authored by Zhou Qufei 周去非 (*jinshi* 1163). For a German translation, see Netolitzky, *Das* Ling-wai tai-ta *von Chou Ch'ü-fei*.

23. Compiled in the Song dynasty by Chen Yuanjing 陳元靚, the extant copies of this title are from the Yuan and Ming dynasties. This title is also discussed in chapter 2.

24. This is a ninth-century collection of miscellaneous tales and records by Duan Chengshi 段成式.

25. A third-century collection of anomaly texts attributed to the proverbially erudite Zhang Hua 張華.

26. Some of the pictures had come from age-old visual conventions. For example, the "Country of [Men with] Holes in Their Chest" appears in stone carvings from early China. See Ma Changyi, *Quan xiang* Shanhai jing *tu bijiao*, 1036–38. The *Luochong lu* may be the earliest block-printed pictorial with a pretension of including all foreign peoples known in Ming China.

27. Note here the link between the terms *yi* and *luochong*, which seem to be used as near synonyms, though perhaps with distinct connotations or conveying different tones.

28. To judge from other editions of the *Luochong lu*, such as Hu Wenhuan's 1593 edition, *ren* 人 here is used as a phonetic prompt for its homophone *ren* 仁.

29. "All four barbarians" refers to "barbarians" of all four directions.

30. What "chesu" 扯嗉 means here is unclear. But the late Ming daily-use encyclopedia *Wanshu yuanhai* rephrase it with "chiqi xiayi" 扯起下衣 (to pull up one's lower garment). My translation here reflects this *Wanshu yuanhai* suggestion. See *Wanshu yuanhai*, in *CNRS*, vol. 6, p. 187.

31. The *Song shi* 宋史 recorded the mountain as "Shensong" 神嵩 (divine high mountain) instead of "Shenwo" 神窩 (divine nest). See Tuotuo et al., *Song shi*, 40: 487. 14053.

32. The text is corrupt here. The parallel passage in the *Song shi* gives an account that differs in several details. See Tuotuo et al., *Song shi*, 40: 487. 14053.

33. *Yiyu tuzhi*, first entry.

34. For example, *Wuche wanbao quanshu* 五車萬寶全書 and *Santai wanyong zhengzong* added the following text from the *Bei shi* with slight word changes: They take the clothes and curios, horses and carriages the deceased had enjoyed in life, and place them at the grave side. Those assembled for the funeral then compete to lay hold of them and take them away. 取死者生時服玩車馬置墓側，會葬者爭取而去. See Li Yanshou, *Bei shi*, 10: 94. 3116.

35. For example, *Wuche wanbao quanshu* added the following lines (in quotation marks) from the *Hou Han shu*: "They delight in drinking and song and dance . . . they are without promiscuity or thievery . . . gentleness and caution are the essential elements of their folk customs." 喜飲酒歌舞… 無淫盜…以柔謹爲風. See "Dongyi zhuan" 東夷傳 in Fan Ye, *Hou Han shu*, 10: 85. 2818, 10: 85. 2822–23.

36. Li Yanshou, *Bei shi*, 10: 94. 3116.

37. On *haoshi zhe*, see chap. 2, note 90.

38. *Yiguo tuzhi*, third entry. Later editions often use "Zhongguo" 中國 instead of only "guo" 國.

39. The basis for the founding date of 57 BCE is in myth. Seth, *A Concise History of Korea*, p. 37.

40. Ibid., p. 65.

41. Cohen, *East Asia at the Center*, p. 98.

42. The third-century *Sanguo zhi*, for instance, states that "the people of the Wo are located in the ocean southeast of Daifang 帶方." This frame of reference became formulaic in subsequent official histories, the only change being that the reference to Daifang was updated by newer place names in keeping with changes in the administrative geography of the Korean peninsula. For example, The *Song shu* records that "the country of Wo is located in the ocean southeast of Koryŏ." See Chen Shou, *Sanguo zhi*, p. 854. Daifang is one of the commanderies in the Korean peninsula established by the Chinese in the third century; see Shen Yue, *Song shu*, 8: 97.2394.

43. Liu Xu, *Jiu Tang shu*, 16: 199.5339.

44. For an illuminating survey of Sino-Japanese relations that sheds light on Chinese documentation of Japan, including some of the sources mentioned in this chapter, see Fogel, *Articulating the Sinosphere*, particularly pp. 7–50.

45. This illustration can be considered part of a larger field of visual depiction of the ongoing fight against Japanese pirates in the Ming. For extant Ming paintings on fighting the Japanese pirates, see Clunas, *Empire of Great Brightness*, pp. 174–75.

46. Swope, *A Dragon's Head and a Serpent's Tail*, p. 3.

47. "Xiongnu" appears in early Chinese records such as *Shi ji*, referring to an assembly of nomadic tribes and nations that formed a mighty confederacy north of the Han empire (206 BCE–220 CE).

48. This tale can be found in *Youyang zazu* and *Taiping guangji* 太平廣記 (comp. 10th c.). "Nü" 女 is missing from the *Yiyu tuzhi* entry but added here according to the *Youyang zazu* account. The tale itself is a bit murky; according to the *Youyang zazu*, the female divinity of the ocean sends a white deer to escort Shemo to the ocean at night for decades before ending the union. See Duan Chengshi, *Youyang zazu*, pp. 44–45.

49. *Jin* 金 (metal, gold) here serves as a phonetic substitution for *jin* 今 (present days).

50. *Yaoshen* 妖神 is a mistranscription of *xianshen* 祆神.

51. The exact meaning of this and the following line is difficult to follow. According to Jiang Boqin, it refers to the practice of putting an icon, cut from felt, on a saddlebag. Jiang refers to several Tang *sancai* (tricolor glazed ceramic) camels that show an image of a god on the side of the saddle as evidence. See Jiang Boqin, *Zhongguo xianjiao yishushi yanjiu*, pp. 227–31.

52. *The Secret History of the Yuan* is a thirteenth-century work of unknown authorship written in Uighur script.

53. *Yiyu tuzhi*, tenth entry.

54. This sort of origin myth, tracing the beginnings of an ethnic group to an ancient instance of animal/human interbreeding, is quite common in Chinese tradition and elsewhere. Along with the accounts from the *Youyang zazu* discussed below in relation to this *Luochong lu* passage, see for example the account in the fourth-century compilation *Sou shen ji* 搜神記 explaining the societies and customs of peoples of the south and southwest in terms of an ancient instance of human/dog interbreeding: Gan Bao 干寶, *Sou shen ji*, pp. 168–69.

55. The relevant passages from *Youyang zazu* are also included in the tenth-century compendium *Taiping guangji.*

56. For the history of translation, printing, and transmission of *The Secret History of the Yuan* (aka *The Secret History of the Mongols*), see Hung, "The Transmission of the Book"; as well as the following three articles by Bai Tmrbagen: "*Yuanchao mishi* xiezuo guocheng kaolue," "Mingdai shisheng zhulu *Yuanchao mishi* kaolue," and "Qingdai cangshujia zhulu *Yuanchao mishi* kaolue."

57. Tonglaga and Wu Liqun, "Meng Yuan yingyi ti dui *Menggu mishi* fanyi de yingxiang."

58. Duan Chengshi, *Youyang zazu*, p. 45.

59. *Jue* 玃 is defined in traditional dictionaries as a female monkey 母猴 (as, e.g., in *Shuowen jiezi* 說文解字), or as a kind of large ape 大猿 (as, e.g., in *Longkan shoujing* 龍龕手鏡). *Jia* 猳, a variation of 豭, is defined in traditional dictionaries as a pig (as in, e.g., *Guang yun* 廣韻), or as a male pig (as in, e.g., *Shuowen jiezi*). Zhang Hua's *Bowu zhi* 博物志 records a kind of macaque called *jiajue* 猳玃, who captures women to be its wives. See Zhang Hua, *Bowu zhi jiaozheng*, p. 36.

60. Duan Chengshi, *Youyang zazu*, p. 44.

61. Ibid., p. 45.

62. The term "mountain ghost" appears in the "Nine Songs" in the *Chu ci*, a Warring States–era poetic anthology, where it designates a goddess. But at the time when the *Luochong lu* was compiled, the class difference between a *shen* and a *gui* was clear.

63. Modern scholarly efforts at parsing these terms are too numerous to recount here. For one influential early example, see Wang Guowei 王國維 (1877–1927), "Dada kao," in *Wang Guowei ji*, vol. 4, pp. 237–62.

64. One can see this page in a copy of *Sancai tuhui* housed in the C. V. Starr East Asian Library at the University of California at Berkeley.

65. Lü Nan, *Duanxi wenda*, p. 34.

66. Huang Zongxi 黄宗羲 (1610–96), *Ming ru xue'an* 明儒學案, in *Mingdai zhuanji congkan*, vol. 1, p. 11.

67. Yan Congjian's 嚴從簡 (fl. Jiajing to Wanli reigns) *Shuyu zhouzi lu* 殊域周咨錄 gives the name as Ning Gu 寧古. Further study is needed to determine which one is a mis-transcription. See Yan Congjian, *Shuyu zhouzi lu*, in *Guojia tushuguan cang Liuqiu ziliao huibian*, p. 138.

68. This is an alternate designation for the *Da Ming yitong zhi* 大明一統志, discussed in chapter 2.

69. The *luoji* is a whirlpool said to entrap passing ships. In 1895, L. C. Hopkins stated that *luoji* is a book term for what is locally known as *gou* 溝 (the current), the western branch of the *Kurosiwo*. See his "Letter of Mr. L. C. Hopkins to Mr. G. Schlegel."

70. Compiled by Du You 杜佑 (735–812) in the Tang dynasty.

71. *Deep Ocean of Collected Matters* is a Ming text. Extant editions can be dated to the Hongzhi (1488–1506) or Zhengde (1506–22) reigns. See Chen Xianxing and Guo Lixuan, *Bokelai Jiazhou daxue Dongya tushuguan Zhongwen guji shanben shuzhi*, pp. 219–20.

72. *Spectacles of the Starry Rafts* is a Ming text. Its author Fei Xin 費信 (1388–1436?) participated in Zheng He's 鄭和 (1371–1433) famed expeditions to the Indian Ocean in the fifteenth century.

73. Zheng Kaiyang, *Liuqiu tushuo*, in *Zheng Kaiyang zazhu*, pp. 556–57.

74. This Liuqiu memorial was reported in Zheng Kaiyang's treatise. Without corroboration from another source, it remains possible that the Ming writer invented or misrepresented this Liuqiu mission to the Ming court. Further, according to an anonymous reviewer for *Asia Major*, some of the Liuqiu envoys were actually Chinese.

75. Guo Rulin 郭汝霖 (*jinshi* 1553) and Li Jichun 李際春 (ca. 1536–83) were sent to Liuqiu in 1561 to enfeoff another new king, and they consequently composed *Chongbian Shi Liuqiu lu* 重編使琉球錄 (Recompilation of *Records of a Mission to Liuqiu*, preface dated 1561). The section of "Resolving Doubtful Points in the Various Books" from Chen Kan's text remained, and Guo and Li added their own comments to Chen Kan's critique. "Resolving Doubtful Points in the Various Books" again appeared later in Xia Ziyang 夏子陽 (*jinshi* 1589) and Wang Shizhen's 王士禎 *Records*, with Xia Ziyang's own critique added.

76. Lai Zhengwei and Huang Shan, "Xu Baoguang yu *Zhongshan chuanxin lu* kaoshu." Xu reiterated in his preface that "Beyond the standard histories, as for example in Master Du's *Comprehensive Canons*, the *Deep Ocean of Collected Matters*, the *Spectacles of the Starry Rafts*, the *Luochong lu* and so on, the geographical, cultural, and material items recorded are always full of errors and omissions."

77. Lang Ying, *Qixiu leigao*, p. 713. My punctuation is slightly different from the collator's.

78. In a narrow sense, *man* refers to the southern barbarians, as the barbarians of the four directions are known as the western *rong* 戎, the northern *di* 狄, the southern *man* 蠻, and the eastern *yi* 夷. In a broad sense, *man,* like *yi,* can refer to all barbarians.

79. *Record of the Beihu* (lit. north-facing window) is a book on local customs and environment of Lingnan 嶺南 (meaning "south of the five peaks" and including modern-day Guangdong, Guangxi, Hunan, and Jiangxi) by Duan Gonglu 段公路 of the Tang dynasty. The quotation here is actually from *Youyang zazu*, not *Beihu lu*.

80. *Spectacles of "Immortals' Isles"* by Ma Huan 馬歡 describes the countries he visited while on Zheng He's Indian Ocean expeditions. Ma Huan was Zheng He's translator.

81. *Record of Lost Accounts* is a book of anecdotes and strange tales by Wang Jia 王嘉 of the Eastern Jin (317–420).

82. Xu Yingqiu, *Yuzhi tang tanhui*, in *Biji xiaoshuo daguan xubian*, vol. 5, pp. 2756–57.

83. Ibid, p. 2639.

84. This expression originated from Ge Hong's 葛洪 (283–343) *Baopuzi*. When commenting on those who are skeptical about the belief and practice of alchemy, Ge Hong said, "When one sees very little, one feels shocked very often—this is the norm in the world" 夫所見少，則所怪多，世之常也.

85. Cai's office in Chinese is *Guangdong zuo buzheng si shi* 廣東左布政司史. This text is also known as *Dongnanyi tushuo* 東南夷圖説 (Pictures and descriptions of southeastern barbarians). It consists of two parts: *tuxiang* 圖像 (pictures) and *tushuo* 圖説 (text accompanying the pictures). *Dongyi tushuo* seems to be a more rhythmic shortened form of the more precise title *Dongnan yi tushuo.* On Cai Ruxian, see Tang Kaijian, "Zhongguo xiancun zui zao de Ouzhou ren xingxiang ziliao—*Dongyi tuxiang*," p. 24.

86. Some believe this illustration to be the earliest Chinese block illustration of the Portuguese. See Tang Kaijian, "Zhongguo xiancun zui zao de Ouzhou ren xingxiang ziliao—*Dongyi tuxiang*," p. 24. For Sino-Portuguese interactions in early modern history, see, e.g., Ptak, *China, the Portuguese, and the Nanyang.*

87. Cai Ruxian, *Dongyi tushuo*, p. 410.

88. Cai also added another title: the *Wu xue bian* 吾學編 (My studies compilation), possibly unknown to Chen Kan when he listed the questionable books. *Wu xue bian* is a book on early Ming history written by Zheng Xiao 鄭曉 (1499–1566, *jinshi* 1523). The earliest extant edition of *Wu xue bian* is dated 1567.

89. Cai Ruxian, *Dongyi tu shuo*, p. 410.

90. Wu Huifang counted thirty-five extant late Ming daily-use encyclopedias. See her *Wanbao quanshu: Ming Qing shiqi de minjian shenghuo shilu*.

91. Ren Chao 仁潮, *Fajie anli tu* 法界安立圖, in *Xu zang jing* 續藏經, vol. 150, p. 913.

92. A text entitled *Yingchong lu* 瀛蟲錄, attributed to a Chen Qing 陳清, appears in the Ming bibliography *Wan juan lou shumu* 萬卷樓書目. I am unaware of any other mention of such a text or of Chen Qing as its author, and it is unclear whether this *Yingchong lu* is simply a mistranscription of *Luochong lu*. Qian Qianyi's 錢謙益 (1582–1664) *Jiangyun lou shumu* 絳雲樓書目 records a book entitled *Siyi tu* 四夷圖. Whether this *Siyi tu* is related to the *Luochong lu* is a question that requires further investigation. See *Gaochao ben Ming Qing cangshumu sanzhong* 稿抄本明清藏書目三種, p. 379.

93. Here I have in mind the author and readers of the Wanli-era Buddhist treatise *Fajie anli tu* later incorporated into *Xu zang jing*, cited and discussed above.

94. Even if we discount the Ming narrative of Liuqiu protest as evidence of the book's being read in Liuqiu (for some of the documentary issues, see n. 74 above), we do have firm evidence that the book was circulated in Japan, as the following discussion will show.

95. As discussed above, Wang Duanxi and Lü Nan considered these two texts of the same category. Another example of the perceived connection between the two was Zhuang Rujing's preface to Hu Wenhuan's 1593 imprint of *Shanhai jing*, in which Zhuang was all too delighted to discuss the link between the two texts: "This *Illustrations to the Classic of Mountains and Seas* has much that is fetched from the deeps and obtained from afar, which is beyond what eyes and ears can see and hear. I dared not truly believe it. However, once I took the book of *Luochong lu* and viewed (them) together, I realized that beyond the farthest corners and remote lands, there are thousands of aspects and myriad appearances that simply cannot be captured by form and shape. Inside the *Luochong lu* are many tributary countries, those of which documented in books such as *Guang yu tu* (Expanded maps of the world) are certainly verifiable. Hence, the book is not without its reliable sources." See *Shanhai jing tu* 山海經圖, pp. 5–6.

96. *Miaojin wanbao quanshu*, p. 209. This preface also appeared in other encyclopedias, sometimes with minor changes.

97. On this point see note 9 above.

98. Beneath (or along with) the ethnocentric smugness of this formulation lie resonances in the culture of the examination essay and the Four Books on true humanity not as a natural given but rather as something requiring constant effort and striving for moral perfection to be truly realized, as, e.g., in *Mencius* 4B.19: "That wherein the human differs from the beastly is infinitesimally small; the common folk depart from it; the superior person fosters it . . ." 人之所以異於禽獸者幾希. 庶民去之, 君子存之. At this level it is possible to read the preface as implying a critique of those who, despite being blessed by birth in the central domains, are lax in cultivating the true humanity that distinguishes them from the uncivilized "naked creatures." Rather than speculate on authorial intent in this regard, though, perhaps

it is more helpful simply to note that such resonances would have made this preface sound all the more familiar to readers whose perspective was shaped by the broader examination culture.

99. The phrase "wuche" (five carriages) refers to a great volume of texts or great breadth of knowledge. See chap. 2, note 57.

100. Here I draw on Katsushika Hokusai's 1816 book *The Three-style Picture Album* (*Santai gafu*), where he discusses three approaches to drawing: "'grass' drawing emphasizes silhouette and form, 'running' drawing emphasizes significant features, and 'true' drawing emphasizes detail and pattern." See Keyes, *Ehon*, pp. 32–33.

101. See the following section in *Kangxi zidian*: the "chong" radical 虫字部, the "shen" section 申集, in the "Supplement" 補遺.

102. *Tushu jicheng* names *Sancai tuhui* as its source. However, as this chapter demonstrates, *Sancai tuhui*, along with other Ming encyclopedias, used the already extant *Luochong lu* to fill its chapter on foreigners.

103. This statement is translated above.

104. The title "Pictures of Foreign Peoples and Their Local Products" already appeared in a late Ming encyclopedia called *Wanjuan souqi quanshu* 萬卷搜奇全書 (Jianyang: Cunren tang, 1628), but this work still mentions the title "Luochong lu" as well.

105. *Ikoku monogatari*, p. 10.

106. In addition to the hand-copied *nara ehon*, a woodblock print of *Ikoku monogatari* was also produced in early Edo Japan, now preserved at the National Diet Library. Further, the *Sancai tuhui*, which incorporated the *Luochong lu*, also was reworked and printed in Japan.

107. On this topic, see Yonemoto, *Mapping Early Modern Japan*.

108. Sohō sensei koki shukuga kinen kankōkai, *Seikidō zenpon shomoku*, p. 334.

109. See Pelliot and Tokio Takata, *Fandigang tushuguan suocang Hanji mulu*, p. 16, 96, 118; Chŏn, In-ch'o, *Han'guk sojang Chungguk hanjŏk ch'ongmok*, pp. 681–83.

110. Han Ch'i-yun, *Haedong yŏksa*, *juan* 2, p. 3. Han attributed his source to *Sancai tuhui*, which, as this study shows, may be considered a later edition of the *Luochong lu*.

Conclusion

1. For a classic definition of "level distance," see Guo Xi 郭熙 (after 1000–ca. 1090) and Guo Si 郭思 (Song dynasty), "Lin quan gao zhi" 林泉高致, translated in Susan Bush and Hsio-yen Shih, *Early Chinese Texts on Painting*, pp. 168–69.

2. Li Yu's play "Yizhong yuan" 意中緣 (The ideal match) presents such a case of women as deft entrepreneurs in the cultural market of the 17th century. In the play, a courtesan falsifies a fan painting by Chen Jiru and sells it to a monk, who is also an antique shop owner, for a tael of silver. See Li Yu, "Yi zhong yuan," in *Li Yu quanji*, vol. 4, pp. 331–3.

3. For a painting on the same topic of itinerant cultural peddlers, which offers several instructive points of both similarity and contrast to the illustration here in terms of the peddler's interaction with his customers and the kind of place where the peddler sells

his goods, see anon, *Village Painter Showing his Wares*, 16th century, ink on silk, Freer Gallery of Art, Washington, DC. For a reproduction and discussion of this painting, see Clunas, *Pictures and Visuality in Early Modern China*, illus. 69, and p. 120.

4. In this connection I find Dorothy Ko's characterization of late imperial-era book merchants as "architects of cosmopolitan culture" to be quite apt. See Ko, *Teachers of the Inner Chambers*, p. 41.

5. The *Miaojin wanbao quanshu* inserts one additional poem by the Hongwu emperor, "On the New Moon" (Yong xinyue 詠新月), before the poem on the Zhengde emperor.

6. A fourth poem called "Dutang you xianjing" 都堂遊仙境 (The Chief tours the immortal land) is grouped together with other Han Yong–related poems, which may or may not be about Han Yong.

7. As discussed in chapter 1, Xu Zhenjun's poem in the *Huang Ming shixuan* is recorded in other sources as a poem by a Japanese author. If we take, for the sake of argument, the Japanese attribution as the earlier one, then the change of attribution to Xu Zhenjun would serve as another example of an editorial tendency to shift regional focus to Jiangxi. At any rate, the *Huang Ming shixuan* version of this poetic anthogylet reflects an editorial focus on the "Jiangxi—Ming empire" axis of spatial orientation to the exclusion of others.

8. This poem circulated widely in Ming writings, appearing for example in Yan Congjian's *Shuyu zhouzi lu*, Wu Bozong's 吳伯宗 (fl. Hongwu reign) *Rongjin ji* 榮進集, as well as Zhu Yizun's 朱彝尊 (1629–1709) *Ming shi zong* 明詩綜. The authorial attributions varied in these collections.

9. Shunkoen Hanamaru and Okada Gyokuzan, *Ikoku ichiran*, 1799.

10. This is a dimension that this book only touches upon, but it is useful to keep in mind that these Ming books continued to be used in Qing China and beyond. On the use of Chinese texts and books in the global marketplace of cultural goods, see, e.g., Reed and Demattè, *China on Paper*; Hunt, Jacob, and Mijnhardt, *The Book That Changed Europe*. One should note that an important area of study in this regard is Jesuit activities, which have been the focus of a rich body of scholarship. One important compilation of the relevant primary sources in this area has appeared in the series edited by Zheng Ande and Lou Yulie, *Mingmo Qingchu Yesuhui sixiang wenxian huibian*.

11. See, e.g., Fang Yizhi 方以智 (1611–71), *Wu li xiaozhi* 物理小識, 8.18B.

12. For example, Wang Yong points out that Ming-made fans were circulated to Europe via India around the sixteenth century and became the prototype for European-style fans. See Wang Yong, "Riben zheshan de qiyuan ji zai Zhongguo de liubo," p. 129.

13. This decline was observed by Chen Ting 陳霆 (fl. Hongzhi reign) in his *Liang shan mo tan* 兩山墨談 and discussed in Wang Yong, "Riben zheshan de qiyuan ji zai Zhongguo de liubo," p. 126.

14. Wang Ting, "Zhedie shan de shuru yu fangzhi," p. 66; *Sancai tuhui*, in *XXSKQS*, vol. 1234, p. 470.

15. On this, see, e.g., Wen Zhenheng 文震亨 (1585–1645), *Zhang wu zhi*, p. 291. Kai-wing Chow points out that in the late Ming "The amount of 0.1 tael perhaps could fetch the cheapest, decent folding fan in Nanjing. Fans with calligraphy by famous artists, however, cost from one to five taels. A good fan could be pawned for 0.2 to 0.3 taels." See Chow, *Publishing, Culture, and Power in Early Modern China*, p. 47. I am grateful to Huiying Chen for calling Chow's point to my attention.

Appendix 1

1. The lists are compiled based on Xie Shuishun and Li Ting, *Fujian gudai keshu*, pp. 254–56; Zhou Xinhui, *Zhongguo gu banhua tongshi*, pp. 181–82; *Zhongguo gudai banke banhua shi lunji*, pp. 73, 85–86; Qu Mianliang, *Zhongguo guji banke cidian*, pp. 112, 162, 339; Guo Yingde and Wang Lijuan, "*Cilin yizhi, Baneng zoujin* bianzuan niandai kao," pp. 58–61; Chen Duo, "Lun Jian'an banhua yu Jingling banhua de guanxi ji yingxiang," p. 69; Wu Huifang, *Wanbao quanshu: Ming Qing shiqi de minjian shenghuo shilu*, pp. 649, 651, 658, and the author's findings. These lists are provided as an indication of the range of the publications associated with each of these key figures, and are not intended to be exhaustive.

2. Qu Mianliang in his *Zhongguo guji banke cidian*, p. 162, lists this book as having been printed by Shijian tang 師儉堂; Du Xinfu in his *Mingdai banke zonglu, juan* 1, p. 36, lists it as by Yuming tang 玉茗堂; Hou Baipeng remarks in his Pi paji *ziliao huibian*, p. 463, that this is a "Liu Ciquan keben," which could mean that Liu Ciquan was the printer as well.

3. For this fiction and the cult of the *wuxian*, see Cedzich, "The Cult of the Wu-t'ung/Wu-hsien in History and Fiction."

4. The information on Sizhi guan and its printing activities is from Qu Mianliang, ibid, p. 112.

5. This text is better known for its short title *Lu Ban jing* 魯班經 (Classic of Lu Ban). For a study of this text, see Ruitenbeek, *Carpentry and Building in Late Imperial China.*

6. Date according to Guo Yingde and Wang Lijuan, "*Cilin yizhi, Baneng zoujin* bianzuan niandai kao."

Appendix 2

1. This type of writing continued in the Qing; see, e.g., Yeh, *Shanghai Love*; Hershatter, *Dangerous Pleasures.*

2. See especially chapter 2. For a translation and study in Japanese of the brothel instructions in Ming daily-use encyclopedias, see chapter 2, note 44. These instructions also make up part of a fifth *juan* in one edition of *Baoxiao zhuji*, now preserved in the National Library in Beijing. The 1616 *Qinglou yunyu* 青樓韻語 is an example of the "Classic of Whoring" as an individually circulated book.

3. According to Ogawa Yōichi, a hand-copied book of the same title is preserved in Tokyo University, and a block-printed copy is preserved in Academia Sinica, Taiwan. See Ogawa, *Mindai no yūkaku jijō: Fūgetsu kikan*, ii. All quotations of the text in this appendix are from the microfilm of the book preserved at the Joseph Regenstein Library at the University of Chicago.

4. *Piaodu jiguan* (hereafter *PDJG*), *shang juan* 上卷, 1A.

5. *PDJG*, *shang juan*, 2B–3B.

6. *PDJG*, *shang juan*, 3A. The word 賤 is rendered 寧 in the *PDJG* text, and emended here on the basis of a parallel passage in Shen Hongyu's *Hunru pian* 渾如篇.

7. *PDJG*, *shang juan*, 4B–5B.
8. *PDJG*, *shang juan*, 7A–9A.
9. *PDJG*, *shang juan*, 7B.
10. *PDJG*, *shang juan*, 8B.
11. *PDJG*, *shang juan*, 8B–9A.
12. *PDJG*, *shang juan*, 9A.
13. *PDJG*, *shang juan*, 47A, 47B, 48B, 49B, 50B, 51B, 52B, 53B.
14. *PDJG*, *shang juan*, 29A–29B.
15. *PDJG*, *shang juan*, 29A–29B.
16. For a summary of important works on vernacular literacy, see Brokaw, "On the History of the Book in China," in Brokaw and Chow, *Printing and Book Culture in Late Imperial China*, pp. 41–42.
17. For a survey of studies of the *Zhu zi jiali*, see Zhou Xin, "*Zhu zi jiali* yanjiu huigu yu zhanwang."
18. *PDJG*, *shang juan*, 1B–2A.
19. *PDJG*, *shang juan*, 2A. Shen's phraseology here is a characteristically subversive echo of the words Confucius allegedly uttered on completing the *Spring and Autumn Annals:* "Those who will understand me—might this be through the *Spring and Autumn Annals*? Those who will blame me—might this be through the *Spring and Autumn Annals*?" See *Mencius* 3B.9.

SELECTED BIBLIOGRAPHY

Abbreviations

BXZJ	*Boxiao zhuji* 博笑珠璣. Printed by Wende tang 文德堂. During or after Jiajing reign.
CNRS	*Chūgoku nichiyō ruisho shūsei* 中国日用類書集成. Tokyo: Kyūko Shoin, 1999–2004.
HWSZ	*Haiwai guben wan Ming xiju xuanji sanzhong* 海外孤本晚明戲劇選集三種. Shanghai: Shanghai guji chubanshe, 1993.
PDJG	Shen Hongyu 沈弘宇, *Piaodu jiguan* 嫖賭機關. Printed by Deju tang 德聚堂. Ming dynasty.
SBXQCK	*Shanben xiqu congkan* 善本戲曲叢刊. Compiled by Wang Ch'iu-kuei 王秋桂 et al. Taipei: Taiwan xuesheng shuju. 1st–3rd series, 1984; 4th–6th series, 1987.
SKCM	*Siku quanshu cunmu congshu* 四庫全書存目叢書. Ji'nan: Qi Lu shushe. 1995–97.
SKQS	*Yingyin Wenyuange Siku quanshu* 影印文淵閣四庫全書. Taipei: Taiwan shangwu yinshu guan, 1983–86.
XXSKQS	*Xuxiu Siku quanshu* 續修四庫全書. Shanghai: Shanghai guji chubanshe, 1994–2002.

Aleni, Giulio (艾儒略). *San shan lunxue* 三山論學. *Mingmo Qingchu Yesuhui sixiang wenxian huibian* 明末清初耶穌會思想文獻匯編, vol. 7, edited by Zheng Ande 鄭安德 (Andrew Chung) and Lou Yulie 樓宇烈. Beijing: Beijing daxue zongjiao yanjiu suo, 2000.

Bai, Qianshen. *Fu Shan's World: The Transformation of Chinese Calligraphy in the Seventeenth Century.* Cambridge, MA: Harvard University Asia Center, 2003.

Bai Tmrbagen 白 · 特木爾巴根. "Mingdai shisheng zhulu *Yuanchao mishi* kaolue" 明代史乘著錄元朝秘史考略. *Nei Menggu shida xuebao* (Zhexue shehui kexue ban), 1990 (no. 3): 56–63.

———. "Qingdai cangshujia zhulu *Yuanchao mishi* kaolue" 清代藏書家著錄元朝秘史考略. *Nei Menggu shida xuebao* (Zhexue shehui kexue ban), 1992 (no. 3): 83–90.

———. "*Yuanchao mishi* xiezuo guocheng kaolue" 元朝秘史寫作過程考略. *Nei Menggu shida xuebao* (Zhexue shehui kexue ban), 2001 (no. 3): 30–36.

Ban Youshu 班友書. "'Liangtouman' bianxi" 兩頭蠻辨析. *Zhonghua xiqu*, 2001 (no. 25): 78–83.

———. "Qingyang 'gundiao' yuanqi xin lun" 青陽滚調源起新論. *Xiqu yanjiu*, 1993 (no. 47): 96–112.

Berg, Daria. *Carnival in China: A Reading of the* Xingshi Yinyuan Zhuan. Leiden: Brill, 2002.

Berliner, Nancy. "Wang Tingna and Illustrated Book Publishing in Huizhou," *Orientations* 25.1 (1994): 67–75.

Bing Jieyong 兵界勇. "Lun *Tang wencui* 'guwen' lei de wenti xingzhi yuqi daibiao yiyi" 論唐文粹古文類的文體性質與其代表意義. *Zhongguo wenxue yanjiu* no. 14 (May 2000): 1–22.

Boxiao zhuji 博笑珠璣. Printed during or after the Jiajing reign by Wende tang 文德堂.

Bol, Peter K. *Neo-Confucianism in History*. Cambridge, MA: Harvard University Asia Center, 2008.

Bourdieu, Pierre. *The Logic of Practice*. Translated by Richard Nice. Stanford: Stanford University Press, 1990.

Brokaw, Cynthia J. "Book History in Premodern China: The State of the Discipline I." *Book History*, no. 10 (2007): 253–290.

———. *Commerce in Culture: The Sibao Book Trade in the Qing and Republican Periods*. Cambridge, MA: Harvard University Asia Center, 2007.

———. "Commercial Publishing in Late Imperial China: The Zou and Ma Family Businesses of Sibao, Fujian." *Late Imperial China* 17, no. 1 (1996): 49–92.

———, and Kai-wing Chow, eds. *Printing and Book Culture in Late Imperial China*. Berkeley: University of California Press, 2005.

Brook, Timothy. *The Confusions of Pleasure: Commerce and Culture in Ming China*. Berkeley: University of California Press, 1998.

———. "Edifying Knowledge: The Building of School Libraries in Ming China." *Late Imperial China* 17, no. 1 (1996): 93–119.

———. *Geographical Sources of Ming-Qing History*. Ann Arbor: Center for Chinese Studies, University of Michigan, 1988.

———. "Introduction." In *Geographical Sources of Ming-Qing History*. Ann Arbor: Center for Chinese Studies, University of Michigan, 1988, 3–25.

Bush, Susan, and Hsio-yen Shih. *Early Chinese Texts on Painting*. Cambridge, MA: The Harvard-Yenching Institute by Harvard University Press, 1985.

Bussotti, Michela. *Gravures de Hui*: *Étude du livre illustré chinois de la fin du XVIe siècle à la première moitié du XVIIe siècle*. Paris: Ecole française d'Extrême-Orient, 2001.

Cai Ruxian 蔡汝賢. *Dongyi tushuo* 東夷圖説. In *SKCM*, *shibu* 史部, vol. 255.

Cao Ye 曹鄴. *Cao sibu ji* 曹祠部集. In *SKQS*.

Carlitz, Katherine. "Printing as Performance: Literati Playwright-Publishers of the Late Ming." In *Printing and Book Culture in Late Imperial China*, edited by Cynthia J. Brokaw and Kai-wing Chow. Berkeley: University of California Press, 2005, 267–303.

Cedzich, Ursula-Angelika. "The Cult of the Wu-t'ung/Wu-hsien in History and Fiction." In *Ritual and Scripture in Chinese Popular Religion: Five Studies*, edited by David Johnson. Berkeley: Chinese Popular Culture Project, IEAS Publications, University of California, 1995, 137–218.

Cerquiglini, Bernard. *Eloge de la variante: Histoire critique de la philologie*. Paris: Éditions du Seuil, 1989.

Chartier, Roger. *Forms and Meanings: Texts, Performances, and Audiences from Codex to Computer*. Philadelphia: University of Pennsylvania Press, 1995.

———. *The Order of Books: Readers, Authors, and Libraries in Europe between the Fourteenth and Eighteenth Centuries.* Translated by Lydia Cochrane. Stanford: Stanford University Press, 1994.

Chen Duo 陳鐸. "Guanyu 'Jianben' yu 'Jian'an banhua' yanjiu zhong jige diming de wujie" 關於建本與建安版畫研究中幾個地名的誤解. *Wuyi xueyuan xuebao,* 2008 (no. 1): 90–2.

———. "Lun Jian'an banhua yu Jingling banhua de guanxi ji yingxiang" 論建安版畫與金陵版畫的關係及影響. *Nanjing yishu xueyuan xuebao* (meishu yu sheji ban), 2007 (no. 3): 68–69, 98.

Chen Duo 陳多 and Ye Changhai 葉長海, eds. *Wang Jide Qulü* 王驥德曲律. Changsha: Hunan renmin chubanshe, 1983.

Chen Qinghao 陳慶浩 and Wang Ch'iu-kuei (Wang Qiugui) 王秋桂, eds. *Si wu xie huibao* 思無邪匯寶. Taipei: Taiwan da Ying baike gufen youxian gongsi, 1994.

Chen Shike 陳士珂. *Kongzi jiayu shuzheng* 孔子家語疏證. Changsha: Shangwu yinshuguan, 1939.

Chen Shou 陳壽. *Sanguo zhi* 三國志. Beijing: Zhonghua shuju, 1959.

Chen Shulu 陳書錄. *Mingdai qianhou qizi yanjiu* 明代前後七子研究. Nanchang: Jiangxi renmin chubanshe, 1994.

Chen Wuyun 陳五雲. *Cong xin shijiao kan Hanzi: su wenzi xue* 從新視角看漢字: 俗文字學. Zhengzhou: He'nan renmin chubanshe, 2000.

Chen Xianxing 陳先行 and Guo Lixuan 郭立暄. *Bokelai Jiazhou daxue Dongya tushuguan guji shanben shuzhi* 柏克萊加州大學東亞圖書館古籍善本書志. Shanghai: Shanghai guji chubanshe, 2005.

Chen Xuewen 陳學文. *Ming Qing shiqi shangye shu ji shangren shu zhi yanjiu* 明清時期商業書及商人書之研究. Taipei: Hongye wenhua shiye youxian gongsi, 1997.

Chen Yu 陳郁. *Cangyi hua yu* 藏一話腴. In *SKQS*.

Chen Yuanjing 陳元靚. *Shilin guangji* 事林廣記. Beijing: Zhonghua shuju, 1999.

Chen Zhenghong 陳正宏 and Zhu Bangwei 朱邦薇. "Mingshi zongji biankan shilue—Mingdai pian (shang)" 明詩總集編刊史略—明代篇(上). In *Zhong xi xueshu* (1) 中西學術(一), edited by Zhu Liyun 朱立元 and Pei Gao 裴高. Shanghai: Xuelin chubanshe, 1995, 106–27.

Chen Zhi 陳植 and Yang Chaobo 楊超伯, eds. *Zhangwu zhi jiaozhu* 長物志校註. Nanjing: Jiangsu kexue jishu chubanshe, 1984.

Cheng Wanli 程萬里 and Zhu Dingchen 朱鼎臣. *Da Ming chun* 大明春. Wanli reign. Reprinted in *SBXQCK*, 1st series, vol. 6.

Chia, Lucille. "Of Three Mountain Street: The Commercial Publishers of Ming Nanjing." In *Printing and Book Culture in Late Imperial China*, edited by Cynthia J. Brokaw and Kai-wing Chow. Berkeley: University of California Press, 2005, 107–51.

———. *Printing for Profit: The Commercial Publishers of Jianyang, Fujian (11th–17th Centuries).* Cambridge, MA: Harvard University Asia Center, 2002.

———. "Text and Tu in Context: Reading the Illustrated Page in Chinese Blockprinted Books." *Bulletin de l'Ecole Francaise d'Extreme-Orient*, vol. 89 (2002): 241–76.

———. "The Development of the Jianyang Book Trade, Song-Yuan." *Late Imperial China* 17, no. 1 (1996): 10–48.

Chŏn, In-ch'o 全寅初. *Han'guk sojang Chungguk hanjŏk ch'ongmok* 韓國所藏中國漢籍總目. Seoul: Hakkobang, 2005.

Chongke Yuan ben tiping yinshi Xixiang ji 重刻元本題評音釋西廂記. Liu Longtian's Qiaoshan tang 劉龍田喬山堂, Wanli reign. Reprinted in Guben xiqu congkan bianji weiyuanhui, *Guben xiqu congkan chuji*, vols. 3–4.

Chow, Kai-wing. *Publishing, Culture, and Power in Early Modern China*. Stanford: Stanford University Press, 2004.

———. *The Rise of Confucian Ritualism in Late Imperial China: Ethics, Classics, and Lineage Discourse*. Stanford: Stanford University Press, 1994.

Clunas, Craig. *Empire of Great Brightness: Visual and Material Culture of Ming China, 1368–1644*. Honolulu: University of Hawai'i Press, 2007.

———. *Pictures and Visuality in Early Modern China*. London: Reaktion Books Ltd., 1997.

———. *Superfluous Things: Material Culture and Social Status in Early Modern China*. Honolulu: University of Hawai'i Press, 2004.

Cohen, Warren. *East Asia at the Center: Four Thousand Years of Engagement with the World*. New York: Columbia University Press, 2000.

Cui Laiting 崔來廷. *Haiguo gusheng: Ming dai shoufu Ye Xianggao yu haiyang shehui* 海國孤生：明代首輔葉向高與海洋社會. Nanchang: Jiangxi gaoxiao chubanshe, 2005.

Da Ming huidian 大明會典. 1587. Reprint, Taipei: Dongnan shubaoshe, 1963.

Da Ming jili 大明集禮. Jiajing reign. Held in the Japanese and Chinese Classics Collection, Waseda University Library, Japan.

Da Ming lü jijie fuli 大明律集解附例. Taipei: Taiwan xuesheng shuju, 1970.

Da Ming tianxia chun 大明天下春. In *HWSZ*.

Da Ming yitong zhi 大明一統志. Printed by Jixiu tang 積秀堂. Held in the collection of C. V. Starr East Asian Library, University of California at Berkeley.

Darnton, Robert. "What Is the History of Books?" In *The Book History Reader*, edited by David Finkelstein and Alistair McCleery. London: Routledge, 2002, 9–26.

de Bary, Wm. Theodore, ed. *Self and Society in Ming Thought*. New York: Columbia University Press, 1970.

de Magalhães, Gabriel. *A New History of China, Containing a Description of the Most Considerable Particulars of That Vast Empire*. London: Printed for Thomas Newborough, at the Golden Ball, in S. Paul's Church-Yard, 1688.

Deng Guangming 鄧廣銘. "Lun *Siku quanshu cunmu congshu* buyi kanxing" 論四庫全書存目叢書不宜刊行. *Guanming ribao* 光明日報, July 29, 1994.

Deng Wei 鄧瑋 and Deng Xiangyun 鄧翔雲. "Zai lun 'liangtouman'" 再論兩頭蠻. *Xiqu yanjiu* 2006 (no. 1): 267–78.

Dong Jie 董捷. *Ming Qing kan* Xixiang ji *banhua kaoxi* 明清刊西厢记版画考析. Shijiazhuang: Hebei meishu chubanshe, 2006.

Drège, Jean-Pierre. "Materiality and Text Organization in Early and Medieval Chinese Manuscripts." Paper presented at the symposium "Texting China: Composition, Transformation, Preservation of Pre-Modern Chinese Textual Materials" held at the University of Chicago, May 11–13, 2012.

Du Lei 杜磊 and Zhu Chongzhi 朱崇志. "Hu Wenhuan he *Qunyin leixuan*" 胡文煥和群音類選. *Guji zhengli yanjiu xuekan* 2004 (no. 3): 78–82, 89.

Du Xinfu 杜信孚. *Mingdai banke zonglu* 明代版刻綜錄. Edited (參校) by Zhou Guangpei 周光培 and Jiang Xiaoda 蔣孝達. Yangzhou: Jiangsu Guangling guji keyinshe / Yangzhou guji shudian, 1983.

———— and Du Tongshu 杜同書. *Quan Ming fensheng fenxian keshu kao* 全明分省分縣刻書攷. Beijing: Xianzhuang shuju, 2001.

Du Zexun 杜澤遜. "Siku quanshu cunmu congshu chengshu shimo" 四庫全書存目叢書成書始末. *Wen shi zhe*, 1998 (no. 3): 70–73.

Duan Chengshi 段成式. *Youyang zazu* 酉陽雜俎. Collated by Fang Nansheng 方南生. Beijing: Zhonghua shuju, 1981.

Dudbridge, Glen. *Books, Tales and Vernacular Culture: Selected Papers on China*. Leiden: Brill, 2005.

————. The His-yu chi*: A Study of Antecedents to the Sixteenth-Century Chinese Novel*. Cambridge: Cambridge University Press, 1970.

Elman, Benjamin A. "Collecting and Classifying: Ming Dynasty Compendia and Encyclopedias (*Leishu*)." *Extrême-Orient, Extrême-Occident, hors série*, 2007, 131–57.

————. *From Philosophy to Philology: Intellectual and Social Aspects of Change in Late Imperial China*. Cambridge, MA: Harvard University Asia Center, 1984.

————. *On Their Own Terms: Science in China, 1550–1900*. Cambridge, MA: Harvard University Press, 2005.

Epstein, Maram. *Competing Discourses: Orthodoxy, Authenticity, and Engendered Meanings in Late Imperial Chinese Fiction*. Cambridge, MA: Harvard University Asia Center, 2001.

Fan Shuzhi 樊樹志. *Wan Ming shi* 晚明史. Shanghai: Fudan daxue chubanshe, 2003.

Fan Ye 范曄. *Hou Han shu* 後漢書. Beijing: Zhonghua shuju, 1965.

Fang Yanshou 方彥壽. "Songdai 'Jianben' diming kaoshi" 宋代建本地名考釋. *Fujian shi zhi* 1987 (no. 6): 36–39.

Fang Yizhi 方以智. *Wu li xiaozhi* 物理小識, 8.18B. Copy from the *SKQS* held at Zhejiang University.

Fang Zhiyuan 方志遠. *Mingdai chengshi yu shimin wenxue* 明代城市與市民文學. Beijing: Zhonghua shuju, 2004.

Finkelstein, David, and Alistair McCleery, eds. *The Book History Reader*. London: Routledge, 2002.

Fogel, Joshua A. *Articulating the Sinosphere: Sino-Japanese Relations in Space and Time*. Cambridge, MA: Harvard University Press, 2009.

Fracasso, Riccardo. "*Shan hai jing*." In *Early Chinese Texts: A Bibliographical Guide*, edited by Michael Loewe. Berkeley, CA: Society for the Study of Early China: Institute of East Asian Studies, University of California, Berkeley, 1993, 357–67.

Fu Yunzi 傅芸子. *Baichuan ji* 白川集. Tokyo: Bunkyūdō, 1943.

Gan Bao 干寶. *Sou shen ji* 搜神記. Collated by Wang Shaoying 汪紹楹. Beijing: Zhonghua shuju, 1979.

Gao Ming 高明. *Yuan ben Pipa ji* 元本琵琶記. Edited by Qian Nanyang 錢南揚. Shanghai: Shanghai guji chubanshe, 1980.

Gaochao ben Ming Qing cangshumu sanzhong 稿抄本明清藏書目三種. Beijing: Beijing tushuguan chubanshe, 2003.

Gardella, Robert. "Fukien's Tea Industry and Trade in Ch'ing and Republican China:

The Developmental Consequences of a Traditional Commodity Export." PhD diss., University of Washington, 1976.

———. *Harvesting Mountains: Fujian and the China Tea Trade, 1757–1937.* Berkeley: University of California Press, 1994.

Gaskell, Philip. *From Writer to Reader: Studies in Editorial Method.* Oxford, Eng.: Clarendon Press, 1978.

Gu Qiyuan 顧起元. *Kezuo zhuiyu* 客座贅語. In *Gengsi bian, Kezuo zhuiyu* 庚巳編，客座贅語. Beijing: Zhonghua shuju, 1997.

Gu Yanwu 顧炎武. *Ri zhi lu* 日知錄. Shanghai: Shangwu yinshuguan, 1935.

Guben xiqu congkan bianji weiyuanhui 古本戲曲叢刊編輯委員會, ed. *Guben xiqu congkan chuji* 古本戲曲叢刊初集. 124 vols. Shanghai: Shangwu yinshuguan, 1954.

Guo Rulin 郭汝霖 et al. *Guojia tushuguan cang Liuqiu ziliao sanbian* 國家圖書館藏琉球資料三編. Edited by Wang Han 王菡. Beijing: Beijing tushuguan chubanshe, 2006.

Guo Shaoyu 郭紹虞 and Wang Wensheng 王文生, eds. *Zhongguo lidai wenlun xuan* 中國歷代文論選. Shanghai: Shanghai guji chubanshe, 1979.

Guo Yingde 郭英德 and Wang Lijuan 王麗娟. "*Cilin yizhi*, *Baneng zoujin* bianzuan niandai kao" 詞林一枝八能奏錦編纂年代攷. *Wenyi yanjiu* 8 (2006): 55–62.

Guoli Taiwan daxue lishixue xi 國立臺灣大學歷史學系, ed. *Shi xue: Chuancheng yu bianqian xueshu yantao hui lunwen ji* 史學：傳承與變遷學術研討會論文集. Taipei: Taiwan daxue, 1998.

Guwen zhenbao 古文真寶. Sili jian 司禮監. 1583.

Guy, Kent. *The Emperor's Four Treasuries: Scholars and State in the Late Ch'ien-lung Era.* Cambridge, MA: Harvard University Asia Center, 1987.

Hall, John W., and Toyoda Takeshi, eds. *Japan in the Muromachi Age.* Ithaca, NY: East Asian Program, Cornell University, 2001.

Han Ch'i-yun 韓致奫. *Haedong yŏksa* 海東繹史. Kyŏngsŏng: Chosŏn Kwangmunhoe, 1912–1913.

Han Dacheng 韓大成. *Mingdai chengshi yanjiu* 明代城市研究. Beijing: Zhongguo Renmin daxue chubanshe, 1991.

Han Yong 韓雍, Han Yang 韓陽 and Li Kui 李奎, eds. *Huang Ming Xijiang shixuan* 皇明西江詩選. In *Yuzhang congshu* 豫章叢書, compiled by Hu Sijing 胡思敬. Nanchang: Tuilu, 1915–20.

Hanan, Patrick, trans. *The Carnal Prayer Mat.* New York: Ballantine Books, 1990.

Harper, Donald. "The *Analects* Jade Candle: A Classic of T'ang Drinking Custom." *T'ang Studies* 4 (1986): 69–89.

———. "The Textual Form of Knowledge: Occult Miscellanies in Ancient and Medieval Chinese Manuscripts, Fourth Century B.C. to Tenth Century A.D." In *Looking at it from Asia: The Processes That Shaped the Sources of History of Science*, edited by Florence Bretelle-Establet. *Boston Studies in the Philosophy of Science*, vol. 265 (2010): 37–80.

Hayashi Tomoharu 林友春, ed. *Kinsei Chūgoku kyōikushi kenkyū: Sono bunkyō seisaku to shomin kyōiku* 近世中國教育史研究：その文教政策と庶民教育. Tokyo: Kokudo sha, 1958.

He Liangjun. *Si you zhai congshuo* 四友齋叢説. Beijing: Zhonghua shuju, 1997.

He, Yuming. "The Book and the Barbarian in Ming China and Beyond: The *Luochong lu*, or 'Record of Naked Creatures'." *Asia Major* 24, no. 1 (Spring 2011): 43–85.

———. "Productive Space: Performance Texts in the Late Ming." PhD diss., University of California at Berkeley, 2003.

Hegel, Robert E. "Niche Marketing for Late Imperial Fiction." In *Printing and Book Culture in Late Imperial China*, edited by Cynthia J. Brokaw and Kai-wing Chow. Berkeley: University of California Press, 2005, 235–66.

———. *Reading Illustrated Fiction in Late Imperial China*. Stanford: Stanford University Press, 1998.

———. Review article on *Carnival in China: A Reading of the* Xingshi Yinyuan Zhuan by Daria Berg. *Harvard Journal of Asiatic Studies* 63, no. 2 (Dec. 2003): 450–57.

Heijdra, Martin. Review of *Geographical Sources of Ming-Qing History* by Timothy Brook. *Ming Studies* 29 (Spring 1990): 65–69.

Hershatter, Gail. *Dangerous Pleasures: Prostitution and Modernity in Twentieth-Century Shanghai*. Berkeley: University of California Press, 1997.

Hevia, James L. *Cherishing Men from Afar: Qing Guest Ritual and the Macartney Embassy of 1793*. Durham: Duke University Press, 1995.

Hopkins, L. C. "Letter of Mr. L. C. Hopkins to Mr. G. Schlegel." *T'oung pao*, vol. 6 (1895): 529–30.

Hostetler, Laura. *Qing Colonial Enterprise: Ethnography and Cartography in Early Modern China*. Chicago: University of Chicago Press, 2001.

Hou Baipeng 侯百朋. Pipa ji *ziliao huibian* 琵琶記資料匯編. Beijing: Shumu wenxian chubanshe, 1989.

Hou Rongchuan 侯榮川. "Ming chao Zhu Zhifan, Zhu Mengzhen, Pan Zhiheng shengzu nian kao" 明朝朱之蕃，朱孟震，潘之恆生卒年考. *Yulin shifan xueyuan xuebao* 2012 (no. 1): 121–24.

Hsiao, Li-ling. *The Eternal Present of the Past: Illustration, Theater, and Reading in the Wanli Period, 1573–1619*. Leiden: Brill, 2007.

Hu Shi 胡適. *Hu Shi wencun* 胡適文存. Hefei: Huangshan shushe, 1996.

Hu Wenhuan 胡文煥, ed. *Shanhai jing tu* 山海經圖. In *Zhongguo gudai banhua congkan erbian* 中國古代版畫叢刊二編, vol. 1. Shanghai: Shanghai guji chubanshe, 1994.

———, ed. *Xinke Luochong lu* 新刻臝蟲錄. 1593. Reprint, Beijing: Xueyuan chubanshe, 2001.

Hua Wei 華瑋 and Wang Ailing 王瑷玲. *Ming Qing xiqu guoji yantaohui lunwenji* 明清戲曲國際研討會論文集. Taipei: Zhongguo wenzhe yanjiusuo choubeichu, 1998.

Huai Xiaofeng 懷效鋒, ed. *Da Ming lü* 大明律. Beijing: Falü chubanshe, 1999.

Huang Jian 黃堅. *Xiangshuo Guwen zhenbao daquan* 詳說古文眞寶大全. Edited by Xiong Lihui 熊禮匯. Changsha: Hunan renmin chubanshe, 2007.

Huang Lin 黃霖. "*Xixiang ji, Pipa ji, Mudan ting* huiping shulue" 西廂記，琵琶記，牡丹亭匯評述略. Paper presented at the Workshop on New Directions in the Study of Traditional Chinese Drama held November 6–7, 2010, at Stanford University.

Huang, Martin W. *Desire and Fictional Narrative in Late Imperial China*. Cambridge, MA: Harvard University Asia Cener, 2001.

Huang Wenhua 黃文華, ed. *Baneng zoujin* 八能奏錦. Wanli reign. Reprinted in *SBXQCK*, 1st series, vol. 5.

———, ed. *Yuefu yushu ying* 樂府玉樹英. 1599. Reprinted in *HWSZ*.

——— and Xi Xiufu 郗綉甫, eds. *Ci lin yizhi* 詞林一枝. Wanli reign. Reprinted in *SBXQCK*, 1st series, vol. 4.

Huang Yuji 黄虞稷. *Qianqing tang shumu* 千頃堂書目, edited by Qu Fengqi 瞿鳳起, Pan Jingzheng 潘景鄭. Shanghai: Shanghai guji chubanshe, 2001.

Huang Zongxi 黄宗羲. *Ming ru xue'an* 明儒學案. In *Mingdai zhuanji congkan* 明代傳記叢刊. Taipei: Mingwen shuju, 1991.

Hung, William. "The Transmission of the Book Known as *The Secret History of the Mongols*." *Harvard Journal of Asiatic Studies* 14, no. 3–4 (1951): 433–92.

Hunt, Lynn, Margaret C. Jacob, and Wijnand Mijnhardt. *The Book That Changed Europe: Picart and Bernard's Religious Ceremonies of the World*. Cambridge, MA: Belknap Press of Harvard University Press, 2010.

Ikoku monogatari 異國物語. Edo period. Reprint, Tokyo: Koten Bunko, 1995.

Jiang Boqin 姜伯勤. *Zhongguo xianjiao yishushi yanjiu* 中國祆教藝術史研究. Beijing: Sanlian chubanshe, 2004.

Jiang Xingyu 蔣星煜. *Ming kan ben* Xixiang ji *yanjiu* 明刊本西廂記研究. Beijing: Zhongguo xiju chubanshe, 1982.

Jiang Yikui 蔣一葵. *Yaoshan tang waiji* 堯山堂外紀. In *SKCM*, *zibu* 子部, vol. 148.

Jiang, Yonglin. *The Great Ming Code/Da Ming lü*. Seattle: University of Washington Press, 2005.

Jiao Hong 焦竑. *Sushu kanwu* 俗書刊誤. In *SKQS*.

Jing jushi 景居士 (Ba jing 八景), ed. *Yugu xinhuang* 玉谷新簧. 1610. Reprinted in *SBXQCK*, 1st series, vol. 2.

Johnson, David, ed. *Ritual and Scripture in Chinese Popular Religion: Five Studies*. Berkeley: Chinese Popular Culture Project, Institue of East Asian Studies Publications, University of California, 1995.

Juan Da Ming longtou biandu bangxun lüfa quanshu 鐫大明龍頭便讀傍訓律法全書. Printed by Liu Shuangsong 劉雙松 of Anzheng tang 安正堂. Ming dynasty.

Jujia biyong shilei quanji 居家必用事類全集. *Beijing tushuguan guji zhenben congkan*, vol. 61. Beijing: Shumu wenxian chubanshe, 1988.

Kafalas, Philip A. *In Limpid Dream: Nostalgia and Zhang Dai's Reminiscences of the Ming*. Norwalk, CT: EastBridge, 2007.

Kang Chan-soo 姜贊洙. "Zhongguo keben *Guwen zhenbao*" 中國刻本古文眞寶. PhD diss. Fudan daxue, 2005.

Keyes, Roger S. *Ehon: The Artist and the Book in Japan*. Seattle: University of Washington Press, 2006.

Ko, Dorothy. *Teachers of the Inner Chambers: Women and Culture in Seventeenth-Century China*. Stanford: Stanford University Press, 1994.

Lai Xinxia 來新夏 and Gao Weiguo 高維國, eds. *Za zi* 雜字. Tianjin: Nankai daxue chubanshe, 1995.

Lai Zhengwei 賴正維 and Huang Shan 黄珊. "Xu Baoguang yu *Zhongshan chuanxin lu* kaoshu" 徐葆光與中山傳信錄考述. *Fuzhou daxue xuebao* (zhexue shehui kexueban), 2005 (no. 2): 92–95.

Lam, Joseph. "Ming Music and Music History." *Ming Studies* 38 (1998): 21–62.
Lang Ying 郎瑛. *Qixiu leigao* 七修類稿. Beijing: Zhonghua shuju, 1961.
Legge, James. *The Four Books: Confucian Analects, the Great Learning, the Doctrine of the Mean, and the Works of Mencius, with English Translation and Notes*. Shanghai: The Chinese Book Company, 1933.
Li Diankui 李殿魁. "'Gundiao' zai tan" "滾調"再探. In *Ming Qing xiqu guoji yantaohui lunwenji* 明清戲曲國際研討會論文集, edited by Hua Wei 華瑋 and Wang Ailing 王瑷玲. Taipei: Zhongguo wenzhe yanjiusuo choubeichu, 1998, 717–75.
Li Dongyang 李東陽. *Huailu tang ji* 懷麓堂集. In *SKQS*.
Li Fuqing 李福清 (Boris Riftin) and Li Ping 李平, eds. *Haiwai guben wan Ming xiju xuanji sanzhong* 海外孤本晚明戲劇選集三種. Shanghai: Shanghai guji chubanshe, 1993.
Li Ping. "Liuluo Ouzhou de sanzhong wan Ming xiju sanchu xuanji de faxian" 流落歐洲的三種晚明戲劇散齣選集的發現. In *Haiwai guben wan Ming xiju xuanji sanzhong*, edited by Li Fuqing and Li Ping. Shanghai: Shanghai guji chubanshe, 1993, 9–30.
Li Yanshou 李延壽. *Bei shi* 北史. Beijing: Zhonghua shuju, 1974.
Li Yu 李漁. *Li Yu quanji* 李漁全集. Hangzhou: Zhejiang guji chubanshe, 1992.
———. *Rou pu tuan* 肉蒲團. In *Si wu xie huibao* 思無邪匯寶, edited by Chen Qinghao 陳慶浩 and Wang Ch'iu-kuei 王秋桂. Vol. 15. Taipei: Taiwan da Ying baike gufen youxian gongsi, 1994.
Liao Ben 廖奔. *Zhongguo gudai juchang shi* 中國古代劇場史. Zhengzhou: Zhongzhou guji chubanshe, 1996.
Liao Kebin 廖可斌. *Mingdai wenxue fugu yundong yanjiu* 明代文學復古運動研究. Beijing: Shangwu yinshuguan, 2008.
Lin, Li-chiang. "The Proliferation of Images: The Ink-stick Designs and the Printing of the *Fang-shih mo-p'u* and the *Ch'eng-shih mo-yüan*." PhD diss., Princeton University, 1998.
Lin Xiyi 林希逸. *Kaogong ji jie* 攷工記解. In *SKQS*.
Liu Hui 劉輝. *Xiaoshuo xiqu lunji* 小說戲曲論集. Taipei: Guanya wenhua shiye youxian gongsi, 1992.
Liu, Lydia H. *The Clash of Empires: The Invention of China in Modern World Making*. Cambridge, MA: Harvard University Press, 2004.
Liu Ruoyu 劉若愚. *Zhuo zhong zhi* 酌中志. Beijing: Beijing guji chubanshe, 1994.
Liu Shuiyun 劉水雲. *Ming Qing jiayue yanjiu* 明清家樂研究. Shanghai: Shanghai guji chubanshe, 2005.
Liu Xu 劉昫 et al. *Jiu Tang shu* 舊唐書. Beijing: Zhonghua shuju, 1975.
Liu Yeqiu 劉葉秋. *Zhongguo zidian shilue* 中國字典史略. Beijing: Zhonghua shuju, 2004.
Loewe, Michael, ed. *Early Chinese Texts: A Bibliographical Guide*. Berkeley, CA: Society for the Study of Early China: Institute of East Asian Studies, University of California, Berkeley, 1993.
Lowry, Kathryn. *The Tapestry of Popular Songs in 16th- and 17th-Century China: Reading, Imitation, and Desire*. Leiden: Brill, 2005.
Lu Jiye 盧冀野, ed. *Ci xue* 詞謔. Shanghai: Zhonghua shuju, 1937.
Lu Xinyuan 陸心源. *Yigu tang tiba* 儀顧堂題跋. In *XXSKQS*, *shibu* 史部, vol. 930.

Lu Yongqiang 陸勇強. "Song Maocheng shengzu nian kaobian ji qita" 宋懋澄生卒年考辨及其他. *Ming Qing xiaoshuo yanjiu* 2004 (no. 3): 138–40.

Lü Nan 呂柟. *Duanxi wenda* 端溪問答. In *Jingye zi nei pian* 涇野子內篇, collated by Zhao Ruimin 趙瑞民. Beijing: Zhonghua shuju, 1992.

Ma Changyi 馬昌儀. *Guben* Shanhai jing *tushuo* 古本山海經圖說. Ji'nan: Shandong huabao chubanshe, 2001.

———. *Quan xiang* Shanhai jing *tu bijiao* 全像山海經圖比較. Beijing: Xueyuan chubanshe, 2003.

Ma Guojun 麻國鈞 and Ma Shuyun 麻淑雲, eds. *Zhongguo jiuling daguan* 中國酒令大觀. Beijing: Beijing chubanshe, 1993.

Ma Hanqin 馬漢欽. *Mingdai shige zongji yu xuanji yanjiu* 明代詩歌總集與選集研究. Harbin: Harbin gongcheng daxue chubanshe, 2009.

Ma Maojun 馬茂軍. "*Song wen jian* yu *Song wen hai*" 宋文鑑與宋文海. *Daqing shifan xueyuan xuebao* 2006 (no. 6): 87–89.

Ma, Meng-ching. "Fragmentation and Framing of the Text: Visuality and Narrativity in Late-Ming Illustrations to *The Story of the Western Wing*." PhD diss., Stanford University, 2006.

Ma Wenda 馬文大 and Wang Zhijun 王致軍, eds. *Wu Xiaoling xiansheng zhencang gu banhua quanbian* 吳曉鈴先生珍藏古版畫全編. Beijing: Xueyuan chubanshe, 2003.

Mair, Victor H., ed. *The Columbia History of Chinese Literature*. New York: Columbia University Press, 2001.

McDermott, Joseph. "The Ascendance of the Imprint in China." In *Printing and Book Culture in Late Imperial China*, edited by Cynthia J. Brokaw and Kai-wing Chow. Berkeley: University of California Press, 2005, 55–104.

———. *A Social History of the Chinese Book: Books and Literati Culture in Late Imperial China*. Hong Kong: Hong Kong University Press, 2006.

McDougall, Bonnie, ed. *Popular Chinese Literature and Performing Arts in the People's Republic of China 1949–1979*. Berkeley: University of California Press, 1984.

Mclaren, Anne E. "Constructing New Reading Publics in Late Ming China." In *Printing and Book Culture in Late Imperial China*, edited by Cynthia J. Brokaw and Kai-wing Chow. Berkeley: University of California Press, 2005, 152–83.

Meiguo Hafo daxue Hafo Yenching tushuguan 美國哈佛大學哈佛燕京圖書館, ed. *Meiguo Hafo daxue Hafo Yenching tushuguan cang Zhongwen shanben huikan* 美國哈佛大學哈佛燕京圖書館藏中文善本彙刊. Beijing: Shangwu yinshuguan; Guilin: Guangxi shifan daxue chubanshe, 2003.

Meyer-Fong, Tobie. "The Printed World: Books, Publishing Culture, and Society in Late Imperial China." *Journal of Asian Studies* 66, no. 3 (August 2007): 787–817.

Miao Huaiming 苗懷明. *Ershi shiji xiqu wenxian xue shulue* 二十世紀戲曲文獻學述略. Beijing: Zhonghua shuju, 2005.

Miao Yonghe 繆咏禾. *Mingdai chuban shigao* 明代出版史稿. Nanjing: Jiangsu renmin chubanshe, 2000.

Miaojin wanbao quanshu (Myōkin banpō zensho) 妙錦萬寶全書. 1612. Reprinted in *CNRS*, vols. 12–14.

Ming Min Qiji huike Xixiang ji caitu 明閔齊伋繪刻西廂記彩圖. In *Ming Min Qiji*

huike Xixiang ji caitu, Ming He Bi jiaoke Xixiang ji 明閔齊伋繪刻西廂記彩圖，明何壁校刻西廂記. Shanghai: Shanghai guji chubanshe, 2005.
Ming mingchen wanyan xulu 明名臣琬琰續錄. In *SKQS*.
Ming shi 明史. By Zhang Tingyu 張廷玉 et al. Beijing: Zhonghua shuju, 1974.
Ming shi lu 明實錄. Collated by Zhongyang yanjiuyuan lishi yuyan yanjiusuo 中央研究院歷史語言研究所. Taipei: Zhongyang yanjiuyuan lishi yuyan yanjiusuo, 1966.
Miura Kunio 三浦國雄. "'Banpō zensho' shoimon shōron: Minjin no gaikoku kan" 萬寶全書諸夷門小論：明人の外國觀. *Kangakukaishi* 44 (March 2005): 227–48.
Moule, A. C. "An Introduction to the *I yü t'u chih*." *T'oung pao* 27 (1930): 179–88.
Murray, Julia K. "Didactic Illustrations in Printed Books." In *Printing and Book Culture in Late Imperial China*, edited by Cynthia J. Brokaw and Kai-wing Chow. Berkeley: University of California Press, 2005, 417–50.
———. *Mirror of Morality: Chinese Narrative Illustration and Confucian Ideology.* Honolulu: University of Hawai'i Press, 2007.

Nagasawa, Kikuya, ed. *Min Shin zokugo jisho shūsei* 明清俗語辭書集成. Tokyo: Kyūko Shoin, 1974–1977.
Netolitzky, Almut. *Das* Ling-wai tai-ta *von Chou Ch'ü-fei: eine Landeskunde Südchinas aus dem 12. Jahrhundert.* Wiesbaden: Franz Steiner Verlag, 1977.
Nienhauser, William H. et al. *The Indiana Companion to Traditional Chinese Literature.* 2 vols. Bloomington, Indiana: Indiana University Press, 1986–98.

Ogawa Yōichi 小川陽一. *Fūgetsu kikan to Min Shin bungaku* 風月機関と明清文学. Tokyo: Kyūko Shoin, 2010.
———. *Mindai no yūkaku jijō: Fūgetsu kikan* 明代の遊郭事情風月機関. Tokyo: Kyūko Shoin, 2006.
———. *Nichiyō ruisho ni yoru Min Shin shōsetsu no kenkyū* 日用類書による明清小説の研究. Tokyo: Kenbun Shuppan, 1995.
Ong, Walter. *Orality and Literacy: The Technologizing of the Word.* London: Routledge, 1991.
Owen, Stephen. *An Anthology of Chinese Literature: Beginnings to 1911.* New York: W. W. Norton, 1996.
———. "Meaning the Words: The Genuine as a Value in the Tradition of the Song Lyric." In *Voices of the Song Lyric in China*, edited by Pauline Yu. Berkeley: University of California Press, 1994, 30–69.

Pan Fu'en 潘富恩. *Lü Zuqian pingzhuan* 呂祖謙評傳. Nanjing: Nanjing daxue chubanshe, 1992.
Park, J. P. *Art by the Book: Painting Manuals and the Leisure Life in Late Ming China.* Seattle: University of Washington Press, 2012.
Park Sam-soo 朴三洙. "Shilun Hanguo ban *Guwen zhenbao*" 試論韓國版古文眞寶. *Changchun shifan xueyuan xuebao*, 2001 (no. 3): 51–54.
Pelliot, Paul, and Takata Tokio. *Fandigang tushuguan suocang Hanji mulu* 梵蒂岡圖書館所藏漢籍目錄. Beijing: Zhonghua shuju, 2006.
Ptak, Roderich. *China and the Asian Seas: Trade, Travel, and Visions of the Other (1400–1750).* Aldershot, UK: Ashgate, 1998.

———. *China, the Portuguese, and the Nanyang: Oceans and Routes, Regions and Trades (c. 1000–1600)*. Aldershot, U.K.: Ashgate, 2004.

Pu Songling 蒲松齡. *Pu Songling ji* 蒲松齡集. Edited by Lu Dahuang 路大荒. Beijing: Zhonghua shuju, 1962.

Qi Biaojia 祁彪佳. *Qi Zhongmin gong riji* 祁忠敏公日記. Shaoxing: Shaoxing xian xiuzhi weiyuanhui, 1937.

Qian jia shi 千家詩. Ming dynasty. Printed by Zheng Yunlin 鄭雲林.

Qian Nanyang 錢南揚. *Han shang yi wencun* 漢上宧文存. Shanghai: Shanghai wenyi chubanshe, 1980.

Qinding Tianlu linlang shumu 欽定天祿琳琅書目. In *SKQS*.

Qiu Pengsheng 邱澎生. "You shichan lüli yanbian kan Ming Qing zhengfu dui shichang de falü guifan" 由市廛律例演變看明清政府對市場的法律規範. In *Shi xue: Chuancheng yu bianqian xueshu yantao hui lunwen ji* 史學：傳承與變遷學術研討會論文集, edited by Guoli Taiwan daxue lishixue xi 國立臺灣大學歷史學系. Taipei: Tanwan daxue, 1998, 291–333.

Qu Mianliang 瞿冕良. *Zhongguo guji banke cidian* 中國古籍版刻辭典. Ji'nan: Qilu shushe, 1999.

Quan Ming shi bianzuan weiyuanhui 全明詩編纂委員會, ed. *Quan Ming shi* 全明詩. Shanghai: Shanghai guji chubanshe, 1990–.

Rawski, Evelyn. *Education and Popular Literacy in Ch'ing China*. Ann Arbor: University of Michigan Press, 1979.

Reed, Marcia, and Paola Demattè, eds. *China on Paper: European and Chinese Works from the Late Sixteenth to the Early Nineteenth Century*. Los Angeles: The Getty Research Institute, 2007.

Ren Chao 仁潮. *Fajie anli tu* 法界安立圖. In *Xu zang jing* 續藏經, vol. 150. Taipei: Xin wenfeng, 1993.

Rolston, David L., ed. *How to Read the Chinese Novel*. Princeton: Princeton University, 1990.

———. "Sources of Traditional Chinese Fiction Criticism." In *How to Read the Chinese Novel*, edited by David Rolston. Princeton: Princeton University, 1990.

———. "Traditional Fiction Commentary." In *The Columbia History of Chinese Literature*, edited by Victor H. Mair. New York: Columbia University Press, 2001, 940–50.

Rosenfield, John M. "The Unity of the Three Creeds: A Theme in Japanese Ink Painting of the Fifteenth Century." In *Japan in the Muromachi Age*, edited by John W. Hall and Toyoda Takeshi. Ithaca, NY: East Asian Program, Cornell University, 2001, 205–25.

Ruan Xiangyu 阮祥宇, ed. *Yuefu wanxiang xin* 樂府萬象新. In *HWSZ*.

Ruitenbeek, Klaas. *Carpentry and Building in Late Imperial China: A Study of the Fifteenth-Century Carpenter's Manual Lu Ban jing*. Leiden: Brill, 1993.

Sakade Yoshinobu 坂出祥伸. "Kaisetsu—Mindai nichiyō ruisho ni tsuite" 解說—明代日用類書について. In *Wuche bajin* (*Gosha bakkin*) 五車拔錦, pp. 7–30.

Sakai Tadao 酒井忠夫. "Confucianism and Popular Educational Works." In *Self and Society in Ming Thought*, edited by Wm. Theodore de Bary. New York: Columbia University Press, 1970, 331–66.

———. "Mindai no nichiyō ruisho to shomin kyōiku" 明代の日用類書と庶民教育. In *Kinsei Chūgoku kyōikushi kenkyū: Sono bunkyō saisaku to shomin kyōiku* 近世中國教育史研究: その文教政策と庶民教育, edited by Hayashi Tomoharu 林友春. Tokyo: Kokudo sha, 1958, 39–51.

Seth, Michael. *A Concise History of Korea*. Lanham, MD: Rowman and Littlefield, 2006.

Shang Wei. "*Jin Ping Mei* and Late Ming Print Culture." In *Writing and Materiality in China: Essays in Honor of Patrick Hanan*, edited by Judith T. Zeitlin and Lydia H. Liu, with Ellen Widmer. Cambridge, MA: Harvard University Asia Center, 2003, 187–238.

———. "The Making of the Everyday World: *Jin Ping Mei cihua* and Encyclopedias for Daily Use." In *Dynastic Crisis and Cultural Innovation: From the Late Ming to the Late Qing and Beyond*, edited by David Der-wei Wang and Shang Wei. Cambridge, MA: Harvard University Asia Center, 2005, 63–92.

Shanhai jing tu 山海經圖. 1593. In *Zhongguo gudai banhua congkan erbian* 中國古代版畫叢刊二編, vol. 1. Shanghai: Shanghai guji chubanshe, 1994.

Shen Defu 沈德符. *Wanli yehuo bian* 萬曆野獲編. Beijing: Zhonghua shuju, 1959.

Shen Hongyu 沈弘宇. *Hunru pian* 渾如篇. Prefaced by Liu Fu 劉復, edited by Fan Yu'an 范遇安. Beijing: Beixin shuju, 1927.

———. *Piaodu jiguan* 嫖賭機關. Printed by Deju tang 德聚堂. Ming dynasty.

Shen Yue 沈約. *Song shu* 宋書. Beijing: Zhonghua shuju, 1974.

[Shi] Xingjun 釋·行均. *Longkan shoujing* 龍龕手鏡. Beijing: Zhonghua shuju, 1985.

Shinü hua zhi mei 仕女畫之美. Edited by Guoli Gugong bowuyuan bianji weiyuanhui. Taipei: Guoli Gugong bowuyuan, 1988.

Shirane, Haruo, ed. *Envisioning* The Tale of Genji*: Media, Gender, and Cultural Production*. New York: Columbia University Press, 2008.

Shunkoen Hanamaru 寿光園花丸 and Okada Gyokuzan 岡田玉山. *Ikoku ichiran* 異國一覽. Osaka: Naniwa shorin, 1799.

Sieber, Patricia. *Theaters of Desire: Authors, Readers, and the Reproduciton of Early Chinese Song-Drama, 1300–2000*. New York: Palgrave Macmillan, 2003.

Sima Qian 司馬遷. *Shi ji* 史記. Beijing: Zhonghua shuju, 1959.

Sohō sensei koki shukuga kinen kankōkai 蘇峰先生古稀祝賀記念刋行会, ed. *Seikidō zenpon shomoku* 成簣堂善本書目. Tokyo: Min'yūsha, 1932.

Spence, Jonathan. *Return to Dragon Mountain: Memories of a Late Ming Man*. New York: Viking, 2007.

Stone, Charles R. *The Fountainhead of Chinese Erotica*: The Lord of Perfect Satisfaction *(Ruyijun zhuan) with a Translation and Critical Edition*. Honolulu: University of Hawai'i Press, 2003.

Strassberg, Richard. *A Chinese Bestiary: Strange Creatures from the Guideways through Mountains and Seas*. Berkeley: University of California Press, 2002.

Sui Shusen 隋樹森, ed. *Quan Yuan sanqu jianbian* 全元散曲簡編. Shanghai: Shanghai guji chubanshe, 1984.

Sun Chongtao 孫崇濤. Fengyue jinnang *kaoshi* 風月錦囊考釋. Beijing: Zhonghua shuju, 2000.

——— and Huang Shizhong 黄仕忠. Fengyue jinnang *jianjiao* 風月錦囊箋校. Beijing: Zhonghua shuju, 2000.

Sun Xu 孫緒. *Shaxi ji* 沙溪集. In *SKQS*.

Sun Yizhi 孫宜志. "Jiangxi Yiyang fangyan de yinyun tedian" 江西弋陽方言的音韻特點. *Jiangxi jiaoyu xueyuan xuebao* 29, no. 1 (2008): 58–61.

Swope, Kenneth M. *A Dragon's Head and a Serpent's Tail: Ming China and the First Great East Asian War, 1592*–1598. Norman: University of Oklahoma Press, 2009.

Tan Fan 譚帆. *Zhongguo xiaoshuo pingdian yanjiu* 中國小說評點研究. Shanghai: Huadong shifan daxue chubanshe, 2001.

Tanaka Issei 田中一成. *Ming Qing de xiqu: Jiangnan zongzu shehui de biaoxiang* 明清的戲曲：江南宗族社會的表象. Translated by Yun Guibin 云貴彬 and Wang Wenxun 王文勛. Beijing: Beijing guangbo xueyuan chubanshe, 2004.

Tang Kaijian 湯開建. "Zhongguo xiancun zui zao de Ouzhou ren xingxiang ziliao—*Dongyi tuxiang*" 中國現存最早的歐洲人形象資料—東夷圖像. *Gugong bowuyuan yuankan*, 2001 (no. 1): 22–28.

Tang Xianzu 湯顯祖. *Mu dan ting* 牡丹亭. Edited by Xu Shuofang 徐朔方 and Yang Xiaomei 楊笑梅. Beijing: Zhonghua shuju, 1965.

Tonglaga 通拉嘎 and Wu Liqun 吳利群. "Meng Yuan yingyi ti dui *Menggu mishi* fanyi de yingxiang" 蒙元硬譯體對蒙古秘史翻譯的影響. *Nei Menggu shifan daxue xuebao* (Zhexue shehui kexue ban), 2006 (no. 4): 32–34.

Tuotuo 脱脱 et al. *Song shi* 宋史. Beijing: Zhonghua shuju, 1977.

van Crevel, M., M. Hockx, and T. Y. Tan, eds. *Text, Performance, and Gender in Chinese Literature and Music: Essays in Honor of Wilt Idema*. Leiden: Brill, 2009.

van der Loon, Piet. *The Classical Theatre and Art Song of South Fukien*. Taipei: Nantian shuju youxian gongsi, 1992.

van Gulik, R. H. *Erotic Colour Prints of the Ming Period: With an Essay on Chinese Sex Life from the Han to the Ch'ing Dynasty, B.C. 206–A.D. 1644*. Introduction by James Cahill, Wilt L. Idema, and Sören Edgren. Leiden: Brill, 2004.

Volpp, Sophie. "Texts, Tutors, and Fathers: Pedagogy and Pedants in Tang Xianzu's *Mudan ting*." In *Dynastic Crisis and Cultural Innovation from the Late Ming to the Late Qing and Beyond*, edited by David Der-wei Wang and Shang Wei. Cambridge, MA: Harvard University Asia Center, 2005, 25–62.

Wagner, Peter. *Reading Iconotexts: From Swift to the French Revolution*. London: Reaktion Books, 1995.

Wakeman Jr., Frederic E. *Telling Chinese History: A Selection of Essays*. Edited by Lea H. Wakeman. Berkeley: University of Berkeley Press, 2009.

Wang Anqi 王安祈. *Mingdai chuanqi zhi juchang jiqi yishu* 明代傳奇之劇場及其藝術. Taipei: Taiwan xuesheng shuju, 1986.

Wang Baoping 王寶平. "Hu Wenhuan congshu kaobian" 胡文煥叢書攷辨. *Zhonghua wenshi luncong*, 2001, vol. 1 (no. 65): 120–45.

Wang Ch'iu-kuei (Wang Qiugui) 王秋桂 et al., eds. *Shanben xiqu congkan* 善本戲曲叢刊. Taipei: Xuesheng shuju, 1984.

Wang, David Der-wei, and Shang Wei, eds. *Dynastic Crisis and Cultural Innovation: From the Late Ming to the Late Qing and Beyond.* Cambridge, MA: Harvard University Asia Center, 2005.

Wang Ermin 王爾敏. *Ming Qing shidai shumin wenhua shenghuo* 明清時代庶民文化生活. Changsha: Yuelu shushe, 2002.

Wang Gulu 王古魯. *Mingdai Huidiao xiqu sanchu jiyi* 明代徽調戲曲散齣輯佚. Shanghai: Gudian wenxue chubanshe, 1957.
Wang Guowei 王國維. *Wang Guowei ji* 王國維集. Edited by Zhou Xishan 周錫山. Beijing: Zhongguo shehui kexue chubanshe, 2008.
Wang Jide 王驥德. *Qulü* 曲律. In *Wang Jide Qulü* 王驥德曲律, annotated by Chen Duo 陳多 and Ye Changhai 葉長海. Changsha: Hunan renmin chubanshe, 1983.
———. *Xin jiaozhu guwen Xixiang ji* 新校註古本西廂記. In *XXSKQS*, *jibu* 集部, vol. 1766.
Wang Liqi 王利器. *Yuan Ming Qing sandai jinhui xiaoshuo xiqu shiliao* 元明清三代禁毀小說戲曲史料. Shanghai: Shanghai guji chubanshe, 1981.
Wang Qi 王圻. *Sancai tuhui* 三才圖會. In *XXSKQS*, *zibu* 子部, vols. 1232–36.
Wang Qiang 王強. *Huiguan xitai yu xiju* 會館戲台與戲劇. Taipei: Wenjin chubanshe, 2000.
Wang, Richard. "Creating Cultural Artifacts: The Ming Erotica Novella in Cultural Practice." PhD diss., University of Chicago, 1999.
———. "The Publishing of the Ming Novellas and the Print Culture," *Monumenta Serica* 48 (2000): 93–132.
Wang Rigen 王日根. *Ming Qing minjian shehui de zhixu* 明清民間社會的秩序. Changsha: Yuelu shushe, 2003.
Wang Shifu 王實甫. *Jiping jiaozhu Xi xiang ji* 集評校注西廂記. Edited by Wang Jisi 王季思. Shanghai: Shanghai guji chubanshe, 1987.
———. *Xinkan qimiao quanxiang zhushi Xixiang ji* 新刊奇妙全相註釋西廂記. Printed by the Yue family of Jintai in 1498. Reprinted in *Guben xiqu congkan* 古本戲曲叢刊, 1st series. Shanghai: Shangwu yinshuguan, 1954.
Wang Ting 王頲. "Zhedie shan de shuru yu fangzhi" 折迭扇的輸入與仿制. *Dongnan wenhua*, 2001 (no. 9): 62–68.
Wang Wentai 王文泰. "Mingdai ren bianxuan Mingdai shige zongji yanjiu" 明代人編選明代詩歌總集研究. PhD diss., Fudan daxue, 2005.
Wang Xiaodun 王小盾. *Tangdai jiuling yishu: Guanyu Dunhuang wupu, zaoqi wenren ci jiqi wenhua beijing de yanjiu* 唐代酒令藝術：關於敦煌舞譜，早期文人詞及其文化背景的研究. Taipei: Wenjin chubanshe, 1993.
Wang Yinglin 王應麟. *Yu Hai* 玉海. Hangzhou: Zhejiang shuju, 1883.
Wang Yong 王勇. "Riben zheshan de qiyuan ji zai Zhongguo de liubo" 日本摺扇的起源及在中國的流播. *Riben xuekan*, 1995 (no. 1): 115–30.
Wang Yucheng 王育成. *Mingdai caihui Quanzhen zongzu tu yanjiu* 明代彩繪全眞宗祖圖研究. Beijing: Zhongguo shehui kexue chubanshe, 2003.
Wang Zhenghua 王正華. "Shenghuo, zhishi yu wenhua shangpin: Wan Ming Fujian ban 'riyong leishu' yuqi shuhua men" 生活、知識與文化商品：晚明福建版"日用類書"與其書畫門. *Zhongyang yanjiuyuan jindaishi yanjiusuo jikan* no. 41 (Sep. 2003): 1–85.
Wang Zhongmin 王重民. *Guohui tushuguan cang Zhongguo shanben shu lu* 國會圖書館藏中國善本書錄. Washington, D.C.: Library of Congress, 1957.
Wanjuan souqi quanshu 萬卷搜奇全書. 1628. Printed by Cunren tang 存仁堂. Held in the C. V. Starr East Asian Library, University of California at Berkeley.
Wanshu yuanhai (*Bansho enkai*) 萬書淵海. Reprinted in *CNRS*, vols. 6–7.
Wanyong zhengzong buqiuren (*Ban'yō seiso fukyūjin*) 萬用正宗不求人. 1609. Reprinted in *CNRS*, vols. 10–11.

Watson, Burton, trans. *The Complete Works of Chuang Tzu*. New York: Columbia University Press, 1968.

Wen Duanzheng 溫端政 and Zhou Jian 周荐. *Ershi shiji de Hanyu suyu yanjiu* 二十世紀的漢語俗語研究. Taiyuan: Shanxi renmin chubanshe, 2000.

Wen Zhenheng 文震亨. *Zhangwu zhi* 長物志. Edited by Chen Zhi 陳植 and Yang Chaobo 楊超伯. *Zhang wu zhi jiaozhu* 長物志校註.

West, Stephen H. "Time Management and Self-Control: Self-Help Guides in Yuan." In *Text, Performance, and Gender in Chinese Literature and Music: Essays in Honor of Wilt Idema*, edited by M. van Crevel, M. Hockx, and T. Y. Tan. Leiden: Brill, 2010.

——— and Wilt Idema, trans. *The Story of the Western Wing*. Berkeley: University of California Press, 1995.

Wu Bozong 吳伯宗. *Rongjin ji* 榮進集. In *SKQS*.

Wu Huifang 吳蕙芳. *Ming Qing yilai minjian shenghuo zhishi de jiangou yu chuandi* 明清以來民間生活知識的建構與傳遞. Taipei: Xuesheng shuju, 2007.

———. *Wanbao quanshu: Ming Qing shiqi de minjian shenghuo shilu* 萬寶全書：明清時期的民間生活實錄. Taipei: Guoli Zhengzhi daxue lishixue xi, 2001.

Wu Hung. *The Double Screen: Medium and Representation in Chinese Painting*. Chicago: The University of Chicago Press, 1996.

Wu Jingzi 吳敬梓. *Rulin waishi* 儒林外史. Beijing: Renmin wenxue chubanshe, 1958.

Wu Liwei 吳莉葦. "Ming Qing chuanjiaoshi dui *Shanhai jing* de jiedu" 明清傳教士對山海經的解讀. *Zhongguo dili luncong* 20, no. 3 (July 2005): 117–26.

Wu, Yenna. *Ameliorative Satire and the Seventeeth-Century Chinese Novel,* Xingshi yinyuan zhuan—*Marriage as Retribution, Awakening the World*. Lewiston, NY: E. Mellen Press, 1999.

Wuche bajin (*Gosha bakkin*) 五車拔錦. 1597. Reprinted in *CNRS*, vols. 1–2.

Xi Zhengwo 龔正我, ed. *Zhaijin qiyin* 摘錦奇音. 1611. Reprinted in *SBXQCK*, 1st series, vol. 3.

Xiao Dongfa 肖東發. "Jianyang Yu shi keshu kaolue" 建陽余氏刻書攷略. *Wenxian*, 1984 (no. 3): 230–47; 1984 (no. 4): 195–219; 1985 (no. 1): 236–50.

Xiaoxiaosheng 笑笑生. *Jin Ping Mei cihua* 金瓶梅詞話. Wanli reign. Reprint, Hong Kong: Taiping shuju, 1993.

Xie Shuishun 謝水順 and Li Ting 李珽. *Fujian gudai keshu* 福建古代刻書. Fuzhou: Fujian renmin chubanshe, 1997.

Xie Zhaozhe 謝肇淛. *Wu za zu* 五雜組. Shanghai: Shanghai shudian chubanshe, 2001.

Xinkan qimiao quanxiang zhushi Xixiang ji 新刊奇妙全相註釋西廂記. 1498. Reprint Hangzhou: Zhejiang guji chubanshe, 2002.

Xinke chuxiang yinzhu Li Rihua nan Xixiang ji 新刻出像音註李日華南西廂記. Printed by Fuchun tang 富春堂 of Jinling during the Wanli reign. Reprinted in Guben xiqu congkan bianji weiyuanhui, ed., *Guben xiqu congkan chuji*, vol. 33.

Xinke xiuxiang piping Jin Ping Mei 新刻繡像批評金瓶梅. Collated by Qi Yan 齊煙 and Wang Rumei 王汝梅. Hong Kong: Sanlian shudian, 2000.

Xiong Lihui 熊禮匯. "*Guwen zhenbao* de bianzhe, banben yanbian jiqi zai Hanguo, Riben de chuanbo" 古文眞寶的編者、版本演變及其在韓國、日本的傳播. In *Xiang shuo Guwen zhenbao daquan* 詳說古文眞寶大全, by Huang Jian, edited by Xiong Lihui. Changsha: Hunan renmin chubanshe, 2007, 1–30.

Xiong Renhuan 熊稔寰, ed. *Hui Chi yadiao* 徽池雅調. Wanli reign. Reprinted in *SBXQCK*, 1st series, vol. 7.

Xizhou sheng 西周生. *Xingshi yinyuan zhuan* 醒世姻緣傳. Edited by Huang Suqiu 黄肅秋. Shanghai: Shanghai guji chubanshe, 1981.

Xu Huilin 許暉林. "Chaogong de xiangxiang: Wan Ming riyong leishu 'Zhuyi men' de yiyu lunshu" 朝貢的想像：晚明日用類書«諸夷門»的異域論述. *Zhongguo wenzhe yanjiu tongxun* 20, no. 2 (June 2010): 169–92.

Xu Qilong 徐企龍, ed. *Wanshu yuanhai* (*Bansho enkai*) 萬書淵海. 1610. Reprinted in *CNRS*, vols. 6–7.

———. *Wuche wanbao quanshu* (*Gosha banpō zensho*) 五車萬寶全書. 1614. Reprinted in *CNRS*, vols. 8–9.

Xu Wei 徐渭. *Nanci xu lu* 南詞序錄. In vol. 3 in *Zhongguo gudian xiqu lunzhu jicheng* 中國古典戲曲論著集成. Beijing: Zhongguo xiju chubanshe, 1959.

Xu Xuehui 徐雪輝. "Keju changmian yu xiju xiaoguo" 科舉場面與戲劇效果. *Qi lu xuekan* 2 (2008): 123–27.

Xu Yingqiu 徐應秋. *Yuzhi tang tanhui* 玉芝堂談薈. In vol. 5 in *Biji xiaoshuo daguan xubian* 筆記小説大觀續編. Taipei: Xinxing shuju, 1962.

Yan Congjian 嚴從簡. *Shuyu zhouzi lu* 殊域周咨錄. In *Guojia tushuguan cang Liuqiu ziliao huibian* 國家圖書館藏琉球資料彙編, edited by Huang Runhua 黄潤華 and Xue Ying 薛英. Beijing: Beijing tushuguan chubanshe, 2000.

Yang Bojun 楊伯峻. *Lunyu yizhu* 論語譯注. Beijing: Zhonghua shuju, 1980.

———. *Mengzi yizhu* 孟子譯注. Beijing: Zhonghua shuju, 1960.

Yang Huiling 楊惠玲. *Xiqu banshe yanjiu: Ming Qing jiaban* 戲曲班社研究：明清家班. Xiamen: Xiamen daxue chubanshe, 2006.

Yang Zhengtai 楊正泰, annot. *Tianxia shuilu lucheng, Tianxia lucheng tuyin, Keshang yilan xingmi* 天下水陸路程，天下路程圖引，客商一覽醒迷. Taiyuan: Shanxi renmin chubanshe, 1992.

Yao Rong 姚蓉. "Li Wen shengnian bianzheng" 李雯生年辨正. *Wenxue yichan*, 2006 (no. 1): 82.

Yao Shuyi 么書儀, Wang Yongkuan 王永寬, and Gao Mingluan 高鳴鸞, eds. *Xiju tongdian* 戲劇通典. In Zhang Jiong 張炯 et al., eds., *Zhongguo wenxue tongdian* 中國文學通典, vol. 4. Beijing: Jiefangjun wenyi chubanshe, 1999.

Ye Dehui 葉德輝. *Shulin qing hua, Shulin yu hua* 書林清話, 書林餘話. Changsha: Yuelu shushe, 1999.

Ye Dejun 葉德均. *Xiqu xiaoshuo congkao* 戲曲小説叢考. Beijing: Zhonghua shuju, 1979.

Yeh, Catherine Vance. *Shanghai Love: Courtesans, Intellectuals, and Entertainment Culture, 1850–1910.* Seattle: University of Washington Press, 2006.

Yin Qisheng 殷啓聖, ed. *Yao tian yue* 堯天樂. Wanli reign. Reprinted in *SBXQCK*, 1st series, vol. 8.

Yin Zhi 尹直. *Jian zhai suo zhui lu* 謇齋瑣綴錄. Taipei: Taiwan xuesheng shuju, 1969.

Yiyu tuzhi 異域圖志. 1489. Commissioned by Jin Xian 金銑.

Yiyu zhi 異域志. Annotated by Lu Junling 陸峻嶺. In *Zhenla fengtu ji jiaozhu, Xiyou lu, Yiyu zhi* 真臘風土記校注，西遊錄，異域志. Beijing: Zhonghua shuju, 2000.

Yonemoto, Marcia. *Mapping Early Modern Japan: Space, Place, and Culture in the Tokugawa Period (1603–1868).* Berkeley: University of California Press, 2003.

Yong Rong 永瑢 et al., eds. *Siku quanshu zongmu* 四庫全書總目. Beijing: Zhonghua shuju, 1965.

Yu, Anthony, trans. *The Journey to the West.* Chicago: University of Chicago Press, 1977–80.

Yu Huai 余懷. *Banqiao zaji (wai yizhong)* 板橋雜記(外一種). Edited by Li Jintang 李金堂. Shanghai: Shanghai guji chubanshe, 2000.

Yu, Pauline, ed. *Voices of the Song Lyric in China.* Berkeley: University of California Press, 1994.

Yu Weimin 俞為民, ed. *Song Yuan sida xiwen duben* 宋元四大戲文讀本. Nanjing: Jiangsu guji chubanshe, 1988.

Yu Wentai 余文台 (Yu Xiangdou 余象斗), ed. *Ke quanxiang wuxian lingguan dadi huagang tianwang zhuan* 刻全相五顯靈官大帝華光天王傳. 1631. Reprint, Taipei: Tianyi chubanshe, 1985.

———, ed. *Santai wanyong zhengzong* (*Sandai ban'yō seisō*) 三台萬用正宗. 1599. Reprinted in *CNRS*. Tokyo: Kyūko Shoin, 2000.

Yu Xian 俞憲, comp. *Sheng Ming baijia shi* 盛明百家詩. In *SKCM, jibu* 集部, vol. 304.

Yuan Ke 袁珂. Shanhai jing *jiaozhu* 山海經校注. Shanghai: Shanghai guji chubanshe, 1980.

Yung, Bell. "Model Opera as Model: From *Shajiabang* to *Sagabong*." In *Popular Chinese Literature and Performing Arts in the People's Republic of China, 1949–1979*, edited by Bonnie McDougall. Berkeley: University of California Press, 1984, 144–64.

Zeitlin, Judith T., and Lydia H. Liu, with Ellen Widmer, eds. *Writing and Materiality in China: Essays in Honor of Patrick Hanan.* Cambridge, MA: Harvard University Asia Center, 2003.

Zhang Bowei 張伯偉. "Xuanben yu yuwai Han wenxue" 選本與域外漢文學. *Nanjing daxue xuebao* (Zhexue, renwen kexue, shehui kexue), 2002 (no. 4): 81–89.

———. "Yuwai Haiji yu Zhongguo wenxue yanjiu" 域外漢籍與中國文學研究. *Wenxue yichan,* 2003 (no. 3): 131–39.

Zhang Dai 張岱. *Tao'an mengyi* 陶庵夢憶. In *Tao'an mengyi, Xihu mengxun* 陶庵夢憶，西湖夢尋, collated by Xia Xianchun 夏咸淳 and Cheng Weirong 程維榮. Shanghai: Shanghai guji chubanshe, 2001.

Zhang Faying 張發穎. *Zhongguo jiayue xiban* 中國家樂戲班. Beijing: Xueyuan chubanshe, 2002.

———. *Zhongguo xiban shi* 中國戲班史. Beijing: Xueyuan chubanshe, 2003.

Zhang Hua 張華, *Bowu zhi* 博物志. In *Bowu zhi jiaozheng* 博物志校證. Collated by Fan Ning 范寧. Beijing: Zhonghua shuju, 1980.

Zhang Jiong 張炯 et al., eds. *Zhongguo wenxue tongdian* 中國文學通典. 4 vols. Beijing: Jiefangjun wenyi chubanshe, 1999.

Zhang Weibao 張偉保, ed. *Mingdai wenxue "fugu yu gexin" yantaohui lunwen ji* 明代文學復古與革新研討會論文集. Hong Kong: Xinya yanjiusuo, 2001.

Zhang Xiumin 張秀民 and Han Qi 韓琦. *Zhongguo yinshua shi* 中國印刷史. Hangzhou: Zhejiang guji chubanshe, 2006.

Zhang Zhihe 張志和. "Zhu Dingchen ben *Sanguo zhi shizhuan* tankao" 朱鼎臣本三國志史傳探考. *Ming Qing xiaoshuo yanjiu* 2004 (4): 196–205.

Zhang Zhigong 張志公. *Chuantong yuwen jiaoyu jiaocai lun—ji mengxue shumu he shuying* 傳統語文教育教材論–暨蒙學書目和書影. Shanghai: Shanghai jiaoyu chubanshe, 1992.
Zhao Hankun 趙含坤. *Zhongguo leishu* 中國類書. Shijiazhuang: Hebei renmin chubanshe, 2005.
Zhao Jingshen 趙景深. "*Qiu ye yue*" 秋夜月. In *Yuan Ming nanxi kaolue* 元明南戲考略. Beijing: Zuojia chubanshe, 1958, 125–35.
Zhao Qi 趙岐 and Sun Shi 孫奭. *Mengzi zhushu jiejing* 孟子註疏解經. Taipei: Guoli gugong bowuyuan, 1986.
Zheng Ande 鄭安德 (Andrew Chung) and Lou Yulie 樓宇烈, eds. *Mingmo Qingchu Yesuhui sixiang wenxian huibian* 明末清初耶穌會思想文獻匯編. 60 vols. Beijing daxue zongjiao yanjiu suo, 2000.
Zheng Kaiyang 鄭開陽. *Liuqiu tushuo* 琉球圖說. In *Zheng Kaiyang zazhu* 鄭開陽雜著. 1693. Reprint, Taipei: Chengwen chubanshe, 1970.
Zheng Kesheng 鄭克晟. "Mingdai Ganxi zhongfu yu Jiangxi shidafu" 明代贛西重賦與江西士大夫. In *Ming Qing shi tanshi* 明清史探實. Beijing: Zhongguo shehui kexue chubanshe, 2001, 86–102.
Zheng Ruoyong 鄭若庸. *Lei juan* 類雋. 1578. Reprinted in *XXSKQS*, *zibu* 子部, vol. 1236.
Zhongguo guojia bowuguan 中國國家博物館, ed. *Zhongguo guojia bowuguan guancang wenwu yanjiu congshu* 中國國家博物館館藏文物研究叢書. Shanghai: Shanghai guji chubanshe, 2006–.
Zhongguo lishi bowuguan 中國歷史博物館, ed. *Zhongguo lishi bowuguan* 中國歷史博物館. Beijing: Wenwu chubanshe, 1984.
Zhongguo meishu quanji bianji weiyuanwei 中國美術全集編輯委員會, ed. *Zhongguo meishu quanji* 中國美術全集. 60 vols. Beijing: Renmin meishu chubanshe, 1984–89.
Zhongwai jiaotong shi ji congkan 中外交通史籍叢刊. Beijing: Zhonghua shuju, 1958–, reprint, 2000–.
Zhou Huabin 周華斌 and Zhu Lianqun 朱聯群, eds. *Zhongguo juchang shi lun* 中國劇場史論. Beijing: Beijing guangbo xueyuan, 2003.
Zhou Wu 周蕪. *Huipai banhua shi lunji* 徽派版畫史論集. Hefei: Anhui renmin chubanshe, 1984.
Zhou Yubo 周玉波 and Chen Shulu 陳書錄, eds. *Ming dai min'ge ji* 明代民歌集. Nanjing: Nanjing shifan daxue chubanshe, 2009.
Zhou Xin 周鑫. "*Zhu zi jiali* yanjiu huigu yu zhanwang" 朱子家禮研究回顧與展望. *Zhongguo shehui lishi pinglun* vol. 12 (2011): 432–46.
Zhou Xinhui 周心慧. *Zhongguo banhua shi conggao* 中國版畫史叢稿. Beijing: Xueyuan chubanshe, 2002.
———. *Zhongguo gu banhua tong shi* 中國古版畫通史. Beijing: Xueyuan chubanshe, 2000.
———. *Zhongguo gudai banke banhua shi lunji* 中國古代版刻版畫史論集. Beijing: Xueyuan chubanshe, 1998.
———. "Zhongguo gudai xiqu banhua kaolue" 中國古代戲曲版畫考略. In *Guben xiqu banhua tulu* 古本戲曲版畫圖錄. Beijing: Xueyuan chubanshe, 1997.
———, ed. *Guben xiqu banhua tulu* 古本戲曲版畫圖錄. 5 vols. Beijing: Xueyuan chubanshe, 1997.

———, ed. *Xinbian Zhongguo banhua shi tulu* 新編中國版畫史圖錄. 11 vols. Beijing: Xueyuan chubanshe, 2000.

Zhu Chongshou 祝重壽. *Zhongguo chatu yishu shihua* 中國插圖藝術史話. Beijing: Qinghua daxue chubanshe, 2005.

Zhu Chongzhi 朱崇志. *Zhongguo gudai xiqu xuanben yanjiu* 中國古代戲曲選本研究. Shanghai: Shanghai guji chubanshe, 2004.

Zhu Liyuan 朱立元 and Pei Gao 裴高, eds. *Zhongxi xueshu* (1) 中西學術(一). Shanghai: Xuelin chubanshe, 1995.

Zhu Wanshu 朱萬曙. *Mingdai xiqu pingdian yanjiu* 明代戲曲評點研究. Hefei: Anhui jiaoyu chubanshe, 2002.

Zhu Xi 朱熹. *Yuding xiaoxue jizhu* 御定小學集註. In *SKQS*.

Zhu Yizun 朱彝尊. *Ming shi zong* 明詩綜. In *SKQS*.

Index

Harvard-Yenching Institute Monograph Series

(titles now in print)

24. *Population, Disease, and Land in Early Japan, 645–900*, by William Wayne Farris
25. *Shikitei Sanba and the Comic Tradition in Edo Fiction*, by Robert W. Leutner
26. *Washing Silk: The Life and Selected Poetry of Wei Chuang (834?–910)*, by Robin D. S. Yates
28. *Tang Transformation Texts: A Study of the Buddhist Contribution to the Rise of Vernacular Fiction and Drama in China*, by Victor H. Mair
30. *Readings in Chinese Literary Thought*, by Stephen Owen
31. *Remembering Paradise: Nativism and Nostalgia in Eighteenth-Century Japan*, by Peter Nosco
33. *Escape from the Wasteland: Romanticism and Realism in the Fiction of Mishima Yukio and Oe Kenzaburo*, by Susan Jolliffe Napier
34. *Inside a Service Trade: Studies in Contemporary Chinese Prose*, by Rudolf G. Wagner
35. *The Willow in Autumn: Ryutei Tanehiko, 1783–1842*, by Andrew Lawrence Markus
36. *The Confucian Transformation of Korea: A Study of Society and Ideology*, by Martina Deuchler
37. *The Korean Singer of Tales*, by Marshall R. Pihl
38. *Praying for Power: Buddhism and the Formation of Gentry Society in Late-Ming China*, by Timothy Brook
39. *Word, Image, and Deed in the Life of Su Shi*, by Ronald C. Egan
40. *The Chinese Virago: A Literary Theme*, by Yenna Wu
41. *Studies in the Comic Spirit in Modern Japanese Fiction*, by Joel R. Cohn
42. *Wind Against the Mountain: The Crisis of Politics and Culture in Thirteenth-Century China*, by Richard L. Davis
43. *Powerful Relations: Kinship, Status, and the State in Sung China (960–1279)*, by Beverly Bossler
44. *Limited Views: Essays on Ideas and Letters*, by Qian Zhongshu; selected and translated by Ronald Egan
45. *Sugar and Society in China: Peasants, Technology, and the World Market*, by Sucheta Mazumdar
49. *Precious Volumes: An Introduction to Chinese Sectarian Scriptures from the Sixteenth and Seventeenth Centuries*, by Daniel L. Overmyer
50. *Poetry and Painting in Song China: The Subtle Art of Dissent*, by Alfreda Murck
51. *Evil and/or/as the Good: Omnicentrism, Intersubjectivity, and Value Paradox in Tiantai Buddhist Thought*, by Brook Ziporyn
52. *Chinese History: A Manual, Revised and Enlarged Edition*, by Endymion Wilkinson
53. *Articulated Ladies: Gender and the Male Community in Early Chinese Texts*, by Paul Rouzer

54. *Politics and Prayer: Shrines to Local Former Worthies in Sung China*, by Ellen Neskar
55. *Allegories of Desire: Esoteric Literary Commentaries of Medieval Japan*, by Susan Blakeley Klein
56. *Printing for Profit: The Commercial Publishers of Jianyang, Fujian (11th-17th Centuries)*, by Lucille Chia
57. *To Become a God: Cosmology, Sacrifice, and Self-Divinization in Early China*, by Michael J. Puett
58. *Writing and Materiality in China: Essays in Honor of Patrick Hanan*, edited by Judith T. Zeitlin and Lydia H. Liu
59. *Rulin waishi and Cultural Transformation in Late Imperial China*, by Shang Wei
60. *Words Well Put: Visions of Poetic Competence in the Chinese Tradition*, by Graham Sanders
61. *Householders: The Reizei Family in Japanese History*, by Steven D. Carter
62. *The Divine Nature of Power: Chinese Ritual Architecture at the Sacred Site of Jinci*, by Tracy Miller
63. *Beacon Fire and Shooting Star: The Literary Culture of the Liang (502–557)*, by Xiaofei Tian
64. *Lost Soul: "Confucianism" in Contemporary Chinese Academic Discourse*, by John Makeham
65. *The Sage Learning of Liu Zhi: Islamic Thought in Confucian Terms*, by Sachiko Murata, William C. Chittick, and Tu Weiming
66. *Through a Forest of Chancellors: Fugitive Histories in Liu Yuan's* Lingyan ge, *an Illustrated Book from Seventeenth-Century Suzhou*, by Anne Burkus-Chasson
67. *Empire of Texts in Motion: Chinese, Korean, and Taiwanese Transculturations of Japanese Literature*, by Karen Laura Thornber
68. *Empire's Twilight: Northeast Asia Under the Mongols*, by David M. Robinson
69. *Ancestors, Virgins, and Friars: Christianity as a Local Religion in Late Imperial China*, by Eugenio Menegon
70. *Manifest in Words, Written on Paper: Producing and Circulating Poetry in Tang Dynasty China*, by Christopher M. B. Nugent
71. *The Poetics of Sovereignty: On Emperor Taizong of the Tang Dynasty*, by Jack W. Chen
72. *Ancestral Memory in Early China*, by K. E. Brashier
73. *'Dividing the Realm in Order to Govern': The Spatial Organization of the Song State*, by Ruth Mostern
74. *The Dynamics of Masters Literature: Early Chinese Thought from Confucius to Han Feizi*, by Wiebke Denecke
75. *Songs of Contentment and Transgression: Discharged Officials and Literati Communities in Sixteenth-Century North China*, by Tian Yuan Tan
76. *Ten Thousand Scrolls: Reading and Writing in the Poetics of Huang Tingjian and the Late Northern Song*, by Yugen Wang
77. *A Northern Alternative: Xue Xuan (1389-1464) and the Hedong School*, by Khee Heong Koh
78. *Visionary Journeys: Travel Writings from Early Medieval and Nineteenth-Century China*, by Xiaofei Tian

79. *Making Personas: Transnational Film Stardom in Modern Japan*, by Hideaki Fujiki
80. *Strange Eventful Histories: Identity, Performance, and Xu Wei's* Four Cries of a Gibbon, by Shiamin Kwa
81. *Critics and Commentators: The* Book of Poems *as Classic and Literature*, by Bruce Rusk
82. *Home and the World: Editing the Glorious Ming in Woodblock-Printed Books of the Sixteenth and Seventeenth Centuries*, by Yuming He
83. *Courtesans, Concubines, and the Cult of Female Fidelity*, by Beverly Bossler
84. *Chinese History: A New Manual*, by Endymion Wilkinson
85. *A Comprehensive Manchu-English Dictionary*, by Jerry Norman